LET ME

BE

CLEAR

LET ME
BE
CLEAR

Barack Obama's War on Millennials,
and One Woman's Case for Hope

KATIE KIEFFER

CROWN
FORUM
NEW YORK

The cataloging-in-publication data is available upon request.

ISBN 978-0-8041-3975-5
eBook ISBN 978-0-8041-3976-2

Printed in the United States of America

Jacket design by Michael Nagin
Jacket photography by Deborah Feingold

10 9 8 7 6 5 4 3 2 1

First Edition

To my heroines
My 100% Irish grandmother, a woman of wondrous wit.
My 100% German grandmother, whose laughter
bubbles like champagne.

and

To the memory of my heroes
My grandfathers—a magnanimous Marine and
a stouthearted sailor.

CONTENTS

Dear Barack Obama,

Let me begin by borrowing one of your favorite phrases. Let me be clear: I am a young American and I am writing on behalf of my generation. We are the Millennial Generation and we are 95 million strong. I am writing to request accountability for victimizing us for your political gain. You promised us jobs, hope, and change. In the end, you followed through only on the "change."

You duped Millennials into voting for you not once but twice and implemented unconstitutional decrees that robbed us of the opportunities that we deserve. We are the first generation of Americans to be financially worse off than our parents. Your puerile policies and pomposity have rendered it nearly impossible for us to achieve the American Dream.

You chatted it up with our favorite hosts like Fallon, Leno, and Stewart; you seemed like a nice, regular guy and Millennials trusted you. You saturated social media with false hope. You endorsed voyeuristic YouTube videos by Hollywood celebrities targeted at college students for your presidential campaign.

With the aid of your teleprompter, you traveled the college-campus circuit, promising us that you would help us find jobs when we graduated and that you would make college more affordable; you encouraged us all to go to college and twisted our arms to take out massive loans. Meanwhile, your administration was profiting off our backs.

Law school students acquired colossal debt and passed the bar exam only to end up working as coffee baristas; Ivy league graduates applied for third-rate jobs just to get by; and youth abandoned their dreams as nurses, doctors, and surgeons to take mind-numbing but higher-paying office jobs within the government.

You told us that you were reforming health care and making it more affordable, but you did not tell young medical students how hard it would be for them to care for their patients or make a profit as physicians under Obamacare. We thought you were being "transparent" when you told us we could keep our doctor and our health-care plan if we liked it; we didn't realize you had your fingers crossed behind your back.

You promised to create 7 million new jobs and to help entrepreneurs of my generation become "the next Steve Jobs." Then you hardly worked on the economy at all; you spent nearly twice as much time on the golf course as you did in economic meetings.[1]

Meanwhile, my generation of highly educated Americans was underemployed and drowning in the student debt that you advised us to take out. Our credit was terrible; we couldn't buy homes and we often had nowhere to turn but our parents' basements. We put off marriage, and many of us will delay parenthood for so long that we may never see our own grandchildren.

You sent young men and women into hopeless battles where they had their limbs blown off by savage brutes and earned an epidemic of PTSD.

When these brave troops returned home, you withheld their benefits and imprisoned them unjustly—sending them spiraling into suicidal depression.

You rendered my entire generation defenseless and vulnerable to terror and violence; you attacked our Second Amendment rights; you threatened to hunt us down with lethal drone force; you allowed young Americans to die in easily preventable terror attacks.

Your administration lied to my friends about guns in order to buy their votes. You did not just mislead; you are culpable for setting us against each other and creating an aura of distrust that clouds our relationships; you are accountable for promoting gun regulations that left us susceptible to mass violence in our schools and workplaces.

You were the Executive Con Man of one gigantic pyramid scheme where young people hustled to knock on doors and "get out the vote" in both 2008 and 2012 only to be forgotten by you. Once elected, you prioritized getting down in a dance-off with Usher;

jetting off to play eighteen holes with Tiger; and eavesdropping on journalists with Holder.

You shirked responsibility for the misery you imposed on my generation. Your economic, social, and national security policies have left both literal and metaphorical bloodstains on your hands for killing the hopes, careers, and dreams of young Americans for your own political gain.

Your administration's lies and incompetence anger me on my own behalf and on behalf of my friends and our parents. You have done such extensive damage to my generation that I decided to share and expose our story. You are now accountable to us. I expect you to read this book; I believe you will find it quite eye-opening.

Sincerely,
Katie Kieffer

OPERATION PICKUP LINE

1

B ill Clinton beguiled any attractive young woman who struck his fancy as he made his way through two terms in the White House. Barack Obama outdid Clinton during his own dual presidency, beguiling young men and women alike without leaving even one stained navy blue dress to mark his trail. Obama worked remotely—using slick and dirty pickup lines to attract youths to his brand and then turning around and crushing the careers, hopes, and dreams of millions of young Americans.

Obama's greatest presidential legacy is also his biggest scandal: Obama literally robbed the cradle. He seduced the Millennial generation into voting for him not once but twice. He captured 60 percent of the eighteen-to-twenty-nine vote in 2012 and an even larger share of the youth vote (66 percent) in 2008.[1] Unlike a young person who could at least find maturity and support in an older partner, Millennials who voted for Obama were left with a shell of a man who had less maturity than they; a man who promised to help them land jobs and pay for college only to leave them jobless while he teed off with his bad boy playmates.

Because He Could

Why did Obama con 95 million young people? For the same reason President John F. Kennedy preyed on an attractive young intern. And for the same reason Clinton said he became an expert in extramarital affairs and dress staining: "Just because I could."[2]

Because he could, one summer afternoon in 1962, President John F. Kennedy treated nineteen-year-old White House press office intern Mimi Alford to a swim and two daiquiris. Before she knew it, her "first time" was taking place on first lady Jacqueline's bed. Kennedy continued the affair until his assassination. Alford recounts the liaison in her memoir, telling how Kennedy once put her in the "unforgivable" position of pressuring her to perform a sexual favor on one of his aides—while he observed.[3] To think many people worried that Kennedy would take his orders from the pope.

Because he could, President Clinton invited White House volunteer Kathleen Willey into a private Oval Office hallway where he groped her breasts and then placed her hands on his privates. This was not consensual. Clinton's eighteen-month affair with White House intern Monica Lewinsky was consensual. Still, she was quite young, he aggressively encouraged the affair, and he was her boss, not to mention the president of the United States. Clinton relied on Lewinsky's constant adulation, frequent "non-sex," and willingness to become his cigar holder to boost his fragile ego. Eventually, he exercised a shakedown effort on both Willey and Lewinsky to influence their testimonies after stories of his fondling leaked.[4]

Many paths lead to the White House. Obama decided to take the path that had been blazed by a long line of cheaters, seduction masters, and swindlers. He was a careful student of Kennedy and Clinton, quickly picking up on their least-becoming traits and using his knowledge to build himself into a far bigger player. As far as we know, Obama was never a player in the sense that Clinton and Kennedy were; Obama was a whole new kind of player.

As if there was any doubt, Clinton outright told us that he lived "parallel lives."[5] As he racked up rendezvous, Clinton utilized a special calendar to track the days on which he actually behaved himself.[6] Obama was more guarded; he kept his wild cards close to his vest and his second life is just now coming to light.

Only, Obama did not use his sway to get White House interns to carry out sexual favors; he used his power to extort votes from young swing voters. From Obama's perspective, it must have been more titillating than a swinger club: after young people gave him their votes, he returned their favors with official and unofficial policies that destroyed their social, cultural, and economic opportunities.

Groupies will go to their graves arguing that Kennedy and Clinton made mistakes in their private lives but were excellent leaders overall. Groupies can't make this argument for Obama. The reverse is true: he led a wholesome-looking private life and made colossal public mistakes that set back an entire generation—forever.

No one can defend Obama's actions (as they tried for Clinton) by saying: "It's none of our business. Even if he was president, it was still his private life!" Obama did not seduce one busty babe in a bathroom; his quest was 30 percent of the U.S. population.

When a sober man makes the same public promises over and over again, and then signs policies that break these promises, he is operating with careful calculation. Obama knew what he was doing and he was not acting under the influence of a fine Scotch whiskey.

We had every right to *expect* our presidents to behave with integrity. Think about it. We gave these men and their families free rent for eight years in a mansion, we paid for their vacations; we handed them the most powerful and high-profile job on earth; we fetched them in limousines; we flew them cross-continental in Air Force One, and we supplied them with an army of chefs, bodyguards, and assistants to attend to their every whim. It is silly to defend presidents after they abuse their power and bite the hands that fed them—*our* hands.

No matter what Obama, Clinton, or Kennedy's groupies say, big shots *are* capable of leading with fortitude. Certainly, not every power-ful, burdened, charismatic, and handsome male has become a con man just because he could.

Case in point: Steve Jobs. The late cofounder of Apple possessed comparable power, charisma, and good looks to those of Kennedy, Clin-ton, and Obama. As the billionaire entrepreneur who built Apple into the world's most valuable company, he could have scored with his choice of paramours. Jobs juggled a global business empire with family life *plus* the strain of pancreatic cancer. He honored his commitments: He was loyal to his wife Laurene through their twenty-year marriage; he led Apple with integrity; he received the first National Medal of Technol-ogy from President Ronald Reagan; he barred porn on Apple apps when his competitors did the opposite; he advised Clinton to come clean on Lewinsky, and he told Obama to stop ripping off the American dream with his policies.[7] Jobs made some mistakes as a young man, but he was not a hypocrite. He sincerely repented of his omissions and matured into a devoted father, faithful husband, and businessman of integrity.

We could also bring up Presidents Ronald Reagan or George Wash-ington as examples of big shots who were also good guys. But because Jobs was a registered Democrat, we now have a case for powerful men to behave with integrity that no liberal can tear asunder.

Reflecting on the legacies of our three most charismatic Democratic presidents in recent memory, the question becomes:

Who was the biggest con man?

1. **Kennedy:** For bedding an intern willing to play naughty nurse behind the back of a married mother?
2. **Clinton:** For coaxing sexual favors from a young coquette throwing him kisses in public and teasing him with her thong at the office?[8]

or

3. **Obama:** For taking advantage of the hope and trust of an en-tire generation of young Americans and permanently setting them back economically, morally, and socially.

Our answer is obvious.

Kennedy lured. Clinton decoyed. Obama hunted big game. He could and so he did.

Who Are the Millennials?

B aby Boomers had many children: Millennials comprise about 30 percent of the U.S. population. Historians Neil Howe and William Strauss popularized the term "Millennial Generation." Most people agree that Millennials were born between the late 1970s and the early 2000s.

Most Millennials remember exactly where they were when the twin towers of the World Trade Center fell on September 11, 2001. They remember Clinton's affair and impeachment trial and G. W.'s bullhorn speech at Ground Zero, and the majority of them voted for the first African American president.

They are techies. For the first generation to grow up contemporaneously with the Internet, e-mailing is a given and texting is instinctive. Millennials were babies when Microsoft, IBM, and Apple were having "babies": new operating systems like Windows 95, OS/2, and Mac OS. When Millennials wake up in the morning, they instantly check their smartphones; they were the earliest adopters of social media like Facebook and Twitter; they do not keep photo albums, but they do Instagram their lives; they grew up with fifth-generation video-game consoles like Sony PlayStation and Nintendo 64 and with J. K. Rowling's *Harry Potter*, Stephenie Meyer's *Twilight* series, and *The Hunger Games*. YouTube and reality television made them famous (think pop star Justin Bieber)—and infamous (think Bieber when caught on camera at a New York club squirting a photo of President Clinton with blue cleaner fluid and shouting: "F—k Bill Clinton!"). Technology has made Millennials' lives an open book—their pranks go viral as fast as their successes.

Transparency is huge for Millennials. Given the technology they grew up with, it is no surprise that experts say this generation places a high value on being included in a stream of back-and-forth communication with their friends, peers, and colleagues.[9] Millennials also are budding pioneers; entrepreneurship appeals to them, as does the ability to trail-blaze within an existing company. Quick and observant learners, many strive to soak up every bit of information around them, and they are so eager to grow (right now!) that they pique their supervisors, who kindly coach them on patience.

Millennials have been dismissed as "lazy narcissists." Realistically, Millennials are fiscally conservative and socially libertarian, and their number one issue is the economy.[10] Experts say Millennials resemble Americans growing up during the Depression era—using coupons, shopping for deals, and embracing an organic, do-it-yourself lifestyle.[11] MTV released a study in 2013 revealing that 75 percent of fourteen- to seventeen-year-olds worry about the economy's impact on their future.[12] Fourteen is too young to be so anxious, but our youths are not blind; they know their future is murky and are economically wary.

Despite fielding stress at a tender age, Millennials have big hearts; many are willing to donate their time and services to the community or the armed forces. They excel when their families and mentors give them the benefits of high expectations, freedom, and leadership. But when their mentors exploit them for profit, their natural talents wilt and they tailspin into tabloid tonnage or exchange their reputations for quickie claims to fame like "I was the first guy eliminated from *The Bachelorette*!"

* * *

IF you are a Gen Xer, Baby Boomer, or a member of the Greatest Generation, you experienced your own set of challenges. Many of you fought for the freedom that Millennials enjoy today. Through your hard work and perseverance, you built many of the great American companies that will employ Millennials in the future—from the ground up. You also experienced what it was like for America to *dominate* and be *respected* around the globe. You tasted a freer America. You knew that if you were industrious and honorable, you could achieve the American dream. You want this life for your children and grandchildren, who are Millennials.

Americans of all ages now have a common desire: to pursue and achieve their hopes and dreams. To advance toward this goal, we must uncover the untold story of how Obama ripped off the American Dream for the Millennial Generation. In telling this story, we will encounter lessons, alternatives, and solutions to move us toward freedom and fulfillment.

Once Upon a Christian Community Organizer

M any years ago, in the windy city of Chicago, there lived a young man named Barack Obama. His friends called him Barry and he called himself a follower of Jesus Christ.

Barry was a "community organizer" and part of his job was to help poor black men living in Chicago's South Side find work.

Community organizing *sounded* like a benevolent profession, especially to Millennials who grew up volunteering. In 2007, young swing voters hearing that a former "community organizer" named Barack Obama was running for president were given the impression that he had dedicated his life to serving his neighbors. It almost sounded like Obama had worked at an orphanage rocking forsaken infants to sleep, or at an animal shelter spoon-feeding milk to kittens. Far from it.

Millennials did not realize Obama's true motivation for becoming a community organizer. Here's what they *didn't* know: After completing his undergraduate work at Columbia University, Obama worked briefly as a research assistant for a mid-Manhattan consulting house to pay off his student loans and then began aggressively applying for community organizing roles. Obama was an Ivy League graduate who could have worked in a Manhattan firm. Instead, he sought $10,000 per year and a car allowance to leave New York in 1985 for the South Side of Chicago to "community organize" and live like a pauper. Obama essentially viewed his time in Chicago as a political boot camp where he would learn how to influence people as a politician someday and become more powerful than he could ever be as a Manhattan lawyer. When Obama moved to Chicago, he was hired and trained by the followers of a man named Saul Alinsky. Soon, Obama was training others in the Alinsky method, which taught that the ends justify the means and the ultimate end was power—an overthrow of the system for the sake of overthrowing the system.[13] Obama's assistant community organizer, Johnnie Owens, recounted that Obama's "house and his bookshelf" featured books about power, including Alinsky's *Reveille for Radicals*.[14]

Alinsky's philosophy was: Obtain "power" by determining the "self-interest" of your audience. Once you understand their self-interest, use your power to overthrow the prevailing free-market cultural, economic, and political structures (which you perceive as onerous) using *whatever means necessary*. The Alinsky method encouraged community organizers to rouse the poor and middle class by making them feel discontented, angry, and victimized, and to view the wealthy and successful as their enemies. Of course this is irrational: If success is ostracized, how will you rise toward success? If job creators are the enemy, how will you find a job? Alinsky's idealistic method failed to explain how the new "overthrown" society would work in reality. But Alinsky's method succeeded in helping Obama learn how to manipulate the self-interest of his audience so *he* could rise from pauper to power broker.

On the campaign trail, Obama told our young people *his* version of his community organizing days: "I dedicated myself to discovering his [Jesus Christ's] truth and carrying out his works."[15] The testimonies of Obama's friends reveal that he saw political organizing on Chicago's South Side—a low-paying and dangerous job—as a way to gain two assets for his political pipe dream: the trust of the black community and experience organizing people.[16] Owens observed: "He had larger ambitions in mind" and "In retrospect it was clear he was hoping to gain some organizing experience and he was willing to take a low pay grade to get it."[17]

Barry quit the Chicago community—without helping blacks find jobs. Jerry Kellman was the man who read Obama's application to community organize for the Developing Communities Project in Chicago's

South Side, and he helped Obama land the job in 1985. Kellman made the mistake of admitting to the *New York Times* in 2008 that by the time Obama left Chicago for law school, they had accomplished: "nothing that would change poverty on the South Side of Chicago."[18] Obama left his South Side brothers as poor as ever, after using them as guinea pigs. He walked away with a political cache: a stockpile of ideas for convincing people to embrace him as their leader.

In 1988, Barry turned his back on Chicago and set off for Harvard Law School, always keeping his eye on the White House.

Let the Bribing Begin

C linton used pickup lines to entice young Monica into living at his beck and call, even on Easter Sunday. His charming words sunk so deeply into Monica's head that she began hinting to friends that the president might marry her.[19] Barry was far sleazier than Bill. He used pickup lines to crawl into the heads of an entire generation of young Americans. He offered guarantees that he would help them achieve their most personal dreams. As a special bonus, he offered young people exclusive access to a "celebrity"—him.

Obama's community organizing days—as well as his time teaching at the University of Chicago, as we'll explore in chapter 4—taught him how to present himself as whatever man his audience wanted him to be, *to speak to their innermost self-interest* and promise jobs, peace, and affordable health care that he would never deliver.

A former law school student of Obama's observed to the *New York Times* that when he heard Obama speak on the campaign trail: "it's at a level so much simpler than the one he's capable of."[20] Simple indeed. Obama dusted off his teleprompter and began delivering speeches proffering young people their ideal world.[21]

HE PROMISED: *"This campaign must be the occasion, the vehicle, of your hopes, and your dreams . . . . I want to win that next battle—for better schools, and better jobs, and health care for all"* ... *"Not just with words, but with deeds ... by providing this generation with ladders of opportunity that were unavailable for previous generations."*

WHAT HAPPENED: Millennials became the first generation of Americans to do worse economically, educationally, and culturally than their parents.

HE PROMISED: *"And I'll be a President who ends this war in Iraq and finally brings our troops home; who restores our moral standing . . . [who unites] America and the world against the common threats of . . . terrorism and nuclear weapons; climate change and poverty; genocide and disease."*

WHAT HAPPENED: Obama took over three years to withdraw all U.S. troops from Iraq, he authorized the troop surge in Afghanistan, and U.S. troops were set to remain in Afghanistan through 2014 and potentially beyond.

Terrorists repeatedly and successfully attacked Americans on U.S. soil; American citizens faced the threat of lethal drone force; corporate and military infrastructures were hacked.

Obama addressed "climate change" by encouraging Americans to drive green vehicles before the technology was safe (think exploding electric car batteries)[22] and subsidizing wind turbines that killed over 573,000 birds in the United States annually.[23]

During Obama's two terms, poverty spiked nationwide, including in Obama's hometown of Chicago, and mentally ill individuals incited five of the twelve deadliest mass shootings on record in American history.

HE PROMISED: *"A revamped education system. A bold new energy strategy. A more efficient health care system. Renewed investment in basic research and our infrastructure. These are the pillars of a more competitive economy that will take advantage of the global marketplace's opportunities."*

"What gives me the most hope is the next generation—the young

people whose attitudes and beliefs and openness to change have already made history in this election [by turning out in record numbers for his sermons]."[24]

"*We won't extend the promise of American greatness unless we invest in our young people and ask them to invest in America.*"

WHAT HAPPENED: Young people heard the president say: If you hustle and get out the vote for me, I'll repay you handsomely. Unfortunately, he left them empty-handed.

How did Obama get away with making and breaking so many promises? One word: shortcuts. Let me explain . . .

Out of His League

W hen he signed up to run for president, Barry also re-signed with Baby League Baseball. His 01 jersey was beginning to look like a midriff top. But, what the heck, no one would know, he would wear business casual on the campaign trail!

"His entire life . . . he's never stepped up to the plate and taken full swings," said a former University of Chicago colleague, describing Obama to the *New York Times*.[25]

The colleague said Obama avoided challenges and growth opportunities during his twelve years of teaching—refusing to take a stand by publishing a single legal opinion, and limiting his communications with the university's conservative-leaning faculty.

Obama was virtually unknown in 2007. Despite serving as a U.S. senator and teaching law, he was not a household name and his "community organizing" credentials were underwhelming. He needed to make his name go viral so he could win over young swing voters. So, he broke with tradition and decorum by aggressively campaigning on late-night television, feverishly courting voters through social media, and downplaying the radical policy changes he planned to make as president. Once elected, he continued to dodge serious issues, becoming the first sitting president of the United States to appear on a late-night comedy show and repeatedly glossing over the facts for the sake of a rosy picture.

Barry appeared on comedy shows some fourteen times prior to his first election and a dozen more times prior to his second election. Michelle got in on the action too, sometimes appearing with her husband but doing the lion's share of her appearances solo.

Obama was playing T-ball when he should have been playing baseball (talking to the real press and taking hard questions). Of course, Millennials did not realize he was playing T-ball; to young people, he seemed like a regular guy. He was endearing himself to them by appearing on the shows that they watched.

Despite the confidence he *projected*, Obama was insecure in the strength of his ideas and thus refused to let himself be challenged. There was nothing *inherently* wrong with Obama doing a few appearances on late-night television. That said, he should have balanced his featherweight appearances with more hard-hitting appearances on programs where seasoned journalists with a wide range of worldviews would *challenge* his ideas and compel him to explain his *game plan* for achieving his idyllic promises.

Imagine if Obama had been brave enough to repeatedly face veteran journalists who posed challenges for him: "Senator Obama, please articulate your step-by-step plan for how Obamacare will make health care higher in quality and lower in price." Obama would have fallen flat on his face: "Ah, um, yes. Well, you know, if you like your plan you can keep it! For folks listening at home, I am totally committed to making health care more affordable. Rather than buying into Fox News bias against me, let's keep a civil tone and focus on what we can all agree on, such as . . . aaahh . . . March Madness?!"

Typing and Casting Spells

C *lickity, click, click.* Against their own better judgment, journalists turned themselves into "typing wizards," using their words to weave masterful articles and news segments that cast Barack and Michelle as rock stars and role models. Obama was greatly enabled by this dragoon of typing and broadcasting enchanters who left young people spellbound.

An October 2008 Pew Research poll showed that: "By a margin of 70%–9%, Americans say most journalists want to see Obama" win.[26] Unfortunately, while most first-time voters *knew* the media favored Obama, they were too young to *question* the media's love affair with Obama. Eighteen-year-olds voting for the first time in their short lives lacked the benefit of experience to know that politicians' words cannot be taken at face value. Journalists knew better; most had years of experience analyzing American politics and reporting on elections, yet they only told young people about Obama's glamorous side—not his radical side. For example:

- Obama opposed the Born Alive Infant Protection Act, which guaranteed medical care to a baby that survives an abortion; he also favored partial birth abortion. The conventional media alerted Millennials to Obama's inhumane views just three times in the two years before his first election, according to Media Research Center.[27] And, young people heard next to nothing about Obama's tight relationship with Bill Ayers, a founder of a militant organization called Weathermen that is responsible for killing police officers and blowing up U.S. government buildings.[28]

  Instead, young people heard enchanting words like these:
  – "Obama is a rock star!"—NBC's Andrea Mitchell in 2004.[29]
  – "It seems reasonable to expect that he can bridge all the other divisions—and answer all the impossible questions—plaguing American public life."—Joe Klein in *Time* in 2006.[30]
  – "I have to tell you . . . the feeling most people get when they hear Barack Obama's speech . . . . I felt this thrill going up my leg" and Obama gives "the kind of speech I think . . . people in the last year of college should see before they go out in the world."—MSNBC's Chris Matthews in 2007 and 2008.[31]

—"He is a rock star! . . . Obama can do no wrong! Sexy! Sexy! Sexy!"—Ana Marie Cox on MSNBC in late 2006.[32]

* * *

BARRY had a far bigger ego than JFK or Clinton, who, though hardly humble, *did* deliver their presidential victory speeches with their wives, families, and vice presidents at their sides. On November 4, 2008, Obama gave his victory speech in Grant Park, Chicago. There was one person on the stage—him. Barry was not about to share the limelight with those who helped him win!

The next day, two *Newsweek* reporters, Evan Thomas and Jon Meacham, discussed Obama's speech with Charlie Rose on the *Charlie Rose Show*. Most Americans have forgotten this interview or never heard it, but it offers a rare glimpse into the fact that the conventional media *did* initially notice Obama's penchant to hog the stage; even progressive journalists found it annoying to watch Obama crow and strut like a rooster. Nevertheless, for the next four years, these journalists made the conscious decision to rebrand Obama's vanity as charisma.

MEACHAM: I was very struck watching the stagecraft—and this comes out again and again in the project—in Grant Park [Chicago], he walks out with the family, and then they go away. Biden's back, you know, locked in the bar or something, you know—

(*Rose laughs.*)

MEACHAM: They don't let him out. And have you ever seen a victory speech where there was no one else on stage? No adoring wife, no cute kid—he is the message.

THOMAS: There is a slightly creepy cult of personality about all of this. I mean, he is such an admirable—

ROSE: "Slightly creepy cult of personality?"

THOMAS: Yes.

ROSE: What's "slightly creepy" about it?

THOMAS: It just makes me a little uneasy that he's so singular. He's clearly managing his own spectacle. He knows how to do it. He's a—I think, a deeply manipulative guy—you know, this could be a useful thing in a leader—

ROSE: How so is he "deeply manipulative?"

THOMAS: I think the key moment, to answer your question . . . it's when he was running for—to be the president of the Harvard Law Review. . . . And he realizes that people want to help him. They want to help him. It makes people feel good to help—and this is an important insight for him. Oh my gosh, I have this gift. I have this knack. People are going to want to help—want to help me. I'll let them help me, all the way to the White House.[33]

Barry's necromancers played hocus-pocus for over five years, polishing his image in the eyes of Millennials with magic words like "charisma" and "leader," and never stopped to think that by abandoning their posts as watchdogs of the government and defenders of the First Amendment, they were self-cannibalizing.

When Millennials finally heard from media watchdogs, it was too late. Two days after Obama was reelected in 2012, a Government Accountability Project counsel for whistleblowers tweeted: *"Now am I allowed to criticize Obama on drones & assassination & military commissions & secret memos expanding secret surveillance powers??"*[34] Allowed to? That was in your job description all along.

In the spring of 2013, when the Associated Press and the *New York Times* discovered they were the victims of unconstitutional government probes, the typing wizards finally realized they had been played for fools.

The *New York Times* editorialized on May 6, 2013: "The administration has now lost all credibility . . . Mr. Obama is proving the truism that the executive branch will use any power it is given and very likely abuse it."[35] But by May of 2013 it was too late for the journalists at the *Times* to caution young people against voting for a thug.

Without the typing wizards, Millennials would have realized Obama was self-absorbed, not visionary, and he would never have scored two terms.

Gold Diggers

As Baby Boomers, Barry and Michelle needed to make themselves relevant to Millennials. This was not about evangelizing; this was a numbers game. They figured they could reach the highest number of young people by saturating late-night television and social media and by making themselves famous for being famous. Ironically, in the memoir he released before running for president, *Dreams of My Father*, Obama expressed aversion to the world of fame, wealth, and television—a world he eventually took full advantage of.

Some might argue that Barack and Michelle were simply meeting young people where they were. To this objection, I must emphasize that it is certainly fine if our politicians appear on television or utilize technology. It is admissible for politicians to *naturally* become celebrities in the process of running for the high-profile job of president. But we must draw a line at the *way* our presidents gain notoriety. Our leaders better take care to become celebrities in the Steve Jobs tradition and not in the Barack Obama tradition. Jobs became famous by speaking his mind and creating useful products. Obama became famous by hiding his true motivations, reading scripts, associating himself with louche celebrities, and raising our young people's expectations. Then, he broke his promises as well as systems that already worked well and needed *improvement*—not *overhaul*—like the free-market health-care system.

Further, for their political gain, Barack and Michelle encouraged our young people to form unhealthy habits that they did not tolerate in their *own* family. During Barack's first summer at Columbia University in New York, his mother and sister Maya visited him. He recalls: "I scolded Maya for spending one evening watching TV instead of reading the novels I'd bought for her."[36] On the *Tonight Show*, Obama told Jay Leno that Malia, his older daughter, "got a cell phone, but [both girls are] not allowed to use it during the week just like they are not allowed to watch TV during the week." He said he was not comfortable with his own daughters watching the reality show *Keeping up with the Kardashians*, and "I am probably a little biased against reality TV."

As a presidential candidate in 2008, Obama roared like a preacher: "So many children are growing up in front of the television. As fathers and parents, we've got to spend more time with them . . . and replace the video game or the remote control with a book . . . It's up to us—as fathers and parents—to instill this ethic of excellence in our children."[37] Once he became president, he apparently lost sight of his vision; Obama quarried late-night comedy, technology, and fame for swing votes, as if they were gold mines.

If he was gonna be a gold digger, couldn't he have at least followed the Golden Rule?

A Socialist Who Drinks Beer

Obama appeared on *The Daily Show with Jon Stewart* in October of 2008. Here, he shrugged off rumors that he would implement a "socialist" or "communist" agenda, blaming such assertions on: "hard core Sean Hannity fans that probably wouldn't wanna go grab a beer with me."

Obama wanted Stewart's young audience to think he was the go-to guy to help them "get a job" and so he deadpanned: "the whole socialist argument, that doesn't fly too well with me; the evidence of this seems pretty thin . . . I think they found proof, that when I was in kindergarten, I shared some toys with my friends."

Notice that Obama did *not* go on late-night television and tell young people: "Hey guys, I'm Barack and I have socialistic and borderline communistic plans to redistribute wealth and set up new taxes like

Obamacare that will kill jobs and hurt entrepreneurship!" Rather, he told Millennials that he would bring jobs, hope, and change. On comedy shows, Obama sidestepped charges that he had a socialist agenda by cracking a cute joke about sharing his toys as a kindergartener. Young people tuning in gathered that Obama was a nice guy who would help them find jobs because, as a child, he shared his Legos.

There was a common theme to Obama's late-night appearances: He had virtually no challenge to his record or policies. Comedians would raise the objection de jour, but Obama could take as long as he wanted to respond and then the comedian often moved on to the next question without pushing him to elaborate. Obama seemed to relish the fact that hosts pitched him plenty of lightweight topics having nothing to do with politics or the economy, like sports and Hollywood. This is not to disparage comedians; they were doing their job. Obama was the one playing baseball in diapers.

* * *

DAYS before Election Day 2008, Senator Obama did a massive sales pitch on MTV with reporter Sway Calloway. He assured Millennials that he would improve virtually every aspect of their lives:

> CALLOWAY: You have a gigantic audience that is watching you right now. What can you tell them about the importance of getting out to vote?
> OBAMA: You've got a younger viewership on MTV, so let me be specific to the young people. Every decision that is going to be made in this election, or by the next president, is going to have an enormous impact on your lives. We've talked about some of them: your ability of whether you are going to afford to go to college, whether we have got an economy that's creating jobs for the future, whether we've got a tax code that is fair and gives everybody a chance at a better life . . . are we continuing with two wars and how does that impact young people who are typically the ones who are fighting wars.

Obama bribed young people to vote for him by making it sound like he would solve all their concerns. He also reassured Millennials that he was *not* a radical or a socialist. Yet, as president he implemented policies that redistributed wealth and surprise, surprise, the result was the *nightmare* of the fantasy he promised.

*   *   *

BARACK Star rode his young fans like a rock star over a mosh pit—all the way to 1600 Pennsylvania Avenue. But by 2011, Obama began to lose his favorability among young people. This meant that before the 2012 election he needed to spend even more time targeting them on the programs they watched. Late night would again be the perfect place for Obama to promote himself without having to defend his embarrassing record. Consider his October 25, 2011, appearance on the *Tonight Show* with Jay Leno:

Obama defended his decision to unconstitutionally bypass Congress and engage militarily in Libya, saying: "this whole thing only cost us a billion dollars as opposed to a trillion dollars." (Such a frugal man!)

Looking to please everyone, Obama praised both the Occupy Wall Street and the tea party movements. (Oh sure, Barry *loved* the tea party philosophy—so much that his IRS officials targeted tea party groups, barring them from countereducating Millennials!)

Barry made it sound like he and Michelle were basically June and Ward Cleaver. To paraphrase, he told Leno: I'm a principled guy who quit smoking and handles stress by hitting the gym. I'm down-to-earth; occasionally, I'll eat fried chicken and waffles and spill on my tie and oh, by the way, did you know I watch the World Series and I'm friends with—name drop—Will and Jada Smith?!

Why *wouldn't* a young person want to vote for Obama? He assured them that he would solve all their problems if he got four more years and he was a normal guy who drank beer, talked sports, and happened to be friends with movie stars!

*   *   *

OBAMA was not giving late-night comedy appearances for sport; after all, he could have been on the basketball court. He was methodically pursuing Millennial voters by appearing on the shows they watched.

In the course of one week in April of 2012, he appeared on *NBC's Late Night with Jimmy Fallon* and palled around with Jimmy Kimmel at the White House Correspondents' Association dinner. That same week, former White House press secretary Dana Perino pointed out on *FOX and Friends*: "It's where he's most comfortable. He does really well on those shows. . . . You see him on a show like that and you like him. . . . President Bush had just a very different outlook on these comedy shows. He liked them, he respected them, but he never went on them, during his presidency . . . . He just didn't think it was a place where the president should be."[38]

The *New York Times* reported: "Ben LaBolt, a spokesman for the Obama campaign, said the willingness to appear with interviewers like Mr. Stewart, Mr. Leno and Mr. Letterman has to do with reaching out in less conventional ways to undecided voters. . . . Mr. Stewart's network, Comedy Central, coincidentally released a research study this month that asked so-called millennials in what venue they would most like to hear a candidate be interviewed. By a large margin they responded: on a late-night comedy show."[39]

Barry stomped his feet and refused to give up his T-ball glove and play in the major leagues; he was terrified of confronting the press or discussing serious topics like the Benghazi terrorist attack that might showcase his failures. For example, Obama gave an October 24, 2012, *Tonight Show* appearance despite the fact that the Benghazi attack had recently occurred and August 20 was the last time he had held an "open" news conference with the press, according to ABC—and even that could hardly be called a news conference because he handpicked questions from four reporters in the White House Briefing Room.[40] On the *Tonight Show* Obama joked about baseball and Halloween candy. Classic Obama, prioritizing his hunt for votes over his presidential duties.

Days later, on Friday, October 26, Obama did a thirty-minute live special on MTV. Obama told young people that he would make college more affordable and encouraged them to keep taking on debt they could not afford.[41] He promised Millennials that if they voted for him in 2012, he had a "game-changing idea" to resolve their student debt loads. It would be a game-changer all right: a massive Ponzi scheme where students went into record default while the Department of Education pulled in more money from taxpayers than Exxon or Apple reported in 2012 profits.

Young people listening to Obama on comedy shows and MTV thought that he would *help* them find jobs and eliminate their debt.

War

"Obama has the biggest U.S. election army ever assembled," Time *magazine reported in October of 2012.*

E asy victories were so 2008. The stakes were higher by 2012 as young people were more hesitant to vote for Obama. After all, they were still unemployed and living at home.

Barry was in a bad mood,[42] fretting over his prospects for reelection, but Michelle refused to give him even one cigarette break. He decided to take action and stepped up his social media tactics to target youths. He created a "Geek Squad" to handle his tech and social media stratagems and recruited hundreds of Millennial-aged staffers to Obama headquarters in Chicago and increased his "number crunchers" five-fold from 2008, *Time* reported.[43]

When it came to viral fundraising for small donations, Obama made it a little *too* easy for young people to dump their piggy banks into his coffers—especially for someone who claimed he would help students dig themselves out of debt. His Geek Squad developed an app that stored credit card information and allowed repeat donations via single-number texts. Obama raised $500 million online in 2008 and $690 million online in 2012.[44]

Trolling

Fishermen troll for kingfish by gliding through the water with multiple fishing lines loaded with different baits. Likewise, Obama trolled for swing votes in 2012 by baiting 600,000 supporters on Facebook with false promises of hope, jobs, and change. He exploited these 600,000 supporters to share his lies with 5 million of their friends and hook them into voting for him. According to *Time* magazine, Obama's campaign desperately needed "a big youth turnout," and without Facebook trolling, the campaign would have been in "a crisis."[45] Obama's Facebook app enticed young people to urge their friends to vote for Obama and donate to his campaign. Obama's digital director conceded to *Time* that they utilized the Facebook app to convince Millennials to *trust* Obama: "People don't trust campaigns. . . . Who do they trust? Their friends."[46]

Millennials trusted their friends' recommendations and consequently donated their time, money, and votes to Obama's campaign. If only they had known how Obama would betray their trust once elected! Obama's campaign abused Facebook—employing it to dupe young people into believing he would help them find jobs and achieve their dreams. Obama used Facebook as his Millennial Troll Vessel—snaring starry-eyed youths with his lies and then reeling in their votes.

We Know We're Hurting You, We Just Don't Care

Beyond their precious daughters Sasha and Malia, every young person in America was a tool to the Obamas, capable of voting on three important dates. The Obamas' eyes were on the grand prize package: Two terms in the White House, eight years of bankrolled excess, and international fame. Nothing—especially a conscience—held them back from winning.

* * *

BESIDES *Jersey Shore*, MTV was home to reality shows like *Teen Mom* and *16 and Pregnant* that made *Keeping up with the Kardashians* look wholesome. These shows glamorized teen pregnancy—featuring hot girls who landed six-figure reality show gigs after getting knocked up and becoming felons. Gals like nineteen-year-old Jenelle Evens (arrested for assault) and twenty-one-year-old Amber Portwood (pleaded guilty to domestic battery).[47] Did Obama care that he encouraged young women to tune in to MTV, where they would find "role models" like Portwood and Evens?

Heck, no! Obama perfectly timed his appearances on MTV before the 2008, 2010, and 2012 elections.

The *New York Post* revealed that Obama was so crazed with MTV that his Get Out the Vote campaign picked up the phone and called MTV Scratch (MTV's ad agency) in the summer of 2011 asking for advice on how to reach out to Millennials. Young people were losing interest in Obama and growing angry over the high unemployment situation. Obama's campaign asked MTV: "Can you tell us how we should be talking to them?"[48] MTV reportedly turned the predators down.

The Obamas knew the long-term consequences of their actions. It had to cross their minds: *We're encouraging other parents' children to do everything we gloat about forbidding our own children to do!* While the Obamas made it a family affair to read classic American novels like *Tender Is the Night* and *Catcher in the Rye* with their daughter Malia, they were pushing classic American trash on other youths.[49]

A 2009 Stanford study revealed that multitasking across various forms of media (texting and watching TV simultaneously) impaired the cognitive abilities of college students. Other experts revealed that media multitasking can hold young people back from high-paying jobs by damaging their analytical skills, while social media use deprives youths of sleep, thereby stunting their ability to transfer short-term memory into long-term memory.[50]

Again, there is nothing wrong with appearing on TV or using social media. The problem was *how* Obama used these mediums. He asked young people to tune in to questionable networks and spend unhealthy doses of time on Facebook. Then, he led them to believe that he would *help* them in profoundly personal ways. After he hooked them with his promises and reeled in their votes, he filleted and fried their dreams for dinner.

Tweeting for Victims

In 2008, exit polls revealed that Obama won about two-thirds of the vote among eighteen- to twenty-nine-year-olds and Senator John McCain only took 32 percent. According to the *New York Times*, 70 percent of Obama's 19 million Twitter followers were "fake" or "inactive" or purchased fans leading into the 2012 campaign.[51] In violation of Twitter's policy, fake accounts could be created by a spamming computer (bot) or culled from inactive accounts, and then sold to anyone looking for a shortcut to boost their following. Anyone can follow you on Twitter, so having a "fake" or spam follower does not guarantee that you bought that follower. That said, the fact that the *vast majority* of Obama's followers were fake does not reflect well on him.

Celebrating the Kill: The 2012 Post-Election Bash

What would be the most appropriate place for Obama to celebrate his viral victim campaign? Facebook and Twitter, #obviously.

On November 6, Obama posted an image of him and Michelle hugging with the caption "Four more years." This image broke social media records, becoming the most Liked post in Facebook history and the most retweeted photo of all time on Twitter. There is nothing wrong with a sentimental photo. This particular photo put visual icing on the cake of a long, calculated campaign and was another staged photo opp that primarily boosted the Obamas' celebrity image.

Breaking these records speaks to the importance of social media sites in electing Obama and the shallowness of his campaign. Obama's campaign encouraged young people to become media zombies and consumers of celebrity rather than cerebral learners. Five years into his presidency, in August of 2013, a University of Michigan study found that using the social media site Facebook led to feelings of unhappiness and self-loathing.[52] The longer people used Facebook, the more their unhappiness became apparent. When used for long stretches of time, sites like Facebook and Twitter, which invite users to compare themselves on superficial levels, can stunt psychological development. The Obamas should have encouraged more moderate usage of social media throughout their campaigns; instead—as pop star Katy Perry would say of herself—Barack and Michelle were "part of the problem."

I Kissed a Girl and . . . Obamacare *Passed*?

Nike and Rolex look for celebrities to boost their brand. Obama also sought celebrities to pitch his brand. Except his brand did not front a legitimate company offering quality goods or services. His brand was a front for a pyramid scheme.

Stars eagerly offered to help Obama build his brand. Some celebrities no doubt thought they were using their star power to "help" young people, but Obama was using *them*, like hex keys, to screw Millennials. Eva Longoria, Jay-Z, Beyoncé, Will Ferrell, Lena Dunham, Scarlett Johansson, and Katy Perry were some of the celebrities who endorsed Obama in 2012.

Perry is a talented songbird, but she was the textbook example of celebrities falling hard for Obama and then using their influence to sway young people to vote for a man they hardly understood. When she wasn't performing her hit single "I Kissed a Girl," Perry was telling *Rolling Stone*: "Our priority is fame, and people's wellness is way low. I say this knowing full well that I'm a part of the problem. I'm playing the game, though I am trying to reroute. Anyway, not to get all politically divulging and introspective, but the fact that America doesn't have free health care drives me f—ing absolutely crazy, and is so wrong."[53]

The president signed Obamacare into law in March of 2010 and *Rolling Stone* interviewed Perry in mid-2011, yet the health-care problem persisted in her mind. "This is a big f—ing deal" were the words Vice President Joe Biden used to describe the same state of affairs that Perry said drove her "absolutely f—ing crazy."

Once Obama was reelected, Perry still had more to say on political stories she had not been following. The day after a jury found George Zimmerman "not guilty" on all counts, @katyperry tweeted:

"Ugh, my tummy turns. RT "@RonanFarrow: American justice: still colorblind (as long as you're white)."

Perry deleted the above tweet after more informed members of Twitter reminded her that Zimmerman was not white, but half Hispanic.

Hollywood Insider reported that 16 percent of under-thirty-five voters found Perry to be a "credible" political spokesperson (this was a lot considering only 1 percent of voters aged thirty-five to forty-four considered her credible).[54] Too bad cute Katy was chattering rather cluelessly about what she was endorsing.

Desperate Hispanic of Hollywood

Desperate Housewives star Eva Longoria signed on to cochair Obama's 2012 campaign. With Longoria whispering in his ear, advising him to talk to Congress and Hispanics "in an emotional manner" and as if he were speaking to "family," Obama won almost 75 percent of the Hispanic vote in 2012.[55]

Obama knew that by 2012, 40 percent of Millennials would be nonwhite.[56] So, during his first term, in the spirit of the Dream Act, he became the first U.S. president to offer work permits to young undocumented immigrants. In retrospect, this move was more about buying votes than helping immigrants.

Longoria likely did more damage than good to the Hispanic community by pushing the president to lobby for the Dream Act, which Steve Jobs told his biographer, Walter Isaacson, would not solve the real problem of recruiting talented foreign students to be trained and allowed to remain in the United States as engineers. Jobs said: "The president is very smart, but he kept explaining to us reasons why things can't get done [outside the framework of the Dream Act]. It infuriates me."[57]

* * *

OBAMA'S overall utilization of celebrities in his hunt for swing votes feels desperate. A sex-themed video from *Girls* creator Lena Dunham encouraged college women to vote Obama. In the clip, Dunham compared voting for Obama with having intercourse for "your first time" and Obama posted it on his official campaign YouTube channel. Comedian-actor Will Ferrell released a last-minute video pitch promising young people that he would do anything for them if they would just "vote Obama," including: "eat anything you tell me to: garbage; hair; human toenails; underpants, whatever, I'm serious, I'll do anything to get you to vote; I'll punch myself in the face."

The silver lining was that Ferrell's clip blew Dunham's video out of the water with twice as many hits—almost 5 million—which just goes to show that you don't need to verbally prostitute yourself to get Millennials to laugh.

HBO's *Game Change*, which came out March 10, 2012, satirized the GOP's 2008 vice-presidential pick of Sarah Palin (played by Tina Fey on SNL, Julianne Moore on HBO) and tried to paint the GOP and conservatives as a pack of nitwits. Even unsympathetic journalists like James Poniewozik pointed out in *Time* magazine that the movie: "feels like piling on."

Hors d'oeuvres connoisseur and elitist Hollywood filmmaker Michael Moore helped Senator Obama prep America for Obamacare with his 2007 release of *Sicko*. Moore came to Obama's aid once again by releasing *Capitalism: A Love Story* on October 2, 2012.

By 2013, Obama did not have time for questions about Benghazi from the mother of the Millennial who died in the terrorist attack, but he had plenty of time to chill with celebrities and recruit stars like Magic Johnson, Lady Gaga, Kerry Washington, Amy Poehler, and Katy Perry to help him promote his signature legislation, Obamacare. Obama deserves credit for always putting the biggest thing in his life first—his ego.

The Common (Con) Man

Obama led Millennials to believe that he was different from other politicians—that he was one of them; a common man. Alas, he was a con artist with a hat full of phony fundraising tricks.

Obama sought the votes of young and angry Occupy Wall Streetors who were camping out in parks from New York to California—decrying student debt, unemployment, and corporate greed. He presented himself through both campaigns as the clean-money guy—the people's candidate who would not stoop to accepting large, undisclosed donations from billionaires, lobbyists, and corporations. Then, he took full advantage of the fundraising practices that he publicly frowned upon, particularly in the 2012 election.

In the 2008 campaign, Obama proclaimed that he would not accept unlimited cash from outside groups. On a frigid day in February of 2007, Obama declared his candidacy before thousands of heavily bundled Americans who gathered in the Springfield, Illinois, town square:

> *The cynics, and the lobbyists, and the special interests who've turned our government into a game only they can afford to play. They write the checks and you get stuck with the bills, they get the access while you get to write a letter, they think they own this government, but we're here to take it back. The time for that politics is over.*[58]

In March of 2007, Obama portrayed himself as the biblical Joshua (who finished where Moses left off and brought God's people to the

Promised Land): "Be strong and have courage, for I am with you wherever you go."[59] On New Hampshire primary night in January of 2008, Obama again likened his campaign to the sacred mission God entrusted to Moses, and reiterated his promise:

> *You can be the new majority who can lead this nation out of a long political darkness . . . who understand that if we mobilize our voices to challenge the money and influence that's stood in our way . . . there's no problem we can't solve—no destiny we cannot fulfill.*[60]

When it came to practicing what he preached, Obama tossed his poetical tablets of stone to the wayside.

In January of 2010 the Supreme Court ruled in *Citizens United v. Federal Election Commission* that outside groups such as corporations were the same as individuals regarding the right to free speech. Essentially, the Court ruled that corporations and unions could finance campaign elections without a spending cap and by an 8–1 majority also ruled that campaigns should disclose their spending.

Barry protested this decision by becoming the first sitting president to insult the Supreme Court during a State of the Union address:

> *With all due deference to separation of powers, last week the Supreme Court reversed a century of law that, I believe, will open the floodgates for special interests, including foreign corporations, to spend without limit in our elections.*

Justice Samuel Alito shook his head and seemed to mouth: "Not true, not true." As Democrats cheered; Obama continued to disrespect the Supreme Court:

"I don't think American elections should be bankrolled by America's most powerful interests or, worse, by foreign entities," Obama sniffed. "They should be decided by the American people."

Soon, Obama would be exploiting *Citizens United* for all it was worth—while hiding this from the young people who cast their 2012 votes thinking he was the clean-money guy. By the spring of 2013, *Time* was reporting how Obama had broken many of his own fundraising rules. For example, Obama made three promises regarding fundraising at the 2012 Democratic National Convention:

1. No corporate money would be accepted. *(FEC filings later revealed that corporate monies had played a role in funding the DNC.)*
2. The campaign would disclose donations quickly. *(Obama's campaign broke this pledge in the final days leading up to the convention.)*
3. Convention donations would be capped at $100,000. *(This was violated by the corporations that helped Obama break promise number one.)*

* * *

OBAMA told throngs of young people at the Charlotte, North Carolina, Democratic National Convention that he was different from: "the people with the $10 million checks who are trying to buy this election." But before he said this, he had accepted a roughly $10 million check in the form of a postelection loan settlement from Duke Energy.[61] Beginning in 2011, Duke Energy CEO Jim Rogers began contributing to the Obama campaign. Rogers's personal donations to the convention would total $100,000. Almost immediately after he began cutting checks for Obama, Rogers began to receive a questionable level of access to the White House before Obama's reelection. Rogers also served as a cochair of the DNC host committee.[62]

This may help explain why Duke was able to snag the approval of no fewer than six regulatory boards to become one of the lobbying leviathans that Obama had raged against as a candidate: On July 2, 2012, Duke merged with Progress Energy to become America's largest electric utility company.[63] Crony capitalism strikes again!

* * *

WITH one hand raised, the other resting on the Bible that Michelle held before him, Obama took the presidential oath in January of 2013. At his inauguration, as the perfect final touch on Campaign Common (Con) Man 2.0, Obama dropped his promises of swift disclosure, uncapped donations, and grabbed corporate donations by the fistful from the likes of Microsoft, AT&T, and Centene Corp.[64]

For a man who promised young people he would sweep Washington clean from the cobwebs of greed, he spun a plethora of his own webs.

"He's the only one who knows the truth—and he never tells the truth," Lewinsky once said of Clinton.[65] Unlike Clinton, Obama will not be able to keep his vices a secret. Barry moronically decided to rook young people in public instead of behind closed doors as Billy did. The truth is out.

FIRED BEFORE THEY
EVEN INTERVIEWED

2

Clinton seemed unapologetic for the way he permanently damaged the life of young Monica Lewinisky. When CNN's Wolf Blitzer asked Clinton whether he cared that Lewinsky's "life has been changed forever" shortly after the affair became public, Clinton said: "That's good."[1] Even years later, when he wrote a memoir so thick and heavy it could be used as a free weight at the gym, Clinton penned that he was the victim of: "a four-year $40 million investigation [that] had come down to: parsing the definition of sex."[2] Willie whimpered that right after the affair broke he slept on a couch while vacationing in Martha's Vineyard with his wife and daughter Chelsea and he continued to sleep on an "old couch" at the White House for at least two months after the affair.[3] Such harsh chastisement it was, dozing on a couch.

Obama was not only unapologetic for his far weightier crime of swindling millions of innocent young Americans, he was proud as a peacock.

Each generation of Americans should experience a better life than the previous generation. Unfortunately, Millennials struggle to overcome lower levels of personal income and wealth and higher rates of poverty, unemployment, and student-loan debt than their parents at the same age, according to a March 2014 Pew report.[4] Yet, Barry patted himself on the back and took credit for a "huge recovery" despite the fact that not one of his major recovery promises came to fruition.

If you thought Bernie Madoff was a con man, it may not be long before you think a penitentiary could be a nice setting for Barry Obama to contemplate his crimes.

Obama took office during a severe economic recession. As a candidate, Barry was quick to blame the recession on Bush and, less than two years into his own presidency, he was just as quick to take full credit for a recovery: It's "Recovery Summer!" Obama and Biden cheered during the summer of 2010. (He had to say *something* to reconvince young people to vote for him.) But he was frighteningly slow to show the "fruits" of his recovery, namely jobs. In ten post–Great Depression recessions, it took an average of twenty-five months for the economy to recover the jobs lost during the recession.[5] In contrast, sixty-seven months after the Great Recession began, Obama's economy still had not recovered its jobs. Every state (except for North Dakota) posted a jobs deficit.[6]

Even worse, after Obama's nearly $1 trillion economic stimulus package passed in February of 2009, guess what, the economy got worse. *Forbes* reported that we experienced the longest post–Great Depression period of unemployment equal to or greater than 9 percent (thirty months) and the longest period over 8 percent (forty-three months).[7] During Obama's first five years in office, poverty rose by almost 31 percent to the highest level on record with the Census Bureau: 49.7 million in poverty.[8] In October of 2012, Michelle Obama went on D.C. hip-hop radio station WPGC 95.5 and said: "I mean, we are seeing right now that we are in the midst of a huge recovery. Right? Because of what this president has done." Michelle's hot air only sounds cool if you rap it.

Let's walk through Obama's legacy of a nonrecovery and broken recovery promises one by one. These were the guarantees he offered to young people to assure them he would grow their incomes. In truth, their votes cost them their lifelong earning potential.

First Broken Recovery Promise

Obama promised on the 2008 campaign trail that, as president, he would oversee "new policies that create the jobs and opportunities of the future"[9] and, once elected, he began his first term by promising Congress "my economic agenda . . . begins with jobs."[10]

Drum roll . . . We're still waiting for all those jobs you promised us, Mr. Obama!

Mimi Alford and Monica Lewinsky both describe themselves as playing the "Waiting Game" with JFK and Clinton respectively. Mimi would sit in a hotel all morning, wasting her life away, waiting for Jack. Monica refused to leave home and paced by her phone, waiting for Willie to make it ring. Both young women squandered their career potential by waiting for these two presidents. After voting for Obama, Millennials waited for far more than hugs and calls; they waited for *jobs*. By January of 2014, the effective unemployment rate (including those who had given up looking for a job) for Millennials aged 18 to 29 was 15.8 percent![11]

Supposedly, the recession officially ended in June of 2009. But what Obama called an economic recovery looked more like a double-dip recession, or like two scoops of vanilla ice cream sprinkled with spiders and leaking from a broken waffle cone. Compared to all of our previous U.S. presidents since FDR, Obama was in last place on job creation during the "recovery" and he was not creating enough jobs a month (200,000 or more) to put us on the road to permanent recovery.[12] The public policy organization Demos released a report in 2013 showing that the economy would need to create *4.1 million jobs* for eighteen- to thirty-four-year-olds just to return to the number held by that age group before the recession.[13] Recovery was still in the distance when Obama and Michelle were boasting about their "huge recovery" going into the 2012 elections. Once Obama was safely reelected, economic growth lingered around 2 percent. This is because many of the new jobs were low-wage or part-time jobs. During the first seven months of 2013, part-time jobs accounted for 77 percent of job growth.[14]

Under Obama, employers took their sweet time hiring new workers, but employers were not to blame—they were fighting to survive and felt uncomfortable taking chances on employees without experience. This hesitancy to hire hurt younger people without nest eggs more than older workers.[15] According to the Manhattan Institute: "it is younger workers, not older workers, that have borne the brunt of the employment losses during the recession. Since 2000 the labor force participation rates of workers 55 and over have been rising steadily, whereas the labor force participation rates of workers aged 16 to 24 and workers aged 25 to 54 have been declining."[16]

Economist and bestselling author John Lott explained the situation Obama bamboozled young people into when he substitute hosted *The Jason Lewis Show* on June 14, 2013:

"If there's anything that I think summarizes how bad this economy has been, it's just looking at the number of jobs that have been created or not been created. When the recession started there were 146,300,000 people working in the United States. As of this last month, the latest numbers that we have, is that there are 143,800,000. . . . We have 2.4 million fewer people working now after four years of recovery than we had before things started going south. Now, that's bad, but one way to put it in perspective is that over that same period of time, the number of people in the working age population in the United States has grown from about 223 million to over 245 million; again, we've had about a 15 million increase in the working age population. At the same time, we've had about over a 2.4 million drop in the number of people working. . . . So rather than having almost 10 million people working, we have 2.4 million *fewer* people working. That's a difference of over 12 million there. And it goes a long ways to explaining why the unemployment rate's fallen.

"Unbelievably here, about 80 percent of the drop in unemployment since it hit the peak in late 2009 has been due to the fact that people have given up looking for work, not because they've been able to go and get jobs.

"This is a recovery unlike anything we've had in terms of how slow it's been. . . . 47 months into this recovery, and we've had job growth of just 2.5 percent! It's hard to emphasize how bad that is. That's one quarter of the job growth that you would have had in the average recovery. It's one fifth the job growth you would have had after past severe recessions. . . . There's no previous recovery where . . . you still have fewer jobs than you have prior to the peak even a few years after the recovery."

Clinton and JFK had flaws, but both presidents were more conscientious about spending and inflating the taxpayer's dollar than Obama, who took an *extreme* approach to printing, redistributing, and spending money—even by "liberal" standards. Obama's intense rate of spending made it unfeasible for his economy to generate jobs at a healthy rate.

Even if we had followed Clinton's spending trajectory, we'd be singing AC/DC's "Back in Black" instead of the song Obama wrote for us, "Ledger in Red." As Lott put it: "If you take the spending at the last year that Bill Clinton was president and have it grow for inflation and the growth in population so that the amount of money spent by the government *per person* stayed the same in real terms, we would have had a surplus of $100 billion last year rather than a deficit of $1.1 trillion . . . [and] I mean, I thought government spending was too large then."

Or, if Obama had responded to the economic mess he "inherited" the way JFK reacted to the recession and high unemployment that he "inherited," our young people would also be better off. Like Obama, Kennedy initially tried a series of Keynesian attempts to stimulate the government through spending taxpayer dollars. He increased housing subsidies and government construction projects and expanded unemployment benefits and food stamps.[17] Unlike Obama, when these efforts failed, Kennedy ignored his own economic advisers, who were telling him to spend more.[18] He worried that government spending would weaken the dollar and invite inflation.[19] Kennedy initiated two massive, *permanent* tax cuts. In contrast to Obama, who wanted to keep taxing the rich, Kennedy tried to reduce the tax burden of *all* Americans, including wealthy job creators. His legislation (passed after his death) cut the bottom federal income tax rate from 20 to 14 percent and the top rate from 91 down to 70 percent. Soon, the economy was roaring back. JFK's second set of economic policies, which put more freedom in the hands of consumers and entrepreneurs, is directly responsible for what *Forbes* calls the "great 1960s boom" where "growth from 1961 to 1968 was an outsized 5.1% a year, unemployment went below 4%, and the Dow crossed 1000 for the first time."[20]

Obama's redistributive economic policies were cavalier even in comparison to previous presidential seducers.

* * *

LET'S continue to put Obama's jobless disaster into perspective. American Millennials in the twenty-five- to thirty-four-year-old range who were out of college and looking for work were having a harder time in 2011 (two years into Obama's "huge recovery") finding jobs than young people in other leading economies; this age cohort had a better chance of finding work in Canada, Great Britain, Japan, France, Sweden, Russia, and Australia than in America.[21] And it was also not becoming easier to become "the next Steve Jobs," as Obama led young entrepreneurs to believe in his 2012 State of the Union Address: there were more new billionaires coming out of China than the United States in 2012, according to *Forbes*. Obama's gift to the Millennials who voted for him was to make them a global laughingstock.

Obama seemed uninterested in fulfilling his promises to create jobs. He spent his campaign promising to cut spending and create jobs. After he safely secured his second term, he said that *more spending* was the solution, and jobs were nowhere to be seen.

Second Broken Recovery Promise

On the '08 campaign trail, Obama assured Millennial voters that he was unwilling to lose "this generation" to "poverty"[22] and he promised to "restore balance and fairness to the American economy after years of Bush Administration policies that tilted the playing field in favor of the wealthy and well-connected."[23]

The first black president's legacy will be that he helped the rich get richer and the poor get poorer. Young people became the poorest of all and, among young people, blacks and women fared the worst. It is angering, ironic, and sad to realize that the same groups of people who voted for Obama in droves—anticipating a better life—had the hardest time finding jobs and escaping poverty.

We want a society where the poor and the middle class are continually advancing because when these groups advance, it is a sign that society as a whole is progressing. ONLY THE RICH advanced under Obama. An April 2013 Pew report analyzing the first two years of the economic recovery found that 93 percent of American households experienced a 4 percent drop in their average net worth while the richest 7 percent of households experienced a 28 percent increase in their average net worth.[24] Fed chairman Ben Bernanke's Federal Reserve policy contributed to this situation. About two months before the 2012 elections, the Fed announced its third round of quantitative easing (QE3), which included buying bonds at a pace of $85 billion a month. One year later, in the fall of 2013, Bernanke persisted with his $85 billion a month bond-buying binge with no sign of stopping. Quantitative easing policy encouraged the stock market to rally. Unfortunately, rising stock prices primarily helped Wall Street firms and wealthy individuals because the richest 10 percent of the population owns about 80 percent of all stocks.[25] In 2011, Bernanke promised that his program would "promote economic growth" and "lead to higher incomes."[26] He was wrong. By the middle of 2013, economic growth was rising at the anemic rate of less than 3 percent and incomes were still failing to keep up with inflation.

QE's boon to the stock market is why the wealthy were buying designer handbags and jewelry (sales of luxury items jumped 12 percent in 2012) while the average American struggled to pay for gas and groceries.[27] In 2012, the top 10 percent of income earners took in the *highest* share of the country's income *in one hundred years.*[28] The Federal

Reserve Bank of St. Louis reported in May of 2013 that while 91 percent of the wealth lost during the recession was reacquired, this recovery mostly benefited the wealthy, while average household wealth was still *down* 55 percent.[29]

Besides his easy-money policy, Obama's administration attempted to "stimulate" the economy with a big-government tonic. Progressives said the stimulus failed because it wasn't large enough. Nice try. That's like saying a movie with a boring plot failed at the box office because its budget wasn't big enough to dress its dullness up with special effects. The stimulus was a bust because it took money out of the economy and the hands of consumers and redirected it toward programs that failed to create jobs (such as Obama's green jobs program, which we'll discuss momentarily). A better way to stimulate the economy would have been to lower the corporate income tax rate: Obama maintained the highest corporate income tax rate in the world, which automatically made it unattractive and noncompetitive to do business in America.

Millennials in particular were hurting. Over one third of all Millennials lived at home. Incomes for young people ages twenty-five to thirty-four living with their parents were 43.7 percent below the national poverty threshold. Another example of how young people were hurting, especially those from lower-income families, was their inability to find paid internships. In many fields, an internship is the surest way to advance into a full-time job because internships give corporations the chance to put a young person through an "extended interview" before taking the risk of offering them a job. During Obama's anemic recovery, *Time* reported a trend in which poor and middle-class youths were squeezed out of internships because corporations could only offer unpaid internships. Basically, you needed to be from a wealthy family in order to afford to take an internship, and this set many Millennials back because experience or connections are necessary to get your foot in the door. "It's slavery almost," a twenty-one-year-old black intern on her seventh internship, of which only four were paid, complained to *Time*.[30]

* * *

UNHEALTHY numbers of young people in their prime working years, particularly less educated single women without children and African American men, began dropping out of the work force during the Great Recession and Obama exacerbated the bleed.[31] Economists were wringing their hands, trying to understand why. It was not a mystery; it was Obamanomics at work.

By 2012, the number of blacks (27.2 percent) and Hispanics (25.6 percent) in poverty was more than twice that of non-Hispanic whites (9.7 percent) and there were over 5 million more women than men in poverty according to the official U.S. Census data.[32] Obama helped the vulnerable by rendering them more vulnerable.

Barry's Rock Band: Black Men Not at Work

Men at Work was a cool Aussie band. Barry played covers of all their hits, especially "People Just Love to Play with Words." Barry called his band Black Men Not at Work.

In both campaigns, Obama specifically targeted the African American community. He asked his brothers to vote for him and he left them empty-handed. In 2012, 13.8 percent of blacks were unemployed—up from 10.1 percent in 2008, before Obama took office and "recovered" our economy.[33] Blacks continued to experience the highest levels of unemployment compared to all major racial/ethnic groups under the first black president. For the past fifty years (1963–2012), black unemployment in America has been consistently higher than white unemployment.[34] Blacks voted for Obama hoping they would do *better*, not worse.

Black men, especially young black men, struggled disproportionately under Obama. For years, the proportion of the population who are working (the employment–population ratio) has been the lowest for black men in comparison to men of other races, and this problem festered under Obama. In 2008, the employment–population ratio for black men was 63.9 percent; in 2012 it fell to 58.3 percent.[35] "For young blacks—the most politically misled people in America—the out-of-work number is between 40% and 50%," bemoaned Daniel Henninger in the *Wall Street Journal*.[36] In 2008, 24.7 percent of Obama's black brothers and sisters were in poverty and this number rose to 27.2 percent in 2012; in contrast, the number of non-Hispanic whites in poverty rose by about one percentage point, from 8.6 percent to 9.7 percent; the number of Asians in poverty decreased slightly; and the number of Hispanics in poverty rose from 23.2 percent to 25.6 percent.[37] Under the first black president blacks experienced the greatest rise in poverty of any ethnic group or race between 2008 and 2012.

A white mother. A black father. Obama could have promoted racial unity; he was a living and breathing example of racial harmony. *The New Yorker* gushed that Obama's "most visible attribute" was "the color of his skin." Instead of creating harmony, Obama whisked the pot. He gave speeches scaring Americans into believing that "racial stalemate" persisted, such as his March 2008 stump speech in Philadelphia, Pennsylvania, where he said: "This is where we are right now. It's a racial stalemate we've been stuck in for years."[38] He dug up imaginary dirt from the past, claiming the "Reagan Coalition" grew out of "anger" and accusing "conservative commentators" of building "entire careers" by ignoring "racism."[39] He insisted on employing old images of bigotry instead of leading us *forward* and reaching across the aisle in friendship, booming in an October 25, 2010, midterm election stump speech in Rhode Island: "We don't mind the Republicans joining us. They can come for the ride, but they gotta sit in back."

"Stalemate" is a word that drops unnaturally from the mouth of a black man whose parents were a mixed-race couple; a black man who attended two Ivy League schools; a black man who was three months away from becoming the Democratic Party's nominee for president of the United States; a black man who dated at least four white women. "Racial stalemate" hardly describes *this* black man's America.

Never letting the facts get in the way of a good speech, Obama used the word "stalemate" to pretend that racism was rampant in America. He acted like we had not moved past the days when buses and schools were segregated. He used fear instead of love to buy votes; he made blacks feel like *he* would be their advocate; *he* would help them find jobs; they could *not* trust white people. If blacks believed that white people did not have their best interest in mind, it was a boon to Obama. After all, his opponent was a white man.

Comfortably reclining in his man cave at the White House, Obama quickly forgot about his black brothers. Beer in one hand, remote in the other, Obama had stress to release. He could not be troubled with helping other young blacks emerge from poverty and have a shot at success. Chicago's blacks, Obama's closest brothers, were suffering greatly as he began his second term.

Obama's buddy Rahm Emanuel, the mayor of Chicago, had overseen a record year of Windy City violence: The 18.6 percent murder rate was more than twice the murder rate of New York City or Los Angeles; 77 percent of Chicago murders were black-on-black; most of Chicago's homicides took place in the black neighborhood of Austin; and most of the murderers and 44 percent of their victims were *young*—between the ages of 15 and 24. They should have been advancing in school, not shooting up their hood.[40] One mile from Obama's Chicago home, fifteen-year-old Hadiya Pendleton took a fatal bullet in a South Side park after performing with her school band for Obama's inauguration ceremonies a few days earlier.

"To our nation's children, who deserve to grow up healthy and strong and have every chance to pursue their dreams," first lady Michelle dedicated the book that she released with impeccable timing a few months before the 2012 elections. She spoke fondly of growing up on the South Side of Chicago where she and her friends could safely "play outside for hours" and her parents were at peace when she took off on her bike or ventured to Rainbow Beach Park.

Fast-forward to May of 2013. Twenty-year-old Blake Ross was shot to death near Rainbow Beach Park.[41] Poverty and violence were striking young blacks nationwide, and the problem was most obvious in the city of Obama's senatorial constituents and Michelle's neighborhood friends. Compared to 2009, when Obama took office, the data showed increasing numbers of blacks in poverty, unemployed and on food stamps.[42] Whites and Hispanics were poorer and more dependent on government programs too, but, as we've mentioned, blacks were suffering the most from poverty and joblessness and blacks had voted for Obama with the highest hopes for a historic opportunity to have a stronger voice in America. The first black couple had promised all young people, especially blacks, a more peaceful and prosperous world but forgot about them after taking their votes and slipping away to Washington.

She Works Hard for the Money

B arry also targeted young women. He utilized marketing that ranged in tone from gentle to garish—misleading women on the "power" of wealth redistribution.

Remember "Julia," the middle-class white woman who had the picture-perfect life and was supposed to represent the fantastic future of all women under Obama? In the spring of 2012, Obama posted a slide show following the life of a cartoon character named Julia from ages three through sixty-seven. "The Life of Julia" went viral and became part of Obama's drive for female swing votes in 2012, convincing women that Obama's government intervention would help them. In part of the slide show, Obama promised women that, like Julia, they would be able to complete college and land a good job as a "web designer" by age twenty-three and live comfortably. The cartoon boasted that Julia "makes her [student loan] payments on time every month" and can "focus on work" because she has universal health-care coverage.

The Julia hoax worked. Obama won the female vote in both elections. Barry knew the Julia plan was hopelessly romantic, yet he pushed his cute cartoon heroine because she made him look like he *cared*. If

Julia had been a real person, it would have been easier for young women to see that the Fantasy of Julia was not what they wanted. Julia did not work toward big dreams, and instead moved from generic stage to stage like a carefree zombie; she also faced situations that most women would find undesirable, such as raising a baby boy without another parent, notably a father.

Most American women work hard for their money. Moreover, if they are pursuing their talents and dreams, most women *want* to work for their money. Obama created an economic situation where many young women find themselves jobless and their dreams out of reach, despite their work ethic.

Barry began his second term, over 5 million more women than men were in poverty, and the economy was so bad that even the women who had jobs were worried about losing them. A March 2012 poll by Allianz Life Insurance Company of North America revealed that 49 percent (almost half) of American women feared becoming a "bag lady." Even 27 percent of women making salaries of $200,000 or more said they were concerned about falling into homelessness and dire poverty.

Barry, honey, you did not treat the women who voted for you right.

Third Broken Recovery Promise

On the campaign trail, Obama promised to "invest in research and development of every form of alternative energy" so as to "create jobs that pay well and can't be outsourced."[43]

Gabbing about alternative energy would endear Obama to young swing voters. So he did. Obama spent a great deal of your money to brand himself as Mr. Green.

Bush signed the 2005 Energy Policy Act, in theory to boost nuclear, solar, and wind investments and make the United States more competitive with China. Bad idea. Then, Obama came along with his 2009 economic "stimulus" and broadened the program. Bypassing the natural free market, Obama dumped cash into green tech before it was viable. He also played favorites, distributing cash based on political calculations.

Obama's 2009 stimulus created the Section 1705 Loan Program that favored select green companies with very attractive deals. George Mason University's Mercatus Center exposed the fact that while normal government loans require the borrower to pay a "credit subsidy fee" to "prevent taxpayers' exposure," Obama's stimulus package allocated $2.435 billion of taxpayer money to the Department of Energy to cover the credit subsidy fees on many 1705 loan guarantees.[44] Basically, under Obama, many green companies—including green firms run by his buddies—received special loans that are not normally given out, even by the government.

Oh, yes. And Obama gambled on green start-ups with taxpayer dollars despite no clear scientific evidence that humans are responsible for detrimental warming. Scientists with the Nongovernmental International Panel on Climate Change (NIPCC) conducted an independent assessment of the same peer-reviewed science that had been analyzed by the UN-sanctioned International Panel on Climate Change (IPCC). NIPCC scientists reported in October of 2013 that they found "no hard evidence for a dangerous human-caused warming. They find the null hypothesis—that observed changes in climate are due to natural causes only—cannot be rejected. . . . We conclude no unambiguous evidence exists for adverse changes to the global environment caused by human-related CO_2 emissions. In particular, the cryosphere is not melting at an enhanced rate; sea-level rise is not accelerating; no systematic changes have been documented in evaporation or rainfall or in the magnitude or intensity of extreme meteorological events; and an increased release of methane into the atmosphere from permafrost or sub-seabed gas hydrates is unlikely."[45]

Let's review who cashed in to see whether they created high-paying, long-term jobs.

Ivanpah

Throw on your Ray Bans and stare at the sun! Now, imagine looking at the sun magnified twenty-eight thousand times. If you value your eyesight, you may want to avoid glancing at the receivers atop three solar towers rising along the California–Nevada border.

It's the summer of 2013. Over two years after BrightSource Energy received a $1.6 billion stimulus loan, the Ivanpah solar thermal project was still many months from operation. Though Ivanpah was a big risk for taxpayers, it was determined to be eligible for a special 1705 loan. Google was a joint owner of Ivanpah. Perhaps this loan was a way for Obama to "pay back" Google CEO Eric Schmidt for his 2008 endorsement?

To build Ivanpah, four thousand acres of public land, once home to a rare desert tortoise, was converted into the world's largest solar thermal facility. BrightSource committed up to $56 million to relocate and preserve the tortoises. Now four thousand acres are littered with three solar towers, each surrounded by hundreds of thousands of mirrors that fan out into the desert. The towers collect heat from the mirrors and convert the heat into steam, and then electricity. The goal: carbon-free electrical power for 140,000 homes.

Experts warned this massive solar thermal development was not economically competitive with photovoltaic solar technology, let alone against fossil fuels.[46] Our government threw a $1.6 billion Hail Mary pass on Ivanpah when there was a far better option: nuclear power. The advantages of solar thermal power are that it is clean and can produce base-load energy. Nuclear power has both these advantages. Plus, we actually know nuclear works and is extremely safe.

Guess what? Even hipster environmentalists love nuclear power. Environmentalists decided to take a second look at nuclear after the disaster in Fukushima, Japan. Discovering virtually no health backlash from Fukushima—or *any* nuclear accident since the 1986 Chernobyl disaster in Ukraine that resulted in thirty fatalities—one environmentalist became so excited that he released a documentary, *Pandora's Paradise* (2013), *lauding* nuclear energy.[47]

In February of 2012, Obama spoke at the University of Miami in Coral Gables, saying "because of the investments we've made [in] the use of clean, renewable energy in this country . . . thousands of Americans have jobs. . . . We've supported the first new nuclear power plant in three decades. . . . I will not cede the wind or solar or battery industry to China."[48]

Again, never expect Barry to let the facts crimp a good speech:

1. Globally, over sixty nuclear plants are being built. China is building over half of them while the United States has just three on the docket.[49] China is even beginning to export its nuclear expertise, by collaborating on building a nuclear power plant for the United Kingdom.
2. In 2013, Obama oversaw the largest permanent closing of a nuclear plant in over fifty years: the San Onofre plant in Southern California. Retiring San Onofre is set to cost taxpayers at least $1 billion. *Thanks for the bill, Barry!*
3. If you continue reading, you'll see that Barry *lost* quite a few energy jobs. And he blew billions to create a handful of lasting jobs.

You sure look cool in your aviators but it's hard to say if they will protect you from twenty-eight thousand suns. It's even harder to say if Ivanpah will create thousands of amazing jobs.

Fisker

It took $192 million in 'Bama Bucks to develop a plug-in electric luxury, high-performance sedan called the Karma, from automotive corporation Fisker. Retailing at $100,000 each, around two thousand Karmas were built, two years later than promised. A *Consumer Reports* test drive resulted in an embarrassing breakdown and the lowest rating for all luxury sedans.

Fisker considered bankruptcy after the Department of Energy

finally blocked it from continuing to draw on its $529 million loan. Fisker laid off three quarters of its employees in April of 2013. Those were some nice part-time jobs, building the sexiest death trap ever!

In October of 2013, Reuters reported that Fisker still owed the government $168 million and the DOE had put its green-energy loan up for auction. The winner was a Hong Kong billionaire. By December, the government had only recovered $53 million.[50]

A123

Fisker's battery supplier filed for Chapter 11 bankruptcy protection in October of 2012 after drawing down $133 million out of $249 million in Department of Energy grants. Fisker claimed that it needed to stop producing the Karma because of issues with A123's batteries, but Karma's bad Karma clearly extended beyond battery problems.[51]

Reuters reported that a Chinese company won the Obama administration's approval to purchase A123—"beating U.S. rival Johnson Controls Inc (JCI.N) of Milwaukee."[52] So, when Obama said: "I will not cede the wind or solar or battery industry to China," was he bluffing . . . or was he just "burned" by his teleprompter?

First Solar

"It sounds like you're not an American Company," Representative Darrell Issa said to First Solar's CEO after pointing out that most of the company's full-time jobs were located overseas.

First Solar received roughly $3.1 billion in three federal loans in 2011.[53] At least one of these loans, worth $646 million, was a 1705 loan. First Solar applied for two of the loans on the basis of "innovation," defined as creating products that have not been commercialized in America. For one loan, e-mails released to Congress suggest that the DOE manipulated information so First Solar would qualify in the innovative category.[54] For another loan, the so-called innovative portion of First Solar's product was already being made in Colorado.[55] In 2011, First Solar announced that it would be laying off one hundred employees and slashing earnings and revenue estimates. In 2012, First

Solar announced two thousand global layoffs (about 30 percent of its workforce) and, in 2013, 150 new layoffs in the United States. First Solar executives benefited from the $3.1 billion we gave their company, but it's unclear how much the American *taxpayers* benefited from this "investment." In the Kingdom of Crony Environmentalism, the worst were first.

SunPower

SunPower Corp. took a $1.2 billion government loan in 2011 to build a solar project that was only projected to create ten to fifteen permanent jobs (and 350 temporary construction jobs while the site was built).

You read that right: Obama was willing to spend $80 million of your money to create a single permanent green energy job.[56] For this, he expected a high five when he deserved a bop on the head with a tennis racket.

Abound Solar

Abound Solar scorched millions of our dollars to ashes before the Department of Energy cut it off from its $400 million 1705 loan guarantee. The company filed Chapter 7 bankruptcy protection.[57] Cost to the taxpayers? Oh, not much. Just $40 to $60 million.[58]

Evergreen Solar

After receiving $5.3 million in stimulus cash, photovoltaic panel maker Evergreen Solar filed for bankruptcy, fired its U.S. workers, and closed its Michigan plant.[59] *Timber!*

Beacon Power

This beacon of bankruptcy received a $24 million federal stimulus grant and drew $39.5 million on a $43 million 1705 loan guarantee for its energy-storage firm. Beacon Power obtained a buyer and the Department of Energy told Reuters that it "stands to recover more than 70 percent of the taxpayer's investment."[60] We sure hope so.

SpectraWatt

SpectraWatt was supposed to use $500,000 in stimulus money to improve solar technology and ended up filing for bankruptcy.[61] SpectraWatt was sold via auction to Canadian Solar. Obama put his hand over his heart and sang: "O Canada! O Canada! I won't build Keystone . . . but you can have my second-hand solar!"

Solyndra

"I appreciated the chance to tour your plant and to see the incredible cutting edge solar panels that you're manufacturing . . . I also want to give some credit to those guys in the back who have been building this facility so that we can put more people back to work and build more solar panels to send all across the country," Obama said when he toured Solyndra's plant in 2010. Just over a year later, after receiving a $535 million federal loan under the Section 1705 Loan Program, Solyndra went bankrupt. Around a thousand workers showed up to work one morning to find their jobs—poof—gone.[62]

A Solyndra investor e-mailed Obama's chief economic adviser Lawrence Summers in 2009 asking why Solyndra received such a large chunk of cash since Solyndra was not generating a profit. The investor wrote: "While that is good for us, I can't imagine it's a good way for the government to use taxpayer money." Summers agreed that "gov is a crappy vc" (government is a crappy venture capitalist) but added he did not have a better answer.[63] Summers should have answered: From now on, the government will do *nothing*; consumer demand and competition will take their natural course.

Another Solyndra investor, billionaire George Kaiser, seemed less scrupulous. E-mails revealed that Kaiser, also a big Obama donor, brazenly asked the Energy Department and White House for a *second* loan for Solyndra in 2010.[64]

Finally, Summers became concerned enough to send a memo to Obama in October of 2010 outlining his suggestions to reform the loan-guarantee program. But the midterm elections were less than a month away and Obama said no way.[65]

By 2011, it became public that several of Obama's senior officials had been warning him all along that Solyndra was a financial mess and so was the DOE program.[66] However, the White House was hell-bent on using the Solyndra loan to make a grand job-creation announcement.[67] In the end, it was more like a pink slip announcement. To top this off, by December of 2013, the DOE's Loan Department Office website showed that U.S. taxpayers had recovered a total of "$0" on their investment in Solyndra.[68]

Tesla

When Obama was inaugurated in 2008, a billionaire named Elon Musk sat in the front row with his British girlfriend. Many Americans admired Musk, assuming he was a free-market entrepreneur. In fact, once Obama took office, Musk and his electric car company, Tesla Motors, won the stimulus lottery while taxpayers received almost nothing in return. *Slate* outed Musk in 2013, calling the taxpayers' "investment" in Tesla "worse than Solyndra."[69] In 2009, Tesla received a $465 million DOE loan at rock-bottom interest rates, ten times lower than Tesla would have paid on the open market. Amateur hour DOE negotiators failed to demand the option to convert the taxpayers' investment into shares of Tesla stock if the company succeeded. Unlike Solyndra, Tesla's stock performed well and its Model S was rated 2013 Motor Trend Car of the Year. Musk made a 3,500 percent gain on his personal investment in Tesla while the taxpayers gained 2.6 percent, reported *Slate*. Tesla's image and stock took a tumble in November of 2013 on reports that three of its car batteries spontaneously combusted in a six-week time frame. Tesla scrambled to do crisis management, asking the National Highway Traffic Safety Administration to conduct a probe into the fires, and Musk blogged that Tesla would amend its warranty to cover fire damage, while huffing that journalists who dared question his car's safety were "seeking to make a sensation." Spontaneous fires in vehicles that transport human beings are worth journalistic investigation. Without the negative news exposure, Tesla may not have felt pressured to amend its warranty or seek an NHTSA probe. Musk's story seems to be that Tesla's successes were due to his brilliance and its losses were due to nefarious, brainless, and sensationalist columnists. Ultimately, Tesla is an example of how Obama took money out of the economy to gamble on helping the already rich get richer (Musk was worth $6.7 billion in September of 2013), while failing to help the average unemployed young American.

The Department of Inside Influence

I t sounds sweet to say: "Stop beating up Obama. He only made a few missteps," as if Barry were a baby bird learning to fly. Except Obama was *not* a baby bird learning to fly and he made numerous calculated errors.

A better name for the Obama administration's Department of Energy is the "Department of Inside Influence." Obama used the DOE to cut unconstitutional, back-door deals with taxpayer dollars. End result? Joblessness. The *Washington Post* revealed that Obama gave "insider's seats" on the DOE to venture capitalists backing clean-tech firms before the DOE started handing out his stimulus money.[70] For example, clean-tech venture capitalist Sanjay Wagle went from fundraising for Obama in 2008 to an "insider's seat" at the DOE as a renewable energy grants adviser responsible for helping to "oversee the $11 billion renewable energy program under the Recovery Act."[71]

The federal government says that it hires on merit, but isn't it interesting that before working for the Deparment of Energy, some of its advisers worked for firms that would go on to benefit from DOE funds? Before joining the DOE, Wagle worked for a venture capital firm (Vantage Point Venture Partners) with a stake in: Tesla Motors, Brightsource, and Mascoma Corporation.

A man named David Danielson made a move similar to Wagle's, leaving General Catalyst in 2009 to become a program director at the DOE's Advanced Research Projects Agency-Energy (ARPA-E). Danielson's DOE division was explicitly charged with funding emerging technology in energy, yet the DOE denied that he had a hand in the three General Catalyst portfolios that were infused with $105 million 'Bama Bucks.[72]

As we mentioned, Wagle's old firm was tied to a DOE recipient known as Mascoma Corporation. So was Danielson's old firm, through General Catalyst's managing director, Hemant Taneja, who simultaneously served as a director on the board of Mascoma.[73] Mascoma Corporation did not look like a company worth investing in.

Mascoma

"Our company has only been in existence since October 2005 and we have no experience in the markets in which we intend to operate," Mascoma stated as risk factors in its Form S-1 filing with the U.S. Securities and Exchange Commission on September 16, 2011.[74] On paper, Mascoma's profit model looked more like that of a *non*-profit whose largest donor was the government:

"In the year ended December 31, 2011, our total revenue was $10.7 million with government grants and awards constituting 93% of our revenue and sales of pretreatment equipment and services constituting 6% of our revenue. We have incurred substantial net losses since our inception, including net losses of [$105.3 million] . . . . We expect these losses to continue," Mascoma admitted in an amended S-1 filing on March of 2012, stating that it had not achieved and could not predict profitability.[75]

The Obama administration was happy to give Mascoma executives access to *more* money although their SEC filing indicated that they knew as much about biofuels as five-year-olds sucking on lollipops. Mascoma's managment released a press statement on December 14, 2011, announcing that they had already been awarded $20 million in DOE funds and would receive an additional $80 million in DOE funding access for a total of up to $100 million.

That year, Mascoma was granted almost $1 million from the state of Minnesota and pledged to build a cellulosic ethanol plant in Little Falls. Nine months later, Mascoma abruptly exited the project and reportedly returned just $48,000 in funding.[76]

Back to the $100 million: Mascoma Corporation promised to build a hardwood cellulosic ethanol facility in Kinross, Michigan, and create fifty to seventy permanent jobs and 150 temporary construction jobs, but a February 2012 Michigan Economic Development Corporation report would evince they created *three* jobs.[77] By 2013, ground had still not broken on the plant, the new jobs were nonexistent, and Mascoma appeared to be doing as poorly as ever, noiselessly withdrawing its registration for an anticipated initial public offering.[78] In August of 2013, Mascoma reportedly lost its $50 million funding partner, Valero Energy Corporation, and released a statement saying: "Mascoma has completed the detailed design engineering and finalized the engineering, procurement and construction bids for the planned cellulosic ethanol facility in Kinross, Mich. . . . and will not proceed until there is a firm commitment for all the required funding."[79]

Calls during the summer of 2013 to Mascoma's business partner, Frontier Renewable, were answered by a vice president who would not expound on potential reimbursement to taxpayers, saying "We don't discuss finances publicly," but offered a number to reach Mascoma's CEO. The number turned out to be a main line that no receptionist or live person would answer, on multiple attempts in the summer and fall.

Calls during late 2013 to Kinross Township to inquire about plans for the plant's construction went like this:

Q: Hi, I'm trying to learn about Mascoma's plans to build a renewable fuel plant in Kinross. Their main number listed on their website has been disconnected, but their website still says construction plans are on track. Can you tell me who else I can call?

A: They're gone. They've pulled out. They are no longer in Kinross.

Q: Are you sure?

A: Yeah. I should be sure. I'm the City and they aren't here anymore.

Q: Do you know whether the money will be refunded?

A: I have no idea.

When pushed for details, Kinross Township referred the request to Chippewa County Economic Development Corporation. Conversations with the staffer who answered Chippewa County EDC's main line went similarly:

Q: Hi, can you tell me if the Mascoma Corporation renewable fuel plant is being built?

A: No. That's not ever going to happen.

Q: You mean they haven't broken ground?

A: No. All I know is, that is never going to happen.

Q: Do you think they will allocate the money toward something else? Or refund it to the taxpayers?

A: I have no idea.

So Kinross Township and Chippewa County's EDC Office both indicated that the plant was "not happening" as of late 2013. Yet Frontier Renewable's "About Us" section on its homepage was still promising in February of 2014:

Frontier Renewable Resources is owned by Mascoma Corporation, a renewable fuels company, and J.M. Longyear, a Michigan-based national leader in natural resources management.

Frontier Renewable Resources has established a joint venture with Valero Energy Corporation, the nation's largest independent oil refiner and a leading ethanol producer, to develop and operate a first-of-its-kind commercial-scale cellulosic ethanol facility in Kinross, Michigan. The facility will use Mascoma's proprietary consolidated bioprocessing technology platform to convert hardwood pulpwood into 20 million gallons of ethanol per year initially.

Construction is expected to commence within the next three to six months . . . [emphasis added].

It looks like Mascoma received access to piles of 'Bama Bucks, of which they drew down on, at minimum, $33 million,[80] promised to build facilities that would convert wood chips into ethanol and jobs. What role does the revolving door of industry insiders play in the making of such poor funding decisions? It's a question that bears closer scrutiny.

Warren Buffett, Obama's Mistress

Warren Buffett and Barry Obama's intimacy extended beyond the realm of polite acquaintances: Buffett was a bosom beneficiary of Obama's faux investments in energy for future generations.

Criminal presidential affairs do not require bedrooms; they require breaking an oath of office made to the American public. The Constitution prohibits the president or executive branch from making laws or delegating lawmaking to an extra-congressional group like the EPA. Federalist and framer Alexander Hamilton explained in the *Federalist*, No. 78, that Congress controls the purse strings and makes laws while the president merely enforces the laws. E-mails reveal that Obama's administration utilized the EPA to plot with environmental groups, bypass Congress (where Keystone enjoyed bipartisan support), and *destroy* thousands of clean energy construction jobs and dozens of permanent jobs that would have resulted from partnering with our ally Canada to build the Keystone XL Pipeline.[81] Why? Who knows? Maybe because Keystone XL would have hurt his mistress and fundraiser, Buffett.

There was no *environmental* reason for Obama to spend over five years stalling the construction of Keystone XL. Even the president's own State Department thrice declared Keystone XL to be environmentally safe.[82]

A $7 billion jobs and energy infrastructure project, the Keystone XL Pipeline development was approved by Canada's National Energy

Board in 2007. The pipeline was to initiate in Alberta and then traverse six states in the contiguous United States to its final destination of Texas Gulf Coast refineries. One of these six states was Nebraska, home of Barry's lover: the Oracle of Omaha. It's an interesting "coincidence" that every day Obama delayed approval of the Keystone XL was a boon to Buffett and the profit he was pulling from his $26 billion 2009 investment in Burlington Northern Santa Fe Railway Company. Buffett also owned Union Tank Car Company. If we did *not* build Keystone XL, Buffett stood to profit from the *other* way to get Canada's oil to the Gulf: one hundred tank cars and fifteen daily train runs.[83]

Weeks after hosting a campaign fundraiser for Obama in Omaha, Buffett told Fox Business that the pipeline "makes sense," but added that there could be "drawbacks" and concluded "You could build anything and it will create jobs, but that doesn't mean it's a great idea."[84] For the next two years, Obama made no effort to approve Keystone, which is odd given that his righthand man purportedly thought it made "sense." In retrospect, Buffett's comments look more like an effort to deflect attention from his profits and his cozy relationship with Obama going into the 2012 election.

In stalling Keystone XL, did Obama care that railroads are highly dangerous, inefficient, and unreliable as a means of transporting crude oil? (Forty-seven people were killed, at least forty buildings were destroyed, and fuel was lost in the oil train derailment that occurred in Lac-Megantic, Quebec, Canada, on July 6, 2013.) Or, did he care about the fact that pipelines transport more crude at less risk of incurring a leak or spill than railroads, and pipelines take routes located farther from dense population zones, making them safer even when there is a spill? Or, as an "environmentalist," did Obama care that transporting oil by pipeline emits far fewer carbon dioxide emissions than transporting it by train?[85]

Ha! Barry only seemed to care about pleasuring a louse who used capitalism to get rich and then named a progressive tax after himself so he could appear magnanimous while helping Obama con Millennials out of their rightful shot at achieving wealth.

P.S. What else did Obama's mistress know? Hmm. Remember First Solar and SunPower? Okay. Well, Buffett owns a solar power plant that is being developed by SunPower and two projects constructed by First Solar.[86]

Now you know everything worth knowing about Barry and Warren, save for becoming a Peeping Tom—which could take you from the territory of XOX to XXX.

Fourth Broken Recovery Promise

'll end tax breaks that ship jobs overseas, and invest in American jobs,"[87] Obama promised on the 2008 campaign trail.

Before he died, Steve Jobs told Obama exactly how he could stop U.S. tech companies from moving jobs overseas. Obama was a fool to ignore him. The first time they met in person, Jobs bluntly told Obama that his antibusiness policies were putting him on track to become a "one-term" president. Jobs was a Democrat, so he obviously did not ask Obama to commit political suicide. He simply suggested that Obama slash the excessive cost of doing business in America and reduce regulations.[88] (The most palpable cost of doing business in America is the federal and state integrated corporate income tax rate.)

Thrusting his nose in the air, Obama prodded on with his socialist policymaking, paying virtually no attention to Jobs's advice. He maintained the highest corporate income tax rate in the world (approximately 40 percent, according to KPMG),[89] and he ramped up regulations and taxes on businesses (think Obamacare).

Then, after Jobs died, Obama used his pals in Congress like Senator Carl Levin, Democrat of Michigan, to turn public opinion against Jobs's company, making Apple out to be a tax evader. Levin asked CEO Tim Cook to defend Apple's tax strategies at a Senate hearing, accusing Apple of pursuing "the Holy Grail of tax avoidance."[90] In truth, Apple pays its legal share of taxes and nothing more; Apple will not bail out the U.S. government's wasteful spending. Apple has been the biggest taxpayer in Cupertino, California, the site of Apple headquarters, paying $9.2 million in annual taxes in fiscal year 2012/13.[91] Apple paid $6 billion in federal corporate income taxes in fiscal 2012. In order to maximize profits to shareholders, Apple utilized *legal* tax incentives to shift some profits overseas for more competitive tax rates and avoid higher U.S. taxes. In reality, (100 percent legal) tax breaks were the primary reason tech companies like Apple could do *any* business in the United States. It's quite eye-opening to see that despite Obama's huff and puff about reforming the tax code and his party's pursuit of so-called tax cheats like Apple, *his buddies* fared exceptionally well. Citizens for Tax Justice reported in 2012 that General Electric (a beneficiary of the Fed's financial bailout, whose CEO was appointed to chair Obama's Council on Jobs and Competitiveness) and Duke Energy (whose CEO was a big fundraiser for Obama's campaign): "enjoy negative federal income tax rates. That means they still made more money after tax than before tax over the four years [2008–2011]!"[92] Obama's major "action step" to reform the tax code was to become a spectator as his fellow Democrats ostracized a for-profit company (Apple) for following the law and making a profit.

It was easy for Obama's administration to attack big companies like Exxon or Apple because of their high profits. But the fact is that these companies paid a *ton* in taxes, while providing valuable energy (Exxon) or technology (Apple) and creating jobs so that Americans could enjoy a high standard of living. For instance, in 2012, Exxon posted worldwide earnings of $44.9 billion, but paid $12.1 billion in U.S. taxes and $102.1 billion in worldwide taxes.

Tech giants like Apple, Facebook, Oracle, and Cisco moved jobs and profits overseas during the Obama years, as Obama never took Jobs's advice. Barry arrogantly assumed that if he maintained the world's least competitive corporate tax rate, increased regulations, and generally made it *harder* for tech companies to profit at home he would incentivize them to do *more* business in America.

Obama expected for-profits to behave like *non*profits and, as a result, American jobs moved overseas. What a joke.

Fifth Broken Recovery Promise

Obama guaranteed voters that he would "make good on the debt we owe past and future generations."[93]

A paramount reason why Obama's economy failed to recover at a healthy rate by historical standards was his choice to spend more than former U.S. presidents, adding close to $7 trillion to the national debt—an amount projected to reach $10 trillion by the end of his presidency.[94] On the 2008 campaign trail, Barry repeatedly chided Bush's spending. Bush added $4.9 trillion to the national debt over eight years, which is hardly defensible, but it was galling to watch Obama spend at twice Bush's pace after promising the reverse.

Why is the debt such a big deal for young people? Here's why: economists have shown that a high national debt (in our case around $18 trillion) permanently reduces standard of living and incomes.[95] Even further, Obama's unprecedented additions to the national debt will also set back Millennials in some or all of these ways: make higher education, homes, and cars more expensive as interest rates on loans soar; make it harder to save up for retirement by forcing young people to subsidize safety nets that will be unavailable to them when they retire; and make it harder to afford their taxes and living expenses, which must go up (in order to pay down the debt) either directly or indirectly via inflation when the Federal Reserve monetizes the debt.[96]

In February of 2009, Obama signed a $797 billion stimulus package. By 2011, economic experts John F. Cogan and John B. Taylor assessed Obama's stimulus as a failure, pointing out that stimulus packages from Ford, Carter, and Bush had also failed to reinvigorate the economy.[97] This is because, in simple terms, the government has no money of its own and does not create wealth; the government only pushes your money around and spends it carelessly, such as on luxurious conferences for line-dancing IRS employees instead of the way a young person would spend it—on food and rent.

The following week, Bermudan journalist Roger Crombie asked the question that was obvious to the rest of the world in the *Royal Gazette*:

Would Obama have done less damage to future generations of Americans if he had just "done nothing?"[98]

Because he did not follow through on his promise to substantially reduce our historic budget deficit, America's triple-A credit rating was downgraded from AAA to AA+ for the first time in history by Standard & Poor's (S&P) under Obama's watch on August 5, 2011. Congress raised the debt ceiling on August 2 and only agreed to cut spending by $2.4 trillion over ten years. (Obama had ignored S&P's warning in April of a pending downgrade and its advice to cut spending by at least $4 trillion.) This downgrade put the United States on par with New Zealand, a bucolic country that is less than 1 percent developed thanks to government bureaucracy; a land where Hollywood goes to shoot movies and where young New Zealanders cannot buy homes.[99]

Looking back, we can see that the Great Recession (December of 2007 through June of 2009) hit young people hardest. Young people today are historically worse off than previous generations. A Pew Research Center study found that the median net worth of households headed by Millennials (under age thirty-five) dropped 68 percent between 1984 and 2009.[100] To rephrase, in 2010 dollars, the median net worth for young people dropped from $11,521 in 1984 to just $3,661 in 2009. Meanwhile, Americans over the age of fifty-five saw their net worth increase over this same time period, with those over sixty-five experiencing a 42 percent increase in net worth. The housing market crash and student loan debt were big contributors to the disparate drop in wealth among Millennials—and experts predict that this wealth gap will persist for years if not *forever*, particularly as Millennials' taxes increase to pay off their share of the public (national) debt.[101]

Syndicated talk radio host Jason Lewis says: "The sad fact of the matter is judgment day most likely will arrive on the watch of today's young people. And those who are attempting to do the right things will wind up paying the most. What a lesson."

Barry did not make good on his debt promise to Millennials; he basically stole their credit cards and racked up their debt without their consent.

Fore!

When golfing, whiffs sound better than shattering glass. Obama's worshippers can bawl that G. W. Bush teed Obama up for the economic destruction he wrought on young people. But when you're golfing and your caddy tees you up to drive straight through the picture window of a gorgeous home along the fairway, is it your caddy's fault when you step up to the tee and drive the ball—as hard as you can—through the window?

Obama was teed up for some economic adversity, but he should have re-teed his shots; he should have adjusted his swing. There is no use denying that Obama is guilty of hitting ball after ball after ball through economic "windows" of opportunity for young people.

Millennials were unable to find jobs—not because they failed to send out their résumés, but because Obama's policies destroyed the number of jobs in existence and development. Even if five hundred people apply for a job, only one is hired.

Obama lied in 2007, telling young people that he would spend less than Bush, end poverty, and create high-paying jobs, particularly in alternative energy. He lied in 2012 when his campaign told Millennials to give him four more years because he'd created a "huge recovery." Ninety-five million young Americans were effectively fired before they had a chance to interview for the jobs they qualified for—thanks to Barry's policies.

It's maddening. Obama was a bigger fraud than Tiger Woods was off the course. Don't you almost want to pull an Elin Nordegren?

YOUNG AND HELLTHY

3

Yeeeehaaaa! Clinton lassoed his young and pretty prey Monica Lewinsky with gifts like an antique flower pin, Davidoff cigars, and cherry chocolates. Kennedy hogtied Mimi Alford with three special gifts, including diamond-and-gold pins, plus trips to places like the Bahamas, rides on Air Force One, and cruises on the Potomac in the presidential yacht.[1] Presents were the ploy of preference for presidents who seduced young people.

Fiercely competitive, Obama outdid both Clinton and Kennedy in sweetening the deal. (To bait more people, you must be a bigger baiter.) Obama was Alpha Baiter.

Obama tantalized Millennials with a "gift" so big it needed $1 trillion in taxpayer funding. It was a gift he said young people could not live without (health insurance), and it included a special "bonus" (an unlimited supply of items they could already find for a few bucks at the corner store).

> 'Twas the night before Christmas in 2009: Barry tossed his copy of the Constitution into the fireplace, opened a cold beer, and glanced at his phone to see what was the clatter. A text from Pelosi. What could she want? "Hey Prez, Obamacare passed!"

Millennials did nothing to deserve the coal they received that Christmas. Actually, young people did not realize Obamacare was coal because Barry wrapped it up in a gold box with a tag that read: "Free Health Care Until You Are Twenty-Six." He added a life supply of condoms and pills to the box and tied it with a red bow. It didn't look like coal. It looked like your classic over-the-top Christmas present.

Obamacare was not a gift but a *bill* forcing Millennials to bankroll the health insurance of older people instead of saving for their own health-care needs later in life. Plus, Obamacare scared the best and brightest youths away from practicing medicine by placing additional bureaucratic, legal, administrative, and financial obstacles in the way— while burning out some of the finest existing doctors early.

We can all agree to improve health care. We can also agree that we did *not* need to *extirpate* our health-care system to *improve* it. On November 25, 2013, Gallup found that the vast majority of Americans were satisfied with the quality of their current health care (79 percent); happy with its cost (59 percent); and happy with their coverage (69 percent).[2] As Americans, we have a long history of opposing attempts to "improve" health care by putting the federal government in charge of the doctor–patient relationship. President Kennedy urged Congress to pass an early version of Medicare. This was not a great idea, but at least JFK was transparent. He openly campaigned on his Medicare proposal. Once elected, he asked Congress to pass it and it failed. Perhaps if JFK had lied, he would have had more success in passing Medicare. JFK had faults, but he did evince honesty on his health-care agenda. President Clinton likewise tried to ram through a universal health-care plan. His agenda failed to garner support because the drug industry produced a huge PR campaign that tuned Americans in to the truth.

Obama was different. He never let honesty—his own or others'—get in the way of his quest for power. If Obama had not lied about his health-care agenda, he would never have won the youth vote, and he would *never* have been elected. Obama lied about every major aspect of his plan: He claimed there would be no individual mandate (there was!); he said health insurance would become more affordable (it became pricier for Millennials!); he said if young people liked their insurance plan, they could keep it (they received cancellation notices!); he said if they liked their doctor, they could keep their doctor (their doctors retired early!); and he swore off the drug lobby (he got higher than a kite!).

When comedian and talk show host Ellen DeGeneres asked Obama about his plan to reform health care during the February 2008 Democratic primaries, candidate Obama said he would *not* push for a health insurance mandate: "If things were that easy [requiring all Americans to buy health insurance], I could mandate everybody to buy a house, and that would solve the problem of homelessness. It doesn't."[3]

Speaking to the American Medical Association on June 15, 2009, Obama said, "no matter how we reform health care, we will keep this promise to the American people: If you like your doctor, you will be able to keep your doctor, period. If you like your health care plan, you'll be able to keep your health-care plan, period. No one will take it away, no matter what . . . . Now, let me be clear . . . We're not going to need to force you to do it."

Obama rammed Obamacare through Congress and stabbed Millennial voters in the back. *Only if* young people take matters into their own hands will they be able to afford and receive the high-quality and individualized long-term health care they deserve.

It's hell getting old. It's more hell being young. Bet you never heard that from a young person. Until now. There is hell to pay in America if you are young and healthy.

How Obama Conned Millennials:
The Meaning of the Word *Is*

Obamacare has never been ragingly popular or well understood by Americans. Even Congress did not have a chance to finish reading the bill before the president signed it into law as the Patient Protection and Affordable Care Act (PPACA) on March 23, 2010. Gallup reported that the high point in the bill's popularity prior to passing was a favorable rating of 51 percent in October of 2009.[4]

Millennials were particularly confused and ambivalent toward Obamacare. The Henry J. Kaiser Family Foundation released a poll in April of 2013 indicating that 51 percent of young people between the ages of eighteen and twenty-nine were completely unaware that Obamacare had even passed in March of 2010.[5] (In contrast, 42 percent of all ages were unaware of Obamacare's passage.) Instead, 29 percent of young people thought that Obamacare had been repealed by Congress or overturned by the Supreme Court and was no longer law.

This poll shows you that in 2012 most young people did not realize they were reelecting a man who had passed universal health care. Millennials tend to be "fiscally conservative," particularly the younger Millennials who were eligible to vote for Obama for the first time in 2012.[6] Had they understood that Obamacare was effectively a tax and remembered that in 2008 Obama promised not to raise taxes on the middle class,[7] this fiscally conservative generation would have hesitated to hand their 2012 presidential votes to a con man who broke his fiscal guarantees.

Barry made it sound like Millennials were getting a super sweet deal, promising that they would receive health insurance under their parents' plans until they were twenty-six. To an eighteen-year-old voting for the first time, twenty-six probably seemed so far away. A twenty-three-year-old who voted for Obama in 2008 and was debating whether to do so again probably thought: "Awesome! I have three more years of leeway. What's not to love?"

Barry also played to the optimism and volunteer-oriented nature of Millennials, telling them that his health-care platform would help the

poor and unfortunate and make health-care coverage universally affordable to all people.

Finally, the Obama administration misled young people by withholding key information from them. Instead of marketing PPACA as
a package deal, he spoke of the bill's provisions piecemeal, focusing on
items like free birth control coverage and insurance coverage for people
under the age of twenty-six. He pitched the "perks" of the bill and left
out the fine print such as how much young people could expect to pay
and what quality of health-care services they could expect to receive. He
emphasized that he would "be a President who finally makes health care
affordable and available to every single American."[8]

When Census data came out in 2011 showing that the incomes for
Millennials were tailspinning and their unemployment levels were almost twice as high as those of the generations above them, it was clear
that Millennials were hurting economically and must be losing faith in
Obama's ability to help them afford a good life. The Obama administration needed to give Millennials a reason to reelect Barry. So, Secretary of Health and Human Services Kathleen Sebelius made a public
announcement that "the Affordable Care Act is working."[9] (Emphasis
on the word "is.")

How could the ACA be working before it was rolled out? Sebelius defined the meaning of the word "is" in the same amorphous way
Clinton defined "is" when he was asked whether he had any form of sex
with Lewinsky. Gifts. Lies. Whatever it took to make sure young people
voted for Obama in 2012.

* * *

SOME might argue that young people should have known better: if
they weren't texting and playing online games all day long, they would
have realized the truth about Obamacare. But it's hard to blame
eighteen-year-olds and twentysomethings when the Kaiser Family
poll shows that many of their fifty- and sixtysomething parents were
equally confused.

Love it or hate it, we live in a sound-bite society; we all need to do a better job of investigating the news on our own. But, as the leader of our country, the president is especially culpable for misleading the young. Isn't there a passage in the gospels about that? Ah yes, there is:

> *Luke 17:2: "It were better for him, that a millstone were hanged about his neck, and he cast into the sea, than that he should scandalize one of these little ones."*

For the first time in American history, our health-care system is regressing. Thankfully, also for the first time, increasing numbers of doctors are publicly calling the Executive Con Man's bluff.

Obama Never Asked Us: Doctors Speak Publicly for First Time

Nearly three hundred doctors, many of whom have never spoken publicly, agreed to be interviewed and speak their minds on Obamacare for this book.[10]

You may wonder: Why are we hearing from doctors now, *after* the law has passed? Here's why: *Obama never asked them.*

How would you feel if one morning Barry walked into your office and told you how to work? Let's say you're a salesperson. Barry announces: "New rules: You will read a script that *I* give you every time you do a sales call, no exceptions. I'm also eliminating commissions and bonuses; you will all be paid the same amount no matter how successful you are. 'Top dogs' will share with the 'little dogs' because it's not fair that they have the natural drive to work harder and are better salespeople. Don't like those rules? Go to jail."

Your first thoughts might be: "Mr. President, you can't tell me how to do my job! You're not a salesperson. My clients want individualized service, not robocalls. This plan will cause me to hate my job and go broke!"

Well, that's how doctors feel. The president walked in and told them where to go and how to get there and if they didn't like it they could go to jail.

Of the doctors surveyed, 92 percent said that Obamacare would "increase" the amount of "government interference into my relationship with patients." When asked whether Obamacare would be "beneficial" to the long-term finances of young Americans, 90 percent of doctors said "no." Most alarming, 89 percent of doctors said Obamacare would *not* be beneficial to the long-term health of young people because it would raise their costs by forcing them to subsidize care for everyone else, prevent them from saving for their own retirement, and lower the quality of their medical care by scaring good doctors and would-be medical students away from practicing medicine.

It is very telling to survey doctors over two years after Obamacare passed:

> *No one ever asked physicians about health care. No effort was made to diminish the negative effects of medical liability on a physician practice.*
> —GUY RUTLEDGE FOGEL, MD

> *Can you imagine that a government spending unnecessary trillions will revamp an entire system without input from bright and well-trained practicing physicians?* —RONALD FELDMAN, MD

> *I am a self-employed, independent-minded solo practitioner. Hopefully not an endangered species. Perhaps the federal Endangered Species Act would protect me?* —SHAYNE TOLIVER, DO

> *I didn't enter medicine to be a government employee.* —LARRY DOSS, MD

The doctor responses could fill this book. Instead, let's highlight a few more to represent how unhappy doctors are about the government taking over their profession and to illustrate why doctors believe Obamacare will *disproportionately* harm the young and healthy.

Doctors Say Obamacare Hurts Young People Most

"For all Americans who like their health insurance, nothing changes except they will have lower costs,"[11] Obama promised young people on the 2008 campaign trail.

If Clinton had to testify over his equivocation on whether he used cigars as sex toys, don't you think it's about time Obama testifies over the epic lies that he and his administration perpetuated for five years? The truth is that Obamacare was set up so that there would be very big changes for young people:

1. Millennials "who like their health insurance" *cannot* keep it. If their "health insurance" was a daily prayer, time at the gym, a healthy diet, their original catastrophic care plan, and periodic visits to their preferred doctor, they *cannot* keep that plan. They must buy one of Obama's overpriced packages covering services they are too young and healthy to need, or pay a fine. Plus, the doctor that they feel comfortable with and have known for years may become too busy to provide them with the same level of attention—or become burned out and retire early, leaving them to find a new provider.

2. Millennials will have *higher* health insurance costs. In article after article describing Obamacare, the mainstream media led Millennials to believe that *any* individual making less than $46,000 a year would qualify for a subsidy or a reduction in their premium. So, before the Obama administration begins "tweaking" Obamacare in anticipation of the 2014 midterms, we try plugging the salary figure of $45,900 into Covered California's affordable health insurance calculator. (Covered California was the template exchange for all fifty Obamacare state exchanges.) We find out that anyone between the ages of eighteen and forty-seven does *not* qualify for a subsidy at that salary. (Oh really? Young people are subsidizing everyone

else?) You also learn that the monthly insurance premium
will range between $230 for a twenty-one-year-old, $236 for
a twenty-six-year-old, $261 for a thirty-year-old, and $283
for a thirty-six-year-old.

How could Obama call spending three grand a year on insurance
that you won't use "low cost?" These young people are hardly rolling in
it. Many are spending over 7 percent of their annual income on health
insurance.

If you're young and healthy and feel like blowing nearly three grand
a year to improve your health, why not take an annual trip to the south
of France? At least you will inhale a dose of healing sea air.

* * *

"THE main message I want for Californians and people all across the
country, starting on Oct. 1 [2013], if you're in the individual market,
you can get a better deal," Obama promised. Then, he added a dis-
claimer: if you see your premium increase, it's due to insurers "jacking
up prices unnecessarily" or employers asking their employees to make
up for a difference in costs.[12] (In other words: "When premiums go up,
I won't take any responsibility.")

Days before the Obamacare exchanges opened, the administration released a report suggesting that average national premiums for
the standard Obamacare plan would be *16 percent lower* than expected. This was false hope that encouraged young people to rush to
sign up. On October 1, the exchanges rolled out with a grand splash
of chaos: the website did not work and people could not enroll. As
Obama scratched his head, the Heritage Foundation released a report
confirming that the average monthly premium *would* go up for young
people: a twenty-seven-year-old would be paying far more for insurance in nearly every state, with the rate increasing by over 50 percent
in most states.[13]

For all his problems, Clinton never said, "I got burned by an intern"
after his deception before a federal grand jury was exposed. With his

own lies exposed, Obama told MSNBC host Chuck Todd: "I've been burned already with a website." Cry us a river.

* * *

TAKE a listen to how doctors describe Obamacare's impact on young people:

> *This act will force many to make decisions between whether to take a penalty or buy expensive insurance they do not need. Either way, they will be spending hard-earned money on a product they neither want nor need.* —JASON SMITH, MD

> *They are the least likely to suffer catastrophe other than motor vehicle accidents. They will greatly resent the financial implications of Obamacare—that is, if they can get a job!* —SUSAN RUTTEN WASSON, MD

The number one reason why the cost of health insurance increases for young people is that Obamacare implements a three-to-one age ratio for premiums. Historically, the ratio was closer to five-to-one because the oldest (non-Medicare) group tends to use about five times more health care services than the youngest group, says the Heritage Foundation.[14] Obamacare basically tells insurance companies that they may only charge a sixty-four-year-old up to three times the premium they charge a twenty-one-year-old. This artificially forces the premiums that young people pay to increase. A sixtysomething will generally need more health care than a healthy twentysomething, so in order for the insurance company to charge the sixtysomething a reasonable premium, the insurance company will need to jack up the rate for the twentysomething.

Here's a hypothetical example to explain the impact of five-to-one and three-to-one age bands:

Picture that you own an insurance company. You have two thousand members; half are twenty-five years old and half are sixty years old. Last year, your sixty-year-old members consumed $500,000 worth of health care, which averages to $500 each. Your twenty-five-year-old members utilized $100,000 worth of health care, which averages to $100 each. Noticing that the average twenty-five-year-old consistently used far less health care than the average sixty-year-old because of his or her good health, you decide to set rates at $500 for a sixty-year-old and $100 for a twenty-five-year-old. These rates reflect the risks you are assuming for covering your members.

To stay in business, you need to collect $600,000 just to cover all your members' health-care expenses, but with the three-to-one mandate, you cannot charge an amount that accurately reflects the costs and risks for each age group. So, instead of charging $100 of the young people who only use $100 in health care, you must increase their premiums to $150 so that you can charge the sixty-year-olds $450 each. The twenty-five-year-olds are financing the health-care costs of the sixty-year-olds by paying an extra $50, which goes directly toward paying part of the sixty-year-olds' health-care costs. This is called redistributing wealth, or socialism.

Thanks to Obama, Millennials have the choice of buying over-priced insurance or turning into that cheapskate at the holiday party who walks up to the doctor in attendance and says: "Hey, doc! Great tie. So, um, since no one's looking, would you write me a quick prescription on this cocktail napkin? I can't afford another doctor's visit, but I need a refill on my RX. I know it's wrong and we just met, but could you please do that for me. As . . . a friend?"

Doctors Call Obamacare a "Ponzi Scheme" and "Socialized Medicine"

Remember when Barry told young people tuning in to the *Daily Show* that he most definitely was *not* a socialist? Oh no, he was a nice guy who shared his toys! Well, he was lying to Millennials. Obamacare is a "socialist" scam because it puts the federal government in control of your private relationship with your doctor and compels you to pay for this system for both yourself and others whether you like it or not. So say doctors:

It is a Ponzi scheme. —ELAINA GEORGE, MD

Physicians and patients need to realize the Tsunami of Socialized Medicine coming their way with Obamacare. —JAMES RITZE, DO

Patient health care privacy? Forget about it. Obamacare will have the compassion and, now, the political persecution, of the IRS, and the efficiency of the post office. I loved my practice, but I couldn't afford to continue. —ROBERT W. DUPRIEST, JR., MD

Doctors will be on salary, see few patients and make less than government workers until the entire "system" collapses and doctors work for barter or cash. I have traveled the world as an officer of the International College of Surgeons and I have seen it personally over the past twenty years. —DAVID STANLEY, MD

It will benefit crony businessmen . . . Socialism at its worst. —JOHN HUNT, MD

Ever heard of Ponzi? —TOM PEPONIS JR., DO

Millennials thought they were getting free health-care insurance until they turned twenty-six and then affordable insurance for the rest of their life. In reality they were being asked to overpay (extra-high premiums) for a product (comprehensive coverage) that they did not need so that Obama and his political insiders could profit. This is why doctors call Obamacare a Ponzi scheme. Insurance is not for a stubbed toe, a head cold, or a standard test like a chest X-ray for pneumonia. When insurance companies become involved for minor doctor visits, it raises the costs for consumers by raising administrative costs for doctors. To maximize doctor efficiency and therefore allow doctors to care for more people at less cost, we need to eliminate the unnecessary third party. Health insurance should only be for catastrophes.

Millennials never had a chance to hear from doctors—only the Chief Sharer of Toys.

Pimp Daddy Tauzin

In 2008, Obama released a campaign video attacking a man named Billy Tauzin, the CEO of PhRMA (Pharmaceutical Researchers and Manufacturers of America). In the video, Obama blasted Tauzin as a scoundrel who made "$2 million a year" pushing the interests of one of the largest drug lobbies and led viewers to believe that "Barack Obama is the only candidate who refuses Washington lobbyist money."

> It's 2009 and Barry is sitting pretty in the White House. One fine morning, an Escalade with custom rims and tinted windows pulls up to 1600 Pennsylvania Avenue. Tauzin jumps out and strolls up the front lawn, swinging his cane and strutting in his white suit.
>
> Barry glances up from his desk in the Oval Office to see Tauzin standing in the doorway. "Why are you here?" Barry asks, startled. "Don't you remember my campaign promises? You're not supposed to be seen near me." Tauzin smirks and flashes some hefty bills in the president's face. Suddenly, all Barry can see are dollar signs. He tells Tauzin: "Have a seat. I'm listening."

* * *

OBAMA accepted the *most* drug industry money in 2008. An exclusive report produced for *Raw Story* by the nonpartisan Center for Responsive Politics revealed that Obama accepted over $20 million from the health-care industry. To put this in perspective, that's nearly three times the amount the industry gave to McCain. It's not as though Republicans have never benefited from the drug lobby; in fact, they have, and we need overall reform in D.C. However, young people specifically voted for Obama because he promised to be a clean-money guy. This was just another lie. The Center for Responsive Politics' communications director Dave Levinthal explained: "Obama definitely has a relationship with the health sector."[15]

Obamacare passed because Obama jumped in bed with big pharma, whereas Clinton's health-care plan failed because he was not quite as big of a playboy as Obama. In 1993 and 1994, the insurance industry sponsored the huge "Harry and Louise" television ad campaign. In one ad, a couple sat at a kitchen table and pored over their medical bills while complaining that if Clinton's health-care bill passed they would end up "having choices we don't like [which] is no choice at all." The ads were a hit and Clinton's plan flopped. Americans supported *improving* health care, but not via socialized medicine, and they saw his plan for what it was.

Fast-forward to Obama. Billy Tauzin is the president of PhRMA and Obama really, *really* wants to get Obamacare passed. White House chief of staff Rahm Emanuel wonders: Hmm . . . could PhRMA bring back the Harry and Louise commercials, but this time *in support of* nationalized health care? Yes they can! PhRMA gets the exact same actors and runs ads in 2009, showing the now older couple sitting at their kitchen table and praising Obamacare. The *New York Times* quipped that the actors, Harry Johnson and Louise Caire Clark, "are adept at emoting whatever political point of view they are paid to evoke."[16] Tauzin told the media that PhRMA was backing the new Harry and Louise commercials to help the middle class.[17] The truth, which came out in e-mails exchanged between the White House and lobbyists, was that big pharma wanted to ensure it had a say in writing Obamacare. Tauzin's lobbyist concluded: "We got a good deal."[18]

On the campaign trail in 2008, Obama made this promise: "We can bring doctors and patients, workers and businesses, Democrats and Republicans together; and we can tell the drug and insurance industry that while they'll get a seat at the table, they don't get to buy every chair. Not this time. Not now."[19]

WHAT HAPPENED: Big pharma got more than a seat at the table: it was as if Obama invited the CEOs of the major drug companies to a seven-course dinner and then they moved out to seats on the White House patio for Scotch and cigars to close the deal.

Tauzin told the *New York Times* that the president invited him to "come first" to the table. Obama needed an emissary to help bring the private sector onboard with Obamacare. "If you come first, you [big pharma] will have a rock-solid deal," the White House promised Tauzin.[20]

On the campaign trail, Obama also assured voters that he would cut prescription drug costs by doing three things: promoting competition with imports of affordable medicine, encouraging greater use of generics and by allowing "Medicare to negotiate for better prices."[21] Tauzin was able to convince the White House to renege on all three of Obama's promises.[22] Here's how he did it:

Tauzin spent 2009 and the first few months of 2010 cutting back-room deals with the Obama administration, advising the White House on how to write the health-care reform legislation. PhRMA spent about three times as much as the insurance lobby in 2009, dumping $26.2 million into lobbying.[23]

Obama did not want Millennials to discover his relationship with the drug lobby. So Tauzin devised a cover-up. PhRMA created a nonprofit front group for itself called Americans for Stable Quality Care (ASQC). In 2009, ASQC launched a $12 million TV ad campaign selling the public lies about Obamacare. The ads featured attractive men and women playing the roles of patients, doctors, and nurses. A reassuring male voice told viewers: "What does health insurance reform mean for you? . . . It means putting health care decisions in the hands of you and your doctor. It means lower costs . . . Quality, affordable care you can count on."[24]

No mention of the drug lobby. The ads said they were: "Paid for by Americans for Stable Quality Care." Young viewers could only imagine that plenty of doctors and fellow Americans loved Obamacare.

Key portions of Obamacare were not written by Congress; they were essentially written by two individuals with zero constitutional law-making authority: a president and a lobbyist. Tauzin visited the White House no fewer than eleven times and PhRMA sat down with White House staffers like Rahm Emanuel and agreed to drug-friendly verbiage that ended up in the Senate version of the Obamacare bill that passed on Christmas Eve of 2009[25] *and* the final version, which President Obama signed in March of 2010.[26]

The White House defended its tight relationship with the drug industry by suggesting the industry made *cost-cutting* concessions. What cuts? Health insurance costs more for Millennials, who are expected to subsidize Tauzin's deal. What concessions? Big pharma received everything it wanted and more. By 2013, a study by GlobalData of London revealed that the U.S. drug industry would make an additional $10 billion to $35 billion in profits because it had a hand in crafting the legislation.[27]

Tauzin made money talk and Obama listened.

And the Sexiest Tax Award Goes to . . . the Hustler Tax

In 2012, the Supreme Court declared the individual mandate within Obamacare a "tax." It's a tax all right. A tax on being hip, healthy, and hustling. If you're a young person who works hard, Obamacare hits you the hardest from the time your alarm blares off in the morning until the time you crash into bed to catch a few Z's so you can hustle again in the A.M. to pay off Obama's debt and higher health-care costs.

It will raise their taxes. —MICHAEL FLEISCHER, MD

The individual mandate means that young people need to buy insurance or pay a fine. So if you are an entrepreneur and you work for yourself, or you work part-time, or your employer does not offer health insurance, you will pay the Hustler Tax. Even if you opt out and take the penalty, you are still looking at a tax of several hundred dollars. That's several hundred dollars that could have been used to cover the one to three annual doctor visits a young and healthy person might have.

Fireworks

Obama chose the quiet week of July 4, 2013—when most Americans were tuning out the news and enjoying the summer—to postpone the employee mandate portion of Obamacare from taking effect until 2015. (Speaking the language of socialism, Obama called the employee mandate the "Employer Shared Responsibility Payment.")

Public support was growing, even among Democrats, to repeal or delay the individual mandate. Obama could not do this, or the law would loose its teeth. So, he delayed the employer mandate to look like he was compromising. Democratic moneymen were relying on him to help ease his party through the midterm elections, and, if Barry cared about his legacy and future on the speaker's circuit, he needed to keep his party happy.

The Ball Drop

By 2018, with Obamacare in place, 7 million *fewer* Americans will have their health insurance covered by their employers, according to forecasts by the Congressional Budget Office.[28] Insurance is becoming less affordable for business owners because Obamacare asks insurers to cover new benefits, not because insurers are arbitrarily hiking prices. Obama danced around this dilemma, saying his plans would offer "better coverage." But most Americans (69 percent) were already happy with their coverage and didn't consider his fully loaded plans "better" when their employers refused to offer them.

In the fall of 2013, a Public Opinion Strategies poll of four hundred businesses found that 28 percent of companies were planning to pay the $2,000 annual penalty per employee and drop health-care coverage for their employees in 2015 when the employer mandate was reinstated, while 12 percent of nonfranchise companies and 27 percent of franchise companies had gone ahead and exchanged full-time jobs for part-time jobs.[29]

> *Many details would have to be addressed before we moved forward on a [health-care] plan . . . in particular, we would have to make sure that the creation of a new state pool does not cause employers to drop the health-care plans that they are already providing their employees.*[30] —The Audacity of Hope

In retrospect, *The Audacity of False Hope* would have been a better title for Obama's book. *His* health-care plan encouraged employers to drop their corporate insurance plans or, worse still, reduce their employees' hours to part-time.

By November of 2013, Obama had a juicy scandal on his hands and a midterm election a year away. His necromancers in the media had stopped using their words as magic wands to make the public spellbound. *Time* magazine essentially called Obama a whopping liar: "Obama Administration officials *knew* that normal turnover in the individual market would mean that most old plans would end under the new law. But they **never** made this clear at the time, a *conspicuous failure* for an Administration that *promised transparency and candor* would be paramount [emphasis added]."

Days later, Barry's once-trusty wingman Bill Clinton stabbed him in the back. (Bill's ultimate concern was Hillary 2016, not Barry's legacy.) Clinton chided Obama in a November 13 OZY interview that went viral, exposing him as a con man who broke his promise to young people:

> *Third problem is for young people mostly, but not all young, who are in the individual market whose incomes are above 400 percent of the poverty level. They were the ones who heard the promise: "If you like what you've got, you can keep it." I met a young man this*

week who has a family, two children, bought into the individual marketplace. His policy was canceled and one was substituted for it that doubled his premium. . . . He said, "You know, we're all young and we're all healthy." So, I personally believe, even if it takes a change in the law, the president should honor the commitment the federal government made to those people and let 'em keep what they got.[31]

Panic-stricken, Obama held a long news conference on November 14, 2013, where he rambled and bumbled to cover up his lies. His first order of business was to point his finger at web designers and insurance companies.

Self-righteous as ever, he said, "it's important that we're honest and straightforward," and, self-centered as ever, he offered the solution that worked best for him: "the bottom line is insurers can extend current plans that would otherwise be canceled into 2014. And Americans whose plans have been canceled can choose to re-enroll in the same kind of plan."

This was not a solution for anyone except for Obama, and Democrats who were up for reelection. How could insurance companies suddenly turn on a dime and revert to the old system for twelve months, and then switch back again in 2014? A twelve-month delay would help Obama squeak through the midterms but do nothing to resolve long-term issues with Obamacare. Unimpressed with Barry's pageantry and perfidy, *Time* plastered its December 2 cover with the words "Broken promise" and the image of a broken pill tablet with one half etched with the word "Obama" and the other half inscribed with "Care."

Obama went on to further abuse his executive authority by unilaterally altering the law, including further delaying or softening the impacts of the employer and individual mandates. As we look back on Obama's signature policy, it's vital to remember that the goal of Obamacare was never to improve the health care system. Obama repeatedly lied to the public and abused the presidency in order to advance his own political career and the interests of crony capitalism.

Obama had dropped the ball. Again. And for Millennials it was not like watching the ball drop in Times Square.

Docs Say Obamacare Exacerbates Doctor Shortage

While many of us rarely *want* to see doctors, we do *need* them throughout life. We need doctors who are smart and passionate, and have time to listen and a monetary incentive to make the best decisions for our health. What drove doctors and would-be doctors crazy about Obamacare was all the new administrative paperwork, phone calls, and tasks that they did not go to medical school to do.

The future of young doctors is of particular importance to our country. The Association of American Medical Colleges (AAMC) forecasts that by 2015 the United States will have a physician shortage of 62,900 and by 2025 a shortage of 130,000 physicians over all specialties.[32] The aging population, student debt burden, and Obamacare regulations will intensify this shortage by driving physicians away from geriatrics or family medicine and instead toward more lucrative (and less needed) specialties like cosmetic surgery. Of the nearly three hundred doctors surveyed for this book, 87 percent agreed that Obamacare would definitely "discourage talented young people from attending medical school and exacerbate the shortage of doctors and surgeons in the U.S."

Here is what real doctors are saying about the impact of Obamacare on young people who aspire toward careers as doctors:

> *The fact is [medical school] is no longer worth it. The liability, workload, and responsibility keep increasing. The insurance meddling, paperwork, and government bureaucracy keep increasing. The only things that decrease are our independence, our reimbursements, and any public sense of personal responsibility for their own health. My generation of medicine is on a sinking ship. It would be unethical to recruit more passengers.* —MICHAEL SOBIERAJ, MD (age thirty-five)

Most physicians I know have been effectively telling young adults to forget medicine. . . . Almost all are listening. . . . Bright students see the road to medicine as hard, less autonomous and being a serf to the state instead of helping people. They are not blind. —JERRY LITHMAN, MD

Talent is not drawn to a system which attempts to "equalize" all performance. —LIONEL BROWN, MD

A young doctor drowning in medical school debt finds little comfort in adding "MD" after his name as he signs off on prescriptions and struggles to care for his patients while making a profit. Welcome to The Life of Barry, where smart and caring young doctors are expected to work for free. Most doctors don't do it just for the money. Why else would they accrue six-figure debt and spend four-plus additional years studying *after* college when they could be working for the IRS and vacationing in Tahiti on a guaranteed bonus? They're either crazy or hoping for a meaningful career.

The costs for medical school are skyrocketing. Medical education is currently the most expensive of all postsecondary tracks in America. The average medical student graduates with $166,750 in student debt and over one third graduate with in excess of $200,000 in debt. Even after medical students successfully graduate, they struggle to find residencies, which are required to get jobs, and then continue to struggle to profit in their profession due to sliding reimbursements and rising overhead costs from government-mandated administrative work.

Doctors Say Obamacare Puts Most Talented Residents Out of Work

For those brave souls who do venture into medicine, finding a fulfilling job will be an uphill battle—despite the need for doctors. Residencies are in short supply. Also, many residents are specializing in fields that are not their first choice, based on financial cost instead of what kind of medicine they are most drawn to. Last, they are robbed of quality time with their patients because of Big Brother's growing administrative demands. Instead of spending an extra five minutes with their patient, they are cutting face time short so they can fill out Obama's paperwork.

Here is what doctors are saying:

> *The number of medical students is rising while there hasn't been a corresponding increase in the number of residency positions. This is ridiculously shortsighted. The number of practicing physicians can't increase if residency positions remain the same. This is just another example of how poorly conceived the ACA really is.* —KAREN SIBERT, MD

> *Obamacare places emphasis on nursing education and increasing the so-called "physician extenders."... Why would anyone go into primary care when an RN can get a salary, have malpractice covered and shift the responsibility to the doctor?* —MARILYN SINGLETON, MD, JD

Since 1996, government residency training funding has been frozen. Meanwhile, the aging population and Obamacare (adding 32 million new patients) will increase the need for primary-care doctors.[33] So, Obama used taxpayer dollars to increase the demand for health care without providing a plan to meet the demand by properly training residents.

Obamacare will force most U.S. doctors out of private practice and under the umbrella of a large hospital.[34] This business model allows the government to micromanage doctors, curtailing doctor efficiency and morale when they are unable to provide the high level of care they could under a private clinic system. This hospital-driven business model has been shown to lower physician productivity by 25 to 35 percent.[35] "All of this reduced productivity translates into the loss of what should be a critical factor in the effort to offer more health care while containing costs," Dr. Scott Gottlieb writes in the *Wall Street Journal*.[36]

Doctors Suggest Better Solutions for Young People

I t's not enough to prove that Obamacare is one heck of a bad idea. As conservatives and independents, we need to offer our own, *better* ideas. Instead of looking to cutthroat lobbyists for solutions the way Obama did, let's look to *doctors*. Chances are they have excellent ideas for improving the state of health care:

1. Millennials Can Kill Obamacare by Opting Out

> *[Young people] should protest Obamacare now, today, in front of the White House and on the steps of the Congress. More than anything else, we [doctors] need political freedom to pursue our private medical care in the USA. The government needs to be out of medicine totally, completely—and did I mention totally?* —MARK HURT, MD

If you're a Millennial, you are a member of the most powerful force in America. As a generation, we carry the big stick. We crack the whip. If we don't want Obamacare, all we need to do is opt out. That means refusing to enroll in overpriced health-care plans. It also means protesting. We should protest at the level of Occupy Wall Street times ten (and, of course, minus the defecating and raping in parks). Let's avoid unnecessary plastic handcuffs by keeping things aggressively peaceful.

Young people already opt out of health insurance because it is too costly. Obamacare will make insurance even more costly. Unless 2.7 million healthy young eighteen- to thirty-five-year olds enroll through the state exchanges, Obamacare fails.[37] One group that is exempt from obtaining coverage or paying the penalty associated with Obamacare, according to Covered California, is "people who qualify for religious exemptions." Right off the bat, all young Christians and Jews can claim religious exemption as members of religious groups that believe God gave Moses the Ten Commandments and number eight goes like this: "Thou shalt not steal."

Young people who are not religious should cite discrimination for being unable to claim an exemption. After all, Obamacare is not unethical because it violates religion. Obamacare is wrong because it violates *reason*, which all humans share. Reason says: (1) you own your property; (2) your body is clearly your first piece of property; (3) therefore, Obama had no right to tell you how to insure your body.

We can use our votes to elect politicians who will work to replace Obamacare with more freedom in the marketplace so we can *truly improve* health care. In the meantime, there are existing alternatives to Obamacare for young people who wish to opt out and retain some form of catastrophic health insurance. Nonprofit health-care-sharing ministries such as Samaritan Ministries, Medi-Share, and Christian Healthcare Ministries are little-known alternatives that have been in place for two decades and are exempt from Obamacare. These ministries may not be the right fit for everyone but are worth exploration.

2. Let Doctors Compete For Patients

> *Bottom line, until my patients have to start asking me: "Hey doc, how much does all this stuff you're ordering cost?" and I have to start answering that question, nothing will change . . . for the better, that is.*
> —MICHAEL DORRITY, MD

We could lower the cost and improve the quality of health care if the government stepped aside and allowed patients and doctors to take charge. As with any other service, there are consumers and providers in health care. Consumers complain or jump ship to another provider if they are not getting what they want, motivating providers to respond with better service. Unlike in the private marketplace, if consumers complain about Obamacare, overstretched doctors will have no capacity or authority to address their concerns.

Fortune and CNN Money reported in 2013 that health-care reformists could learn from how the free market has improved the cosmetic surgery industry. A two-decades-long study conducted by economist Devon Herrick for the National Center for Policy Analysis found that the prices for cosmetic surgery were increasing at 1.2 points *below* inflation while the prices of all other medical care have risen at twice the rate of inflation.[38]

Consumers pay out of pocket for cosmetic surgery, so they compare prices and review surgeons until they find the best quality at the best price. Because of competition, prices steadily dropped. Competition also drove talented doctors to *keep* practicing instead of retiring early. Unlike physicians burdened by Barry's bureaucracy, cosmetic surgeons find fulfillment in taking ownership over their practice; and they know they will be rewarded monetarily based on their performance. You could not ask for a better scenario for patients or doctors.

3. Concierge Medicine—At the Cost of a Daily Latte

Veteran doctors have already left insurance companies in droves and opted for a "concierge" or "direct pay" method of operation that allows them to provide their clients with better treatment under less stress. The American Academy of Private Physicians' executive director Tom Blue reported that in 2011 [right after Obamacare passed] nearly 25 percent more doctors opted for the direct-pay method.[39] Save for Medicare, many do not accept payments from insurance companies.

Dr. Louis Magdon wrote in the *Journal of American Physicians and Surgeons*: "One idea that has been gaining popularity recently is that of 'concierge medicine.' These doctors contract directly with their patients in order to avoid the burden of third-party payers. Once for only the rich and famous, concierge service is now enjoyed by many people of modest means. For the price of a gym membership or a daily Starbucks latte, many individuals are pursuing an alternative to the assembly-line medicine experienced at their managed-care-contracted doctor's office. These practices offer their patients much longer appointment times, round-the-clock phone and e-mail consultations, and sometimes even house calls."[40]

Concierge care is more affordable because patients do not pay for services unrelated to the care, such as an insurance administrator's time talking to the doctor on the phone and discussing coverage options, a service which is unrelated to the blood draw, X-ray, physical, or vision test. By removing the third party (insurance company) from non-catastrophic care, the price for the care drops. Why? Because the price of care is no longer determined by the administrative cost of dealing with the insurance company and the profit that the insurance company has to make for their services. The so-called "service" that an insurance company provides for noncatastrophic care gives doctors less independence to care for patients as they think best and pulls them away from healing patients to communicate with insurance companies on reimbursement. Even if the physician hires an administrator to handle communication with the insurance company, this does not help patients because the doctor now has to charge the patient more to cover the cost of the administrator.

4. Preventative Lifestyles

> *I do not believe having health insurance coverage improves anyone's health.* —JOSEPH GAUTA, MD

Your health insurance policy won't make you eat well, work out, or manage your stress. Insurance is only beneficial as a safety net against the unpreventable: aging and unforeseen catastrophes. However, when you are young, the best thing you can do for your health is adopt a healthy lifestyle that will help you age gracefully.

It could make sense for a young person to have catastrophic coverage, but, as Dr. Gauta points out, the insurance itself won't save you from the consequences of unhealthy choices such as throwing back ten shots of vodka and then driving; an insurance policy won't "rewind" you back to life if you plow into a cement median.

Living a preventative lifestyle is the most effective and affordable insurance you can give yourself—whether you are eighteen or sixty-eight. If you are accountable for your health, you are more likely to take care of your body. Comprehensive insurance buffers patients from their stake in their own health, making it seem less imperative to develop a healthy lifestyle or make the best of health care when they do end up needing it.

5. Health Savings Accounts

They should be saving for a later date. HSAs coupled with a high deductible plan are a great solution for them. —Tim Ryan, MD

Medical savings accounts allow people to set aside money for their later care while they are young and can be productive. —Stephen Replogle, DO

When you are young, you can and should invest more aggressively and take more financial risks than when you are older. You're only young once and you need to use your youth to build a cache for later.

An HSA (health savings account) is a terrific option for young people. George W. Bush passed a prescription drug plan in 2003 that allowed Americans to use HSAs for the first time. Instead of an employer or insurance company telling a young person to pay for certain services they will never use, the young person decides for him- or herself which health-care services to purchase. Thus, HSAs allow young people to spend only what they need and save the rest for the future.

If you have a high-deductable insurance plan, you may open an HSA. The money is yours. Unlike a 401(k), even if your employer contributes to your account and you leave your company before you are "fully vested," you still keep all the funds in your account. Each year, you may roll over any money you did not spend and use it the following year and you can withdraw everything when you retire. An HSA encourages doctors to compete on price and quality because they know that customers are making their own spending decisions and shopping around for the best price. You do not pay income taxes on the money unless you withdraw it. You can also keep the account through old age and at death transfer any remaining funds to a beneficiary (the transfer is tax free if the beneficiary is your spouse).

A very famous doctor offered a similar solution.

The Black Man Who Solved the Health-Care Crisis (Hint: Not Obama)

Obama is not the only black man to offer a solution to the health-care debate in America. Dr. Ben Carson is the former director of pediatric neurosurgery at Johns Hopkins Hospital. Carson was the first surgeon to successfully separate conjoined twins. He led a seventy-member surgical team for twenty-two hours to operate on twins bonded at the back of the head. Dr. Carson is far more qualified to talk about health-care reform than our Community-Organizer-In-Chief.

At the 2013 National Prayer Breakfast (while Obama sat next to him, nostrils in the air, rudely refusing to clap during his introduction), Carson offered a simple solution to give you control over your own health care—*and* provide quality health care for all members of society, including the poor. Whereas the president needed over nine hundred pages to write a death sentence for private health care, Carson articulated a solution to reform health care in roughly forty-three seconds. Carson said in part:

> *We need to have good healthcare for everybody. . . . We spend a lot of money on healthcare. Twice as much per capita as anybody else in the world. And yet not very efficient. What can we do?*
>
> *Here's my solution: When a person is born, give them a birth certificate, an electronic medical record and a health savings account, to which money can be contributed pre-tax from the time you are born 'til the time you die. When you die, you pass it along to your family members so that when you're 85 years old and you've got six diseases you're not trying to spend up everything; you're happy to pass it on and there's nobody talking about death panels. That's number one.*
>
> *And also, for the people who are indigent, who don't have any money, we can make contributions to their HSA each month because we already have this huge pot of money; instead of sending it*

to some bureaucracy, let's put it in their HSAs. Now they have some
control over their own healthcare.

Carson's plan gives you and your provider control over your health
care instead of ceding control to the government. Talk radio host Rush
Limbaugh explained: "What Dr. Carson's plan says is just take that
money that's already in the health care system that's coming out of your
pocket in the form of taxes—Medicare tax, Medicaid tax, income tax,
all that—and you keep it instead of sending it to Washington."

6. A New Generation of Doctors, Volunteering to Help the Poor

The standard nitwit guilt trip is: "Obamacare is wonderful because it
gives young people a chance to help the old and the poor!" Please. There
are much more effective means of helping the poor. Numerous doctors
are willing to try what history has proven to work best: volunteering.

Young Dr. Magdon says: "I issue a challenge to my generation of
doctors. Let an overwhelming majority of us start and/or participate
in clinics [such as Zarephath Health Center in New Jersey, staffed by
volunteer doctors, nurses, and clerks, funded solely by private donations,
and operating at a fraction of the cost of the federally qualified health
clinics]. Let us truly be our brother's keeper. No one should go without
basic healthcare. Let us do it the right way."[41]

In the early days of America—before the welfare state—doctors
volunteered to care for the poor. Despite that history, Obama never
asked doctors whether they might be willing to keep doing what they
have done for hundreds of years: *volunteer* to care for the poor. If he
had asked, he would have been pleasantly surprised to hear how generous most doctors would be with their time. When doctors volunteer,
they have a better relationship with their patient. Plus, the care is more
streamlined because doctors don't need to jump through a bureaucratic
obstacle course to provide pro bono care.

Once the Obamacare exchanges went into operation, many of the
poorest Americans—those without insurance—found that they did

not qualify for subsidized health insurance. Obama groupies blamed Obamacare's failure to help poor blacks and single mothers on the twenty-six states that opted out of the Medicaid expansion the Supreme Court deemed optional. States were right to balk. We should not be looking for *federal* "improvements" for health care. Instead, we should seek ways to give doctors the freedom they need to provide maximum care for their patients at local clinics and hospitals.

Obamacare failed to help the poor by conflating holding an insurance policy in your hand with guaranteed access to quality health care from a conscientious doctor. Instead, Obamacare left the poor in a situation where they are more likely to be treated by doctors who are overworked, underpaid, and resentful because the government is treating them like babies instead of professionals—*forcing* them to care and to complete unnecessary forms for minor procedures instead of allowing them to *choose* to care for the poor in the most efficient manner, which would allow them to care for more poor people, and more *effectively*.

Of course, if Obama had encouraged doctors to volunteer, he might have lost out on some of Pimp Daddy Tauzin's drug money and a second term in the White House.

* * *

OBAMACARE hands Millennials the burden of using their young and healthy working years to pay for the health insurance of older and sicker members of society. Consequently, Millennials will spoil their own long-term health and capital. Extortion by any other name would smell as fishy.

> *When I graduated from medical school and took my oath, it was to serve patients, not to serve government, not to serve insurance, not to serve a hospital system, and not to serve myself. I have no intention to allow any of those entities to come between me and the patients I have been called to serve.* —JENNIFER POWELL, MD

FLIPPING STUDENTS
THE BIRD

With the hot sun beating on his back and D.C. humidity soaking his white polo shirt, a teenage Bill Clinton elbowed his way through a pack of high school boys to be first to shake JFK's hand.[1] Years later, Clinton included a photo of the occasion in his memoir with the caption: "I'm in the front, right behind the photographer, as President John F. Kennedy addresses the Boys Nation delegates in the Rose Garden on July 24, 1963." That day a photographer named Arnie Sachs took another photo, this one capturing the exact moment when Kennedy and Clinton met—their eyes locked and fingers entwined in a firm handshake.

Sachs could not have known how closely Clinton would follow Kennedy's path; it was simply a fascinating shot of a cheeky youth colliding with the president.[2] Looking back, the meeting Sachs memorialized looks like a warped adaptation of the meeting Michelangelo solemnized in his Sistine Chapel ceiling fresco, *The Creation of Adam*. Michelangelo painted the figurative moment when God's and Adam's eyes locked and God breathed life into Adam as their fingers were about to touch; Sachs snapped the symbolic moment when the original presidential predator infused his energy into the next man to carry on his legacy of luring young people.

Kennedy inspired Clinton. Both men inspired Obama. *The Creation of Barack* involved a process whereby Obama eerily channeled Kennedy and Clinton to achieve his own political goals by punking young people.

Before entering politics, Clinton went to Georgetown and then Yale Law School where he sailed through on the bare minimum, charming some girl into sharing her meticulous notes with him so he could cram at the last minute after playing hooky for most of the class.[3] Immediately after graduating from Yale, because of luck and help from a friendly professor, Clinton landed a position *teaching* law at the University of Arkansas Law School at Fayetteville. Slick Willie went from zero job offers to faculty member at Arkansas Law.[4]

Obama mimicked Clinton's path in academia and milked it for all it was worth. In 1988, Obama left his community organizing post in Chicago and set out for Harvard Law School. After partying, smoking, and relaxing his way through postsecondary, studying when absolutely necessary and often at the last minute, Obama landed a prestigious fellowship at the University of Chicago Law School in 1991 that evolved into a part-time teaching gig at the law school in 1992. How did he get there? On a recommendation from the *Harvard Law Review*'s president.[5]

Luck favored Obama throughout his teaching career. In 1996, Barry was teaching law part-time and serving as state senator. He decided he wanted more cash, so he asked the law school dean for something unprecedented and unearned: Obama insisted on a promotion to "senior lecturer," a distinguished position that had only been granted to two federal judges who had worked full-time for the law school. In contrast, we know thirty-four-year-old Obama had taught *one* seminar, a class he conceptualized, called "Current Issues in Racism and the Law."[6] Nevertheless, the dean went to bat for Obama and he got his way.[7] The *Times* suggested affirmative action played a role in this peculiar promotion: "The newly minted state senator would have added diversity to the law school: at the time, there was only one person of color on the full-time Chicago academic teaching staff."[8] (In any case, one point is crystal clear: again we see that "racial stalemate" hardly describes Obama's life as a black man in America.) In 1996, Obama added "Constitutional Law III: Equal Protection" to his heavy course load and ended up teaching three courses a year until 2004.

Once Obama had a stockpile of students at his disposal, "He tested his [political] ideas in classrooms," a former colleague told the *New York Times*.[9] According to the *Times*, Obama positioned himself as a celebrity. He praised his own physique during lectures and students responded by "referring to themselves as his groupies" and holding fundraisers for him in their apartments when he decided to run against Illinois Republican incumbent Bobby Rush for a seat in the U.S. House of Representatives.[10] Obama lost that primary race in 2000, but his students had helped him gain invaluable experience for his political future.

Would Obama have become such a polished public speaker, even *with* the aid of a teleprompter, had he not won the lottery in terms of a political test tube: twelve years at the University of Chicago where he could test his strategies and messages on law students before he would adapt them for young people in the 2008 and 2012 presidential campaigns? It's highly unlikely.

Kennedy and Clinton relied on mistresses to spike their confidence. But both presidents gained emotionally at the *educational and professional expense* of their young inamoratas. Mimi Alford became hermit-like, avoiding her friends and eventually dropping out of Wheaton College for the sake of sustaining the affair; looking back, she called herself a "headless girl, blinded by the President's power and charisma."[11] Monica Lewinsky also "paid a high price," Andrew Morton explained in the biography she authorized him to write: "I feel that he [Clinton] should have shown more restraint and left it as a flirtation and as an unacted-upon fantasy. . . . It was too much of an emotional burden for someone my age," she told Morton.[12]

Alpha Baiter Barry Obama used young people for more than an ego boost; he used Millennials to win two presidential elections. And

Millennials paid an even higher educational and career price for Obama's political success. After snatching their votes, Obama effectively gave the students who voted for him the middle finger. Let me explain . . .

Obama presented taxpayer-subsidized and federally controlled higher education [even students at private colleges and universities are eligible for federal grants and loans] as the *one and only* route to full success. He acted like he was a savior who would help Millennials afford college at a time when his administration was completely ripping off student borrowers. Millennials took out college or graduate school loans only to be crushed with debt and unable to find jobs when they graduated. Plus, the education they received left them unemployable: Their skills did not match employer needs.

During Obama's presidency, an all-time high of *48 percent* of college students were working in jobs that did not require a four-year college degree, such as janitor, bartender, maid, waitress, retail clerk, amusement or recreation attendant, cashier, and taxi driver.[13] Obama was low enough to buy the youth vote by encouraging an entire generation to borrow money hand over fist and dedicate four years to pursuing questionable degrees only to graduate and find a job market more arid than the Sahara Desert.

Groupies at Gunpoint

Tim Tebow's groupies are groupies by choice. So are Lindsey Stirling's. So are Ivanka Trump's. The fun thing about being a fan of celebrities is that you freely choose to follow them, watch their games, attend their concerts, or buy their fragrances. But Obama made Millennials feel like their survival depended upon raving for him. Obama brought his message to college campuses and utilized the power of intimidation and peer pressure to stiff-arm Millennials into becoming his groupies and eventually voting for him.

There were no guns pointed at their heads, but there may as well have been. The Millennials who became Obama's "groupies" did so under enormous pressure. Obama made Millennials feel like if they didn't buy into his worldview, if they didn't vote for him, they would be gigantic failures: They would forever struggle to pay off their education, find jobs, and achieve success.

Forcing young people to conform to an artificial model of success yields disaster. Young people needed to know *all* of their options for reaching success so they could choose a career trajectory that would minimize their weaknesses and maximize their unique talents and interests. For his political gain, Obama led our young people to believe that there was *one* route to definitive success, so many youths who were better suited for different paths were set up for failure.

Take a listen to a few comments that Obama and Michelle made about higher education on the campaign trail. Remember, the Obamas were celebrities in the eyes of Millennials (thanks to the typing wizards!) and their words carried weight. Notice how the Obamas made it sound as though, if he were reelected, he would make college affordable to *all* young people. This made young people feel comfortable 1) voting for him and 2) taking out unwise student loans.

On the 2008 Campaign Trail:

"Every American has the right to pursue their dreams . . . . When I am President, we will stop passing bills called No Child Left Behind that leave the money behind, and start making real investments in education. That means early childhood education . . . . It also means putting a college education within reach of every American. That's the best investment we can make in our future."[14]

"The chance to get a college education must not be a privilege of the few—it should be a birthright of every single American."[15]

"It's great if you have a job; it's even better if you have a college degree."[16]

As President:

"In the end, girls, that's why I ran for President: because of what I want for you and for every child in this nation . . . . I want them to have the chance to go to college—even if their parents aren't rich."[17] (Obama in a letter to his daughters, *Parade* magazine, January 2009)

"We said, well, how do we make sure that every young person can go to college once they get through high school? And we shifted billions of dollars that were going to banks in the form of unwarranted subsidies and we took that money and we made sure that that money was going directly to student loans and Pell Grants so that young people would never feel as if they were barred from opportunity simply because they didn't come from a wealthy family." (Democratic Senatorial Campaign Committee Dinner, Rockville, Maryland, October 18, 2010)*

"I want every child in Texas and every child in America ready to graduate, ready to go to college, and actually able to afford going to college." (DNC fundraiser, Austin, Texas, May 10, 2011)

"Every single young person who is willing to apply themselves can afford to go to college without taking on hundreds of thousands of debt." (Obama speaking about his second-term goals at a DNC event, June 23, 2011)

"If they've been working hard, if they've gotten the grades to go to college, I don't want them to cut their dreams short because they don't think they can afford it." (Biltmore Hotel, Coral Gables, Florida, February 23, 2012)

Michelle repeated her husband's lofty promises when she spoke at the 2012 Democratic Convention, before a huge crowd that included many Millennials:

"When it comes to giving our kids the education they deserve, Barack knows that, like me and like so many of you, he never could have attended college without financial aid. And believe it or not, when we were first married, our combined monthly student loan bill was actually higher than our mortgage. Yeah, we were so young, so in love and so in debt. And that's why Barack has fought so hard to increase student aid and keep interest rates down—because he wants *every young person*

---

*He made nearly identical statements in Minneapolis, Minnesota, on October 23, 2010, and in Orlando, Florida, on February, 23, 2012.

to fulfill their promise and be able to attend college *without* a mountain of debt [emphasis added]."

The first couple encouraged young people to think that college was necessary for *full* success and led them to feel like their student loans would magically disappear if only Obama was in office. Besides his unhealthy rhetoric, Obama took *actions* to keep rates artificially low; to *look* like he was helping Millennials afford college. Even if Obama was not out to hurt your sons, daughters, and grandchildren, he did not seem to *care* that he hurt them by making them think college was extremely necessary, valuable, and affordable. By restricting or discouraging six paths to success that young people should have had available to them, Obama ensured that young people would turn to his one-size-fits-all model and vote for him twice. They paid a big price.

1. ENTREPRENEURSHIP

"If you've been successful, you didn't get there on your own. You didn't get there on your own . . . . If you've got a business, you didn't build that. Somebody else made that happen." —OBAMA ON THE CAMPAIGN TRAIL IN JULY OF 2012

Obama made Millennials feel like they needed to pay large institutions to give them a piece of paper (diploma) saying they were capable of starting a business instead of going it on their own. Rather than boosting their confidence in their natural talents and encouraging them to innovate, Obama tore budding entrepreneurs down.

Consider a few of the many Americans who became wildly successful *on their own* and *without* college degrees:

- Rush Limbaugh
- Steve Jobs
- Bill Gates
- Michael Dell
- Ralph Lauren
- LeBron James

Now, consider the consequences if these men had wasted their youth in college!

Besides benefittng society, entrepreneurs reap rewards themselves. Entrepreneurs are naturally self-motivated individuals; their deepest motivation comes from within. This means that they will feel the most satisfied in a career where they have the latitude to *push themselves*. In the short run, the freedom inherent in entrepreneurship provides high day-to-day satisfaction; in the long run, this freedom grants the entrepreneur the opportunity to reach his or her full capacity for personal, professional, and financial success. More personal benefits of entrepreneurship can include the liberty to work hardest during the time of day when you feel the most energized; the independence to work as creatively as you can; and the lack of a long daily commute, which multiple studies link to depression, anxiety, and health issues.[18] For certain young people who are self-driven, creative, energetic, and willing to work alone for long stretches—especially in their company's infancy—entrepreneurship is the perfect fit.

Obama will take credit for "creating" a few entrepreneurs with taxpayer money, but, as we know, he generated failures and propped up his wealthy buddies' ventures that did not need propping up. Entrepreneurs—like love—cannot be created from money. A *culture of freedom* can *cultivate* entrepreneurship among young people who are naturally oriented toward this path, as we'll explore further in chapter 10.

2. Skilled Trades

Many Millennials would have been better off skipping the traditional higher education path and working in energy or a skilled trade. Shale gas and oil workers, plumbers, truck drivers, and welders are much needed in America. Plus, by 2013, about 30 percent of associate's degree holders were outearning those with four-year degrees.[19]

In 2012 Obama defended himself, claiming that he had also encouraged young people to attend community colleges. He did make a few token attempts, especially after a Republican presidential candidate called him out in January of 2012. However, his laser focus on the four-year degree helped make trade school seem socially unacceptable: By 2013, CNN Money reported that enrollment was falling at community colleges.[20]

3. TECHNOLOGY

"The Internet didn't get invented on its own; government research made that happen." —OBAMA ON THE 2012 CAMPAIGN TRAIL

Actually, a young man named Bill Joy invented the code for the Internet. He taught himself how to code as a nerdy student hacker, not by working for the government. "Do you know who wrote much of the software that allows you to access the Internet? Bill Joy . . . . Among Silicon Valley insiders, Joy is spoken of with as much awe as someone like Bill Gates of Microsoft. He is sometimes called the Edison of the Internet," Malcolm Gladwell wrote in *Outliers*.[21]

Obama made true innovation in technology difficult by subsidizing so-called "green" technology instead of letting the market develop it naturally. His taxes and regulations also made it challenging for American tech companies like Apple and Cisco to keep general tech jobs in America.

4. LAW

Here's a lawyer joke for you: What happens when the First Couple is a couple of lawyers? Answer: Young law grads will spend nine-plus months searching for work in the legal profession only to end up working as coffee baristas or folding clothes at Macy's.

Right, that wasn't funny (most lawyer jokes are not funny). But this lawyer joke is sad because it is true. With the exception of casework like *Tall Black Coffee v. Skinny Vanilla Latte,* scores of law school graduates failed to find work due to Obama's poor economy and government interference in legal education.

"So, yes, go get that law degree. But if you do, ask yourself if the only option is to defend the rich and the powerful, or if you can also find some time to defend the powerless,"[22] Obama urged students graduating from Morehouse College.

Too bad young lawyers could not find legal jobs that would allow them to pay their *own* bills, let alone have the financial flexibility to work pro bono. In the spring of 2012, the American Bar Association released a study showing that just 55 percent of law school graduates had found jobs necessitating a law degree.[23]

Washington University Law School professor Brian Z. Tamanaha told the *New York Times* that 90 percent of law school students relied on loans to get through law school.[24] He also said that the average cost of attending a private law school jumped from $23,000 in 2001 (Bush era) to $40,500 in 2012 (Obama era). He said tuition at public law schools rose from $8,500 in 2001 to $23,600 in 2012. The average debt for law school students jumped dramatically during the Obamas' time in the White House. In the academic year 2001–2002, the average private law school debt load was $70,000 and the average public law school debt load was $46,500. By 2012, the *ABA Journal* reported that private and public law school debt loads had grown to around $125,000 and $75,500, respectively.[25]

If Obama had not destroyed the U.S. economy, it would have been easier for young lawyers to find employment doing legal work and helping the poor.

5. MEDICINE

You already know from the previous chapter how Obama's policies discouraged aspiring doctors.

6. STAY-AT-HOME PARENT

Millennials could not afford to become parents, let alone stay at home with their children, in Obamaville. We will explore this further in chapters 5 and 6.

* * *

By 2011, Millennials understood that they faced profound economic problems, including student loan debt, and they organized Occupy Wall Street (OWS) protests around the country. But while young OWSers should have been mad at Obama, they took out their frustration on capitalism. Obama fed into the misplaced rage of OWS protestors and pitched a "solution" of more government intervention that he promised would make higher education "affordable."

Obama was selling young people yet *another* Ponzi scheme. He would benefit; they would get crushed. He pushed his one-size-fits-all model of success through government-subsidized higher education more aggressively as the 2012 election drew near.

The Socialist Who Drinks Beer Heads to Campus

Prior to "officially" launching his campaign during the week of April 30, 2012, Obama did a two-day tour to colleges in battleground states and a skit with comedian Jimmy Fallon at the University of North Carolina at Chapel Hill (Obama's administration claimed that this was not to win votes but to help young people get more out of their education).

Students went wild listening to Fallon and Obama go back and forth like best buds discussing Obama's relaxation ritual in the "presidential man cave":

> FALLON: "But what do you do when you and Bo—you get
>   together—you go to the presidential man cave?"
> OBAMA: "We go to the man cave. We turn on *SportsCenter.*"
> FALLON: "Is that what you do?"
> OBAMA: "Yeah. We have a couple'a beers."

(Back in 2008, Obama gave a speech saying that fathers set a bad example for their children by watching *SportsCenter* when he was speaking to voters at the Apostolic Church of God. In 2013 when he was talking to college-student voters, he bragged about ditching his daughters to chillax with Bo and watch *SportsCenter*. Classic Obama, sending different messages to different groups of people.)

In addition to discussing Obama's man cave, Fallon "slow-jammed" (rapped) the news with the president and unwittingly helped him market his student loan Ponzi scheme. Fallon and Obama both grabbed hand mics and the Roots band backed them up as they slow-jammed:

> OBAMA: "What we said is simple. Now is not the time to make
>   school more expensive for our young people."
> (*Huge applause from students.*)
> FALLON: "Ohhh. Yeeaaaah. You should listen to the president. Or
>   as I like to call him, the Preezy of the United Steezy."

Later, CNN host Anderson Cooper asked Fallon how he was able to get the president to slow-jam the news with him. Fallon responded that the president and the White House initially approached him and asked if he would do a "piece with the president" at a college.

What college students had likely viewed as Fallon's idea was actually the brainchild of Obama. Students would not realize that Obama had sold them on a Ponzi scheme until the spring of 2013, *after* they had voted.

* * *

MICHELLE and Vice President Joe Biden joined in on Obama's college circuit in the spring of 2012 including a speech at an all-women's school, Barnard College, on May 14 to curry favor with young female voters who were losing interest in Obama.

Obama encouraged more young people to go to college and take out massive loans—during the middle of the Great Recession and then during his nonrecovery. Many of these youths would have done better to work and save for a year before attending college. Others were better suited for entrepreneurship or a skilled trade.

Despite warnings from his *own administrators* that student debt would hurt the economy, Obama continued to encourage young people to take out needless debt. During the 2012 Democratic National Convention, Obama tapped his idol, Bill Clinton, to help him con young people into voting for him. Clinton was happy to help; it was a chance to return to center stage!

Obama: "If you can't afford to start a business or go to college, take my opponent's advice and borrow money from your parents. You know what, that's not who we are. That's not what this country is about." (Translation: Borrow recklessly. That's what it means to be American!)

Obama: "Millions of students are paying less for college today because we finally took on a system that wasted billions of taxpayer dollars on banks and lenders. . . . I refuse to ask students to pay more for college" (Fact: Students were paying historically high college tuition rates. Also, Obama did not take on the system; he played the system.)

Clinton: "So the president's student loan reform is more important than ever. . . . Now what does this mean? What does this mean? Think of it. It means no one will ever have to drop out of college again for fear they can't repay their debt." (Truth: One month later, when Obama was safely reelected, the *New York Times* reported that nearly 30 percent of students *were* dropping out of college—within six years of enrolling for the first time.[26] Also, it is hard to call student debt an "investment" without a diploma.)

Higher "Profits" Than Apple and Exxon Mobile

Obama bought votes with a student loan campaign in 2012—while using taxpayer dollars to post "profits" for the federal government bigger than those of Exxon Mobile and Apple. Obama left an entire generation burdened with historic student debt in the middle of his "huge recovery" where they could not find jobs to pay back their debt.

Unlike community colleges, enrollment at four-year colleges is up

38 percent from a decade ago. College debt is also historically high: in 2013, the average debt burden was $29,400; in 2003, the average debt burden was about one third of that figure: $10,649.[27]

Obama's administration predicted it would make a whopping $51 billion in "profit" from its student loan program in 2013, reported the *Huffington Post*. This is far higher than Exxon or Apple profits in 2012. But, *unlike* Exxon and Apple, the federal government is not a legitimate company, creating goods or services; it does not technically "profit."

When students defaulted on their loans, the federal government cashed in bigger than Steve Jobs's company did by selling actual, usable products like laptops and tablets. When the federal government says it is "profiting," it is merely advertising the fact that it has succeeded in wrangling money from taxpayers. Plus, bureaucrats in the federal government usually waste the money they seize since they did not earn it themselves and do not understand its value.

The *Huffington Post* wrote: "Regulators and officials at agencies that include the Federal Reserve, Treasury Department, Consumer Financial Protection Bureau and Federal Reserve Bank of New York have all warned that student borrowing may dampen consumption, depress the economy, limit credit creation or pose a threat to financial stability. At $1.1 trillion, student debt eclipses all other forms of household debt, except for home mortgages."

Obama's Department of Education "profited" from student debt in two ways. First, there was a historically high spread between the government's funding costs (the yield on ten-year Treasuries, which had been under 2 percent since the summer of 2011) and the rates on federal Stafford loans made by the Department of Education, which had been around 6.8 and 7.9 percent. The spread between these two allowed the federal government to post a killing ($50.6 billion) off student loans.[28]

Second, Obama's Department of Education benefited by unscrupulous debt collection and pushing young people into default. Under Obama's watch, the Department of Education escalated its practice of using shady nonprofit organizations to oversee student loans. The agents at these "nonprofits" made six-figure and seven-figure salaries in 2011.[29]

The agents had a financial incentive (receiving commissions of up to 16 percent of the loan amount) to push students into default rather than to prevent default via counseling, which only yielded agents a kickback of 1 percent of the borrower's loan.[30]

Despite the fact that complaints about student debt collection abuse spiked 41 percent in 2011, Obama continued to push his "go to college" mantra through the rest of his dual term and tell students that he was reforming the student loan program. It wasn't until he was safely re-elected and his Department of Education was under fire for looking like the "world's croniest company," that he addressed his administration's ruthless debt collection tactics.

Beginning in May of 2013, the maximum fee an agent could collect on a student default dropped from 16 to 11 percent and agents were encouraged to put students into more flexible monthly payment plans than before. But this was too late to help many students who were already drowning in debt. Obama's Department of Education nearly doubled its profit off of student debt between 2011 ($27.5 billion)[31] and 2013 ($51.6 billion). No wonder he waited so long to look into his student debt collectors!

Which Way Does the Wind Blow?

In July of 2013, the interest rate on federal loans was set to double from 3.4 percent to 6.8 percent. Obama proposed a budget plan that tied interest rates to the market. Then, House Republicans proposed tying interest rates to the market. *Uh-oh. This is not good,* thought Obama. *I can't look like I agree with Republicans!*

Obama gathered a group of students behind him, "as backdrop," quipped the *New York Times,* and chided House Republicans for proposing to tie rates to the market: "It fails to lock in low rates for students next year. That's not smart. It eliminates safeguards for lower-income families. That's not fair."[32] Eventually, both congressional Democrats and Republicans ignored a finicky president and passed a bill that tied all student loan interest rates to market rates (instead of having Congress arbitrarily force the rate down). Caps were added to prevent the rate from rising above 8.25 percent for undergraduates and 9.5 percent for graduates. Obama, apparently unable to make up his mind, signed the bill and praised it as "a sensible, common-sense approach to keeping student interest rates at a reasonable level so that young people have a better opportunity to go to college."

In fact, this proposal did little to make college more affordable. Tying rates to the market is an improvement in that it shows students the true cost of college and thus might dissuade some youths from wasting four years and six figures on college when they could be building up their own business or acquiring a trade. But, this bill did not make college more affordable. To make college more affordable, colleges need to *cut costs* and *increase their value*. Otherwise, it's still a lousy investment in terms of time, money, and energy.

Barry, unfortunately, did nothing substantial to make college a better *investment*. This isn't to say that he should have. The solutions for cutting the cost of college will come from students and the colleges themselves, as we will discuss. But he should not have misled young people to think that he would help them achieve educational and career success when all he did was take a hefty cut off of their poor investment: instead of a commission, he took their votes for reelection.

The Mafia

Obama needed help ripping off students and pressuring them to become his groupies at metaphorical gunpoint. His vixens and henchmen in academia helped him every step of the way. Barry had many sly and soft-footed allies in the halls of universities across the country; their expertise was killing Millennials softly.

We want a *balance* of conservative, independent, and liberal professors in American colleges and universities so that students are exposed to *diverse* ideas—*not* only *liberal* ideas. The number of college professors who identified as liberals increased under Obama. Every three years, the University of California at Los Angeles Higher Education Research Institute conducts a national survey of college educators. In the 2007–2008 academic year, 55.8 percent of college professors claimed to be liberal. By the 2010–2011 academic year 62.7 percent of college educators self-identified as liberal and only 11.9 percent self-identified as conservative.[33]

Under President Obama, educators with little credibility besides their "celebrity" found their way into the halls of America's finest institutions of higher learning. Meet a few distinguished members of the Obama Mafia:

MICHAEL ERIC DYSON: When this Georgetown University professor of sociology wasn't inoculating students in the classroom, he was hypnotizing them on cable TV. Dyson appeared on MSNBC's *Martin Bashir* program on May 30, 2013, and said Attorney General Eric Holder "shouldn't give up his office. What he should understand is he is the chief law-giver of the United States of America so to speak. He's the *Moses* of our time and at least for this administration."

Dyson made these comments in the wake of the botched Fast and Furious gun-running program *and* revelations that Holder violated the Constitution and the Department of Justice's own regulations by approving subpoenas for the phone records of journalists from the Associated Press, the *New York Times,* and Fox News.

At first the comparison between Moses and Holder seems blasphemous. But then you realize that Moses spoke to God in the form of a burning bush . . . and Holder bushwhacked the Constitution. They're practically twins!

SALAMISHAH TILLET: This University of Pennsylvania professor one-upped Dyson by going on MSNBC in June of 2013 and suggesting that all white people who are pro-life are responding "to that sense that there's a decreasing white majority in the country and that women's bodies and white women's bodies in particular are obviously a crucial way of reproducing whiteness, white supremacy, white privilege. And so I think it's just a kind of clamping down on women's bodies, in particular white women's bodies, even though women of color are really caught in the fray."

Basically, she called all white pro-life people racist. Tillet might have had a point, except more women of color have abortions than white women. So by opposing abortion, pro-life whites are actually encouraging *more* nonwhite births.

ELIOT SPITZER: Had lots of girlfriends: Call girls—he prosecuted prostitution rings as the governor of New York and then got busted for being a top client for the now-defunct high-end Emperor's Club escort agency. Activist girls—Obama's Supreme Court nominee Elena Kagan was his good friend. School girls—Spitzer taught a weekly seminar called Law and Public Policy from 2009 through 2012 at City College in Manhattan. He told the college gals (and guys) that they could call his cell phone anytime with "homework questions." One of his female students told the *New York Times* that she enjoyed his class but "he didn't really seem to know what he was doing. . . . He kept asking us, 'What do other professors do?' "[34]

JOHN MICHAEL BAILEY: This psychology professor at Northwestern University taught a controversial human sexuality class in 2011. He invited his students to an after-class presentation where he asked Chicago sex-tour guide Ken Melvoin-Berg to demonstrate the use of a sex toy called a "f—ksaw" on a nonstudent, naked female to the point of orgasm in front of 120 students, according to the school's newspaper, the *Daily Northwestern*.[35] (Though 120 students may sound like a lot, there were 600 students in the class so 480 had better things to do, apparently.) At a different after-class event, students listened to a panel of convicted sex offenders. Bailey still teaches, just not *that* human sexuality class.

ELLEN LEWEN: University of Iowa professor Ellen Lewen specialized in studying "same-sex relationships" at the University of Iowa. The Association of Queer Anthropology awarded her with a prize in 2009 for her book *Gay Fatherhood: Narratives of Family and Citizenship in*

America. You would think after all the time she spent studying gay and lesbian anthropology that she would be a very tolerant person. However, like many liberal professors, Lewen was very close-minded.

In April of 2011, Lewen opened her school e-mail account and found a creative recruiting blast from the campus College Republicans inviting students to attend its "Conservative Coming Out Week." As an expert on lesbians and gays, she jumped to the only logical conclusion you can come to if you live in a bubble, which is: *Republicans hate gay people!*

Lewen instantly fired off a response to the College Republicans recruitment e-mail: "F—k you, Republicans!"

Lewin is still on the University of Iowa's payroll and we have not heard a peep from America's Top Civility Cop, Barack Obama.

SHARON SWEET: Brevard Community College teacher Sharon Sweet encouraged her students to sign pledges saying that they would vote for Obama in November of 2012. The pledge said: "I pledge to vote for President Obama and Democrats up and down the ticket." She is a registered Democrat and pushed liberal campaign materials on her students. She has been fired by the college and will likely appeal.

DARRY SRAGOW: Also in the fall of 2012, an adjunct political science professor at the University of Southern California (USC) named Darry Sragow pressured his students to vote for Democrats by going on long rants during class where he called Republicans "racists, old white men, losers and stubborn sons of bitches."

DEANDRE POOLE: In March of 2013, a student was reportedly suspended for refusing to stomp on a piece of paper that said "Jesus" on it at Florida Atlantic University. When FAU decided to renew Poole's contract, Church of All Nations Pastor Mark Boykin of Boca Raton, Florida, told WPTV, "What next, spitting on the cross you get tenure?"[36]

BILL AYERS: Obama has mutely stood by while known terrorists like Bill Ayers have advanced in places of higher education. Ayers is a founder of a militant organization called Weathermen that is responsible for blowing up buildings and killing police officers.[37] Minnesota State University Moorhead recently appointed Ayers as the 2013 College of Education and Human Services "visiting scholar." Ayers is friends with Obama. Obama even had a fundraiser in Bill's living room.

BERNARDINE DOHRN: Bill Ayers's wife is a former co-conspirator in Weathermen. Dohrn worked at the same law firm as Michelle Obama and now teaches at Northwestern University. Her name once graced the FBI's Ten Most Wanted List.

KATHY BOUDIN: This friend of Bill Ayers spent twenty-two years in federal prison for her role in an armored car robbery that resulted in the deaths of two police officers and a Brink's guard, and now she is an assistant professor at Obama's alma mater, Columbia University, in the School of Social Work. She was also named the 2013 Sheinberg Scholar-in-Residence at NYU Law School.[38]

Professors of Pop

Why else was it so wrong for Obama to pressure Millenials to pursue four-year degrees? After all, the common view is that a college education guarantees more long-term success. It was wrong because the *quality* of a college education had severely deteriorated.

Today, young people are not studying a solid liberal arts core curriculum. They are not learning how to write and think critically by taking courses in subjects like literature and composition, U.S. history, science, math, and economics.

A 2011 GfK Roper survey found that 80 percent of recent college graduates (ages twenty-five to thirty-four) say that they think a core curriculum mandating classes in traditional areas such as foreign languages, math, science, economics, writing, and history *should* be required at all four-year institutions.[39] Having spent a few years in the workplace, these young professionals value and desire the strong foundation of a core curriculum.

Most major institutions of higher education—including Ivy League schools like Brown University (zero core subject requirements), Yale, and Harvard (two core subject requirements)—do not mandate a full liberal arts curriculum.[40] Instead, students are given the "freedom" to pick and choose from a wide range of classes that might be fun for the professors to teach but not very helpful in preparing young people to think, write, analyze, or compute for business.

Consider a St. Catherine University course titled "The Music and Image Monster: Lady Gaga in Context" where the professor struts around the classroom with pink-and-black polka dot fabric flowers attached to her eyeglasses for a "costume" while lecturing students on the "messages" within the music of Lady Gaga and Beyoncé.

Students should develop a sense for how human thought and culture developed by analyzing classical masters like Mozart, Aristotle, or Sandro Botticelli so they can formulate original ideas rather than merely analyzing their own culture with courses themed around television shows like *The Wire* (University of St. Thomas) or the rapper Jay-Z (George Washington University). After all, the GfK Roper study shows that most young people are glad they took or *wish* they had taken a core curriculum once they enter today's workplace!

Mafia Boss

These horror stories illustrate the sort of "education" for which Obama was convincing young people to take out six figures in debt. He knew Millennials were not necessarily investing in their careers (after all, many of them still struggled to write coherent paragraphs after graduation). Rather, by attending college and amassing debt they were investing in *Obama's* political future. Further, these stories illustrate that Obama's elitist allies in academia robbed young people of more than money and a solid education—in many instances they also denied them their First Amendment rights.

Obama gave the May 5, 2013, commencement address at Ohio State University and used his celebrity to charm young people into trusting the federal government unconditionally instead of being vigilant against tyranny as the Founders wanted:

Unfortunately, you've grown up hearing voices that incessantly warn of government as nothing more than some separate, sinister entity that's at the root of all our problems; some of these same voices [such as your parents and commentators like Rush Limbaugh] also do their best to gum up the works. They'll warn that tyranny is always lurking just around the corner. You should reject these voices . . . . The founders trusted us with this awesome authority.[41]

In this speech and throughout both of his presidential terms, Obama has conned students with this overall message: *Don't* listen to your parents or the true messages of the Founders; *do* go into default and line the Department of Education's coffers and *definitely* spend your borrowed money helping perverts rehab themselves in the classroom.

Barack Hussein Obama II was the mafia boss. He was the top decision maker and the head of the crime family of America's worst professors. He traveled from campus to campus, conning young people into going into debt and becoming his groupies.

Millennial voters listening to Obama had no idea what they were "buying." They could not imagine that the president of the United States would pledge that his policies and ideas would grant them success and reduce their debt when in fact they would not. Young people did not realize that the collegiate system had basically become a national PR firm for Obama's administration, which partly explained why he wanted them to attend college. After all, they certainly were not going to learn how to be good little socialists if they were off on their own like Steve Jobs, geeking out in their parents' garages and launching entrepreneurial ventures.

Help Wanted: College Grads Who Can Write Three Paragraphs

College students were not graduating with employable skills during the Obama years. A major complaint from employers about new

Millennial hires with college degrees was that they lacked the ability to write or speak professionally, concisely, and analytically. "It's a new work-force issue. New graduates can't write a three paragraph e-mail, although they can convey a clear message in 140 characters [a Tweet]," an IT fellow at Rice University's Baker Institute told the *Houston Chronicle*.[42] The problem became so widespread that even Ivy League MBA students were struggling to write: "Employers and writing coaches say business-school graduates tend to ramble, use pretentious vocabulary or pen too-casual emails," explained the *Wall Street Journal*.[43]

Millennials were graduating with phenomenal technology skills, most of which they developed on their own by virtue of growing up in a high-tech era. Yet, employers and HR professionals lamented the Millennials' lack of ability to *apply* their technology skills to the real world of business (data crunching is worthless if you can't analyze the data). And you will never make a sale for your company if your writing and speech do not transmit the value of your company's products or services.[44] Even MBAs struggled to communicate professionally. Obviously, Obama was wrong when he told young people higher education was a sure-fire investment in their futures.

By the summer of 2013, Obama had finished buying votes and he could finally focus on his campaign promise to help reform higher education. His "solution" to cut the cost of higher education was to introduce a "rating system" to publicly shame colleges with low graduation rates, low graduate earnings, high tuition costs, or high graduate debt into improving in order to receive federal financial aid. While embarrassing colleges on these factors might encourage them to cut costs, it won't improve the *quality* of education. Nor will it solve the cultural problem of every youth feeling pressured to get a four-year degree and acquire debt. Plus, this rating system did nothing to help Millennials who were already drowning in debt after helping Obama win reelection. Real reform will come from students, parents, and boards and trustees, as we will discuss in more detail in chapter 10, not from the government.

Common Snore

By the time a young person enrolls in college, professors expect that they know how to write a paper, deliver a five-minute presentation, and do basic math calculations without a tutor. You don't need to be a rocket scientist to know that if a young person does not learn how to read, write, and think analytically in high school, he or she will be stunted for perpetuity. Unfortunately, Obama brought extreme government regulation into public school classrooms and yanked power away from parents, making it harder for Millennials to succeed in college and beyond.

For example, the Common Core State Standards were a set of guidelines that Obama pushed on states. Common Core, which should be called Common Snore because it is so mundane, began as a set of common or national standards for English and math, compelling teachers to follow a certain pace and curriculum for all students. The "goal" was to raise overall standards and create consistency across state borders. Unfortunately, the standards were substandard.

A Stanford professor on the Common Core Validation Committee said he could not sign off on the math standards because they included "actual [ratio and rate] errors" and were "as non-challenging as possible."[45] The English standards encouraged teachers to replace assigned reading in classic literature with government informational texts such as presidential executive orders and EPA guidelines.[46] Instead of challenging young minds to think imaginatively by interfacing with illustrious writers like Homer, Fyodor Dostoyevsky, or Jane Austen, students were to read monotonous and unconstitutional government regulations!

Common Snore's supporters said that state participation was optional, but this was not exactly true. The standards were approved by the administration and funded by the federal government. Obama's administration effectively bribed states with a share of $100 billion in stimulus funds from the 2009 Recovery Act if they agreed to adopt the standards. Common Snore might work if children were programmable toys who came to life via computer animation. But every child learns differently and thus education is most effective when it is personalized and controlled at the local level.

Why do you think homeschoolers consistently outtest students at public schools? A 2009 exploratory study by University of St. Thomas Professor Michael Cogan compared students who had attended home, public, private, and Catholic high schools and then entered a medium-sized doctorate-granting institution in the Midwest. Cogan found that the homeschooled students were very well prepared for college, entering with the highest ACT composite scores and the highest high school GPAs. Once in college, the homeschoolers continued to outperform their peers, achieving higher first- and fourth-year GPAs.[47]

The homeschoolers excelled because they had *minimal* government-induced structure and maximum one-on-one attention. Homeschooling parents have enormous freedom to teach the way they see fit, allowing their students to learn without limit. Unshackled by arbitrary restrictions, homeschooling parents also may discipline and control their students without worrying that they might "offend" ten-year-old Johnny by telling him that his fashion choices of tiaras, tutus, and fuchsia nails are distracting.

Mothers who opposed the implementation of Common Core in their local school districts received sexist and racial sneers from Obama's administration. On November 15, 2013, Secretary of Education Arne Duncan told school superintendants: "It's fascinating to me that some of the pushback [to Common Core] is coming from, sort of, white suburban moms who—all of a sudden [are informed by us that]—their child isn't as brilliant as they thought they were and their school isn't quite as good as they thought they were, and that's pretty scary." As a young woman who was homeschooled through the eighth grade by "a white suburban mom," I appreciate that she knew my learning style better than any Big Brother administrator ever could and consequently empowered me with a robust curriculum. I absolutely credit my mother's foundational lessons for preparing me for success in high school and college.

If Mr. Duncan ever takes a pause from delivering male chauvinistic lectures to read the entire U.S. Constitution and search for the word "education," he won't find it. Our founders did not anticipate an America where *any* politician, particularly the president, would trump parents on the way their children are taught. Parents, not the government, are the determining factor in whether children learn. Whether a child attends school inside or outside the home, it is up to parents to make sure the child is doing his or her homework and progressing.

Since parents have the best understanding of their children's natural talents and interests, they can also play a vital role in encouraging them to look into both traditional and nontraditional career tracks. Parents can help reform our culture of institutional elitism and student debt by encouraging their sons and daughters to pursue their natural gifts once they graduate from high school, or college if they go. Common Snore is another example of the way Obama pushed a one-size-fits-all approach to education from kindergarten through college, to the students' disadvantage. We need to reform our educational system, but we clearly cannot trust politicians to reform *any* level of education; we'll need to rely on our own ingenuity.

Reagan wanted to help students learn and reduce wasteful spending by eliminating the Department of Education. Obama used rhetoric, celebrity comedians, the Department of Education, and college professors to flip students the bird.

THE NEW
"SHACKING UP"

5

Judith Campbell was a beautiful woman with famous friends. After meeting JFK through Frank Sinatra, Judith struck up an affair that lasted until the FBI director warned President Kennedy about wiretapping evidence that he and Judith were "shacking up."[1] That was enough to put an end to Jack and Judy.

Under Obama, "shacking up" took on a new meaning for young people, and it became so common that it lost its shock value. For 36 percent of Millennials, "shacking up" meant living with their parents because they were burdened by student loan debt and unable to find full-time jobs. For a second segment of Millennials, shacking up meant living in a "shack" (a tiny apartment barely large enough for one person) because they could not afford the mortgage or rent on an adequate living space. For a third segment of Millennials, it meant "shacking up" with roommates who could help them pay rent when they would have preferred to live alone. For the few Millennials who *were* home owners, it meant losing 55 percent of their household wealth as home values fell.[2] Five years into Obama's presidency, home values were still 25 percent below their prerecession peak, *even after* accounting for a 12.2 percent increase between May of 2012 and May of 2013.³ In other words, there was no housing recovery. Finally, for Millennial home owners who had recently lost their jobs, it meant living on the precipice of foreclosure with underwater mortgages; you could say their homes were morphing into shacks.

In all of these cases, the new "shacking up" was a practice that Millennials engaged in against their will. Young people lost their independence because they did not have the opportunity to become independent. Obama charmed young people into voting for him and then he made a huge financial mess, forcing an entire generation of Americans to "shack up" against their will.

Generation after generation of young Americans has made the natural transition into adulthood by buying homes of their own. For forty years, from 1968 to 2007, the number of young adults living with their parents remained "relatively constant" in America, according to Pew Research.⁴ By Obama's fourth year in office, things changed: a record 36 percent of people between the ages of eighteen and thirty-one lived at home with Mom and Dad.⁵

Many parents have felt embarrassed when their children shack up before marriage. And many parents felt embarrassed when their children practiced the new "shacking up"—but for very different reasons. Conservatives and independents value responsibility, freedom, and self-sufficiency. It was very hard for these parents to witness their children struggling to find jobs. It was heartbreaking for them to think that their smart and talented children were living at home in their late twenties and early thirties instead of moving on with their lives.

It's also natural for parents to resent the fact that they were footing the bill for their unemployed or underemployed adult children while the president was shuffling around the White House in his bunny slippers sipping beer, and the economy was not recovering normally. The new "shacking up" was a financial burden that Baby Boomers had not been counting on as they entered what were supposed to be their "golden years."

Obama's economy even got so bad—there were no jobs and thus no homes to be had—that young people were living with their *grandparents*. In 2011, 8 percent of children were living with their grandparents, a forty-year high.[6]

How did our young people find themselves in such a financial pickle? Did Obama take too many catnaps in his comfy hammock swinging from Hawaiian palm trees?

When asked to account for our economic straits, Obama's story is that "big business" was to blame for the housing crisis and he "inherited" it from his predecessors. Obama was giving young voters a warped history lesson, but they were too young to know this. They bought Obama's story that business was at fault for the financial crisis and voted for him, hoping he would clean up corruption and make home ownership more affordable. If only Millennials had looked backward in time, they would have seen right through him!

While there certainly were unscrupulous real estate brokers, lenders, and mortgage bankers who took advantage of loose government policies, they did not *cause* the real estate bubble of 2006 or the recession that began in 2007. The entire recession and the woes of the real estate industry can be traced back to *government intervention*, not capitalist greed on Wall Street.

Left to its own devices, the free market works wonderfully. The market *can* benefit from some standards. But standards are the opposite of the extreme government intervention that we witnessed during the Clinton years and the radical government intervention that we witnessed during the Obama years.

Obama created an unhealthy system where a segment of the Millennial generation is now growing up dependent on their parents for survival. Obama's policies are teaching a subset of Millennials to think that they are owed something for doing nothing, and specifically that the *government* owes them something for doing nothing and will bail them out even if they make massive financial mistakes down the road.

This chapter is the untold story of financial events that enabled Obama's self-indulgent vote buying.

Answering Henry's Dare

Let's start from the beginning. Before Clinton's time, you might remember another Democratic president named Jimmy Carter who passed a law called the Community Reinvestment Act (CRA). Carter passed this law during his first year in office (1977), no doubt hoping it would help him win votes and secure a second term. The CRA basically said that in order for banking institutions to receive FDIC insurance, they had to prove they were providing credit in every community where they were chartered. This was a way to force banks to lend money to low-income or racial-minority individuals who were financially unqualified for home ownership. Democrats would get credit for putting more people into homes; banks would have to deal with the mess if they defaulted. The CRA was not enforced enough to substantially damage the economy or win votes for the Democrats because a Republican named Ronald Reagan beat Carter in 1980. In the 1980s, private banks continued to operate quite independently from government entities like Fannie Mae and Freddie Mac: about "75 percent of all loans were made by banks that held on to them," former Housing and Urban Development secretary Mel Martinez told the *New York Times*.[7]

George H. W. Bush took office after Reagan and caved to the Democratic Congress by passing the Housing and Community Development Act of 1992. This legislation artificially loosened home ownership requirements even further.

When Clinton became president, he took full advantage of Carter's and Bush's relaxed home ownership policies by relaxing them even further. There was no way Clinton was going to be a one-term president like Carter. He got right down to business and enlisted the help of a man named Henry Cisneros, who became America's first Hispanic HUD secretary. Why did Clinton enlist Cisneros in his quest to become a two-term president? Two reasons: First, like Clinton, Cisneros was loose with the truth. Second, Cisneros was so starstruck that he would be willing to submit his own political aspirations to Clinton's.

Slick Willie felt these traits made Cisneros the perfect quarterback to help him score reelection in the next big presidential campaign.

Cisneros once told the *New York Times*: "I've been waiting for someone to put all the blame at my doorstep."[8]

Well you got your wish, buster. Today is your lucky day. Because it is impossible to indict Obama for ravaging the American Dream for 95 million Millennials without first indicting you. Here you go!

The Henry Dream: Girls and Government

So who was Henry Cisneros? Many Americans have never heard of Cisneros, but he was basically Clinton's political pawn. His political career began with four terms as mayor of San Antonio. Then, he served as secretary of housing and urban development during Clinton's first term. The Clinton administration used Cisneros to help Billy win votes. Clinton and Cisneros's loose home ownership policies are the reason why the housing market collapsed. Then, Obama expanded upon Cisneros's policies, which is the reason why Millennials could not afford to buy homes.

Cisneros helped Clinton tinker with the economic and financial markets and change housing rules and regulations. They were playing with fire. Rules were in place for sound economic reasons but Clinton led voters to believe that these rules were "discriminatory," so they needed to be artificially loosened. Obama picked up where Clinton and Cisneros left off, trying to win votes from young home owners by further tinkering with home ownership standards. The housing markets got worse and worse, exposing Clinton and Obama for making policy decisions based on collecting votes and garnering political support instead of making housing more accessible and affordable as they had promised.

* * *

WHILE Henry's pretty wife was in Texas carrying his third child in her womb, Henry was miles away cozying up to his staffer Linda Medlar on a carriage in Central Park.[9] A San Antonio TV reporter witnessed Henry's mother shedding tears when asked whether she believed her son's claim that he was not having an affair.[10] She said no, she did not believe her son.[11]

Henry was bored by the American Dream. He felt like yawning when the topic came up. Couldn't people talk about something other than the millions of young Americans who wanted a shot at buying homes with front lawns and garages? Henry liked to close his eyes and daydream about putting all these God-fearing and decent people—these "American Dreamers"—to work for *him*. In Henry's dream, young, poor, and disadvantaged Americans helped Henry get what Henry wanted.

And Henry wanted two things. First, he wanted multiple female companions to feed his insecurities.[12] Whenever he was feeling frisky, Henry wanted to dial the car phone in his orange Volkswagen Beetle and have several women at his beck and call. But these women ultimately did not motivate him to destroy the economy, although Linda did eventually demand $4,000 a month for life.[13]

The second and more destructive thing that Henry wanted was political power. Cisneros busted his tail campaigning in Clinton's first presidential campaign. Both Bill and Hillary came to like Henry and took his political advice.[14] This was not surprising. The three of them had something in common: they valued political power over love and truth. After Clinton won the presidency, he wanted to pay Cisneros back for his loyalty on the campaign trail, so he named Cisneros to be his HUD secretary in 1993. Clinton *said* he nominated Cisneros because he wanted "the most diverse administration in history."[15] That was obviously not the reason since America's first Hispanic HUD secretary went on to prey on first-time Hispanic home buyers.

FBI agents performed a background check on Cisneros before his Senate confirmation hearing. He gave false statements to the FBI, including drastically lowballing the amount he paid to Linda. It was not until the fall of 1994, when Linda went public with her secretly tape-recorded phone conversations, that the FBI realized Cisneros had lied. Attorney General Janet Reno assigned a special prosecutor to the case who indicted Cisneros on eighteen counts in 1997. Luckily for Henry, Linda had repeatedly lied to the FBI and was sitting in prison on unrelated charges of money laundering and bank fraud, so the special prosecutor's key witness (her) was an unreliable witness.[16] Cisneros got off with a $10,000 fine. Clinton granted both Henry and Linda a presidential pardon in 2001.

His entire life, Cisneros seemed above the law. He was a superstar among Democratic politicians. But Cisneros has committed far bigger transgressions than lying to the FBI about his extramarital affairs, transgressions he has never been held accountable for:

1. Helping Clinton destroy the real estate market and cause the Great Recession.
2. Helping Obama exacerbate the economic crisis and prevent the housing market from recovering, thus shutting Millennials out of the American Dream.

Clinton got in way over his head in his efforts to make home ownership more affordable. Obama had a bigger ego than Clinton so he took on *even more*. Looking back, it is both laughable and frightening to see how much power over the marketplace Clinton and Obama assumed they could handle. Neither man had any business experience worth mentioning, yet they both assumed they could command the entire financial system on their own. In their pride and self-worship, they bit off more than they could chew, sold their idyllic plans to young voters, and left Millennials and their parents to live with the consequences.

Cisneros's First Day

Imagine Clinton and Cisneros meeting for a working lunch in the White House one fine day in 1993. The following is a hypothetical conversation based on what we know of these two big rascals.

"We sure have some nice interns in the White House, especially
that curvy redhead who says she can keep her mouth shut,"
Clinton says, lost in thought.

"Do you want to be a one-term president or a two-term president?" Cisneros inquires with a growl.

"Two-term, of course," chuckles Clinton.

"All right. Then you need to stop chasing skirts and start chasing
votes. As in millions of votes from young people who want to
buy homes but can't afford to."

"Show me your plan, chief."

The Plan

HUD secretary Cisneros whispered that plan into President Clinton's ear, a plan that would invariably endear Clinton to young,
poor, and minority voters and help him secure a second term. The plan
would involve destroying the housing market and the overall economy.

Cisneros named his plan the National Home Ownership Strategy.
It called for drastically easing mortgage restrictions for first-time home
buyers.[17] These loose policies included relaxing appraisal rules, eliminating the five-year stable income requirement for first-time buyers,
and lowering the standards of Fannie Mae and Freddie Mac. Working
closely with the mortgage industry, HUD allowed lenders "to hire their
own appraisers . . . [which] inflated appraisals."[18]

On June 5, 1995, Clinton gathered a handful of young home owners
as props and gave a heartwarming speech from the White House East
Room laying out the National Home Ownership Strategy. He started
by sharing the story of how he convinced Hillary to marry him by buying "an old, old, very small house" for $20,500. Then, he told voters
that he ran for president because he wanted to "restore" the American
Dream. He said his strategy "will not cost the taxpayers one extra cent.
It will not require legislation. It will not add more Federal programs

or grow Federal bureaucracy. . . . I say to millions of young working couples who are just starting out: . . . we want you to be able to own your own home."[19]

In 1999, during his second term, Clinton also expanded the CRA by exerting enormous pressure on Fannie Mae to make loans to unqualified buyers. The *New York Times* wrote: "In moving, even tentatively, into this new area of lending, Fannie Mae is taking on significantly more risk, which may not pose any difficulties during flush economic times. But the government-subsidized corporation may run into trouble in an economic downturn, prompting a government rescue."[20] Eventually, the economy *would* spiral downward, and Obama would be the president to attempt a government rescue.

Clinton's policies had a devastating ripple effect on the entire economy. Foreclosures sprang up, consumer spending went down, the credit markets froze, and jobs disappeared. Rather than permanently increasing home ownership, his loose policies temporarily opened the doors to home ownership to an additional 10 percent of the U.S. population that did not qualify by historical standards to become home buyers.

By forcing Fannie and Freddie (aka the taxpayers) to guarantee extremely risky loans, Clinton was setting the entire economy up for collapse. As more homebuyers entered the market, the demand for homes increased. Plus, at the same time that demand was rising, appraisal values were being inflated. Combine these two and you've got an artificial and unsustainable rise in home prices.

Clinton and George H. W. Bush were able to tinker with the economy because they had the luxury of coming into office after Reagan, a strong believer in the free-market system. The Reagan administration prepared a wonderful gift for the two that followed: a vibrant economy. The nonpartisan National Bureau of Economic Research reported that Reagan's policies unleashed the "longest sustained period of prosperity in the 20th century" from 1982 to 1999.[21]

The second Bush administration unfortunately failed to change many of Clinton's destructive policies. Home prices peaked in 2006, resulting in a massive real estate bubble. In 2008, the Bush administration bailed out Fannie and Freddie instead of letting them collapse under the weight of their risky lending and high losses.

By the way, it's okay for Republicans to admit that Bush and his son made a few mistakes. After all, good Republicans have admitted their mistakes before:

> ABC NEWS CORRESPONDENT SAM DONALDSON: "Mr. President, in talking about the continuing recession tonight, you have blamed mistakes of the past and you've blamed the Congress. Does any of the blame belong to you?"
> PRESIDENT REAGAN: "Yes, because for many years, I was a Democrat."[22]

Most Americans have no memory of Reagan blaming economic problems during his first term on the high inflation and unemployment that he inherited from Jimmy Carter. This is one reason why it was so frustrating, years later, to keep hearing Obama blame his predecessors. At some point, the president needs to *look* forward instead of making campaign signs that say "forward." At some point, the sitting president needs to move on and *lead*.

The 2000s: Cisneros Quietly Keeps Ravaging the Housing Market

Cisneros never actually went away when he left HUD in 1997 to save Clinton further embarrassment in the wake of his indictment. He temporarily disappeared to Los Angeles for a few years and worked for the Spanish-language media giant Univision Communications. Around the end of Clinton's second term, Cisneros returned to San Antonio. By this time, San Antonio locals had forgotten about what a scoundrel he was.

He immediately dove into the crony private sector, where he made a pile of money screwing new home buyers with the same loose home ownership policies he had helped Clinton implement. He partnered with a large builder (KB Home) and started his own real estate development company called American CityVista. He also joined the board of Countrywide Financial in 2001.

Cisneros did incredible damage to the economy and housing industry while he was on Countrywide's board. Countrywide was America's largest mortgage lender and Fannie Mae's number one client. Even after you account for Bush's lax oversight and awkward attempt to "reform" the system by pledging more money to Fannie and Freddie, Cisneros was still at the wheel of the destruction.

When Cisneros sat on Countrywide's board, he was not in charge of organizing the corporate picnic. He was on a committee that "oversaw compliance with legal and regulatory requirements."[23] Under Cisneros's watch, Countrywide ramped up risky subprime lending considerably, and multiple audits uncovered abusive practices.[24] He left Countrywide's board on October 24, 2007—minutes before everything went bust. He told the *Times* he had no memory of the abuses he ostensibly oversaw. How convenient.

No wonder his Mexican-born mother cried. In addition to ripping off Hispanics from the comfort of Countrywide's boardroom, America's first Hispanic HUD secretary preyed on Hispanics as a developer. For example, he teamed up with Fannie Mae to market one of his initial projects, called Lago Vista, to the Hispanic community, offering no closing costs and zero down. He also promised plenty of trails, trees, and a lovely lake, which the *New York Times* reported never materialized. Foreclosures sprung up in Lago Vista and crime, theft, and "marital turmoil" became common among dwellers struggling to make their payments.[25]

By October of 2008, Henry had helped build over seven thousand homes. He made millions off his shady involvement with Countrywide and his lemon developments like Lago Vista.[26] Cisneros's failed experiment shows that government intervention in housing induces financial hardship.

Nut Job

If Bill Clinton and Barack Obama were animals, they would be squirrels, because they loved ACORN. The Association of Community Organizations for Reform Now was a nonprofit activist group that professed to focus on helping the less fortunate. ACORN's projects included low-income housing advocacy and voter registration. After a series of public scandals, ACORN's parent organization was effectively shuttered in 2010, but many state branches reorganized and continued operation.

ACORN's early headquarters building was an old funeral home in New Orleans.[27] This was appropriate because ACORN played a role in the death of housing. Investigative journalist Matthew Vadum wrote an entire book explaining how "ACORN is a non-profit version of Enron" that utilized "Enron-style accounting."[28] In *Subversion Inc.*, Vadum writes: "The intra-network transactions of ACORN Housing are the most troubling because out of all of ACORN's affiliates, it is the most dependent on taxpayers for support and has a long history of abusing taxpayer funds."[29]

Cisneros and ACORN worked closely and continuously from the Clinton era up through the Obama era. ACORN supported both men's political careers early on, so it is no surprise that Clinton and Obama felt pressure to pay ACORN back when they gained power. ACORN endorsed Clinton in his early political days. Clinton greatly expanded the CRA to create artificial quotas for low-income buyers and transferred HUD funds to sketchy groups including ACORN that used the money to shame banks into giving risky loans to minorities before they were financially ready for home ownership.[30]

Under Clinton, ACORN Housing pretended to use all of its government funding for noble causes like "mortgage counseling" when, in fact, AmeriCorps inspector general Luise Jordan reported that ACORN Housing used taxpayer dollars to recruit for ACORN.[31] Instead of helping minorities and low-income buyers work themselves out of foreclosure, ACORN was increasing its income from membership dues.

Banks felt intense pressure to make risky loans during the Clinton years. Not only did they have the government's CRA officials on their back, but they paid off community organizing groups like ACORN that were threatening to destroy their public image if they hesitated to hand out loans to every low-income minority who said, "I want a house!" In the end, the public blamed the banks for the crisis and Clinton rode off into the sunset looking like a handsome cowboy who left America with a surplus.

Obama represented ACORN as its lawyer in a 1995 lawsuit.[32] He got very upset when Republicans pointed this out, but he had already publicly confessed his love for ACORN:

> *I've been fighting alongside Acorn on issues you care about my entire career. Even before I was an elected official, when I ran Project Vote voter registration drives in Illinois, Acorn was smack dab in the middle of it, and we appreciate your work.*[33]—OBAMA SEEKING ACORN'S ENDORSEMENT FOR HIS PRESIDENTIAL CAMPAIGN IN 2007

Obama received even more help from ACORN than Clinton did in his early political days, because he hired an ACORN group to help him campaign in 2008, and Vadum suggests that ACORN's work was crucial to helping Obama overtake Hillary and snag the Democratic nomination.[34] Once he became president, he followed Bill Clinton's example by nominating a HUD secretary (Shaun Donovan) with deep ties to ACORN.[35]

How about Cisneros? Where was he during the Obama years? Ol' Tex was back in the saddle, shooting a commercial for a rebranded version of ACORN Housing called the Affordable Housing Centers of America. Cisneros cooed that he was "so pleased that the work will continue, the work of supporting families and helping them get into homes."

Rawhide

Everyone knows Barry is a Chicago boy. So, he must like the Blues Brothers movie. He must admire how actor John Belushi had the moxie to tell the mayor of Chicago he'd like to "drive a car through the lobby of Daley Plaza. Right though the window."[36] He must love the car-chase scene and the sound track. Especially "Rawhide." You can just see Barry cranking that song up so loud, so often, that Michelle tells him to go buy ear buds.

As we look back on his legacy, it's hard to understand why Obama did the things he did because his actions are so contrary to common sense. For all we know, he could have been listening to "Rawhide" when he decided that the way to solve the housing crisis was to rope, throw, and brand the taxpayers like cattle. He would keep the young, unemployed, and low-income voters (who paid little to nothing in taxes) happy by telling them he would help them buy homes they couldn't afford.

* * *

A LIGHTBULB went off for Obama in 2007. It occurred to him that Millennials were too young to know many (if any) details of Carter, Cisneros, and Clinton's intervention in the housing market. He could tell young people *his* version of the financial crisis and they would never know the difference! So he did. He blamed Bush and Republicans for causing the entire crisis. There was nothing wrong with directing some blame at Republicans. There was a huge problem with pretending that Carter, Cisneros, and Clinton were Republicans. The other problem with Obama's story was that he left out *his* role because he wanted young voters to think that he had "inherited" the entire crisis. Long before he became president, Obama was part of the problem. As a senator, Obama was the second-highest recipient of lobbying funds from Fannie and Freddie.[37]

Less than two months after he was inaugurated president in 2009, Obama went on the *Tonight Show* with Jay Leno to discuss the financial crisis. It's a laugh to read the transcript now because Obama was shaking his finger at the same unethical behavior he would end up practicing.

Leno made the mistake of asking Obama to "tell people what happened." (How the financial crisis happened.) Instead of blaming the government, Obama blamed private banks and insurance companies for following the bad laws the government put in place. Then, he said: "Now, the question is, who in their right mind, when your company is going bust, decides we're going to be paying a whole bunch of bonuses to people? And that, I think, speaks to a broader culture . . . this general attitude of entitlement."

Obama was not done preaching: "But there's a moral and an ethical aspect to this, as well. And I think that's what has gotten everybody so fired up."

Tip: When a con man starts telling you what's moral and ethical, buy another gun.

It is concerning that Obama failed to acknowledge the role that detrimental government policies played in creating the financial crisis. Instead, he blamed everything on banking and business, using political platitudes along the lines of "those greedy bankers" and "vile corporations." Young people watching the *Tonight Show* were left without the true historical narrative, and so Obama misdirected their anger at businesspeople instead of politicians like himself, and Clinton before him, who were looking to buy votes.

Promotions for Piggies

On the *Tonight Show*, Obama made a point of singling out AIG as a company that distributed hefty bonuses while it was "going bust." He said: "The main thing [is] we're going to do everything we can to see if we can get these bonuses back . . . . people were able to take huge, excessive risks with other people's money, putting the entire financial system at risk." He promised, "I think that we have a big mess on our hands . . . but it is going to get solved."

Blah. Blah. Blah.

By the fall of 2009, CNN Money was reporting that Obama's Pay Czar, Ken Feinberg, was granting "special exemptions" to three AIG employees on bonuses tallying around $16 million.[38] This is partly why we were *still* in a "big mess" well into Obama's second term. In 2010, Feinberg declined to pursue a refund on the $1.6 billion in incentives that taxpayers had spent to bail out executives at firms like Wells Fargo, Goldman Sachs, and Bank of America because he was afraid they might *sue*.[39]

Feinberg's excuse for not going after the $1.6 refund for taxpayers is a hoot. On the *Tonight Show* in 2009, Leno had posed exactly this possibility to Obama, who laughed it off saying, "So sue me, right?" Leno agreed: "I mean the federal government is in debt a trillion dollars. We're broke—[go ahead and] sue us."

Obama was all talk and no follow-through on the bonuses. All he cared about was pleasing the crony capitalists who could contribute to his 2012 campaign.

"Huge, Excessive Risks" with Your Money

As usual, Barry wanted to outdo his predecessors. He grabbed the one tool left in the barn—the bullwhip—and told taxpayers to bail out borrowers and lenders. Despite what he told Jay Leno in 2009, Obama did *not* think it was "unethical" or "immoral" to take "huge, excessive risks" with other people's money—if *he* was the one doing the risk taking. As you read through this timeline, you will notice how Obama, in his arrogance, got in way over his head and tried to control the markets.

FEBRUARY 2009: Obama bypassed Congress and used his Treasury Department and housing agencies to authorize the Homeowner Affordability and Stability Plan. But he also realized that his bullwhip was not strong enough to keep Americans in line if they knew it was a $275 billion bailout.

So he said his plan would cost taxpayers $75 billion. He skimmed over the part about how he was raiding the U.S. Treasury for an additional $200 billion and pumping that money into Fannie and Freddie. This was the easiest and dirtiest way to tax the taxpayer without calling it a tax. The plan included subprograms "HARP," "HAMP," and "Making Home Affordable."

In total, this $275 billion bailout was supposed to help 9 million home owners avoid foreclosure.[40]

Anyone struggling with a mortgage was encouraged to call the HOPE Hotline: 1-888-995-HOPE. Facing foreclosure? Need hope? Dial it up, baby! But Americans were very confused about whether they qualified for mortgage assistance and, if so, under which program. The HOPE Hotline began ringing off the hook. A HOPE counselor wrote in to the *Chicago Tribune* complaining that they were receiving too many confused callers and told the newspaper to publish an explanation of who qualified to call the hotline. The *Tribune* complied, but with a bit of snark, saying, "the HOPE Hotline is there to lend a helping hand to all."[41]

Obama's little helpers seemed a tad perturbed by the prospect of doing their jobs and fostering hope. Ho, ho, hopeless!

FOURTH QUARTER, 2009: Fannie Mae posts a $5 billion write-down on low-income tax credit investments and $11.9 billion in credit losses.

FEBRUARY 2010: Ya! Ya! Rawhide! As if the $225 billion weren't enough, Obama throws his bullwhip and demands that taxpayers pump $7.6 billion into a new initiative called "The Hardest Hit Fund" to help families on the verge of foreclosure.

Piggybacking on the president's tomfoolery, Fannie Mae begs for $15.3 billion to cover more losses.

AUGUST 2010: The *New York Times* reports that Making Home Affordable is sputtering.[42] In reality, MHA was what real estate experts call "extend and pretend." It temporarily softened the blow of foreclosures without purging the system and immediately dealing with the reality of numerous troubled loans. Obama's economy looked healthier than it really was since banks were carrying loans longer without marking them down. But, up to three quarters of recipients of loan modifications were forecasted to re-default.[43]

In 2010, HBO comedian Bill Maher defended Obama by saying, "I have my issues with this president, but he did inherit a mess like no other president. He is the maid after Led Zeppelin has been in the room."

Obama a *maid*? Ha! The King of Gospel-Bashing, Bill Maher, was off his rocker.

Obama was like a little boy who never grew up and learned to take the long-term view. As president, he took office in the middle of a housing mess. But he did not want to clean it up. He wanted to bodysurf in Hawaii and party with Jay-Z. So, instead of purging the economy of risky loans and cutting back on spending, he encouraged banks to make more risky loans and he increased spending. He made things look good for a while, but he was putting off and aggravating the problem.

AUGUST 2011: Standard & Poor's Ratings Services downgraded the credit ratings of both Fannie Mae and Freddie Mac from AAA to AA+, citing the mortgage giants' "direct reliance" on the federal government.[44] The taxpayers completely own Fannie and Freddie, so every time Obama pumped money into them, he was simply robbing Peter to pay Paul. S&P was unimpressed by this volatile arrangement.

SEPTEMBER 2011: Young people who would normally be buying homes are living at home. Americans bought fewer homes during the peak buying months of March through August of 2011 than they had in the previous fifty years.[45]

Some people were hoping the Fed's extension of low short-term interest rates would fuel the economy, but that could not happen without jobs. High unemployment is tied to higher defaults. High unemployment also scares first-time home buyers away from the market. Without jobs, interest rates could be zero and the real estate market would still flounder.

THIRD QUARTER, 2011: By this point 28.6 percent of all American home owners were underwater, meaning they owed more than their home was worth. This was up from 23.2 percent in 2010, reported Bloomberg News.

NOVEMBER 2011: Obama cracked his whip and forced taxpayers

to pony up. Again. Fannie Mae received about $53 billion between the time she began whining in February of 2010 and November of 2011. Yet she still wanted more, seeking $7.8 billion to cover yet *more* losses.

JANUARY 2012: The 2012 election is just months away and Obama is losing favor among the key voters (Millennials) who helped him win in 2008. At this time, American Enterprise Institute columnist James Pethokoukis speculates that there is a secret refinancing plan underfoot called the "January Surprise."

Rush Limbaugh spends his January 5 show highlighting Pethokoukis's piece. Within hours, the Obama administration tells Bloomberg it has "no plans for a new mass mortgage refinancing program." The next day, Limbaugh described Obama's apparent reversal of plans for a "January Surprise" on his show: "TARP 2 . . . in one fell swoop, it would be buying the election. It'd be a $1.2 trillion stimulus plan, cut $400 to $500 a month off of everybody's mortgage payment, and all you have to do to qualify is be three months current. Now the regime says: No, no, no, no, no such plan. No such plan!"

The *Wall Street Journal* reported that the White House quietly dropped this alleged plan after the conservative media unearthed it for what it was—a plan to buy votes from young people by pushing them into home ownership before they were financially ready.

APRIL 2012: Remember Obama's Hardest Hit Fund? The special inspector general for TARP, Christy L. Romero, released a report indicating that—due to Treasury mismanagement, since the "Treasury is the steward over TARP [programs like HHF]"—only 3 percent of the $7.6 billion fund had been used to help prevent foreclosures.[46] The fund had been in place for two years and only aided 30,640 home owners. Foreclosures increased in the first quarter of 2012 in over half of America's largest metro areas.

OCTOBER 2012: Obama tells Millennial voters in an October 5 speech in Fairfax, Virginia: "Today, I believe that as a nation, we are moving forward again. We're moving forward." And in an October 17 campaign speech in Mt. Vernon, Iowa: "Foreclosures are at their lowest point in five years. Home values are back on the rise."

MARCH 2013: The Urban Institute, which the *Los Angeles Times* hails as "America's Leading Liberal Think Tank," released a study pointing out that "the government's response to the housing crisis—which led to low interest rates" disproportionately hurt young homebuyers "because their lack of equity denied them access to lower-cost loans" and because they held far fewer annuities, which grew in value as interest rates dropped, compared to older Americans.[47] The Urban Institute predicted that Millennials could become "more dependent" than all previous generations because of their financial setback.

MAY 2013: Obama's HUD secretary Shaun Donovan announces the renewal of the "extend and pretend" program HAMP through 2015. This meant that, heading into the 2014 midterms, foreclosure stats would not look as bad as they truly were.

Fannie Mae posts a record "profit" of $59 billion by doing some fancy accounting: applying tax credits from losses on delinquent loans to its 2013 taxes and thereby claiming an increase in profits—which did not make much sense because Fannie Mae does not "make" money, it only takes money from taxpayers. Plus, Fannie Mae owed the taxpayers billions of dollars for bailing it out. That is called being broke.

Meanwhile, home values are still 25 percent below their prerecession peak in July of 2006.

JUNE 2013: Recent research shows the rising home values Obama raved about in 2012 were a joke.

First, this rise was only a blip of 12.2 percent and values were still down 25 percent. Second, ordinary Americans were not benefiting. The *New York Times* DealBook explained the upward blip in home prices: Huge real estate investment firms like the BlackStone Group were gobbling up tens of thousands of residential properties in distressed markets like Las Vegas and Phoenix.[48] These firms were hoping to rent the properties and then flip them for a large profit when home values rose enough. Third, another reason home values kept inching up was because Obama had renewed HAMP's "extend and pretend" practices, thereby allowing banks to delay writing down the foreclosed properties they were holding at full value on their books.

Millennials looking for first-time homes were most likely to say they wanted (and could afford) a fixer-upper or a very basic living space. Unfortunately, institutional investors were scooping up nearly 70 percent of these properties.[49] The true unemployment rate was closer to 15 or 16 percent when you factored in all the Americans who wanted to work but had given up looking. This is why big investors, not young people, were buying homes. Obama could not take credit for helping more Millennials achieve the American Dream. He did anyway. In July, he claimed we were in a "recovery."

Billionaire entrepreneur and real estate guru Sam Zell was unimpressed with Obama's claim that housing was recovering. Zell explained how the concentration of investor acquisitions in "selective markets" like Phoenix made things look good for the "short term." He predicted that "the Kumbaya that I'm hearing with reference to the single family housing market, I don't think will meet the test of time."[50]

JULY 2013: Lawrence Yun, chief economist for the National Realtors Association, reports that the national home ownership rate has dropped to "its lowest level in 20 years": 65.2 percent.[51] He predicts it will continue to drop even if the job market recovers because young people living with their parents will rent before they buy a home. This came on the tails of a *New York Times* story putting the home ownership rate for Americans *under the age of thirty-five* at 37 percent—5 percent lower than before the recession and hardly Michelle's "huge" recovery.[52]

Meanwhile, the $275 billion bailout program had failed miserably to close the floodgates on foreclosures. Good thing Obama kept renewing HAMP and HARP! In July, CoreLogic reported that the national foreclosure rate was *over twice* as high as before the recession.[53]

AUGUST 2013: Super Barry swoops down and proudly urges the Senate to endorse his "bipartisan plan" to "reform" Fannie and Freddie. Except his plan was a belly laugh. *New York Times* financial columnist Floyd Norris pointed out months earlier that the plan was developed by a bipartisan commission including . . . drum roll . . . Henry Cisneros! Norris describes the plan thus:

"Uncle Sam remains the ultimate guarantor for most home mortgages. . . . [The plan] would phase out Fannie and Freddie—something that is politically necessary—but replace them with something that sounds sort of similar. The new organization would be called a 'public guarantor.' It would guarantee that investors in mortgage-backed securitizations would not lose money, much as Fannie and Freddie now do."[54]

In other words, Obama's plan to reform Fannie and Freddie was to *rename* Fannie and Freddie. A great idea if you want to win the midterms and a terrible idea if you are sincerely interested in freeing taxpayers from having to bail out mortgage giants.

Barry's Val-Ley Girl

In September of 2013, Obama entrusted his adviser Valerie Jarrett with scolding businessmen for lingering financial problems instead of taking responsibility for his excessive regulations that were preventing the economy from recovering to prerecession levels. Sending Someone Else to Do His Dirty Work and Scolding Businessmen = Barry's Modus Operandi.

Matthew Williams, chairman of the American Bankers Association, told the *Omaha World-Herald* about a phone conversation he had with Jarrett. Apparently, Jarrett chided Williams, "You [bankers] can do one thing [to help us]—make [mortgage] loans."[55]

Jarrett's ignorance "appalled" Williams. Banks would be making loans if they could. It's their *business*. She acted like bankers had conspired to set their voicemail greetings to "out of office" and then lock themselves up in their vaults to play poker.

Jarrett morphed into a "Valley Girl" who could, like, totally not understand how her boss's excessive regulations hurt folks on Main Street. Williams informed Valley Girl that Obama's administration had "created roadblocks," making it unfeasible for banks to make loans.[56] He conceded that commonsense regulation is "indispensible" but maintained that banks were struggling to comply with the stringent regulations in the Dodd-Frank Act.

The next real estate bubble will go just like Valley Girl's hot pink bubble gum. *Pop!*

* * *

IN his second term, Obama kept boasting of gains in home values, yet the housing market and the American Dream were still on death's doorstep because his economy was not creating enough jobs. Young couples were not buying homes; instead, big investment firms were buying homes and renting them out to young couples. As the *Wall Street Journal* put it: "Those gains would look better if they were supported by an economy that was adding more high-paying jobs. Until that happens, the housing sector faces a less predictable path."[57]

Ta Da! Young, Hellthy, and Homeless

Yun's prediction came true. Many of those college grads who did move out of their parents' homes during the Obama years were renting apartments with friends, *not* buying homes or condos on their own. The *New York Times* highlighted college grads apartment hunting in NYC and no one seemed to be self-sufficient: A young man was living at home to save up for a rental he would share with friends. A group of three young friends settled for a duplex in a high-crime area—the only place they could afford. An unemployed young lady would have been in trouble, but she was fortunate to have parents willing to cover her half of the $3,500-a-month rent on a two-bedroom apartment in Manhattan's East Village.[58]

In Chicago, the scene looked just as dismal: Growing numbers of residents under the age of thirty-four were bunking up with roommates when they would have preferred to live independently.[59] *Chicago Business* highlighted three twentysomething college graduates living together in Wicker Park who joked that they had been together for so long they were practically in a "common law" marriage. They were getting on each other's nerves and expressed interest in buying their own places but could not afford to split up. Likewise, a young Chicago woman who gave up her own apartment and moved in with friends after losing her job said, "people are having to stick together to survive."[60]

From the Big Apple to the Windy City, young people found depression and stagnation instead of hope and change. If they were not compelled to shack up with their parents, young people were dependent on other people—living longer than usual with roommates, in smaller than ideal spaces while making short-term investments based on fear of the condo and housing market. It was ridiculously hard for millions of young adults to develop a sense of independence, get married, start a family, or even own a dog bigger than a Chihuahua.

Before the Great Recession and Obama's nonrecovery, your typical first-time homebuyer was a thirty-year-old with a history of student debt. This was because the government was smaller, the market was freer, and a college degree was worth more. However, 2013 marked the first time in a decade when thirty-year-olds with a history of student loan debt were less likely than those without to buy homes and the first time in a decade that college debt held young people back from obtaining home loans.[61] Also, the Pew Research Center reported more college students than non–college students living at home with their parents in 2013.[62] High student loan payments were draining the money Millennials would have applied toward monthly mortgage payments.[63] Some recovery!

Drinking the *Cosmo*

Let me pour you a drink after all this talk about the death of the American Dream. Loosen up and have a cocktail. But please, don't make it a cosmo.

While young people struggle to navigate the new reality of shacking up with Mom and Dad, many conventional journalists preach resignation and encourage Millennials to give up their dreams of independence.

Women's magazines like *Cosmo* helped cover for Obama's economic destruction by making young women feel like it was totally normal to live at home. It's safe to say that these publications influenced the way many young women viewed their life and culture. The median age of a woman reading the *New York Times* or the *Wall Street Journal* was mid-fifties whereas the median age of a *Cosmo* reader was early thirties.[64] *Cosmo* was America's top-selling women's magazine, reaching 18 million readers monthly.

"Dating a Guy Who Lives at Home"

In this article, *Cosmo* advised girls to not write off a guy who lives at home: "Don't assume he's broke," they cautioned, and "help him with his job search." Young men were 8 percent more likely than young women to live with their parents, according to a 2013 Pew study.[65] *Cosmo* should have advised girls to be *angry* about the fact that their boyfriends could not get jobs in America, encouraging them to write letters to Congress and demand spending and regulatory reform. But *Cosmo* advised young women to resign themselves to the effects of Obama's economic policies; to be sheep instead of bold, informed, and independent women.

"How to Get Some When You Live at Home"

Cosmo editors offered young women "tips" to maximize their fun while their parents were footing the bills.

"Five Ways to Survive Moving Back In with Your Parents"

This article told young women that for "every hour" they spent around their parents, they should spend two hours "venting about them" with their friends.[66] Also, young people should set their own rules for behavior in their parents' house and be sure to take full advantage of free homemade meals. What a great message: Girls, if you don't have a job, stay with Mom and Dad, eat their food, boss them around, and gossip about them.

The "feminist" response to the new shacking up was "make the best of it," even if "making the best of it" involved young women turning themselves into disrespectful brats. This does not sound very pro-woman, because all young women need mentors to advance in their careers and no one will want to mentor or promote a little monster. But, then again, *Cosmo*'s favorite female member of the Obama administration was Ms. Valerie Jarrett—Valley Girl—who *Cosmo* interviewed in the October 2013 issue to offer young women her career tips.

As a young woman, it is concerning to see how Obama's administration collaborated with *Cosmo* to profit by selling young women lies about economic success. Sure, if the only thing you know how to do in life is boss your parents around, then, yes, the ideal career would be that of Valley Girl, who bossed businessmen around from nine to five. But women will not find intellectual or financial reward in becoming, like, totally twits.

Five years into Obama's dual presidency we had a situation where millions of Americans in their twenties and thirties were living at home without full-time jobs and missing out on vital years for professional and personal growth, years they would never get back. *Cosmo* was perpetuating this vicious cycle by encouraging our young people to assume a false sense of security instead of spurring them toward actions that could *improve* their situation, such as adopting entrepreneurial mindsets and delving into civic engagement.

Millennials who were "shacking up" with their parents were not doing so by choice. Our Millennials *wanted* to use their unique talents— and most were trying hard to do so—but there were not enough full-time jobs to go around during Obama's "huge" recovery. It would have been fine for *Cosmo* to help young women find a silver lining in this unfortunate situation, but it was reprehensible for *Cosmo* to encourage girls to *create* a silver lining by manipulating their parents and prioritizing poetic crushes over career advancement.

In Obama's idle economy, millions of young people (who voted for him hoping he could turn the Great Recession into the Roaring 2000s) were unable to fulfill their internal drive to move on with their lives. Meanwhile, they felt the depleting tug of pop culture titans like *Cosmo* pressuring them to abandon their dreams and find fun and fulfillment in complacency and dependency. It's no wonder our young people ended up with a bad case of the blues . . .

Depressed? Don't Blame Barry, Keep Hope!

Many Millennials are experiencing psychological and emotional damage due to living at home. Many are fighting off clinical depression. Meanwhile, Obama has kept reminding young people that he "inherited" the economic crisis instead of taking responsibility for perpetuating the crisis and sending young people to the shrink. A study by the University of Alberta found that "the longer they [university graduates] stay at home, or if they return home, the more likely they are to experience symptoms of depression," reports *Science Daily*.[67]

Dr. Victor Schwartz, medical director of the Jed Foundation, which focuses on reducing youth suicide and depression, warned in a column for the *Huffington Post* that "clinical depression" was threatening many young people. He said that moving back home is a blow to self-worth after a young person spends four years working toward a career and building an independent lifestyle as a college student, away from home. He pointed out how it is psychologically crushing for a young adult to drop his or her dreams, develop a new career plan, and go back to living like a child, dependent on Mom and Dad for food, transportation, and shelter.[68]

Stress becomes debilitating when you cannot do anything to mitigate its source. This is the sort of stress that millions of Millennials faced under Obama. Mike Hais, author of *Millennial Momentum*, told *USA Today*: "Millennials are growing up at a tough time. . . . Even though, in most instances, it's not their fault—the economy collapsed just as many of them were getting out of college and coming of age—that does lead to a greater sense of stress."[69]

A Stress in America study released by the American Psychological Association in February 2013 revealed that

- stress increased for 39 percent of Millennials in 2012. Millennials' stress levels were increasing more than those of any other generation.

- 52 percent of Millennials (more than any other generation) reported lying awake at night because of their stress loads.
- millennials were most likely to report that their stress was related to work, job stability, and money issues.[70]

To be fair, not every Millennial was sniffling on a couch and squeezing a teddy bear. Despite living with their parents and being priced out of the American Dream, many Millennials expressed optimism. "Among young adults who are not working and say they don't currently have enough income, 75% are confident they will have enough income in the future," Pew Research reported in 2012.[71] The *Los Angeles Times* reported in July of 2013 on a surprising trend where recent college graduates—drowning in debt and facing an uncertain job market with historically high youth unemployment—were voicing sentiments like those of one twenty-two-year-old UCLA grad who expected a "really bright future."[72] The *Los Angeles Times* went on to relate that certain "experts" were concerned that Millennials' hopeful outlook for their future "could be an illusion, veiling the erosion of job security or fueling risky overconfidence." The most rational way to explain this phenomenon is that their parents were preventing them from feeling the pain of homelessness that they would have felt by living off their own nonexistent incomes. This is not to decry young people who lived at home or the parents who helped them. For millions, living at home was their only mode of survival, and thank goodness for their generous parents! This simply helps explain why some young people were not as angry at the government as they should have been.

Historically, each generation of Americans born since the Great Depression has grown wealthier than the preceding generation. The net worth of Americans over the age of forty-seven doubled between 1983 and 2010 while the net worth of Americans under the age of thirty-seven stagnated, according to a 2013 Urban Institute report.[73] In other words, after the housing crisis, Millennials were "living in the eighties," financially speaking, and could not keep up with the rising cost of living. Based on their *own* income, 45.3 percent of those living with their parents were well *below* the poverty threshold for all single people under the age of sixty-five during Obama's third year in office. Young people living with their parents were technically homeless and would have been out on the streets if their parents did not house them. The fact that they lived with their parents merely masked how poor they truly were and indicates how badly this generation fared compared to previous generations. Plus, how will Millennials ever be able to repay the generosity of their parents by caring for them as they age unless they are first able to care for themselves?

"I can't be sorry for life," Cisneros once told the press.[74] Yet Henry Cisneros spent the prime years of his life looking like he was helping people while he was actually hurting people. That was worth being sorry for.

Obama and his lovers in the media conned young people into thinking that living in substandard conditions—with parents, with tons of roommates, or in tiny spaces—could be fun and freeing. Keep on voting for Obama. Keep giving him more chances. *Keep hope!* For his part, Obama never bothered to explain his choice to take credit for a housing recovery while he was actually ravaging the American Dream for the Millennial generation. He got what he wanted; he conned Millennials into voting for him twice and landed two terms in the White House.

Lighthouses

You do have hope. It just won't come from Obama or his plans to take money from one group and give it to another that won't even know how to spend it in their own best interest. Hope lives in Americans like you and me who will get involved and speak up. You can become a "lighthouse," guiding yourself, your politicians, and your peers out of the gloom and doom and into the calmer waters of can-do optimism and self-sufficiency.

"The message of can-do optimism is magic," talk-show host Rush Limbaugh said on his August 8, 2013, show. Limbaugh was discussing a recent poll showing that, nearly five years into the Obama administration, an astonishing 53 percent of Democrats and 27 percent of Republicans believed that the American Dream was "dead." Limbaugh said: "People just resign to it. That to me is unacceptable."

Rush was right. We can't throw up our hands and resign ourselves to losing the American Dream. We need to start calling "politicians" what they actually are—non-revenue-generating employees—and remember they are working for us. The moment our employees steal from our companies and our bank accounts, we need to fire them. Otherwise, they will keep embezzling. If we are aggressive and upbeat, politicians will start policing themselves and the American Dream will remain achievable for all future generations.

Keep smiling. Can do. Go get it!

WHY FATHERS MATTER

6

J ack and Bill were our playboy presidents and Barry was Mr. Family Guy, right? Not exactly. Only Barry enlisted a team of exotic male dancers to help him buy votes from 95 million young people and shimmy his way into the White House. Let me explain . . .

JFK was a flawed husband and father. But he had some values, and he *did* love America. Clinton likewise left much to be desired as a husband and a father. Only Chelsea can say how she feels about her father and she appears to love him deeply. But many of Clinton's trysts became public while he held the most powerful job in the world, throwing his daughter into a very uncomfortable situation. In contrast, Obama abused his power and disrespected the office of president by missing his chance to be a role model of relationship values for *all* our young people. This particularly hurt our young women, who were often left to raise children in his fragile economy—alone.

The president of the United States is the most powerful world leader. We can expect anyone who holds this office to behave as a role model for our young people and project integrity because we bankroll their salary, security, entertainment, transportation, food, and rent; we elect them with our votes; and we hand them our trust.

How has Obama fared in exemplifying a healthy, moral family life? Many people take it for granted that Obama is a wonderful father. And, speaking strictly aesthetically, he is. He is the picture-perfect father: doting on and devoted to his daughters and loyal to their mother. Yet, outside his four-person family unit, Obama has done enormous damage to fatherhood in America. Barry positioned himself as a rakish rock star and a pseudo-preacher instead of an honorable president.

Let's explore how Barry let his addiction to charming young voters outweigh his presidential duties to enforce the Constitution and bolster role models, especially wholesome father figures for our youths.

Fathers never get enough credit for the value that they bring to society. We have a concerning need for fathers in America, especially in the black community. As the most powerful, elevated, and well-financed father in the world and as the first nonwhite American president, Obama had an unprecedented opportunity to help Millennials by promoting fatherhood among all races. Certainly, previous presidents could have done more to promote fatherhood. Still, there is no denying that the voice of the first black president—one who was also a father himself— carried particular weight. Plus, he was a trained community organizer and his area of "expertise" was supposedly reaching out to the black community. Instead, Obama used his voice and policies to diminish the importance of fathers.

Women Want Fathers

Not every young woman has a brother. Not every young woman finds or wants a husband. Pew Research reported in 2011 that just 51 percent of all adults eighteen and over are married compared to 72 percent in 1960.[1] (We'll explore how Obama helped to keep marriage out of reach for Millennials later in this chapter.) However, every young woman needs and desires a male role model in her life. *Every* woman wants a father.

One of the best things that we can do for women as a whole is encourage men to be good fathers and father figures. Pink ribbons are plastered on everything these days from yogurt lids to NFL uniforms. And certain "find the cure" organizations appear to be taking longer than necessary to find healing remedies because they squander their funds on nonresearch projects (think questionable grants to Planned Parenthood), leaving women on their own to find the cure to breast cancer. Yet not every woman gets breast cancer (a horrible condition and certainly worthy of honest research funding). Fathers, in contrast, are important to the health and development of all women. All rational women see the value of men as fathers. Even many lesbian couples ask "godfathers" to be male role models for their adopted children.[2] So, yes, *all* women want fathers.

Ideally a "father figure" is a woman's biological father or the biological father of her child if she is a mother herself. But not always. A friend, adoptive father, uncle, grandfather, or brother can become a male role model for a woman if her biological father dies or ducks out of her life. Some biological fathers abandon their daughters; they get a young woman pregnant and then leave her to change the baby's diapers (after kindly offering to pay for an abortion, of course).

Chapter 1 mentioned the late cofounder and CEO of Apple, Steve Jobs, as a powerful Democrat who faced an extraordinary level of stress in his life and yet managed to live with personal and private integrity, unlike Obama. Jobs's example was used to show that it is entirely possible for "big shots" to be role models. Well, Jobs *did* make one major personal mistake in his early life, and his reaction to it is relevant here because many of our young fathers may have similar regrets. As a young man, Steve Jobs impregnated his on-and-off girlfriend, became scared, and refused to be an active father for the first ten years of his daughter's life. Jobs eventually assumed his proper role as a father and he deeply regretted his early behavior. Jobs told his biographer, Walter Isaacson,

"I wish I had handled it differently. I could not see myself as a father then, so I didn't face up to it. But when the test results showed she was my daughter . . . I agreed to support her until she was eighteen and give some money to Chrisann [his ex-girlfriend] as well. I found a house in Palo Alto and fixed it up and let them live there rent-free. Her mother found her great schools which I paid for. I tried to do the right thing. But if I could do it over, I would do a better job."[3]

If Obama had held up father figures like Jobs as examples instead of exotic male dancers (more on them in a bit), our young men would have been inspired to treat our young women with more dignity. When our young men make mistakes, they would be inspired to resolve them as Jobs did, instead of digging themselves into deeper holes like Obama's celebrity friends. When Obama employed Jobs's name in his 2012 State of the Union Address (after Jobs was dead and could not protest), it was to convince young voters that his policies would help them "become the next Steve Jobs," and we all know how well that panned out!

A girl's father shapes how she sees herself and the type of mate to whom she eventually finds herself attracted. Research indicates that a girl whose biological father abandons her when she is young will prematurely reach sexual maturity and end up feeling abandoned, prone to behavioral and health problems, and sexually insecure.[4] This insecurity could lead her to attach herself to smooth-talking knuckleheads who use her and lose her.

Fathers who only have sons are just as important: When men raise good sons, they do their sons' future girlfriends, wives, and grandchildren a huge favor. Fathers have the unique power to prevent or encourage bad behavior: When a young man cheats on his wife, it is often because he saw his father cheat on his mother, confirms a 2011 study from the Charles University in Prague. JFK saw his father cheat and then he cheated. Clinton's father and stepfather were womanizers and then he cheated. Obama's biological father and stepfather were philanderers, and he has cheated on millions of Millennials instead of his wife.[5]

Major research shows that the woman and child both fare better when the woman is married to the father when the child is born. A nationally representative Princeton University study overlapping the Bush and Obama administrations found that 65 percent of unmarried couples were separated within five years after the birth of a child. Absence of a father took a toll on the mothers and children: five years after the parents split, the fathers saw their children once a month, *at most.*[6] According to the Fragile Families and Child Wellbeing Study Fact Sheet featured on Princeton University's website in 2013, "Children born to unmarried parents do not fare as well as children born to married parents. Single mothers and mothers in unstable partnerships engage in harsher parenting practices and fewer literacy activities with their child than stably married mothers. Family instability also reduces children's cognitive test scores and increases aggressive behavior. The increase in aggression is especially pronounced among boys."[7]

Young women who voted for Obama were not told this in the "Life of Julia" animated slide show, where Obama promised his presidency would allow women to be like Julia and raise a perfectly behaved baby boy like her cartoon son "Zachary," *without* a father figure.

Super Models

Look out, Gisele Bündchen! The Obamas are storming down the runway! They say they're no ordinary models—they're *super* models.

"Barack's life is a good road map for young people," Michelle Obama told a reporter from the *Minneapolis Star Tribune* on October 14, 2008.

It is not surprising for a wife to speak highly of her husband. It *is* surprising and repugnant to witness a middle-aged married couple who are vying for the most powerful position in the world—*not* the role of a Victoria's Secret Angel—strutting and puffing as if they are God's gift to humanity when their words and actions are delineative of barnacles, leeches, and bottom feeders.

Mr. and Mrs. Obama thought themselves paragons, but their *actions* expose them as cowards. They didn't bother to habitually behave like role models themselves or to champion other strong role models for young people, especially youths in their own community. If the Obamas believed "Barack's life was a good road map for young people," they should have helped young people figure out how to follow his path (i.e., *how* a young black man growing up in the South Side of Chicago could obtain a solid education, land a reliable job, and also become a devoted and present father to his children). Barack and his wife should have proffered a "compass" in the form of *consistent* words and actions to guide youths out of social misfortunes. Instead, they gave Millennials a "compass" that was unusable because 80 percent of the time its needle pointed west when it should have pointed north. The Obamas' erratic behavior, which we will expose, misdirected young people who were trying to dig themselves out of unfortunate situations and predicaments that disproportionately impacted the lives of black youths, such as the fact that 73 percent of black children are born without a committed father. Obama's groupies probably won't like hearing that statistic from a white woman, since they also did not like hearing it from a black man.

African American cable TV host Don Lemon did a segment for CNN in July of 2013 where he made a big point of seconding statements made a few days earlier by Bill O'Reilly on Fox News. (O'Reilly had said, "Right now, about 73 percent of all black babies are born out of wedlock.") Lemon received flack among his own community for saying:

> *Black people, if you really want to fix the problem [of violence within the black community] . . . More than 72 percent of children in the African-American community are born out of wedlock. That means absent fathers. And the studies show that lack of a male role model is an express train right to prison and the cycle continues [emphasis added].*[8]

On Father's Day 2008, candidate Obama gave a rousing speech at a black church in Chicago. This speech helped Barry get elected by endearing him to the black community. He promised his people—his black brothers and sisters—that he would "break the cycle" of black children without devoted fathers:

We need fathers to realize that responsibility does not end at concep-
tion. We need them to realize that what makes you a man is not
the ability to have a child—it's the courage to raise one. . . . I know
what it means to have an absent father, although my circumstances
weren't as tough as they are for many young people today. . . . I
know the toll that being a single parent took on my mother . . . So
I resolved many years ago that it was my obligation to break the
cycle *[emphasis added]*.[9]

In 2008, Obama won the black vote by 91 percentage points; in
2012, he won the black vote by 87 percentage points.[10] It is disheartening to look back and realize that Obama used his own people to get
elected; he made money and gained power off of his disadvantaged
brothers and sisters; he bought the White House with the help of their
votes. There was nothing stopping him from utilizing his historic opportunity to help his people and yet he passed up his chance.

First off, many of Obama's economic policies disproportionately
hurt young blacks, as revealed in chapter 2. In this chapter, I will discuss some of the ways Obama hurt his people by *omission*. He had a
historic chance to help his people advance by directly and repeatedly
addressing absent black fathers, both inside the black community and,
from miles away, in his televised addresses. Unfortunately, he was silent
and still. When he did speak, he often used his voice to prop up black
celebrities who endorsed violent, demeaning, or unhealthy lifestyles.
Other times, he used his voice to fan racial tensions instead of using
his own mixed racial heritage to promote color-blind friendship among
young Americans.

Obama would argue that he *did* promote responsible fatherhood.
After all, his administration posted "Tips and Activities" to Fatherhood
.gov and encouraged fathers to sign an online "Presidential Fatherhood Pledge." Obama also included government funding for fatherhood
programs in all of his budget proposals. The online resources would
have been a terrific idea, assuming bad fathers trolled the Internet for
parenting tips from sites that end in .gov (not likely). The government

funding would have been a swell plan if he knew it would work (he did not). Obama continued Bush's experiment of allocating millions of taxpayer dollars toward fatherhood outreach, despite Princeton University reporting in 2010 that "it is disappointing that the BSF program [Bush's 'Building Strong Families'] had no effects overall" . . . and that, partially due to fragmentary evaluation, "no one has any idea whether these programs are working."[11] So, yes, Obama helped promote healthy fatherhood. By taking shots in the dark.

Five years into his presidency, the sociocultural situation for young blacks was dire. In 2013, the Guttmacher Institute released a study showing that black teenage girls were having abortions at a rate that was twice as high as Hispanic teens and four times higher than white teens.[12] As noted above, 73 percent of blacks were born with absent fathers. Black women were far more likely than women of any other major racial group to be running a family household "without a spouse present" according to the U.S. Bureau of Labor Statistics.[13] Lastly, while levels of cohabitation were higher for all young women, in part due to the economy, young black women were more likely than young white women to experience a pregnancy during their cohabitation. Pregnancy itself is not a "burden," but Princeton's research indicates that a father swiftly abandons a woman who has his child outside of marriage, which leaves the woman with a task that was meant for two, not one, and most of these young women were black.

Certainly, these trends were in place before Obama took office and he does not deserve *all* the blame. That said, he deserves *enormous* blame for failing to do the easiest and most effective things he could have done: speak directly to black men in impoverished black communities; be a good role model; and use his and his wife's celebrity to hoist up other familial role models.

The Obamas were not minor celebrities; they were *the* celebrities. More Americans looked up to them than to anyone else, which presented a historic opportunity. By the end of 2012, a *USA Today*/Gallup poll found that Americans ranked Obama as their "most admired man" in the world and Michelle as the "second-most-admired woman" in the world, beating contenders such as the pope and Rev. Billy Graham by a landslide.[14] Barack and Michelle could have used their celebrity voices to promote loving, dual-parent relationships, particularly among blacks; unfortunately, they were having too much fun getting their swagger on to act like adults, not to mention the First Couple.

Obama could have gone into the black community and said: "Black men: You need to step up to the plate. If you're going to father all these children, then you need to be a father." Two short sentences, just like that. Repeated over and over by Obama. It would have been so easy for him to do and the impact would have been enormous.

In late February 2014, Obama gathered a group of young men of color from Chicago around him at the White House and, as cameras flashed, signed a memorandum establishing a task force called "My Brother's Keeper," to mentor at-risk young black men. Obama's staged remarks fell short of holding absent black fathers accountable and were too little, too late. "Mr. Obama's remarks come as the end of his time in office is in sight, with the president mindful of the legacy that his administration will leave behind . . . ," admitted the *New York Times*.[15]

Unfortunately, Obama fell into the rut of pandering to blacks. From the very beginning, he developed the campaign slogan "Yes We Can," because Michelle convinced him it would resonate with black neighborhoods in Chicago where he needed to build a support base. She murmured: "The brothers and sisters will get it, Barack."[16] These two blacks used their own people to get ahead and then did virtually nothing for them. They also venerated the gangster life of pimps and pistols, encouraging negative role models who would only mislead their community.

Barry's Exotic Male Poll Dancers

How did Barry win elections? With poll dancers, baby!

Barry ran a club called Barry's Exotic Male Poll Dancers. He and his dancers had a busy schedule, working the polls and convincing a majority of Millennials to vote for him in two consecutive presidential elections. Obama made himself look like a celebrity by surrounding himself with celebrities who unfortunately happened to be hollow father figures. He told *Rolling Stone* that these men were "good" guys and "great businessmen" with "great talents" who had "shifted the culture."[17]

Rap, hip-hop, and pop are all-American music genres with roots that include African American blues and Appalachian folk melodies. Obama unfortunately had a gift for singling out the pop, hip-hop, and rap entertainers with serious parenting issues while forgetting to hold up black fathers who were worth emulating. Obama made decisions based on political calculation, not the best interest of young people.

Meet the exotic male dancers who shimmied the polls for Barry's campaign:

SNOOP LION (FORMERLY SNOOP DOGG): Obama's true colors shone through when he felt comfortable with his audience and before he launched his presidential campaign, such as a 2004 speech he delivered to the fans of a popular Chicago hip-hop radio station. Obama was caught on camera boasting about how he played Snoop Dogg's hit single "Drop It Like It's Hot" so frequently while driving in the car with his three-year-old daughter that she began singing her own version. "Drop It" is the perfect song to lull a three-year-old to sleep in a car seat: pimps, hoes, bitches, AK-47s, pistols, and the N-word on repeat. Snoop and other rappers have a First Amendment right to say whatever nonsense they want, but this does not justify a politician who lives off the taxpayer dime, like Obama, in promoting Snoop as a role model for our youths.

Grinning, Barry bounced to "Drop It" while the crowd screamed: *"Obama! Obama! Obama!"* Barry seemed proud that he was raising his little girl to potentially idolize men who treated AK-47s like squirt guns. Barry did not want hunters with firearm licenses and safety training to own semi-automatic firearms and store them in locked safes. But he was more than happy to sing lullabies about pistol-whipping pimps to his tiny daughter. Will someone please nominate this man for Father of the Year?

In 2008, Snoop told the *Daily Record*: "I'm not down with the Republican or Democratic Party—I represent the gangsta party," and

Obama's affection for Snoop's music makes you think he's down with the gangsta party too.[18] In 2012, the Dogg (now with the new stage name Snoop Lion) went online and posted a list of reasons to vote for Obama.[19] These included:

- "He is a black [N-word]."
- "He's hugged Beyoncé before and sniffed her neck."
- "Michelle got a fat a**."

In 2012, Snoop premiered his documentary *Reincarnated* at the Toronto International Film Festival and told the press: "They need to give Obama four more years, man . . . . [Bush] gave him a house where the TV didn't work, the toilet was stuffed up."[20] In the film, he sighs: "I know Obama wants me to come to the White House, but what the f—k can I perform?"[21] Snoop Lion had an ounce more sense than Barack Star, who thought Snoop was suitable for toddlers.

USHER: The year 2004 was a big one for Usher's six-pack abs, rolling hips, and louche lyrics. The R&B singer-dancer's hit single "Yeah!" ranked number one on the charts for a staggering twelve weeks straight. His other number one hits, "Confessions" and its follow-up, "Confessions Part II," brought in piles of cash. Sounding more like he was fist-pumping than folding his hands in remorse, Usher "confesses" to his girlfriend about cheating on her with his "chick on the side" who is "three months pregnant" so "give me another chance," 'cause "it's about us." When the press interviewed Usher for his opinion on a celebrity who allegedly two-timed his wife, Usher said: "He's cheating on her? That happens, man. Everybody's confessing nowadays."[22] Usher built his brand, and his bank account, by glamorizing betrayal.

In "Yeah!" Usher shouted about trolling for women at clubs and demanding sexual favors from strangers on the spot: "Rowl! These women all on the prowl, if you hold the head steady I'mma milk the cow." A tad sexist but, oh well! The song made Usher rich, plus attracted the attention of Obama. In Usher's world, that was like winning the Super Bowl.

According to Usher, the "first time" he met Obama was "in 2004" when they were "kind of rolling" in Obama's ride after "campaigning all day, all over the place."[23] Usher was hungry, so he grabbed the only chow in Obama's car—a candy bar—and shoved it down. A pro at sweetening the deal, Obama had more than candy bars for Usher; he had promises too. Usher told MTV that Obama promised him: "Anything I can do to support you, I'll do so."[24] In return, Obama hoped that Usher would help him tap the youth vote. Usher agreed. That candy bar was *scrumptious* and there were more where it came from!

Usher kicked off his 2008 " 'Usher for Obama" tour with a song and music video called "Hush ft. Barack Obama." Usher mixed Obama's image and speech with his own lyrics encouraging young people, especially young blacks, to get out and vote. Nearly everyone in the music video is a young black person who is either "living hard," "homeless," or disenfranchised, like a young black woman who thinks she will never have a voice in Washington and "it's a waste of time to vote." Then, we see Usher cruising up to a voting poll place in his Escalade, where he is swarmed by paparazzi cameras. He's cool, so he does the cool thing and votes, presumably for Obama. Meanwhile, we hear Obama's speech playing over Usher's catchy beat: "It's time for us to change America, and that's why I'm running for President . . . I am my brother's keeper. I am my sister's keeper. That's the promise we need to keep. . . . You can decide whether we're gonna travel the same war path or whether we will chart a new course that offers real hope for the future." The video ends with one word: "Vote." Usher helped Obama con his young black brothers and sisters into thinking he would help them "fly." What young blacks voting for the first time did not realize is that Obama was a terrible pilot and the flight would end in a crash.

Usher tried reading the Constitution—until he realized it was full of articles—and then went back to peddling the playboy life. He released "Foolin' Around" in 2010 to cash in on his deeply profound justifications for marital infidelity: "Guess that's just the man in me. Blame it on celebrity." In 2011, *News of the World* asked Usher whether he wanted his two sons to follow in his footsteps. "Shamelessly!" responded Usher.[25] Recently divorced, in the same interview he declared he was taking a "pause for the cause" from dating and building his "hit list" of "a few people I'm interested in." Obama had a kill list of most wanted terrorists. Usher had a hit list of most wanted women. They made a cute couple.

Besides campaigning for him, Usher performed at Obama's 2008 and 2012 inaugural events. During the rowdy 2012 inaugural after-party at the White House, Obama tried to impress socialites by "getting down" with Usher for a "dance off."[26] It was their final show together after four years of poll dancing.

LUDACRIS: Obama singled out Ludacris as a father and rapper that he knew personally and who he thought highly of as a businessman. Obama conceded to *Rolling Stone* in 2008 that Ludacris and other rappers should improve their lyrics, but, in the same breath, he said they improved the culture by reducing racial division: "I am troubled sometimes by the misogyny and materialism of a lot of rap lyrics, but I think the genius of the art form has shifted the culture and helped to desegregate music. . . . I know Jay-Z. I know Ludacris. I know Russell Simmons. I know a bunch of these guys. They are great talents and great businessmen, which is something that doesn't get emphasized enough."[27]

Obama was actually perpetuating a ceiling on the opportunities and achievements available to black men by encouraging them to pursue wealth and success in Ludacris's industry. He was effectively encouraging them to think small and limit their potential instead of thinking big. How many businessmen wear bulletproof vests to work? 50 Cent does. How many businessmen worry about dying in a tragic drive-by shooting like Tupac? Ludacris and Snoop Lion undoubtedly do. Not the best career to encourage a young black man to pursue.

When MTV asked Ludacris what he thought about Tiger Woods cheating on his wife, he laughed and said it was "very entertaining" and he could identify because he had similarly cheated on his girlfriend.[28] Ludacris was so funny. Funny *sounding*. There are many phenomenal black fathers and black businessmen out there and yet our president chose to label Ludacris as "great" because he could help him win votes.

JAY-Z AND BEYONCÉ: Okay, okay, pop artist Beyoncé is technically a woman but her hit single "If I Were a Boy" makes you think that she thinks she is a man. Plus, she was rapper Jay-Z's other half and both she and her husband were tight with the Obamas, which makes it hard to talk about him without talking about her. A friendship blossomed in Manhattan in 2007 at a swanky Obama fundraiser. Jay-Z and Beyoncé attended, and Obama begged Beyoncé for her pinup and signature: "I never do this, but can I ask for your autograph?" and, after flashing a smile for the camera with her at his side: "I want a copy of that picture!"[29]

Jay-Z endorsed Obama for president and they have remained close ever since. He and his wife were treated to a VIP tour of the White House, including a controversial visit to the Situation Room. Beyoncé sang for the Obamas' first dance during his first inauguration and belted out "The Star-Spangled Banner" at his second inauguration.

Mr. and Mrs. Jay-Z Carter vacationed in Cuba for their anniversary in the spring of 2013—you know, that communist country run by a dictator whose people love him so much that they risk their lives, paddling on makeshift rafts, to get here? After the trip, Jay-Z made the mistake of boasting about it in a rap called "Open Letter":

> *Boy from the hood but got White House clearance.*
> *Obama said: "Chill, you gonna get me impeached."*
> *But you don't need this sh*t anyway, chill with me on the beach. . . .*
> *You know whenever I'm threatened, I start shooting. (Bang!)*
> *Catch a body [murder someone], head to Houston ["home base" to*
>   *evade repercussions].*

Obama spokesman Jay Carney told the press that Obama had "nothing to do" with the Carters' Cuban excursion. Carney added that Jay-Z probably said White House clearance instead of Treasury clearance, because: "I guess nothing rhymes with Treasury."[30] Which *could* make sense, except nothing in Jay-Z's rap rhymed with "White House," and he still used "White House."

Jay-Z had a baby daughter whom he named Blue Ivy Carter. After

Blue was born, Obama said he called Jay-Z up and "I made sure that Jay-Z was helping Beyoncé out and not leaving it all with Beyoncé and the mother-in-law."[31] Obama couldn't bother to mingle with absent black fathers in Chicago's hoods, but he could make personal phone calls to black fathers whose wives made enough money to hire fifty nannies. Just as Obama used his policies to leave the rich get richer and young blacks poorer, he plied his prestige to elevate multimillionaire black fathers even higher while neglecting to use his stature to "break the cycle" for disadvantaged black fathers.

Jay-Z rapped about Blue in his hit single "Holy Grail":

Blue told me remind you ni**as
F**k that sh*t y'all talking 'bout, I'm the ni**a

Jay-Z told BBC1 Radio he's a "writer" and these verses are a "metaphor."[32] Uh huh. Nice try, bro. You're right up there with Shakespeare.

Jay-Z told MTV about his rap-writing process for songs, such as his single "I Know": "The first thing I do, I say, 'What is the song saying?' For me ["I Know"] sounded like heroin."[33]

In another song, "Roc Boys," Jay-Z raps about un-stepped (raw) heroin.

I get away with murder when I sling yay
Heroin got less steps . . .
That means it ain't stepped on, dig me?

Barack kept Mr. Heroin at his side and had him make many Obama campaign videos, including a video that ends with the official Obama-Biden logo and the Jay-Z lyrics "Turn my music high, high, high, high!" Jay-Z was endorsing Obama, and, in return, Obama was endorsing Jay-Z, his lifestyle, and his lyrics. It's how you barter for votes!

Obama tapped Jay-Z to make appearances at his campaign events, such as one in November of 2008 before a stadium of young people, predominantly black, to whom he said: "I wanted to let you know. You guys all go out and vote. . . . Like for too long we were excluded from the American Dream. . . . Obama's runnin' so we all can fly!"

Heroin is hard core. Heroin is not tobacco or marijuana; it's not a drug you could glamorize in good conscience, knowing it is safe to use recreationally or medicinally. By 2012, a survey found that the number of young adults dependent on heroin had increased in recent years by 100 percent. By September of 2013, *Teen Vogue* was reporting that the average age of heroin death victims had dropped dramatically, to ages eighteen to twenty-five, after historically sitting between ages forty to forty-five.[34] These young lives were cut short, but at least they had cast their votes for Hope and Change. Obama could take credit for helping them fly, just not the way they had expected.

Jay-Z prided himself in his "metaphors." A good father chooses a good mother for his offspring and Jay-Z's choice of Beyoncé could be a metaphor for his fathering skills. No one did soft porn better than soft-drink spokeswoman Beyoncé. She could shake her bootay like nobody else and the more families watching her at the Super Bowl halftime show, the faster she could shake it. The most unfortunate part was that Beyoncé's brand was associated with our American president when she twerked her tush onstage.

First Lady Michelle made it well known to *People* that if there were anyone else in the world that she could be, "I'd be Beyoncé." On Twitter, she said: "@Beyonce Thank you for the beautiful letter and for being a role model who kids everywhere can look up to.—mo." Obama backed his wife up, flattering his pinup girl at an intimate Manhattan fundraiser hosted by Jay-Z and Beyoncé that injected $4 million into his 2012 coffers: "Beyoncé could not be a better role model for my girls because she carries herself with such class and poise and has so much talent."[35] Yes, Beyoncé could multitask by oscillating her derrière at high speed while throwing back shots of liquid sugar. *Such* a classy, graceful, and ingenious craft.

This was confusing for young people who admired the First Lady's opinion. Michelle did not want her daughters exposed to the raunchier side of pop culture but her role model was a sex symbol married to a coarse rapper. Michelle wrote a book telling young people to replace "sugary drinks with water, low-fat milk and 100 percent fruit juice."[36] Beyoncé did a huge commercial for Pepsi where she refuels mid-workout by slugging down a sugary drink. No one needs a busybody First Lady telling kids they can't drink soda while her self-declared role model is making millions telling young people to "live for now!" and pack a soda pop in their gym bag instead of a water bottle.

Michelle played both sides. As her husband's reelection drew near, she released her gardening book showing mothers how she was teaching their children to be healthy, and meanwhile she was giving their children encouragement to live like Beyoncé. Quixotic equation: Votes from Moms + Votes from Millennials = Obama's second term.

Michelle's brother once described her as a sore loser.[37] Well, her role model was a sore *winner*. After Romney lost the presidential election, Beyoncé posted a picture on Tumblr that said: "TAKE THAT MITCHES."

The Obamas' intimate friendship with the Carters placed an unworthy mother-figure and an unhealthy father-figure on a pedestal as role models for young people and the black family.

Stripped

Are black children and black families any better off today because of Barack and Michelle? The blood that stained the streets of Chicago and the sounds of gunshots that pierced the Windy City spoke for themselves. These were the stains and sounds of the gang violence that the Obamas glamorized through their rapper pals, Barry's Exotic Poll Dancers, to win the votes of Millennials.

Compared to popular white presidents like Kennedy, Reagan, and Clinton, it was Obama who had the strongest ability to say that black entertainers and black fathers who get rich off songs that treat women like meat and AK-47s like toys are anything but cool. He blew this opportunity by promoting Snoop Dogg, Usher, Ludacris, and Jay-Z as role models and by benefiting from their help on Election Day. Barry gained significant mileage from his boys wearing gold chains and diamond studs and working the polls, teasing young people into handing over their votes.

Does a stripper love her audience? No, she just wants their money. Still, at least she's transparent about it and does not strip in front of children. The two major differences between Barry and a hardcore stripper were: he pretended he wasn't one, and, he damaged fatherhood by effectively doing his show for toddlers.

"My Son"

B esides propping up the worst examples of fatherhood, Obama also used his voice as a black father figure in a way that instigated more racial divide. This may not have been his intent, but he did not seem to care if it was the by-product of his puerile behavior. Let me explain . . .

Young people of all colors are murdered every day. For example, on March 21, 2013, an eighteen-year-old black man shot a thirteen-month-old half-Hispanic baby in broad daylight. His "offense" was sitting in his stroller while his white mother pushed him down the street in Brunswick, Georgia. Hardly anyone heard about baby Antonio Santiago.

On June 26, a seventeen-year-old Colombian man named David Guerrero was walking to work at 6:30 a.m. when a fifteen-year-old white gang member named Konrad Schafer stalked Guerrero and shot him because it would be "fun."[38] One week later, the fifteen-year-old's twenty-year-old black buddy David Damus shot another young man for no reason. The fifteen-year-old finished things off by slitting their second victim's throat.

Oh, you're just hearing about these killings now? Don't you see, their lives did not matter because the stories behind their deaths were harder to spin into profit and power. Politicians and journalists are lazy.

Politicians want to win affection and votes with minimal effort. Journalists want to make money without spending hours of research.

The press (and then Obama) made sure everyone knew—all day, every day, for months—how a twenty-eight-year-old Hispanic man named George Zimmerman killed a seventeen-year-old black boy named Trayvon Martin. It was a made-for-TV story that the typing wizards could make quick and reliable money on if they pretended Zimmerman was a middle-aged white man: Black boy with Skittles and iced tea shot by armed white man! Black teen carrying sugar murdered by white man carrying pistol!

The press gave a flying squirrel about Trayvon's life; his story meant money. And there's no use denying that his story, rehashed around the clock, came at a price: We never heard about anyone else's life and we were left with the impression that racism is rampant in America.

An eyewitness named John Good testified that he saw Martin pummeling Zimmerman in an MMA-style "ground and pound" mount on the evening of February 28, 2012, in Zimmerman's neighborhood. This was backed up Zimmerman's claim that Martin mounted him and began punching him and smashing his head onto the concrete. During the altercation, Martin caught sight of Zimmerman's weapon, which was holstered at his hip, and yelled: "You're going to die tonight!," indicating that he planned to use Zimmerman's gun against him. At that point, Zimmerman reached down for his gun and shot Martin in self-defense. Another witness for the defense, Dr. Vincent Di Maio (a highly renowned and published expert on gunshot wounds and forensic pathology), testified on the bullet's trajectory: "This is consistent with Mr. Zimmerman's account [t]hat Mr. Martin was over him, leaning forward, at the time that he was shot."[39] He also said that the injuries on Zimmerman's face and head were consistent with punches and the assault Zimmerman had described to the police.

A six-member jury found Zimmerman not guilty on all counts. Even the one jury member who struggled with the verdict, telling ABC News she felt Zimmerman "got away with murder," but "you have no proof he killed him intentionally," said she did not think the case should have gone to trial because "I felt this was a publicity stunt."[40] Months later, Zimmerman would have various encounters with the law, from speeding tickets to apparent domestic disputes; he was not a perfect man, but his flaws do not negate the events of that evening, the one-sided reporting, or the way the president responded by justifing Martin and attacking the American jury system immediately after Zimmerman was declared innocent.

A few days later, Obama surprised the nation by singling out this murder for a national television conference:

> *You know, when Trayvon Martin was first shot I said that this could have been* my son. *Another way of saying that is Trayvon Martin could have been me 35 years ago. And when you think about why, in the African American community [but not in the Hispanic or White community] at least, there's a lot of pain around what happened here, I think it's important to recognize that the African American community is looking at this issue through a set of experiences and a history that doesn't go away. There are very few African American men in this country who haven't had the experience of being followed when they were shopping in a department store. That includes me. . . . Things are getting better. . . . It* doesn't mean *we're in a* post-racial *society [emphasis added].*

Within weeks of Obama's televised remarks, two murders took place:

AUGUST 16, 2013: Two black boys and one white boy, ages fifteen, sixteen, and seventeen, killed a twenty-two-year-old white Australian baseball player named Christopher Lane. The white seventeen-year-old drove his car through a wealthy neighborhood and they spotted Lane jogging. The boy sitting in the back seat pulled his trigger and shot Lane. The police chief said the boys told him they shot Lane because "We were bored and decided to kill somebody."

Two days after the not-guilty verdict in the Zimmerman trial, one of the black teens, James Francis Edwards, tweeted: "Ayeee I knocced out 5 woods [prison-speak for "whitey"] since Zimmerman court!:) lol sh*t ima keep sleepin sh*t! #ayeeee"

Five days after Obama's speech, he tweeted: "N***a of chief keef [a rapper named Chief Keef] don't drop almighty SOSA [refers to a Chief Keef song where he compares himself to *Scarface*'s villain Alejandro Sosa] or something by #Monday I'ma put hands on every wood [whitey] I see until they drop lol @ChiefKeef"

Three days before becoming "bored" and murdering Lane: "With my n***as when it's time to start taken life's"

AUGUST 21, 2013: A month after the president's speech, two black sixteen-year-old boys, Demetruis L. Glenn and Kenan Adams-Kinard, robbed and beat to death an eighty-eight-year-old World War II veteran.

The president said nothing about either tragedy. He was busy pitching his message to college students when Lane died, so he told an aide to tell Lane's parents he was thinking about them. How thoughtful!

Just a few months later, a new phenomenon afflicted America from coast-to-coast: knockout game assaults. On November 26, 2013, Fox News's Sean Hannity reported twenty-seven "documented incidents" of knockout game assaults in "ten states, coast to coast," with "six of them resulting in death." These attacks, typified by a young black person "knocking out" a nonblack stranger, such as a young person or a grandmother, with a sucker punch and then leaving them for dead. While many conventional journalists denied or ignored the trend, the black community *did* recognize these attacks were taking place. The Reverend Al Sharpton penned an editorial for the *Huffington Post* labeling knockout games "racist" and the "biggest form of cowardice." And, three days after Hannity's report, a mostly black crowd of Brooklyn residents rallied in East New York to oppose the assaults: "We are asking our mothers to make a recommitment to pay more attention to our children," said Brown Memorial Baptist Church member Leticia Smith.[41]

Where was Obama? Busy as a bee: enjoying his Thanksgiving vacation and pardoning a turkey named Popcorn. Why didn't he join his black churchgoing brothers and sisters at their rally in Brooklyn? Why didn't he take five minutes to denounce these "games" and encourage racial unity? Obama could have encouraged interracial friendship by deploring black-on-nonblack violence with as much zeal as he exhibited after Martin's death. Unfortunately, he said nothing. Maybe Reverend Sharpton was wrong. *Obama's silence* was the "biggest form of cowardice" in America.

Our president failed to use his mixed racial heritage and all that he had accomplished in America with that heritage (i.e., Ivy League college and law school degrees and presidency of the United States) to bring us together and promote strong families. Instead, he used his voice as a black father figure to pretend that young blacks, young whites, and young Hispanics could not get along and this did not help anyone. It only hurt all families, especially black families. The president's special message for black men was not to encourage them to step up to the plate and be committed fathers. His special message for black men was: "As I said, I could be your father. Whites are racist. Don't worry, we'll keep our victim status and move nowhere."

Mr. Terrific

As president, Obama fulfilled his self-imposed "obligation" of talking to young black fathers by spending time with a multimillionaire black father who also happened to be a pro golfer. Thanks to some juicy texts, we all know how that black father turned out. Obama invited Tiger Woods to speak at his January 2009 inaugural ceremonies and welcomed him as a White House guest that spring. After Woods's scandal broke, our president publicly rebranded Tiger as "terrific" and barred the press corps from observing as he golfed eighteen holes with Mr. Terrific. Nice work, Barry. Bet Momma Nordegren would love to take you to the driving range, test her new Calloway, and thank you for befriending her children's father!

Preacher Man

B arry was a preacher man. A sweet-talkin' preacher man. Yes he was, he was, oh yes he was.

Our Constitution is silent on marriage. It is not the executive's role to become a pseudo-preacher and attack or promote faith-related beliefs. Unfortunately, besides positioning himself as a rock star, Obama also positioned himself as a wannabe preacher, using the executive branch to endorse gay marriage, when he should have remained *silent* and left marriage up to individuals and states to decide, per the First and Tenth Amendments. C'mon, he knew better! Wasn't he supposed to be the big "constitutional lawyer?"

In 2004, Obama was asked whether he thought Americans had an innate right to marry, and he answered, "I don't think marriage is a civil right." Going into the 2008 election, he favored heterosexual marriage. In 2010, he said his views were "evolving." A few months before the 2012 election, he conveniently reversed his views: "It is important for me to go ahead and affirm that I think same-sex couples should be able to get married."

Why did Obama wait until 2012 to express support for gay marriage? Did he suddenly "care" more about equality? What changed? Here's what changed: He was losing support among young swing voters and he needed to win them back. In 2008, 54 percent of the Millennial Generation expressed support for gay marriage, but the majority of the population (51 percent) opposed gay marriage. So, Obama had nothing to gain overall by supporting gay marriage.[42] But, by 2012, 64 percent of the Millennial Generation favored gay marriage and, most importantly, only 43 percent of the overall population opposed gay marriage.[43] So, he could score some political points by making a few remarks about gay marriage. One thing is clear: Obama was never for gays, just like he was never for young people or blacks.

As a young person, it is very concerning that Obama, a self-professed "constitutional law professor," knowingly misled our young people for his own personal gain. By repeatedly presenting himself as a constitutional expert, Obama led our young people to believe that it would be in the interest of equality if the executive branch were involved in marriage. This is absolutely not the case. If the executive branch exerts itself into our churches and bedrooms, it hurts everyone's equality—gay and straight.

The U.S. Constitution considers us with respect to our humanity and American citizenship, not our sexuality. The federal government does not need to be involved in sex or marriage—homosexual or heterosexual. Constitutionally, all Americans should have the freedom to marry in their own places of worship. It does not make sense for the federal government to define marriage because so many Americans believe that marriage is a personal and/or religious *benefit*, not a "right." If a particular state decides to formally legalize gay marriage, this is constitutional albeit unnecessary bureaucracy. And, such state laws *must* allow for religious and free speech exemptions to protect the First Amendment rights of others.

A common point raised by those who favor a federal involvement in marriage is that gays should receive the same federal benefits as heterosexual couples. In the past, Americans have agreed to support tax benefits for heterosexual married couples in the interest of promoting our population growth and ensuring that children are raised with two parents. As our society becomes more diverse, if we wish to continue such tax benefits for traditional marriage, perhaps these should only be state and local tax benefits and not federal tax benefits. Hereafter, Americans who support traditional marriage as well as those who support gay marriage will be best served by a president and a federal government that stay out of our bedrooms and churches. We all need to safeguard our First Amendment rights to free speech and freedom to publicly express our faith as well as our Tenth Amendment states' rights if we desire true equality.

Obama should have used his expertise on the Constitution to educate young people on how the First and Tenth Amendments protect our human dignity and equality—instead of abusing his knowledge by misleading them to think that gays were victims. Gays are not victims just as I am not a victim because I am a woman.

For the sake of winning votes, Obama led our young people—especially young women and gays—to think that they would be "more equal" if the federal government recognized the "right" to female birth control and gay marriage. And, if we actively lobby for the federal government to give us something (i.e., a marriage certificate) at the expense of another person's First Amendment rights, then we become aggressors (not victims) seeking superiority, not equality.

Congress shall make no law respecting an establishment of religion, or prohibiting the free exercise thereof; or abridging the freedom of speech, or of the press; or the right of the people peaceably to assemble, and to petition the government for a redress of grievances. —First Amendment to the U.S. Constitution

The powers not delegated to the United States by the Constitution, nor prohibited by it to the States, are reserved to the States respectively, or to the people. —Tenth Amendment to the U.S. Constitution

The First Amendment protects our *right* to free speech and to publicly express our faith, but is silent on *benefits* like marriage, which means that per the Tenth Amendment, states alone have the constitutional power to regulate marriage.

Constitutional law professor Barry Obama told our young people the exact opposite. He led our young people to think that the federal government could make people more healthy, moral, and equal. This idea is flawed because it ignores the fact that the first piece of private property that every American owns—from the moment of conception—is his or her own body. Natural law or reason tells us that we are solely responsible for our own bodies and the Fourth Amendment affirms this natural, God-given right. Owning our body means we have the right to free speech and religious practices—as long as we do not use wrongful force against another.

The government can only protect individual liberty. Liberty allows for the competition of ideas whereby all individuals voice their beliefs in the public square so that the most rational and moral ideas can rise to the surface.

Our president attacked the Constitution in the name of equality and encouraged our young people to think of gays as victims so that he could position himself as a problem solver and equality promoter. We are already equal before the Constitution, in its original meaning. Warping the Constitution is not a win for gays; it was a lose-lose situation because gays need the Constitution too. Obama knew this, but he was more interested in tracking opinion polls and "evolving" in the direction that would buy the most votes from young swing voters. There's creationism; there's Darwinism; and then, there's Obamaism.

Men and Women Want Options

Every young person wants a wide range of lifestyle and career options. Only in a healthy economy will all women truly be able to choose whether or not to become mothers, and to choose between being working and stay-at-home mothers. And men are no different.

New research shows that men have a biological clock that ticks even faster and louder than that of women. The longer a male waits to sire a child, the higher the chances that his child will be born with autism, schizophrenia, a low birth weight, or prematurely. While men are fertile until they are sixty-five and even beyond, it is ideal for a man to sire a child when he is younger.

Going back to the time of King Henry VIII of England, society has blamed women for anything that goes wrong in childbirth. But three 2012 studies (two in *Nature* and one in the *American Journal of Men's Health*) revealed that sperm, not eggs, are the primary donors of mutations. *Time* magazine reports the findings: "On average, a 20-year-old male passes 15 to 25 such genetic typos on to any child he fathers; for a 45-year-old, the figure is 65. Mothers, no matter how old they are, pass along only about 15."[44]

Our young people grew up with high hopes, hoping to come of age in a time when they could choose from an expanse of life paths. They voted for Obama *precisely because* they trusted him to help them fulfill their hopes. Sadly, unless we reverse directions, Millennials today will be permanently set back by Obama's pallid economy and the culture he and Michelle created, a culture hostile to family life. Our daughters, sons, and grandchildren now feel forced to delay marriage and parenthood because of our anemic economy. As the government grew larger under Obama, record numbers of men and women found that their lifestyle options were limited.

Marriage seemed risky and unaffordable when young people factored in the cost of a wedding (around $28,000 in 2012) plus the potential cost of raising a family on top of their student debt, homelessness, and/or uncertain job situation. Parenthood seemed even more unaffordable. Young women who did become pregnant often did so without the benefit of committed fathers, and Obama played a role in aggravating this problem, as discussed earlier.

A healthy economy, one that fosters choice and provides freedom for all Americans, is one where everyone—from the poorest to the richest—is steadily doing better. Under Obama, only the rich did better. The number of Americans freely *giving up* their U.S. citizenship jumped at least *eightfold* between 2008 and 2013 because of Obama's unfriendly tax policies.[45] Meanwhile, businesses dropped expansion plans that would have generated new jobs due to the anticipated costs of Obamacare; 36 percent of young adults were living with their parents; the average household wealth dropped 55 percent, and the bulk of the new jobs created were part-time or low-paying gigs.[46]

Here are the facts:

- The birthrate dropped during the Great Depression, but it dropped to its lowest point on record under Obama.[47]
- Between 2009 and 2010, the marriage rate dropped to record lows, and the steepest decline was among young people who could not afford to get married: The marriage rate for all American adults dropped by 5 percent while the marriage rate for young

people between the ages of eighteen and twenty-four dropped by
13 percent.[48]

- Thirty-four percent of young people delayed parenthood, marriage, or both because of the economy, the Pew Research Center found in its 2012 study *The Boomerang Generation.*[49]
- Sixty-nine percent of unmarried Millennials want to marry, but say they feel deterred by their lack of a "solid economic foundation," according to a March 2014 Pew Research report.[50]

In the last chapter, we exposed Obama's hand in prolonging the housing crisis. One reason Millennials were not marrying or having children was because they were under water in student debt and could not afford to move out of their parents' basements or small rentals. Their homes were too small to share. Young people have historically driven suburban growth in America as they leave their apartments in the cities to form their own families and seek roomier homes with fenced-in backyards, yet *Time* magazine announced in 2012: "For the first time since the 1920s, U.S. cities are growing faster than suburbs."[51]

Numerous Millennials *did* have children. However, by 2013, about half of all American children were born out of wedlock as the economy discouraged young people from marriage, and, statistically, the fathers of these children are likely to be unstable and uninvolved.[52]

Someone could counter: "Women don't need a marriage certificate to have a father figure in their lives!" This is technically true and also irrelevant. The fact remains that if a woman wants to have a child and she wants her child to grow up with a father, the data illustrates that she is far more likely to achieve this goal if she is married than if she is cohabitating.

In April of 2013, the Centers for Disease Control and Prevention released its first-ever report on cohabitation in the United States.[53] This new CDC study suggests that the economy plays a very large role in young women's decisions to cohabitate: the highest percentage of women choosing cohabitation were very young (under age twenty), minorities (black or U.S.-born Hispanic), and poorly educated (without a high school diploma). These more vulnerable subgroups of women were also more likely to experience a pregnancy during their first year of cohabitation compared to cohabiting women who were of white or Asian descent or had higher educations.

According to this study, most cohabitations still do not result in marriage, even those that have lasted for three years. Whether they end in marriage or not, they don't last long: in 2002, the average cohabitation lasted twenty months. In the years 2006–2010, the average cohabitation lasted 22 months. So, if a young woman becomes pregnant, she is likely to end up with a screaming, pooping, fatherless baby to care for and no alimony prospects as she tries to hold down a job.

In Obama's tight economy, more young couples knew they would need both parents to be working in order to provide for a family, which delayed marriage and parenthood. The numbers of older first-time dads is on the rise in the United States and globally. In addition to divorce, *Time* reported that "the poor economy [appears to be] causing men to delay fathering children."[54]

No guy thinks about marriage or children when he is eighteen and voting for the first time. Most guys just assume those options should be *available* to them when and if they want to choose them. Young men who voted for Obama did not realize that his spending and redistributive economic policies would make marriage and parenthood financially unfeasible for many of them. Unfortunately, when our young men do have the financial means to become fathers, it will be later in life, and they will face greater chances of siring children with health issues. Even if their children are healthy, Millennials who become fathers will do so later, meaning they could miss out on experiencing one of a father's greatest joys, grandchildren.

* * *

OUR young people grew up taking it for granted that marriage or parenthood would be *options* for them in their twenties and thirties, just as those lifestyles were options for their parents and grandparents at that age. Unfortunately Obama's policies and rhetoric took these options off the table for our youths, until later in life.

Why didn't Obama leverage his high-profile, picture-perfect marriage to promote committed fatherhood among our young people, especially young black men? Simple. He did not seem to care about our young people. He only cared about snatching their votes and winning two terms in the White House.

Obama's economic policies, rhetoric, and failure to courageously take a stand in support of fatherhood hurt Millennials, especially young blacks, by limiting their lifestyle choices. Specifically, more young women were burdened with raising children without the fathers who sired the children, and more children were growing up without father figures. These young women and their children are at a historic disadvantage going forward. Additionally, more young people were unemployed or underemployed and lived in tiny spaces or at home and consequently were unable to make two major choices that previous generations could: marriage and parenthood.

JFK and Jacqueline kept his weaknesses to themselves. Clinton also tried to keep his escapades quiet. To his credit, Slick Willie never jumped on top of the White House roof with a megaphone and shouted: "I define marriage as 'until death do us part' as long as the man still has girlfriends." Only Obama broadcast his bad examples of fatherhood from sea to shining sea.

STEAMROLLING
THE FOXHOLES

7

True Stories of Obama Abandoning His Warriors

O n a brisk October day in Chicago during 2007, Obama ascended a podium on the campus of DePaul University. His hair dark, the whites of his eyes bright, his complexion vernal, he needed to convince this youthful crowd that he was not a baby face but a wise leader. He also knew these students opposed the Iraq War, so he endeared himself to them by calling the war a "big mistake" and accusing Bush of lying. That part was easy. The hard part was convincing these students that he, a young man without a military record, could lead on foreign policy. So, he brought out his secret weapon: JFK. Obama had compared himself and his "courage" to that of JFK's before, in his book *The Audacity of Hope*. On this autumn day, Obama expounded on this comparison— capitalizing on the fact that DePaul students were too young to remember JFK's military record.

Obama asked JFK's former speechwriter, Ted Sorensen, to introduce him as "the only serious candidate for president."[1] In his introduction, Sorensen emphasized that Obama would be as capable on foreign policy as JFK, who, at age forty-three, was the youngest elected president. Next, Obama spoke, repeatedly employing Kennedy's name as well as a

JFK quote about the "pursuit of peace." The imagery clicked, especially with the typing wizards in the conventional media who needed a literary device to help them cast a jejune and calculating community organizer as a competent and courageous superstar.

All along the campaign trail that led him to the White House, Obama and the typing wizards likened his courage to Kennedy's. Let's take a look at the presidential military legacy that Obama stepped into and see how he and Kennedy *actually* match up.

* * *

As a young man, JFK volunteered for combat duty in the U.S. Navy and shipped to the South Pacific, where he served with tremendous courage as a commanding officer.

Around two-thirty in the morning on August 2, 1943, Kennedy was commanding the motor torpedo boat *PT 109* when a fast-moving Japanese destroyer sliced Kennedy's small vessel in half. The destroyer zoomed ahead, oblivious to the wreck in its wake. Without losing a beat, Kennedy shredded his codebook, ripped off his pants and boots, and swam to help two injured crewmen who were struggling in the water.[2] Forgetting his chronic back pain, Kennedy spent three hours helping these two men back to what was left of *PT 109*'s hull. As his head bobbed above the waves, Kennedy spotted an island. The speck of land was Plum Pudding Island and it was three miles out.[3] Kennedy rallied his ten surviving comrades (the destroyer had killed two) to swim with him toward the island. JFK operated like a hero, towing an injured comrade to the island by gripping the man's life jacket strap in his teeth as he swam for five hours.[4]

Alas, there was no food or drinking water waiting for them on Plum Pudding Island. A weaker man would have said: "Screw the Sugar Plum Fairy, this is hopeless." Not Kennedy. He repeated his teeth-hauling process with his injured mate the next day as he led them all on a swim to a second island. Safely there, the trust-fund kid took charge like an Eagle Scout, carving a request for help on a coconut shell and enlisting natives to find a rescue crew. All eleven men survived. Kennedy's back pain worsened considerably after this heroic feat and he retired from the navy on physical disability in 1945. He was awarded a Navy and Marine Corps Medal and a Purple Heart Medal. JFK later described his service in the U.S. Navy as an accomplishment that made his "life worthwhile."[5]

Bill Clinton was always ready for action, just not the kind you find in combat. Clinton did everything he could to avoid lifting a finger. With a draft notice in his hand, Clinton concocted a plan to dodge without looking like a dodger. Clinton lied to the colonel who oversaw the University of Arkansas' ROTC board, promising to enroll in the army ROTC after completing his studies at Oxford if the colonel would waive his draft notice.[6] But when Clinton left Oxford, instead of enrolling at the University of Arkansas Law School and joining the ROTC, he enrolled at Yale Law School. The colonel felt hoodwinked: "In retrospect I see that Mr. Clinton had no intention of following through with his agreement to join the Army ROTC."[7] Clinton said he opposed the Vietnam War for moral reasons. It seems like the moral thing to do would have been to express his opposition earlier. Clinton could have spent a night in prison and committed civil disobedience for his beliefs, Henry David Thoreau style. Nope. Billy was not *that* passionate about his moral opposition to war. It was easier to lie. The second time he was available to be drafted, he lucked out and received a high draft lottery number. Clinton never served in the military.

While Willie was having phone sex with a girl so young she could have been his daughter, the men and women he employed at the FBI and CIA were working hard to track bin Laden. Hank Crumpton, a former top counterterrorism CIA officer, told CBS News how he felt when the CIA notified the Clinton administration of a perfect chance to kill Osama bin Laden in 1999, and was promptly shut down: "The frustration was enormous."[8] Had Clinton authorized precision force against Osama bin Laden in 1999, we would have nipped that lunatic in the bud and 9/11 may never have happened. Quick and dirty. Over and done. Avoiding scores of American deaths and a decade of war in the Middle East. Unfortunately, Clinton was too busy drooling over

Monica and maintaining his antiwar persona to let a sniper put a bullet through bin Laden. Being liked was more alluring to Clinton than being feared, even if his popularity jeopardized national security. Objective Republican historians concede, however, that Clinton's administration deserves credit for retaining a strong intelligence community.[9]

In 2000, George W. Bush said in a debate against Al Gore: "If we don't stop extending our troops all around the world and [conducting] nation-building missions, then we are going to have a serious problem coming down the road and I'm going to prevent that." That was before 9/11. G. W. took us into Afghanistan and Iraq after 9/11 and kept us in both countries for nation-building missions. In retrospect, after G. W. routed the Taliban in Afghanistan, he could have taken some of his own advice from 2000. We do need to name the elephant in the room: G. W. kept us in the Middle East longer than even *he* said he would. That said, the troops *loved* G. W. They could sense his sincerity, his respect for their work, and his zeal for fighting terror.

Now, let's move on. Whether you are a hawk or a dove, the point to laser-focus on as we uncover Obama's success at conning Millennials into voting for him is this: By 2008, young people—the crucial swing voters—were tired of war and looking for a harbinger of peace. To them, John McCain sounded like an ornery battle-ax whereas Hawaiian surfer boy Barry sounded like a fun guy who would end the wars.

Obama became president and behaved like a major-league bum toward the U.S. military. There is no need to qualify that statement with an asterisk. There is no use softening the blow. Obama disrespected and abused the military. As commander in chief, he steamrolled the young people who served their country from Middle Eastern foxholes.

* * *

THE worst kind of commander in chief is the one who sits at home in his chair while he sends others to face challenges he would never face himself; one who is so politically correct that he betrays his own troops to appease foreign governments; one who leaves men behind. Barack Obama was this kind of commander in chief.

As commander in chief, JFK respected the armed forces and took their lives and his leadership role seriously. He never dreamt of treating the troops like toys and worked tirelessly to avoid war with the Soviet Union. Clinton was not brave, but he did not send thousands of young people into impossible situations while he played golf, only to strip disabled Marines of their medical benefits or accuse army commanders of murder and throw them in jail if they fired at the Taliban. Only Obama was that screw-happy. Overall, Obama's foreign policy appeared to be: Send more young Americans into chaos without sufficient resources and then cover it up.

Before he ran for president, Obama wrote a book as a way to groom the public's perception of him. In the book, he utilized his favorite comparison—to JFK—to intimate that they shared a common courageousness.[10] Since the book became a bestseller, it was very helpful in portraying Obama as hero, without him doing anything heroic. Obama detailed how, as a legislator, he would reflect on a passage from JFK's book *Profiles in Courage* before he cast his votes. He also wrote "JFK [was] . . . mindful of his heroism in war but perhaps pondering the more ambiguous challenges ahead—the quality of courage. In some ways, the longer you are in politics, the easier it should be to muster such courage . . . [and] courage itself may be seen as calculation. I find comfort in the fact that the longer I'm in politics the less nourishing popularity becomes."[11] The message Obama gave his readers was subtle yet clear: *I have the courage of JFK.* JFK was "mindful of his heroism" and Obama was mindful of his own lack thereof, which is why he linked himself to JFK in the first place.

Barry must have smoked something other than Marlboros and slurped a supersized narcissism smoothie as he wrote this book. Here he was, a man who never served in the military, linking his courage to that of a man who battled shark-infested waters, towed an injured sailor for five hours with his teeth and permanently injured his back while rescuing ten men in the South Pacific. Hobnobbing with wonks over poker games by night and voting "yay" or "nay" on bills by day from the comfort of a leather chair is not courageous, it's cushy.

In addition to branding himself as a courageous hero in his tome, Obama used his speeches to sell young voters on promises of peace. He knew that Millennials, as a group, tend to favor less interventionist foreign policies over "building the U.S. empire" abroad. So, Obama used his teleprompter and his oratorical talents to convince young people to vote for him in both 2008 and 2012 by promising to end the war in Iraq and start bringing home the troops in Afghanistan.

Lip Service

If Monica Lewinsky had done what she was planning to do and taken her navy blue dress to the drycleaner, many Americans would never have believed that Clinton was a liar. With Obama, there were no visuals to help demonstrate his dishonesty. There were no "blue dresses." With Obama, it took more digging into the facts to realize: Whoa. This guy just says whatever he thinks will make him sound good.

The only military service Obama ever performed was lip service. He convinced young people to vote for him by using his lips to form persuasive sentences about ending war and creating peace. Gearing up to run for Senate in 2004, Obama publicly opposed the war in Iraq, calling it a "dumb war . . . based not on reason but on passion."[12] He didn't say this because he had an unyielding moral opposition to war. In truth, Obama was on the fence about coming out against Bush's war until Michelle pointed out that he would win political favor with African American voters as well as Chicago donors.[13]

When he ran for president, Obama continued his lip service, promising to bring all U.S. combat troops home from Iraq within sixteen months. When he declared his candidacy in February of 2007, Obama led Millennials to believe that he would solve "a war with no end" with "diplomacy, and strategy and foresight."[14] He sighed over "young lives" lost in a conflict that was a "tragic mistake" and pitched "a plan that will bring our combat troops home by March of 2008." Michelle panicked when Bill Clinton questioned the authenticity of her hubby's opposition to the war, at one point tearing her nails through the air while declaring: "I want to rip his eyes out!"[15] Barack and Michelle were a team of calculating pugilists who painted themselves as courageous peacemakers.

In March of 2008, the combat troops were still in Iraq and he was in Philadelphia, Pennsylvania, delivering a new version of his message before an audience at the National Constitution Center, saying that as president he would "bring them [the troops] home from a war that never should've been authorized and never should've been waged . . . we'll show our patriotism by caring for them, and their families, and giving them the benefits they have earned."[16] Many consider this speech to have played a key role in Obama's election because so many people watched it on YouTube (over 1.2 million in a twenty-four-hour time span) or on television or heard about it another way; Pew Research reported that 85 percent of Americans had heard about this speech, making it "arguably the biggest political event of the campaign so far."[17]

As president, Obama was tardy on his promise to end the war in Iraq. He dawdled along, prioritizing action items like walking Bo, putting with Tiger, and dribbling with Timothy Geithner. He reduced the number of troops in Iraq to under fifty thousand in August of 2010 and took until December of 2011 to officially end the Iraq war.

Afghani Morphine

Poppy fields hid crouching American soldiers in Afghanistan; row after row of pink and white flowers also hid the secret ingredient to opium's euphoria: morphine.

Once he became president, Obama decided to ramp things up from lip service to injecting the American public with morphine. He took out his figurative needle and syringe (his words and foreign policy decisions) and used them to drug Americans to think that our troops would be safe under his leadership, even if he sent three times *more* troops into the foxholes of Afghanistan.

Obama is responsible for tripling the number of troops in Afghanistan, after he promised to bring our heroes home. Under his leadership, there was a concerning increase in American service people committing suicide, Taliban attacks in Afghanistan, and "red-on-blue" or "insider" attacks where Afghan "ally" forces turned on and killed the American forces who trusted and trained them.

Obama did not *need* to send thirty thousand more troops into Afghanistan in 2009; he did it anyway. And the troops paid the price. They fought impossible battles—even dying at the hands of the Afghan forces that they trusted and trained. And the Taliban grew as strong as ever; the longer Obama kept troops in Afghanistan, the greater the blowback. So, Obama had to work his words extra hard—injecting enough syntactical morphine to help young swing voters (who were becoming disheartened with his performance) forget their conscientious objections to the pain of war and feel euphoric enough to vote for him again in 2012.

He knew he had to make Millennials believe that he had routed the Taliban in Afghanistan and would be bringing home the troops. In his September 6, 2012, National Democratic Convention speech, he said: "We've blunted the Taliban's momentum in Afghanistan, and in 2014, our longest war will be over. . . . I'll use the money we're no longer spending on war to pay down our debt and put more people back to work—rebuilding roads and bridges; schools and runways. After two wars that have cost us thousands of lives and over a trillion dollars, it's time to do some nation-building right here at home."[18]

His lips were performing gymnastics with the facts, entrancing young people to perceive him as a competent commander in chief. In truth, suicides were soaring among the troops. Taliban and insider attacks against Americans were on the rise and he conveniently forgot to mention his plans to keep troops in Afghanistan past his 2014 pull-out date.

At the DNC, Obama failed to mention the human cost of his wars—the troops who were dying, or returning without limbs. Fewer Americans died during the eight years Bush oversaw the war in Afghanistan than during the three years following Obama's troop surge, when thirteen thousand Americans were injured or killed.[19] "The world becomes a very different place when you lose a limb," Boston Medical Center rehabilitation director Karen Mattie told the *Chicago Tribune*.

Obama's claim to be winding down war and focusing on roads and bridges was odd given his Pentagon's recent lifting of the ban on women in combat, which most likely will lead to a requirement for all young women to sign up for the Selective Service at age eighteen. If he was planning to pull us out of war, why did he need to recruit even more young people onto the front lines?

His claim that he planned to use the money he was "saving" on pull-out to pay down the debt was another tall tale. Obama's CIA had a practice of handing secret bags of cash to Afghan leader Hamid Karzai. This practice continued well beyond the 2012 election. Such an ethical way to spend the "savings"—by handing it back to the man who befriended our enemies and also accepted cash from Iran, namely Karzai![20] The *New York Times* reported that Karzai may have used CIA cash to bribe and consequently fund Taliban warlords.[21]

Obama neglected to mention the ways he would keep wasting money in Afghanistan such as shredding and scrapping $7 billion in military equipment in the summer of 2013.[22] American troops sometimes put their lives at risk and patrolled on foot in order to "save" expensive equipment like Mine-Resistant Ambush Protected (MRAP) armored vehicles that cost $1.5 million apiece and guarded troops from roadside bombs. For what? So Obama could have fun shredding MRAPs and dumping billions down the drain?

Because of his expert lip service, Obama won two elections and got away with treating the military like dirt without getting impeached. Fortunately, this chapter is a gift to all the skeptics; a gift to all the doubting Thomases; a gift to all the Americans who still think Obama is a nice guy. Here is the blood and gore. Here are Obama's blue dresses.

The Presidential Man Cave

There is a "presidential man cave" at the White House—a place where the president relaxes. Each incoming president redecorates the man cave according to his tastes.

No historian recalls a conversation where Kennedy asked his interior decorator to go for a "gentlemen's club look" when redecorating his presidential man cave. But it's easy to imagine JFK telling his redecorator: "Please include a revolving library bookcase door. Good to let visiting dignitaries assume I'm reading Aristotle if I decide to invite a young lady up for a daiquiri."

Heading into his second term, Ronald Reagan moved his man cave to the "Second White House," a rustic ranch atop a high, windy hill forty-five minutes from Santa Barbara. His wife Nancy as well as world leaders joined him in relaxing at the ranch. By car, it was a long, winding, uphill trek to the ranch. Any dignitary hoping to cure his car sickness with five-star comfort was surely disappointed: It was a cowboy's club. The amenities were horses, fresh air, and big sky.

Clinton was too impatient to bother with redecorating or relocating the presidential man cave. If he had gone for a style it would have been "the gentlemen's club look" like Kennedy. Clinton efficiently repurposed various White House corridors and the Oval Office bathroom—wherever he and his lover happened to be together—as his man cave.

When Obama became commander in chief, he knew he was not a real cowboy. He also was not a playboy.

BARRY: Hmm. I wonder how I should decorate my man cave. Should I plan on inviting guests or just make it a place for me to relax alone. Bo! Come here. What do you think?

Bo: Grrrrrr. Roof! Roof!

BARRY: What? Use the man cave for a Military Bum's Club? Bo, you're brilliant! Of course! I behave like a bum. My top brass act like bums. And we need a place to rest our bums after a long day. I should seek your advice more often. (*To himself*): A Military Bum's Club! I love it. But it must be exclusive. No way will I be including those second bananas fighting for me in the foxholes of Iraq and Afghanistan. My man cave will be a place where I devise plans to make myself feel like a man by steamrolling the Millennials in the military.

This may sound like fantasy, but the fact is that Obama did have a network that can be figuratively described as the "Military Bum's Club." He and some of his top brass collaborated to achieve their political ends by making life hell for young people serving in the military.

The top brass included:

- Former secretary of state Hillary Clinton
- Former defense secretary Leon Panetta
- Marine Corps commandant General James Amos

The worst of these three was Hillary. Hillary convinced Obama to let her run around finding young American soldiers to metaphorically kick in the bum. There is not space to mention all the young people who served in Middle Eastern foxholes when Obama was commander in chief. So, we will highlight three stories to help illustrate how Obama and his top brass mistreated the military. I am exposing these stories to prevent future commanders-in-chief from making Obama's mistakes.

Sergeant Bowe Bergdahl

While other five-year-olds were learning to print their names, Bowe Bergdahl was learning to shoot a .22 rifle.[23] He grew up in Hailey, Idaho—just east of the Smoky Mountains. His natural habitat featured ten-thousand-foot peaks, lithe mountain goats, and breathtaking cerulean lakes. Bowe had a strong faith in God and a deep love for his family. Homeschooled by his parents for six hours a day, he developed a love for ethics and philosophy.[24] He was curious about everything and learning excited him. A free spirit, as a teenager, he loved to jump on his dirt bike and explore.

Bowe enlisted in the U.S. Army toward the end of 2008 because "he honestly thought he could help the people of Afghanistan," according to his father. He deployed to Afghanistan in 2009 and, about two months later, twenty-three-year-old Bowe disappeared from his base on June 30, 2009. He became the first American service member to be captured by the Taliban during the war in Afghanistan. For over four years, Bowe sat in the hands of Taliban thugs who physically tortured him while Obama drank cold beer with Bo in his presidential man cave. (To be fair, "Bo" and "Bowe" are pronounced the same and perhaps this confused Obama, especially after several beers.)

No one knows the specifics of how Bowe was captured, but the Taliban released several videos proving he was alive and in their hands. What we do know is that at the time of Bowe's disappearance, he was extremely frustrated by a notable lack of discipline in his unit; things got so out of hand in Bowe's group that a British documentary filmmaker captured it on camera for the *Guardian*.

Bowe was a mountain man and by-the-books geek who had prepped for deployment by dissecting military manuals, learning the Pashto language, and exploring ways to educate Middle Eastern girls. Unfortunately, in Afghanistan, he found himself surrounded by many men who did not share his conscientiousness; the unit was a poor fit for his personality and morale. Overwhelmed by a feeling that he could not utilize his talents in Afghanistan, he sent what would be his last e-mail to his parents: "You are cut down for being honest . . . but if you are a conceited brown nosing shit bag you will be allowed to do what ever [sic] you want, and you will be handed your higher rank."[25] It appears that he intended to formally leave the army but in his immediate frustration, instead of committing suicide or overdosing on meds like other depressed soldiers, he may have done his version of the same thing.[26] Unnamed members of Bowe's unit claimed he broke protocol by slipping away alone as the sun prepared to rise on the morning of June 30 with his journal and without a weapon. No doubt, he was hoping to find some respite in the Afghan mountains that reminded him of Idaho's topography. Whatever the truth regarding his disappearance, we know the Taliban captured him that morning.

Days later, the U.S. military had an opportunity to make an exchange for Bowe that involved handing over fifteen Taliban who were jailed in Afghanistan plus a pecuniary bounty. Why didn't Obama authorize this exchange? After this initial opportunity to broker an exchange, the Taliban expressed interest in releasing Bowe on conditions such as the release of five prisoners in Guantánamo Bay and the United States pulling out of Afghanistan. Why didn't we find a way to broker a deal on *our* terms? We were reportedly handing cash to Karzai that he was in turn handing over to Taliban warlords, so why didn't we tell Karzai: "Get your hinder in gear and help us make a deal or no more money." Why, three years later, was *Rolling Stone* reporting that Obama's cabinet members Secretary of State Hillary Clinton and Defense Secretary Leon Panetta were holding up an exchange for political reasons?

Bowe's mother and father kept a low profile, especially at first, trusting the Obama administration would quickly broker their son's release. In 2012, when Bowe's meek parents finally complained that the president had not even *called* them since their son's 2009 capture, Obama put down his putter and picked up his phone.[27] Why did Obama make a speech to soothe the parents of the deceased Trayvon Martin when he could not take time to meet with Bowe's parents when they were in Washington, D.C., to rally for their son's release? Young Americans of all colors are murdered every day, yet our president singled out Trayvon's parents for a special speech that was broadcast around the world. A young American was captured by the Taliban in the course of a decade-long war and Obama acts like it is beneath him to make a peep in public. Could it be that he wanted to hide Bowe from the public before his reelection? C'mon. Let's be real.

In the spring of 2012, Bowe's father sensed that the Obama administration had a "window of opportunity" to broker a deal with the Taliban. In a rare interview, he expressed his biggest concern to *Time* magazine's Nate Rawlings: "that window is not going to wait for a national election to come to an end. . . . I don't think we can count on the dynamics on the ground in Afghanistan to be the same in November as they necessarily are now. This is a war, and war doesn't wait on politics."[28] Bowe's father had good instincts.

Polls were showing that Millennials were losing some enthusiasm for Obama. The president had to know that Millennial swing voters would be outraged if they discovered that a member of *their* generation was a Taliban captive in the war Obama had promised to end four years earlier.

Why did Obama essentially ignore Bowe's plight and devote his 2012 campaign to advertising his one foreign policy win: authorizing Navy SEALs to capture Osama bin Laden? From the way he talked, you would have thought he strangled bin Laden with his own bare hands and the Taliban was history. Meanwhile, hardly anyone knew that Bowe was sitting in the Taliban's hands.

On Tuesday, November 6, 2012, Barack Obama won a second term.

Yellow ribbons dancing in the breeze were a lone sign of hope in the quaint town of Hailey as Bowe's friends and family glanced at their calendars on June 30, 2013—the four-year anniversary of Bowe's captivity and Obama's silence. That month, two thousand people, including many U.S. veterans, gathered at a rally in Hailey to support Bowe's release and listen to Bowe's parents speak publicly. Bowe's father wore all black, plus a black-and-white POW bandanna on his head. His chin hid beneath a bushy beard he had grown in camaraderie with his son, who had developed a beard in captivity.[29] Bowe's mother wore a wide black belt over her light gray dress. She choked up and shed tears while trying to assure Bowe's supporters that she remained "very optimistic." Her husband added: "Mothers all over the world are suffering because of this war, and I don't forget that for even one day."[30] It was like a scene from a funeral, where the attendees are waiting for their loved one to rise from the dead.

* * *

IN Washington, D.C., at a 2013 POW rally, Bowe's father said: "Secretary of State John Kerry and the Secretary of Defense Chuck Hagel should be fully authorized by the President, Barack Obama, to negotiate the safe humane return of the political prisoners held by the Taliban because it is an American principle of *law* and an *ethos*: No man left behind."

No one had the heart to tell Bowe's father that Obama's top three priorities as commander in chief were: Obama, Barry, and Barack, in no particular order. As long as young people in uniform were saluting him with smiles; as long as he could bully the troops into serving as his backdrop for campaign speeches; as long as he was winning elections—in his mind, there *was* "no man left behind."

Obama could have pushed harder to negotiate with the Taliban. He could have devoted a tenth of the time he spent boasting over ousting bin Laden to releasing Bowe Bergdahl. If Obama knew Karzai was taking *our* cash and funding Taliban warlords, then he could have forced Karzai to help broker Bowe's release—or withheld the cash. After telling young voters he would not repeat Bush's mistake of losing "young lives," Obama became the first U.S. president to leave an American soldier to spend his twenties wilting away in Afghan Taliban captivity and torture. When Bowe finally does come home, he will never be able to get those lost years back. Never.

Army Lieutenant Clint Lorance

Clint Lorance grew up in the Texas countryside. His mother and father had him figured out at the age of four. Their son was a caregiver. They watched him play outside with his younger brother, Cody, and Clint never tired of having "Cody play like he got hurt" so he could use his play emergency vehicle to "fix him up," recalled his mother, Anna. His parents smiled as they watched their little boy lead his younger brother in building crosses out of sticks, digging tiny graves, and holding ceremonies for critters and birds that died in the family's pasture.

Anna said: "We are not a wealthy family with money but a very wealthy family with love. We taught our children that 'can't' is not a option. If it can be done by others, then you can do it as well."

No one in Clint's family had gone to college and Clint was determined to go. He was naturally studious and inquisitive. He divided his time between poring over history and legal books (for fun); working at one of his three jobs; and learning to defend his community through an after-school program called the Greenville Police Explorers. Clint *had* to learn, engage, and give. His heart was the size of Texas and his mind was racing at two hundred miles an hour.

Shortly after he enrolled in community college, the United States invaded Iraq and he felt a growing obligation to serve his country. Clint decided to temporarily sideline his lifelong goal of completing college. The day he turned eighteen, he walked into the Greenville, Texas, recruiting station and enlisted in the U.S. Army. "It was like he felt he wasn't doing what he could if he did not make that stand," said Anna. "When he left for boot camp, I was so proud—but so broken."

Before long, Clint was thriving. He kept his mother informed of all his accomplishments and award certificates. Now, she has them all with her in Texas, "two notebooks full." "They were sent from his superiors requesting his promotion. All stating his excellent performance and being highly recommended as an outstanding young man. Not one bad word or one bad report." Clint's superiors described him as trustworthy, highly skilled, very organized, and by-the-book (a vital trait in the military, where order and respect for leadership keep everyone safe and on mission during the fog of war). Two years into his military career, Clint was already a sergeant.

Clint's grandmother began noticing an extra $250 in her bank account every month. She told Anna: "I don't know who it's coming from, but it says it's coming from the Army." Clint's grandfather had recently passed and, without telling anyone, Clint had assumed the role of financially helping his grandmother despite knowing his grandfather had left her with enough. He did it "out of pure respect," said Anna.

When Clint returned from Iraq, he enrolled in the army ROTC program at the University of North Texas. In May of 2010, he became the first Lorance to earn a college diploma. He immediately received his commission as a second lieutenant in the army infantry and trained in Fort Benning, Georgia. In March of 2012, he deployed to southern Afghanistan, where he became frustrated because he was sitting behind a desk instead of serving in action. Soon, Clint volunteered for combat duty. Anna wished Clint would stay put: "I did not want him out there [in combat] as I felt, as his momma, that he was safe there in his placement."

One day Anna's telephone rang. It was her son, saying he would be replacing a wounded lieutenant on a very dangerous mission in a remote part of Afghanistan's Kandahar Province in late June of 2012. Anna was worried but Clint was energized: "Mom, pray that I can bring all the soldiers back home to their families." Clint would be commanding a rifle platoon where several men had recently been killed and morale was low. The region was so saturated with insurgents that the local population of civilians had moved away. If you did see a human being, your first thought was: *Taliban*. Mines were everywhere; one wrong step and you were breakfast for vultures.

That was where Clint was headed. He was up for the challenge but he took extra precautions to prepare himself. In the days before he took command, he crammed every minute with gathering maps and all the information on the region that he could find. Clint was also aware that in the beginning of July, Obama's generals were officially launching a nebulous program called "Afghan in the Lead." Clint wanted more clarity on what "Afghan in the Lead" entailed and he asked his company commander for guidance. The commander's answer offered little help: "If the Afghans don't want to patrol, we don't patrol."

What did that mean? If the Afghans were feeling lazy, were the Americans supposed to let themselves get creamed or were they supposed to pick up the slack? Or, if the trigger-happy Afghans felt like fighting, were the Americans supposed to blindly follow, even when it violated common sense? Clint did not know but he was too respectful to query his commander in this way. He had tried his best to prepare. It was time to leave for his new command.

Clint was not anticipating the welcome he received at his new platoon on June 28. A soldier greeted him by asking: "What's your [first] name?" Clint responded: "What do you mean, my name is Lieutenant Lorance and that is how you will address me." The previous platoon leader had replaced military order with a casual atmosphere where everyone was on a first-name basis. Clint was like a new football coach walking into a locker room where the old coach had lost his clout by becoming everyone's buddy. This is not how the army trains soldiers to behave and this is not how Clint played ball. His subordinates could sense he was there to lead, not shoot the breeze, and they disliked him immediately.

Clint gathered his platoon members together and promised them: "I will see to it that you all get home to your families with both of your legs." Unfortunately, they were unfamiliar with his serious style and mistook him as speaking down to them and criticizing their previous leader. They disliked him even more. Four days later, July 2, Clint led his platoon on their first patrol together. (Keep in mind that July 2 was *one day* after the "official" start date of "Afghan in the Lead"—July 1, 2012—so, Lieutenant Lorance and his troops were very new to the program.) They set out for a village that had been overrun by the Taliban. Clint and his men were walking through a field on foot holding mine detectors in front of them as they walked. (Looking back, they could have traveled more safely in the MRAPs that Obama would eventually shred, but the army had trained them to "save" those vehicles because they were so expensive.) U.S. Army helicopters were circling overhead.

As they approached the village, Clint's soldiers radioed him that they had spotted three Afghans on a motorcycle coming down the road. This was Clint's first time commanding an active-duty platoon; he had barely forty-eight hours' worth of experience under his belt and he had to think fast and make a call. He knew that the road had a sharp turn and the motorcycle was going at a fast pace, thirty-five to forty-five miles per hour, pointed at his men. There was no way the motorcycle was making the turn; Clint knew it was headed for the field where he and his men were patrolling.

In the span of a few seconds, a flood of information passed through Clint's head. He knew that a few days before his arrival a member of his new platoon had been fatally shot in the neck while patrolling in this same village. He also knew that a common tactic of the Taliban was to utilize "spotters" on motorcycles who communicate sightings via ICOM walkie-talkies and carry grenades, which they toss at American forces. Finally, from local intelligence reports, Clint knew that the only inhabitants who used this road were Taliban, and the helicopter pilots were communicating with Clint via radio and reporting that there were enemy combatants on the road whose description exactly matched those of the motorcyclists.

After weighing this information, he did what he felt would save the most lives. Unfortunately for him, this involved departing from "Afghan in the Lead." He knew his Afghan fighters were poor shots and had a tendency to be trigger happy. There was a wall behind the motorcyclists and Clint did not want to rely on his Afghan marksmen on the small chance that there were civilians behind the wall. Instead of letting the Afghans "lead," he authorized them to stand down and ordered his highly trained American snipers to engage and take out the motorcyclists. The first shot fired missed and the motorcycle stopped. Clint ordered a second engage and two of the men were killed. The third man ran through the village and escaped out the other side. A few minutes later, Clint's platoon killed two confirmed Taliban fighters, captured a third Taliban fighter who was driving a motorcycle, and captured and injured a fourth Taliban fighter. The two they captured tested positive for gunshot residue on their hands, indicating they had recently fired a weapon.

Later, when Clint's men searched the first two deceased Afghani motorcyclists, they reported finding a razor blade, scissors, a flashlight, and a round, empty gourd but no grenades. Although they were reportedly unarmed and without ICOM radios, the motorcyclists were likely

Taliban spotters since Clint's platoon had taken out four confirmed Taliban right behind them and ICOM had been spotted from a rooftop. We don't know what the third motorcyclist who escaped carried; there is a good chance it was ICOM or grenades. Still, the fact that these two men were unarmed was *used* to cause a stir, and army headquarters further claimed that the two men Clint captured were "innocent" despite testing positive for gunshot residue and behaving suspiciously like all Taliban fighters in the region.

Perhaps Clint's platoon conspired to get rid of him. Perhaps the Afghan forces ratted him out to the Afghan government for violating "Afghan in the Lead." Call it mutiny; call it politics; call it whatever you want. But a few hours after Clint returned to his base, the army put him on suspension and took his weapon away with no explanation. For five days, he sat puzzled. What had he done wrong? Next, he was hauled to brigade headquarters and from there to Kandahar, where he sat idle for two months with no explanation. When his deployment ended, on September 23, 2012, he was shipped back to Fort Bragg, North Carolina, where he would be reassigned to administrative duties. By this time, Clint was very concerned. When he landed in North Carolina, he caught the first plane to Texas. He had to speak with his family before they heard some wild version of his story on TV.

Anna was guiding a watering hose over her flowers on that sunny September day. Out of the corner of her eye, she spotted a car winding up her road. Then she saw the red lieutenant's cap on the driver. Anna dropped her hose and ran. "Dad! Dad! It's Clint!" she hollered toward the barn where Clint's father was working. Anna met her son's car before he could put it in park. "He picked me plum off the ground and gave me a big 'ole hug. He really had no choice, I jumped up in his arms for that big 'ole hug. We were so shocked that he was in Texas. We had planned to go see him in North Carolina in a couple days."

Clint gathered a family meeting that evening and told them the whole story of what occurred during his deployment. He said he thought there would be no charges but his family was very frustrated. They could not believe he had been relieved of his duties without explanation. He had served honorably in the army for ten years! Never a bad word and suddenly this? They remained optimistic.

But on January 15, 2013, Clint was general court-martialed. A general court-martial, for those not familiar with the military, is the most serious type of court-martial. It is convened by a general and reserved to try felonies, the most serious criminal cases. Punishment can include the death penalty in a worst-case scenario or lengthy imprisonment and a permanent criminal record in a best-case scenario.

If the army wanted to slap Clint on the wrist for misinterpreting "Afghan in the Lead," there were three lesser disciplinary processes it could have considered and did not: special court-martial (generally the maximum sentence is one year in prison and the conviction usually counts as a misdemeanor); summary court-martial (a nonjudicial proceeding that, even with a conviction, does not count as criminal either in or out of the military); and Article 15 (a nonjudicial proceeding referred to as "Office Hours" in the Marine Corps).

During Clint's court-martial, a colonel was asked whether he knew what "Afghan in the Lead" meant and he responded that he did not know. If a colonel did not know, how did the Obama administration expect a lieutenant to know?

If Clint had been killed that day, the military would have draped the American flag over his body and brought him home in honor. Wasn't it the same military under the same commander in chief that practically did cartwheels through a shower of champagne after Obama made the oh-so-hard call to take out bin Laden? Clint had made a similar call, and without a roomful of advisers coaching him. Obama did not have to worry about bin Laden whipping a grenade in his face if he made the wrong call. Clint did. Instead of calling Clint a murderer, the military should have called him a hero. For his leadership under pressure, Clint certainly is worthy of the title. His platoon ousted four Taliban fighters and two motorcyclists who had to be Taliban spotters since civilians had abandoned the village and Taliban fighters were right behind them.

Clint knew he was innocent and he pleaded innocent. In the courtroom, he turned around toward his family and said: "Promise me you will all remain strong and positive. I did my best and we will all get through this. It's out of our control." Clint listened as his platoon members testified against him in order to avoid their own charges. A jury charged Clint with murder and sentenced him to twenty years in prison, forfeiture of all pay, and dismissal from the army.

Obama would not tell us how many innocent children and civilians his drone missions killed in the Middle East. But we know he authorized seven times more drone strikes than Bush and we know humanitarian watchdog groups like the Bureau of Investigative Journalism estimate the number of civilian and children deaths by Obama's drones as three hundred to seven hundred between January of 2009 and January of 2013. In the spring of 2013, Obama tried to justify civilian deaths by his drones: "As Commander-in-Chief, I must weigh these heartbreaking tragedies against the alternatives. To do nothing in the face of terrorist networks would invite far more civilian casualties." Obama told us he was a Christian. He must have been familiar with the Lord's Prayer: "Forgive us our trespasses as we forgive those who trespass against us." By his own standards, shouldn't Obama be sitting in prison for twenty years, without pay?

War, by definition, is messy. "Murder" in the civilian sense makes no sense in war. Innocent people are killed, unintentionally, during war and it is not murder. It's the dark side of war that Obama unnecessarily escalated by authorizing a troop surge and drone strikes in Afghanistan. You do not need to serve in a war to understand this. You can use your noggin.

Obama never tried to understand the messy side of war. He kept his world tidy and compartmentalized. His housekeeper was there to pick up his socks and make his bed when he felt lazy. He kept his hands clean and blamed others for the dirty deeds he authorized.

Please *do* tell us, Mr. Obama: How did it make you feel to send soldiers into impossible situations and then imprison them? Did this make you feel like a man?

Marine Sergeant Robert Richards

M ost of us have no idea what war is like—we can't possibly judge a wounded warrior. But the media asked us to judge Marine Sergeant Rob Richards after he and three of his comrades—in the heat of the moment and under incomprehensible stress—urinated on the bodies of dead terrorists in Afghanistan.

This is the true story of Sergeant Rob Richards. He is a severely disabled Marine sniper, war hero, and Purple Heart recipient. He spearheaded innovative tank operations in Afghanistan and saved countless American lives on the battlefield. On his third deployment to Afghanistan, Rob was videotaped in a July 2011 incident where he and three fellow Marines urinated on the dead bodies of Taliban thugs. Rob never intended for the video to go public. Unfortunately, before the video could be destroyed, another Marine obtained a copy of the video and eventually sold it to TMZ in 2012. From there, the video went viral on YouTube.

As the video views escalated, the conventional media started blowing the story out of proportion and suddenly the Marine Corps had a scandal on its hands. Of the four officers shown in the video, two were higher ranking than Richards. The Marine Corps let these higher-ranking Marines off the hook and gave them their awards and promotions. For no apparent reason, the Marine Corps chose Richards and his family to be its scapegoat.

The Obama administration and the media dragged Rob and his family through a circus of slander for nineteen months. He faced up to two years of imprisonment and the loss of his retirement and medical benefits for his involvement in the video incident. In return for his sacrifice and service, Richards faced jail time for making a human error under the stress of war.

Rob's Untold Story

Rob's mother, Catherine Richards, told me: "I can't remember a generation of our family that hasn't been in military service. Rob wanted to be a Marine ever since he put toys in a Toys For Tots box when he was eight years old. He loves the Marines." His wife, Raechel Richards, told me: "He's so, *so* humble. He doesn't see himself the way others see him [as a hero]. He loves the Marine Corps; he wanted to be like his grandfather who retired after twenty years in the Army."

Rob joined the U.S. Marine Corps in January of 2007. He married the love of his life, the sweet, smart, and beautiful Raechel in April of 2007. Rob was happy. He was pursuing his dreams and had his best friend at his side.

Rob quickly began advancing through the ranks of the Marine Corps. He was a natural leader and his instructors and peers told his mother, "Rob is phenomenal, just phenomenal." Rob's empathy, bravery, and intelligence shone through in every new challenge he took on and he was selected for the First Battalion, Sixth Marines Sniper Platoon in August of 2007, just a few months after enlisting. That same month, he was promoted to corporal and named the team leader of his platoon.

Navy Nurse: "He Can't Talk"

Rob was deployed twice to Afghanistan. In March of 2010, during his second deployment, his mother received a call that she will never forget: "Military moms live with a cell phone and an extra battery at all times. I had just gotten back from a business trip. I got a call at 6:00 a.m. that woke me up. When I answered, they told me: 'We need to inform you that your son is critically wounded.'" Catherine paused before she added: "I've not gotten over that. We moms have our own form of PTSD."

Rob had been on foot patrol when he was severely wounded by an IED. A quarter-sized hexagonal nut ripped through the sheath of his carotid artery and then lodged itself in his neck, permanently destroying his Adam's apple and vocal cords. Rob's body is still full of shrapnel from this IED injury and to this day he deals with persistent back pain and PTSD.

Immediately after the IED injury, Rob was hoisted up into a chopper and flown to Germany, were doctors determined that he had a traumatic brain injury (TBI). The German doctors recorded the TBI, but, for whatever reason, Rob's doctors back in America overlooked this. Despite repeated questioning by Rob's family about whether he may have incurred brain trauma, his family did not learn he had a TBI until Raechel pored through his medical records in early 2013. Rob became an unknowing victim of the epidemic of misdiagnoses within the U.S. military. Raechel says: "We asked over and over again. They kept saying he didn't have brain trauma. He wasn't ever treated for the TBI. There are certain drugs that can worsen TBI which he probably took."

From Germany, Rob was rushed via medevac to the National Naval Medical Center in Bethesda, Maryland. Rob was not able to speak, so his nurse called Catherine and said: "He can't talk. I will put the phone up to his ear and he will scribble down his message on a pad." Rob's first words to his mother were "I LOVE YOU MOM." His nurse took a photo and sent it to Catherine; the image went viral as countless Americans cheered for Rob to heal.

After several weeks in Bethesda, Rob devoted all his energy to healing. Because he did not know he had incurred a TBI and because he was so loyal to the Marines, he was committed to going back and was deployed a third time to Afghanistan. Catherine said: "I would have pushed harder for him to go into retirement [if she had known about the TBI. He could have gotten out but he elected to return. We were asking all these questions, and the doctors at Bethesda were saying, 'No, he's perfectly fine.'"

"He has survivor's guilt, even to this day," said Raechel. "At Bethesda, we saw double amputees. We saw Marines who had lost all their limbs. For Rob, having all of his limbs and taking his retirement? He couldn't live with that. He wanted to go back; he reenlisted."

So, Rob could have walked away from the Marines after his second deployment with an honorable record and guaranteed benefits for life— but he chose to go back into the lion's den of Afghanistan and fight alongside his brothers for his country. Little did he know that the media and top military brass would betray him by turning him into a tool for profit and a scapegoat when he returned from his third deployment.

They Blew Up My Buddy, Then Strung His Limbs from Trees

Rob went to Afghanistan for the third time in March of 2011. During this time, he developed an innovative tactic whereby snipers would lie on top of tanks so that they could extend their line of sight to four miles out. Major General John Toolan praised Rob's innovation on the official *Military Times* blog and credited Rob's idea for allowing individual snipers to get "upwards of 100 kills" in ten days.[31]

In Afghanistan, Rob and his sniper team witnessed horrors that you and I will never understand or see: one of their close buddies (Sergeant Mark Bradley) died in the hospital from an IED; another comrade lost both legs to an IED and then enemy insurgents strung his legs up in tree branches. On top of this all, Rob was dealing with brain trauma (although he did not know it).

Raechel told me the (real) story that the liberal media never told us about the fateful day leading up to the video of Marines urinating on the Taliban bodies. She told me it was a particularly intense and stressful day; Rob and three of his teammates "were in dangerous territory. They had been tracking these guys for a while and had identified the insurgents who hung their friend's parts from trees."

En route to find these three insurgents, Rob and his team encountered three armed enemy personnel walking with an eight-year-old boy. Rob said: "I shot and killed all three of the [insurgents], and the boy sat there for maybe a minute or two in shock, screaming over one of the dead bodies which we found out later was likely his father. He then picked up the AK-47 and at first I did nothing. [Suddenly,] he chicken winged it [tucked the stock under his armpit] and took it off safe. He aimed and [I could tell] he had a decent amount of practice, probably taught to him by his now-dead father. I realized that even if he was a poor shot, a stray bullet or two could wound or kill me or one of my guys. So I shot him once in the chest." When the child aimed the AK-47 at him, Rob had to make a quick and difficult decision—shoot and wound the child out of self-defense or lose a fellow Marine. As Raechel put it: "Children flock to Rob and they love him. I know the type of stress he must have felt having to shoot at this child. He had to make a choice." Rob initially felt bad for the boy and so instead of shooting him a second time, fatally: "I ordered my engineer to blow a hole in the compound wall and go retrieve the boy. He did so and when the boy was brought in the compound he was screaming, calling my corpsman an 'infidel.'" This behavior angered and frustrated Rob: "I guess I knew that this boy would just grow up and become another terrorist." Nevertheless, he and his team treated the child and ultimately saved his life. The child's family retrieved him weeks later, never thanked Rob, and the boy was soon seen back in the same area with a radio, helping the enemy.

That was the sort of stress Rob was dealing with on the day of this video incident.

When Rob and his three fellow Marines finally found the insurgents—the terrorists who had treated their friend's body parts like Christmas tree ornaments—they released the pain and grief they were feeling by urinating on the dead savages. Then, in the heat of the moment, a fifth Marine captured the act on camera.

But that was it. They never intended for the video to go public. They never expected American media elitists who have never fought a day in their life in a real war to judge them. Catherine says, "The whole release of the video was a big surprise to them."

As the threat of imprisonment loomed over her son, Catherine asked the public to "try to put yourself in their shoes. The pain, the grief they are going through during this moment. Try to put this in the context of other crimes. We have drug dealers that are back on the street, unpunished. I think he's been punished enough. His family loves him and will stand beside him. I would trade places with him. Let my son heal and get the stress and the PTSD off of him."

In March of 2013, Rob underwent a preliminary Article 32 hearing for allegedly conducting himself contrary to good order and discipline and for violating a general order. After this hearing, Rob and Raechel were left in limbo regarding the next steps. In May of 2013, Rob faced a general court-martial trial where he could potentially lose his rank and all of his retirement and medical benefits and serve up to two years in jail.

One of the frustrating things for Raechel about Rob's charges was that they had nothing to do with the Taliban-urinating incident. For instance, there was an allegation that he did not wear his helmet (most snipers don't wear their helmets because they get in the way). Another allegation was that Rob did not have 100 percent observance on his target when he threw a grenade over a wall.

Raechel said, "Apparently, when you throw a grenade, you have to continuously see the person . . . but this might get you blown up. These rules of engagement are set up for failure. It makes me so sad to see because we have lost so many friends who probably wouldn't have died had it not been for these silly rules of engagement."

"Crush" Them

During this process Rob did not always face a general court-martial. In early 2012, Rob's prospects looked bright. A prominent three-star general, Lieutenant General Thomas Waldhauser, volunteered to oversee the cases of all four Marines involved in the video incident, including the case of Sergeant Richards.

Raechel told me they were "so blessed" to have the help of their defense team: Lieutenant Colonel Guy Womack and Geoff Womack as well as Captain Robert Boudreau, USMC, the detailed military counsel appointed to Sergeant Richards's case. As a former active-duty Marine himself, Lieutenant Colonel Womack had a phenomenal passion and commitment to both the U.S. Marine Corps and defending justice. For nineteen months, these three attorneys fought for Sergeant Richards.

"We already had plane tickets purchased," Raechel recalled. "We anticipated a pretrial agreement with Waldhauser in February of 2012 and we were planning to go out to California, where he was overseeing Central Command" and get everything squared away. The (anticipated) agreement was basically this: Rob would leave the Marine Corps but he would retire honorably, with medical benefits and without any criminal record. This seemed fair considering Rob's enormous contributions of mind, body, and spirit to the Marine Corps.

Then the unthinkable happened. General James Amos, Commandant of the Marine Corps, met with Waldhauser in the Middle East in early February of 2012 and told him he wanted to "crush" all five Marines involved in the video incident. He wanted Waldhauser to make all the Marines stand general court-martial and be discharged from the Marine Corps. Waldhauser stood his ground. He told Amos he did not feel their behavior rose to the level of general court-martial. The two generals separated and continued their travels. Within four hours of their meeting, Amos sent word to Waldhauser that he was being removed from the case. Richard's case was reassigned to another general, Lieutenant General Richard Mills. For the past year and a half, the Richards defense team fought to get Sergeant Richards the nonjudicial forum he would have received had Lieutenant General Waldhauser not been removed from the case.

"He [Amos] had a general who was unafraid to do what was right and was not being influenced. He *attempted* to commit undue influence by advising Waldhauser to give the Marines a general court-martial. Then, by removing Waldhauser from the case, this actually constituted undue influence," Womack explained.

Womack described Amos as the "number one [ranking] Marine in the world." It is disheartening to think that the world's most powerful Marine committed undue influence and led our Marines by such a terrible example. In 2013, Amos fired several Marines on what appeared to be his whim after they made trivial mistakes. Clearly, Amos was a hypocrite. "Is he going to fire himself? Because he actually committed undue influence," Womack wondered. "If he holds them accountable, why not hold himself accountable?"

"You're Being Retired Out"

On Monday, April 29, 2013, Rob and Raechel received a phone call from the IPAC Retirement Division of the Marine Corps telling them "You're being retired out." Raechel and Rob were flooded by a huge sense of relief and hope—believing that the trial had been dropped and that Rob could retire honorably and with full medical benefits. Rob's grandfather told Raechel, "Rob sounds happy for the first time." Catherine added, "For the first time in a year-and-a-half, I could hear him smiling over the phone." But, two days later, the Marines called back and said they had made "a mistake." Shock and heartbreak overcame Rob and Raechel; they had already begun the process of turning over their active-duty cards. Raechel says, "For two days, we thought it was over. Rob finally felt like 'I can work on my resume.' After the second call, he fell right back into a dark place. He can't move on with his life. Stress worsens the PTSD. His memory is not where it should be. He loves the Marine Corps. I have letters from the Marines telling us that he is a hero and if we ever need anything, they would be there. He feels betrayed, like 'I sacrificed my mind, my body.'"

Because of Amos's unethical intervention, for nearly nineteen months, the Richards defense team worked hard to clear Rob's name and allow him to retire honorably (noncriminally) and with the medical benefits he needed to treat his war injuries.

In the summer of 2013, the Womacks threatened to file a motion for undue command influence against Amos and have Waldhauser sign it. As soon as this happened, Amos had a change of heart. He obviously did not want to deal with the embarrassment and so (via Mills) he offered the Richards a summary court-martial instead. An SCM is a completely nonjudicial and noncriminal proceeding, leaving Sergeant Richards with no criminal record at all. Richards would be allowed to medically retire with honorable discharge. The Richardses graciously agreed.

At last there was a positive resolution: they came to a settlement agreement in which he was reduced one stripe and allowed to retire medically in the fall of 2013 at 100 percent disability with full pay and health benefits for the rest of his life. This positive resolution can be attributed to Rob's upright character; his past record of honorable service in the Navy; the professionalism with which he and his family conducted themselves in the face of trial; and the nineteen months his defense team spent in a steadfast quest for justice.

"Semper Fidelis"

War is jacked up. As Raechel put it, "Things are lovely on a textbook level, but this is real life." Real war is not what the media perceives it to be. Real war does not occur in a vacuum; real war is bloody, gruesome, and mind-blowing. For most of us, the biggest daily stress we face is a traffic jam or meeting the boss's deadline. We finish a "hard" day's work in our air-conditioned office, treat ourselves to a burger and beer, and then flip on the TV. We see a story about a soldier "misbehaving" overseas—such as a soldier urinating on the body of a dead terrorist—and the media asks *us* to *judge* that person.

Unless you have been there and fought in the foxholes of Iraq or Afghanistan, you have no idea what it's like to see your comrades have their limbs blown off by Middle Eastern thugs who throw acid in their wives' faces and arm their innocent children with machine guns as if they were decoys for a duck hunt. Rob and his Marine comrades were thrown into an impossible situation. They were asked to follow rules of engagement that would put them in danger. The brain is the most important organ in the human body. Rob's brain was traumatized during this incident. He and his fellow Marines used common sense and took actions out of self-defense to the best of their ability. If we expect Marines to do the impossible, we need to give them some leeway—because *no one can do the impossible.*

It is not right to throw people into impossible situations—into war—and expect them to behave the same way they would in an office job. The U.S. Marine Corps needs to fulfill its "Semper Fidelis" motto and be "always faithful" to the men and women, like Sergeant Richards, who have literally given everything they have to the armed forces.

The Grand Finale: Treating Marines like Butlers

When Barry was a young man, he went through a phase where he went for lingering runs every day. His girlfriend at the time, who was not running daily, decided to challenge her boyfriend to a short dash through a local park for the fun of it. To his embarrassment, she beat him.[32]

On May 16, 2013, Obama was delivering a press conference in the Rose Garden with the Turkish prime minister. Obama and the prime minister were each standing at separate outdoor podiums when it began to sprinkle. There was not a huge crowd and it was not a major conference; the president could have easily moved everyone indoors. Instead, Obama looked around for a servant. He did not call an aide or an intern. Oh no. Obama waved his hand over to the Marines in attendance: "I am gonna go ahead and ask, folks, why don't we get a couple of, ah, Marines, they're gonna look good next to us." Two marines hurried over with umbrellas and held them above the president and prime minister as they completed the press conference.

CNN has it on tape. Obama had "forgotten" to show basic respect to his Marine Corps before the umbrella incident, such as the time he returned a Marine's salute with a handshake instead of a salute. His behavior said: I'm Obama; I'm the celebrity; I'm the JFK-esque war hero who never served in a war; Marines are my serfs. This time, Obama disrespected the Marine Corps by asking Marines to break their own rules. The Marine Corps Manual specifies that a male Marine may never carry an umbrella while in uniform. Marines are not servants. Marines are warriors. Politicians, including the president, are paid public servants. It was very disrespectful for the president to position a Marine, as former U.S. Air Force Lieutenant General Thomas McInerney put it, to: "look like a butler."[33] "The President has stood in the rain before without an umbrella and a Marine would generally stand there without holding an umbrella." Retired Marine Lieutenant Colonel Guy Womack said: "It really offended me, and I am sure it offended many other Marines."

If you're like most people, the word "Marine" makes you think of an American soldier dressed in blues with the heart and physique of a fighter. Unlike Obama's old girlfriend, the Marine holding the umbrella over Obama's head could not challenge his obnoxiousness with a friendly physical competition like an arm-wrestling match. He had to stand with a perfect poker face, feeling raindrops hit his $700 uniform as he held an umbrella over the head of a man who was once beat by a girl.

The Verdict

The stories of Sergeant Rob Richards, Lieutenant Clint Lorance, and PFC Bowe Bergdahl are powerful and heart-wrenching. Moreover, they are not anecdotal, or "one-off" examples. The abuse these three men experienced is characteristic of the ways Obama mishandled foreign policy and abused the military.

1. Missions Impossible

Our troops do not get to decide where they serve. Rather, our troops serve bravely wherever they are sent. Obama promised to bring our troops home. Instead, he kept them in the Middle East longer, authorized a troop surge that *tripled* the number of troops in Afghanistan, and asked our bravest youths to perform in unworkable conditions with unreasonable rules of engagement and then threatened them with imprisonment for tiny mistakes. It's hard to fight against suicide bombers. What are you supposed to do—turn *yourself* into a suicide bomber?

As his reelection neared, Obama took a trip to Afghanistan in the spring of 2012 and made a big TV announcement (from Afghanistan) claiming that the "tide has turned" and the Taliban had weakened. He was just moving his lips. Around that time, Representative Mike Rogers, Republican of Michigan, and California Democratic senator Dianne Feinstein took their own trip to Afghanistan. Feinstein came back and told CNN: "I think we'd both say that what we've found is that the Taliban is stronger."

On May 16, 2013, six Americans were killed in a car bomb attack in Afghanistan. The attack was performed by a suicide group who said they formed in response to Obama's plans to keep troops in Afghanistan past 2014. This was the fifth episode of deadly insider attacks against Americans in the first five months of 2013. Anti-American sentiment and episodes of fatal blowback against American troops soared under Obama. "Insider attacks rose sharply in 2012, with 64 deaths in 48 attacks, more than in any previous year," a spokesman for the international coalition in Afghanistan, Captain Dan Einert, relayed in the *New York Times*.[34]

2. A Suicide a Day

More soldiers died from suicide than from combat in the stressful deployments to Afghanistan.[35] *Time* magazine highlighted stories of suicide, including that of Ian Morrison. On Morrison's *sixth* attempt to obtain help from government therapists, he waited nearly an hour before giving up and committing suicide. It is heartbreaking to consider the level of depression that Morrison felt. He loved his wife and she was extremely supportive, but the emotional burden of war slowly broke him. His final text to his wife before shooting himself in the neck was: "STILL on hold."[36]

Soldiers were 40 percent more likely to commit suicide if they were facing disciplinary action, like Sergeant Richards faced.[37] Richards hung in there, thanks to his character, faith, supportive wife, family, and defense team. But not everyone was blessed with such a strong support network, and the thought of going to prison and being publicly dishonored seemed worse than a bullet that would turn it all off.

War, especially after soldiers return home and have time and solitude to reflect, is a constant mental challenge. Suicides were also high among non-active-duty service members: Suicide is a multi-headed fiend but the prospect of unemployment during a down economy on top of military budget cuts at a time when reservists faced the prospect of deploying to a new war with fewer resources (think Syria) were reasons non-active duty troops could feel hopeless. This depression would only worsen if it were treated improperly.

3. Military Drug Abuse and Misdiagnoses Rise Under Obama

Sergeant Rob Richards was one of many unknowing young victims of the epidemic of misdiagnoses within the U.S. military that escalated under Obama's negligent watch. (To be fair, it's difficult to keep one eye on a golf ball and another on Afghanistan.)

An in-depth investigation by Paul John Scott for *Men's Journal* uncovered that "American soldiers (active soldiers as well as retired) have never been more medicated than they are now: In 2010, more than 213,000 service members (roughly 20 percent of active-duty military) were taking medications the military considered 'high risk'—from epilepsy drugs to psychiatric pills like Seroquel. But what's more incredible is that Seroquel and other antipsychotics are expensive (as much as $10 a dose) and not proven to be effective in treating the very conditions for which the military and VA most often prescribe them: insomnia and PTSD."[38]

Renowned New York psychiatrist and author Dr. Peter Breggin testified on February 24, 2010, before the Veterans Affairs Committee of the House of Representatives on "Exploring the Relationship Between Medication and Veteran Suicide." Breggin testified: "I'd say it is near-criminal to send young men and women off to combat with a 180-day supply of drugs that can cause an increase in violent suicide." Obama paid little attention to Dr. Breggin's warning.

It was not until February of 2012 that the Pentagon took real notice of the problems antipsychotic drugs prescribed for PTSD were causing American troops. Dr. Jonathan Woodson sent a notice to military treatment facilities asking them to exercise caution and increase monitoring when prescribing antipsychotics such as quetiapine (Seroquel) and risperidone. Quetiapine, for example, was being prescribed for PTSD regardless of the fact that it had *never been shown* to effectively treat PTSD.[39]

4. Mistreatment of Young Veterans

On the 2008 campaign trail Obama used his lips to make sweet-sounding promises to veterans. I will "care for our veterans," recognize them with a "homecoming," and "honor their valor by providing the care they need and rebuilding the military they love," he said.[40] (The only true part of his promises to veterans was his subtle omission of his own love for the military.)

In 2012, he hit the repeat button on "Barry's Best B.S. from 2008" and released an ad called "Sacred Trust." Looking into the camera lens, Obama said: "And when they come home we have a sacred trust to make sure that we are doing everything we can to heal all of their wounds, giving them the opportunities that they deserve to find a job and get the education that they need. It's not enough just to make a speech about how much we value veterans. It's not enough just to remember them on Memorial Day."[41]

Unfortunately, the "Sacred Trust" ad was what he said it wasn't: just a speech. A 2013 membership survey conducted by the Iraq and Afghanistan Veterans of America found that 75 percent of veterans rated President Obama's performance on improving the lives of veterans as "fair" or "poor."[42] Five years into his presidency the unemployment rate for post-9/11 veterans was far higher than the civilian rate: 9.9 percent for male veterans and 10.3 percent for female veterans.[43]

Many Iraq and Afghanistan veterans waited extensively for the Department of Veterans Affairs to reimburse them for the costs of mental and physical injuries they incurred while serving. An inspector general visit to the VA's regional office in North Carolina resulted in a 2012 report that the building was overflowing with "37,000 claims" and that "The excess weight of the stored files has the potential to compromise the structural integrity of the sixth floor of the facility. We noticed floors bowing under the excess weight to the extent that the tops of file cabinets were noticeably unlevel throughout the storage area."[44]

Sergeant Richards and Lieutenant Lorance were two of the many young men who returned from war only to be denied their pay and retirement benefits. This was stressful for the veterans and their families, plus they had to set up defense funds and ask the community to help them fight for their benefits and defend their reputations.

5. Breaking Mothers' Hearts

A woman does not endure nine months of hell, the pain of childbirth, and the alternating pains and joys of raising a child for eighteen years so that a strange man sitting in the White House who has neither met her child nor lived through the stress of war can instantly destroy her child's life.

Obama said he supported a woman's right to end her baby's life. Well, he also supported *his* right to end her baby's life. If your twenties fade away as Taliban captives physically torment you, if you sit in jail for twenty years, or if you are stripped of your reputation, honor, and ability to work—your life is over. You will never reach your full potential unless you have phenomenal willpower (like Sergeant Bergdahl, Lieutenant Lorance, and Sergeant Richards) combined with friends and family helping you restart.

"This discredits my son's whole life. Yesterday, I saw my son's mug shot and I want to tell you it broke my heart," said Clint's mother Anna on August 22, 2013. Through the phone, her voice betrayed the tears welling in her eyes.

"If you knew my son! The media didn't dig deep enough in the story to find out what went on that day. They never saw who these guys really were as humans," said Rob's mother, Cate. "Before *I* even knew *my son* was involved in this incident, I saw Hillary Clinton on TV judging him. When this story first came out, the most vocal person against my son was Hillary. Panetta made perfunctory statements. Obama kind of hides."

Jani Bergdahl. Anna Lorance. Cate Richards. These mothers deserve Purple Hearts for the way Obama and the top brass in his metaphorical "Military Bum's Club" abused their Millennial babies who fought his war and dug his foxholes.

WHERE THERE'S
A NONSMOKER

J FK enjoyed smoking four to five fine cigars a day. Bill Clinton also loved fine cigars and special prosecutor Kenneth Starr subpoenaed him to discuss his interesting method of smoking them. After their little chat, Clinton began smoking cigars without relying on an intern.

People say: "Where there's smoke there's fire." That may be true. But where there's a smok*er*, there's generally nothing to worry about. What you see is what you get: a man or a woman smoking. There's smoke; there's no fire. Where there's a *non*smoker, now that's where you want to watch out. That's where you may find a virtual forest fire. Especially if the nonsmoker is a recent quitter; a man who quit because his wife told him to; a man who once belonged to a marijuana-smoking group called the Choom Gang; a man whose colleagues in community organizing knew he was stressed when he smoked two Marlboros in rapid succession.[1] This is the description of a man on the rebound and Obama fit this description perfectly.

JFK and Clinton were both smokers. Obama started out as a smoker but became a nonsmoker for political reasons and went downhill from there. If we use "smoking quality" to rank these three presidents in terms of how well they succeeded at keeping your children and grandchildren safe from terrorism,

- JFK's success would be signified by a Petit Upmann Cuban cigar.
- Clinton's mediocrity would be signified by a Swisher cigar.
- Obama's failure would be signified by a candy cigarette.

From Russia with Love

Obama loved to wield JFK's name to brand himself as a national security expert. He enlisted JFK's former speechwriter Ted Sorensen to tell students that Obama would exhibit the same acumen that JFK exhibited during the Cuban Missile Crisis: "I have decided that judgment is the single most important quality in a president of the United States. Kennedy had judgment. Obama has judgment."[2] Let's hold Obama to his favorite standard by examining the Cuban Missile Crisis and determining that he failed miserably at decision making in comparable national security crises. Next to JFK, an imperfect leader, Obama's deficiency on national security is abysmal.

JFK described himself as "almost a peace-at-any-price man" and he treated war as a last resort.[3] The closest thing to a terror attack that (almost) happened under JFK's watch was the Cuban Missile Crisis. When JFK learned that the Russians were mounting nuclear warheads onto medium-range ballistic missiles in Cuba, ninety miles away from the tip of Florida, and pointing them at the United States, he authorized a naval blockade of Cuba. Then, he took out his chessboard.

Unlike Obama, whose administration threw strategy, common sense, and ethics out the window when it came to national security, Kennedy kept his mouth shut during the Cuban Missile Crisis and prevented unnecessary American deaths. You never caught Kennedy running around telling the media about his plans to shut down the communists in a pathetic attempt to win fans. Instead, he forced Soviet premier Nikita Khrushchev into a corner, making him guess America's next move and denying Khrushchev the justification of provocation.[4] The Cuban Missile Crisis was a game of chess that the United States won when Khrushchev felt checkmated. Ultimately, JFK did what he was hired to do: keep America safe. JFK also restored America to a position of dominance in the world. He turned Russian–American relations from Siberian ice to the warm feeling you get from drinking Russian vodka.

* * *

FAST-FORWARD to 1998. Americans were adjusting to the news of Clinton's affair with young Monica Lewinsky when two U.S. embassies were attacked by terrorists linked to Osama bin Laden. A dozen Americans and hundreds of other innocent people died. If Clinton had paid more attention to his intelligence community, as we discussed in chapter 7, this tragedy might have been avoided. Alas, Billy had the one-track mind of a flighty girl chaser.

But unlike what Obama would eventually do during the Benghazi terror attack, at least Clinton did not laugh off the 1998 embassy bombings as the result of a "spontaneous protest." He did not jet off to Vegas to play blackjack. Clinton took responsibility, without even being subpoenaed. Three years later, on a bright September morning, al-Qaeda hijacked four planes that ripped through the World Trade Center, the Pentagon, and a Pennsylvania field. President George W. Bush and the city of New York faced bloodshed and destruction that Clinton could have prevented with one sniper bullet in 1999—one hole through Osama bin Laden's forehead. G. W. did not call Clinton a bad dealer; he played the hand he was dealt. Feet planted on a skyscraper reduced to rubble, arm swung over a fireman to comfort, bullhorn to his lips, he pledged: "The people who knocked these buildings down will hear all of us soon . . . . The nation sends its love and compassion to everybody who's here . . . and may God bless America." New York City answered: *USA! USA! USA!*

Bush succeeded in routing the Taliban in Afghanistan. In hindsight, Bush kept U.S. troops in the Middle East for longer than he himself said would be wise, as I mentioned in chapter 7. But America had never experienced anything like 9/11. And never would again. Until the Oval Office welcomed a nonsmoker.

Ashtrays

As a nonsmoker, Obama managed to leave more dirty ashtrays lying around than an absent-minded, chain-smoking professor. Barry made "quitting" smoking look like a very filthy habit.

Barry loved making messes, whether he was packing for Vegas while American diplomats and Navy SEALs burned to death in Benghazi, Libya; threatening Americans with lethal drone force and watching our power grid deteriorate and fall prey to hackers; or leaking confidential security intelligence to al-Qaeda.

On Father's Day 2008, he promised fathers that an Obama administration would make every effort to improve foreign relations so that their children could travel abroad without worrying that "we are hated around the world."[5]

What do you think? Can your children and grandchildren safely travel abroad? Did Obama use 9/11 as a challenge to prevent terror or did he slack off and leave Millennials more vulnerable to terror? And, did he cover up his negligence to win an election? Read these stories about Obama's "ashtrays"—and then decide for yourself.

"Assuming We Don't Die Tonight"

Dusk brings out the stars above Benghazi, Libya, on September 11, 2012. The stars are outshone tonight. Far, far below, a petroleum-based fire blazes bright. The fire is hungrily consuming the U.S. consulate building. All fires emit heat and smoke. Petroleum fires are special; they emit heat, smoke, and lethal cyanide gas.

Picture it: The consulate building is a beast, three football fields long by one football field wide. To defend this baby, you would want a small army. The consulate is decked out with sexy safety features like a nine-foot-high wall topped with three feet of barbed wire and concertina wire but lacks fundamentals like adequate security personnel. Only five American Diplomatic Security (DS) agents are guarding the consulate. Aiding the DS agents are three armed Libyan members of the local "February 17 Brigade," three Libyan National Police officers, and five unarmed Libyan contractors are patrolling the gate.[6] This is why a band of militants is able to easily penetrate the gate tonight with torches and diesel fuel. The chanting fiends dance about, setting fire to the consulate's billowy Middle Eastern furniture and the air turns black with smoke.[7]

The consulate compound is made up of four buildings, including a spacious residence building. Within the residence building, there is a "safe haven." The door to the safe haven is bulletproof but not smokeproof, as it is made of steel bars and not solid steel.[8] The windows are grilled, keeping intruders out but also keeping the safe haven's occupants inside. In the event of arson, anyone locked inside the safe haven will effectively become a steak searing on a hot grill.

Locked inside the safe haven are two American diplomats: the U.S. ambassador to Libya, J. Christopher (Chris) Stevens, and his young colleague, a State Department management officer named Sean Smith. Everyone loved Chris—from the Americans who worked at his side to the local shopkeepers he befriended as he spoke Arabic on the streets. Sean was also loved by his colleagues, who were energized by his sense of humor, quiet confidence, and can-do attitude. "You are as powerful as you want to be," Sean said to encourage a friend shortly before the attack.[9]

Fire safety, including drills and equipment, is part of Safety 101 for any building. Unfortunately, no one provided Chris and Sean with a fire escape plan. They are expected to fight this petroleum fire without basic fire safety equipment and instructed to don body armor, which keeps their bodies extra toasty and rigid—the opposite of what they will want.[10] It is around 10:00 p.m. as smoke rushes into the safe haven.

*　*　*

THAT morning, the Americans had noticed a suspicious man dressed in a Libyan Supreme Security Council police uniform taking photos of the consulate's layout. A complaint reporting the incident was prepared for local authorities, which the ambassador reviewed.[11]

Sean was concerned. After all, this was no ordinary day. It was the anniversary of 9/11. Sean was at the consulate to do IT work, so he was online a lot.[12] He was an avid gamer and when he had downtime, he would play an Internet spaceship game known as EVE Online and chat with his fellow gamers. His EVE Online user name was "Vile Rat." That day, he was chatting with a gamer friend named "The Mittani."

Vile Rat told the Mittani he smelled a rat:[13]

(12:54:09 PM) vile_rat: assuming we don't die tonight. We saw one of our "police" that guard the compound taking pictures

The last message the Mittani received from Vile Rat was: *F—CK. GUNFIRE.*[14]

* * *

SEAN'S instincts were true. Now he and Chris are crawling low on the ground in the safe haven, gasping for air and struggling to see a few feet ahead. Their nostrils flare at the reek of burning furniture and diesel. A DS agent is guiding them out of the safe haven toward an egress window to escape. The DS agent can't see behind him, so as he approaches the window, he is pounding on the floor and shouting—hoping the diplomats can hear and follow.[15]

* * *

THE DS agents risk their lives trying to save Chris and Sean. Over and over, they reenter the consulate through the egress window, come out for air, go back in. By now, the consulate is a furnace. They do not care. Their friends are inside.

All the agents' lungs are filling with thick, black diesel smoke. The agent who tries for the longest collapses and begins vomiting.[16] Another agent refuses to give up until he gives it one last shot. He tears off his shirt, soaks it in the compound's swimming pool, winds it over his head and reenters the inferno.[17]

They find Sean's lifeless body. Chris's body will not be discovered until later.

Grief overwhelms the DS agents but they must flee. They did their best with what an independent report would soon describe as "grossly inadequate" support from Washington. Bullets and rocket-propelled grenades are flying. They fire up their fully armored vehicle and start rolling.

About a mile away, peaceful darkness envelopes an upscale residential compound of four houses enclosed by a concrete wall and a high gate.[18] There is no signage, American flag, or visible peripheral security to make this quadruplex stand out; it blends right in with all the nearby residential compounds.[19] It is almost midnight as the DS agents speed toward this peaceful compound, which is actually a secret CIA annex.

A car chase scene from a movie ensues. The DS agent who had collapsed and vomited from smoke inhalation moments earlier is now in James Bond mode, navigating the armored vehicle through the busy streets of Benghazi while taking fire from militants shooting AK-47s two feet away. He swings up onto the grassy median and cruises into oncoming traffic. As he nears the residential compound, he has two tires blown out and an ominous car following him with its lights off. (A seven-person American rescue team, based out of the CIA annex, returns to the annex close behind the DS agents. This team tried unsuccessfully to rout the militants at the consulate and find Chris's body.) Safely at the CIA annex, they all take defensive positions and plan to quietly wait for help to arrive.[20] Or so they hope.

The Americans have barely pulled into the CIA annex when they are attacked by militants with rocket-propelled grenades and small arms. Somehow, the rebels know this compound disguises something other than sleeping Libyan families. The fight lasts for about an hour and the Americans wait anxiously for reinforcements from Tripoli, who will not arrive until around 5:00 a.m.

Shortly after the Tripoli team arrives, the militants return in full force to the CIA annex. The militants seek American blood, and they want to kill under the cover of darkness.[21] As the faintest rays of morning light emerge, the militants work quickly. They launch mortars onto the rooftop where two former Navy SEALs, Tyrone Woods and Glen Doherty, are defending the compound.

Gregory Hicks, the top surviving diplomat in Libya during the attack and the last person to talk to Stevens on the phone before he died, would later describe the mortar attacks to Congress: "The accuracy was terribly precise."[22] The rebels were experienced. In five swift movements, their mortars killed Woods and Doherty.[23] By 6:00 a.m., the struggle was over. Four Americans were dead and others were severely wounded as the sun rose on the morning of September 12.

Scrubbing the Story

Thousands of miles away, across the Atlantic Ocean, it is 12:00 noon on the East Coast and 9:00 a.m. on the Pacific Coast. By now, most Americans are awake and they have caught bits and pieces of the news from Benghazi. About an hour earlier, while the mortar fight raged at the CIA annex, and just minutes before Doherty and Woods died on the rooftop, President Obama had delivered brief remarks from the White House, announcing the first attack on the consulate and the deaths of the two American diplomats, Chris and Sean.

In his remarks, President Obama suggested that a homemade Internet video that negatively portrayed the Prophet Muhammad was responsible for the attack:

> *Since our founding, the United States has been a nation that respects all faiths. We reject all efforts to denigrate the religious beliefs of others. But there is absolutely no justification to this type of senseless violence. None.*

Secretary of State Hillary Clinton made her own remarks, echoing Obama's, tying the attack to the amateurish video:

*Some have sought to justify this vicious behavior, along with the pro-
test that took place at our Embassy in Cairo yesterday, as a response
to inflammatory material posted on the Internet. America's commitment to religious tolerance goes back to the very beginning of our
nation. But let me be clear—there is no justification for this, none.*

The odd thing was, none of the militants appeared to have seen
the makeshift video. By September 13, a writer for *The New Yorker* was
expressing skepticism:

*Have any of the men who attacked the consulate actually seen the
film? I do not know one Libyan who has, despite being in close
contact with friends and relatives in Benghazi. And the attack was
not preceded by vocal outrage toward the film. Libyan Internet sites
and Facebook pages were not suddenly busy with chatter about it.*[24]

By January 2014, the public would finally find out through declas-
sified testimonies of senior Pentagon officials that Obama's administration *had* learned it was a terror attack—around the same time that Chris
and Sean were fighting the petroleum fire. Then-head of AFRICOM
General Carter Ham testified that he was working at the Pentagon
when he received a call from the AFRICOM Command Center informing him of the attack on the Benghazi consulate within the first fifteen
minutes [around 9:42 P.M. Libya time on September 11]. He immediately notified then-Defense Secretary Leon Panetta and the chairman of
the Joint Chiefs of Staff, General Martin Dempsey, that the attack was
a "terrorist attack" just before they walked into a scheduled Oval Office
meeting with the president.[25]

On September 16, 2012, one week after the attack, UN ambassador
Susan Rice appeared on NBC's *Meet the Press.*

When host David Gregory asked whether Rice could "say definitively" that the Benghazi attacks were "spontaneous," she said: "What
happened in Benghazi was in fact initially a spontaneous reaction to
what had just transpired hours before in Cairo, almost a copycat of the

demonstrations against our facility in Cairo, which were prompted, of course, by the video."

Later in the interview, Gregory inquired: "Was there a failure here that this administration is responsible for?" Rice answered: "David, I don't think so. First of all, we had no actionable intelligence to suggest that any attack on our facility in Benghazi was imminent. . . . We had security in Benghazi, a significant number."

Rice's story was a wild distortion of reality, expressed so eloquently and with enough confidence that people bought it for a few days. But the truth traveled fast. We learned there were just five DS agents at the consulate with the ambassador when he suffocated. We learned that additional staff was denied because the ambassador was supposed to go to the safe haven in the event of an emergency—a safe haven that was actually a "deathtrap," as Jake Tapper put it.[26] We learned that the arson and mortar attacks were led by armed and experienced militants linked to al-Qaeda and Ansar al-Sharia. We learned there was actionable intelligence, months in advance, forewarning the State Department of severe security vulnerabilities at the Benghazi facilities.

Hillary was asked by the House Foreign Affairs Committee: "When did you become aware of Ambassador Stevens' requests [for help] and did he ever personally ask you to be involved?" She testified: "No. No. And, no, any of the requests, any of the cables having to do with security did not come to my attention." This turned out to be false. A congressional report revealed that Clinton had seen and signed (acknowledged receipt of) a security cable requesting backup support, in April of 2012, but then proceded with a security reduction.[27]

Soon, most Americans felt like the White House was not giving them the full story. Anger, embarrassment, and anxiety set in. Americans wanted straight answers. Why wasn't our State Department prepared for an attack on 9/11/12? Why did the State Department, including spokeswoman Victoria Nuland who said she feared Congress might "beat up the State Department for not paying attention to warnings," insist on scrubbing the CIA talking points (changed 12 times) before the White House sent Rice on five major Sunday cable network

programs to claim the Benghazi terror attack was a spontaneous response to a primitive video that the rebels hadn't even watched?[28] Was it
safe to travel? *What was going on?*

Here's what was going on: Obama had less than two months to convince young swing voters that he was their man for the next four years,
and an easily preventable terror attack on 9/11 with American casualties, including Millennial diplomat Sean Smith, looked very, very bad.

Senate Democrats released a report in January 2014 claiming that
the White House and executive branch made "no efforts" to engage in
a cover-up of "facts or make alterations for political purposes."[29] Democrats claimed the Obama administration did not intend to mislead
the public by ascribing the Benghazi attacks to violent protests—even
though Obama's top officials (Panetta and Dempsey) were briefed that
it was a terror attack as they walked into an Oval Office meeting with
Obama. Apparently, the administration didn't want to mislead the public—so they lied to the public.

Barry's Right-Hand Woman

In October of 2012, Clinton said she took "responsibility" for the attacks. Good ol' Hillary, doing her part and taking the heat to help
Barry win reelection!

> *I take responsibility. I am in charge of the State Department.
> 60,000-plus people all over the world. 275 posts. The President
> and the Vice President certainly wouldn't be knowledgeable about
> specific decisions that are made by security professionals.*

So months passed. Obama was reelected. A year passed. Hard answers never came. The White House clamped down on transparency
and the public was left to piece the full story together with the help of a
few bold journalists and whistleblowers.

It is true that Obama was initially unaware of some decisions made by the State Department. This is also irrelevant. He appointed Hillary to his Cabinet. She was his right-hand woman. When it came to stretching the truth, she was just like her husband, only worse. Billy bluffed about sex. Hillie bluffed about bloodshed. Lives depend on the person that our president trusts for national security decisions. Who did Barry trust? He trusted Hillary, and her incompetency led to American deaths. The U.S. Senate Select Committee on Intelligence released a report on January 15, 2014, revealing that there were enough "warnings" and "security shortfalls" to make the Benghazi attacks reasonably "preventable." Clinton's department insisted on altering the CIA talking points, which contributed to Rice's misleading television appearances and in turn delayed the FBI's access to the crime scene (more on this in a bit). The Senate report cited the FBI's "hampered" investigation as a reason why it has been so difficult for the U.S. to bring the perpretrators of the Benghazi attacks to justice.[30] Ultimately, Hillary failed to do her job and keep her employees safe. Further, her cover-up impeded the pursuit of justice for the four Americans who died and their families. Obama must be held responsible for the consequences of trusting Clinton.

Tracking Dogs, Arson Dogs, Cadaver Dogs

Journalists are not just "watchdogs," they also play the role of a K9, tracking down the scents of criminals and their victims. Only a few courageous journalists did K9 reporting on Benghazi.

An independent report commissioned by Hillary Clinton found that "no protest took place" before the attacks and "systemic failures and leadership and management deficiencies at senior levels within two bureaus of the State Department resulted in a Special Mission security posture that was inadequate for Benghazi and grossly inadequate to deal with the attack that took place."[31]

We also learned that Eric Nordstrom, a State Department official and the top security officer in Libya at the time of the attacks, had issued *two* cables to the State Department requesting additional security in the months preceding the attack and was answered with silence both times.[32] Nordstrom testified under oath to Congress:

REP. JAMES LANKFORD: Mr. Nordstrom, before you left as the RSO [regional security officer], did the facilities have the number of security personnel that you had requested?

NORDSTROM: No, they did not.

Rice had been the messenger of Obama and Hillary's cowardice and lies. These lies ticked off a man whom Ambassador Stevens had been making diplomatic strides with: Mohammed Magarief, then the president of Libya. As in, ticked him off big time. Magarief called the attack terrorism. So, when Obama told the world that it was a spontaneous protest, he was effectively branding Magarief as a *liar*. Angry and humiliated, Magarief refused to let the FBI have access to the crime scene until weeks later. You can hardly blame Magarief. He felt like Obama had stabbed him, and his people, in the back. As Hicks testified, the Libyans "took casualties for us that night" and Libyan doctors treated wounded Americans "as if they were their own."[33] Obama may have won the Nobel Peace Prize, but his ego and rudeness led world leaders like Magarief to snub America. Here's how it went down:

Two weeks after the attack, September 26, 2012, Ann Curry of NBC News interviewed President Magarief. Curry asked whether he would classify the attack on the consulate as "an act of terrorism." Magarief answered: "I have no doubt about that. And it's a *preplanned* act of terrorism directed against American citizens." Curry probed: "And you're saying that these [mortars] were fired [at the CIA annex] with such accuracy that this could not have been done by someone who did not have experience? Magarief replied: "Experience. And *knew* what he was doing." Curry pressed further: Do you think the movie had *anything* to do with this attack on the consulate? The president of Libya shook his head: Not on this attack. Not on this attack. It has nothing to do with this attack.

Months after Magarief's interview with Curry, a congressman probed Hillary on why the public was led to believe that the terror attack was caused by an Internet video, and for so long. Hillary acted like she could care less that four Americans had died, throwing up her hands and shrieking: "What difference does it make!?"

Gregory Hicks, who we've already mentioned, testified as a Benghazi whistleblower before Congress. Hicks was a seasoned diplomat with twenty-two years of experience. He was on the ground during the Benghazi attacks. He was also a Democrat who had voted for Obama twice.[34] Clearly, he was a very objective witness.

> REP. PAUL GOSAR: Can I give you the opportunity to respond to that question, "What difference does it make?"
>
> GREGORY HICKS: President Magarief was insulted in front of his own people; in front of the world; his credibility was reduced. His ability to lead his own country was damaged. He was angry. . . . He was still steamed about the talk shows two weeks later and I definitely believe that it negatively affected our ability to get the FBI team quickly to Benghazi. [The unsecured crime scene was off limits to the FBI for seventeen days after the consulate was attacked, Hicks testified.]

Of course it makes a difference. A preplanned terror attack was foreseeable and preventable, meaning that Chris, Sean, Tyrone, and Glen should still be alive.

* * *

OBAMA was over the top in his display of concern for Trayvon Martin's parents, but he showed callousness toward the families of the heroes who died in Benghazi. He acted like he wanted to forget the tragedy as soon as possible. He said next to nothing to shed light on Benghazi; he nominated many of those involved in covering up the attack for *promotion* (think Victoria Nuland and Susan Rice), and he and Hillary both neglected to comfort the next of kin to the victims.

Eight months after Benghazi, on May 7, 2013, CNN's the *Lead* host Jake Tapper interviewed Sean Smith's mother, Pat Smith. Tapper asked Smith what she still wanted to know about her son's death. She said: "Why was there no security for him? When they were supposed to have security, and the security that they did have was called back. It's just, things do not add up and I'm just told lies." Tapper dug deeper: "You have expressed disappointment in the past because President Obama, then-secretary of state Hillary Clinton, then-secretary of defense Leon Panetta, all of them came to you, talked to you, and [since] then you haven't heard from them. Have you heard from anybody in the Obama administration? Have you gotten any outreach or any answers at all?" Smith said: "I got one telephone call from a clerk—that was a couple days after it happened. He was reading to me from the timeline, which I already had, and that was it. And since then all they have told me is that I am not part of the immediate family so they don't want to tell me anything . . . and I don't understand that because I still remember the labor pains, which was quite a while ago!"

Dead Fish and Cue Balls

In October of 2012, there was a special ceremony to honor the life of former Navy SEAL Tyrone Woods after his body returned to the United States. The president and vice president attended the ceremony and walked over to Woods's family afterward. Biden bellowed in a "loud and boisterous" manner: "Did your son always have balls the size of cue balls?" as if Woods's death were a raunchy joke. Woods's father could not believe his ears. He asked, "Are these the words of someone who is sorry?"[35] Everyone knows Biden is one of those jolly jerks who routinely insult people by talking without thinking, so his behavior was not quite as upsetting as the president's behavior. "Shaking hands with him [Obama], quite frankly, was like shaking hands with a dead fish. His face was pointed towards me but he would not look me in the eye, his eyes were over my shoulder," said Woods's father when he described meeting Obama. "I could tell that he was not sorry. He had no remorse." Woods's father was not saying this with odium. He was saying this as a mourning father and firsthand recipient of Obama's coldness who wanted others to know the truth. He would also say, "I'm really not angry, I've forgiven. . . . But it would be nice if, when politicians speak, you wouldn't have to say, well, are they telling the truth or how much of this is true? You shouldn't have to weigh it. Truth is always the best and the most powerful way to express something."[36]

Young people observing this callousness from the commander in chief and his right-hand-woman were left wondering: Why should I pursue a career in international diplomacy if this is how I'll be treated? Why devote my life to becoming a Navy SEAL if my ability to serve my country and utilize my training will be cut short by negligent politicians who leave me to die on a flaming rooftop?

There's a reason why more than one in four Democrats said Obama ought to be impeached over Benghazi.[37]

9/11/13

On this day in history, a car bomb blew up the exact location of a former U.S. consulate in Benghazi. No one died, but the symbolism was clear. Libyans sighed as they walked through the smoldering ruins and picked up lifeless gray birds—doves—that perished in the blast.

> *Make no mistake, the United States will hunt down and punish those responsible for these cowardly acts.* —President George W. Bush on September 11, 2001

Twelve years later, President Obama was in the White House. A Mediterranean coastal city symbolizing American diplomacy had been terrorized on two consecutive anniversaries of 9/11. The tables had turned. Terrorists were hunting down peace.

* * *

ONE year after four Americans died in Benghazi, we still had unanswered questions:

1. Why did the State Department try to prevent the media and Congress from speaking with DS agent David Ubben who was seriously wounded when he fought on the rooftop with Tyrone Woods and Glen Doherty?

2. If there was nothing to hide, why was CNN reporting that the CIA was polygraphing some of its operatives connected to Libya *every month* rather than the standard of every three to four years?[38] What was the agency trying to prevent CIA operatives from telling Congress and the media?

3. When Senator Rand Paul asked Hillary Clinton about a secret gun-tracking program to arm the Syrian rebels during testimony, she said: "I do not know. I don't have any information on that." But if she didn't know anything about a gun-running program, why had the *New York Times* reported that it was Hillary's idea during the summer of 2012 to partner with then-CIA director David Petraeus on launching a covert gun-running program?[39] Hmm.

4. Why, nearly a year after the attack, were journalists like CNN's Jake Tapper and legislators like Senator Rand Paul still asking whether the CIA annex in Libya played a role in smuggling weapons to Syrian rebels? Why couldn't the CIA definitively tell us whether weapons traveling from Libya to Syria accidently landed in the hands of the rebels who stormed the Benghazi facilities? If true, that would be something Obama and Hillary would not want the public to know.

Hillary lied. First, she saw and denied the cable requesting aid. Second, she knew there wasn't a video, and yet she led the public to believe otherwise and then said it made no difference whether her employees died because of a spontaneous video protest or a preplanned terror attack. Third, she apparently brainstormed on a gun-running program to arm the Syrian rebels with the CIA director before the Benghazi attacks.

Hillary did not take an oath before her testimony to Congress, so her lies can't be held against her as perjury.[40] Human courts may not be able to hold her accountable, but that is fine. We don't need to judge her heart: God can handle that.

Four days after her testimony, Obama sat next to her on CBS's *60 Minutes* and said: "I think Hillary will go down as one of the finest secretary of states we've had."[41] You bet she will. *Not.*

Now Hillary is exposed. Stark naked. And it ain't a pretty sight.

Mom! I Got Stung by a Drone!

Children used to run into the house screaming: "Mom! I got stung by a bee!" Those were the good ol' days. Under Barack Obama, a teenage American boy was stung by a drone. He never lived to tell his mother.

Obama authorized a drone strike that killed an innocent sixteen-year-old American boy, Abdulrahman al-Awlaki, and six other civilians including his seventeen-year-old cousin while they ate near a fire pit at an outdoor restaurant in Southern Yemen on the evening of October 14, 2011. Abdulrahman was born in Denver and moved to Yemen to live with his grandfather when he was seven. His father, Anwar al-Awlaki, was the notorious American who betrayed his country by joining al-Qaeda in the Arabian Peninsula. But his teenage son Abdulrahman had no ties to terrorism and he had not seen his father Anwar for two years.[42] Two weeks before Abdulrahman was killed, a different American drone strike killed his father, so the Obama administration could not have mistaken the son for the father; he was already dead.

Why did Obama kill an American citizen and innocent civilians? We never got a good answer.

In February of 2013, NBC News drove Obama to the brink of resuming smoking. NBC revealed a confidential sixteen-page Department of Justice white paper titled "Lawfulness of a Lethal Operation Directed Against a U.S. Citizen Who is a Senior Operational Leader of Al-Qa'ida or An Associated Force."[43] A better title: "President Justifies Killing American Citizens with Drones." The press was irate. They had not spent five years casting spells to enchant Millennials with Obama so he could lounge around the White House in bunny slippers and play with a remote control kill switch!

Barry must have been frantic. *Do I run under my bed and hide? Or, do I take this on full throttle and risk Michelle hauling me off to divorce court when she learns I sent an aide to the corner store for a carton of Marlboros?*

We think Barry went with the first option and cowered under his bed. We already know, thanks to Valerie Jarrett, that he's afraid of Michelle, after all.[44] We also know Attorney General Eric Holder was left to handle the ire of the press and Congress; and, Obama did not give a speech clarifying his position on drones until three months later.

The DOJ white paper was the most articulate justification for murder in American history. Background: George W. Bush launched America's targeted drone campaign. The first targeted killing operation was in Pakistan in 2004 and two Pakistani boys, ages ten and sixteen, were killed along with a band of insurgents. So, drones have been killing thugs and children together for some time and this is concerning.[45] That said, Obama was the first president to use drones to kill American citizens and also dramatically escalate the use of drones that kill innocent foreign civilians and children. Obama was also the first president to write a treatise flat-out claiming that he had the legal right to kill U.S. citizens. Finally, Obama was the first president to authorize the FBI to secretly use drones for domestic surveillance.[46] The DOJ white paper stated that the president or *any* "informed, high-level official of the U.S. government" has constitutional authority to respond to a "threat of violent attack against the United States" by a U.S. citizen in a foreign country *without* "clear evidence." It was unclear who qualified as an "informed, high-level official." Only the president? Congresspersons? Who? In some instances, the paper used the generic term "public official." That could be a postal worker or an NSA snooper trooper. This is why millions of Americans were outraged: *Who does our president think he is?!*

After the DOJ white paper leaked, Senator Rand Paul led a thirteen-hour filibuster in the Senate and #StandWithRand quickly became the most popular hashtag on Twitter, uniting commentators of all stripes, from CNN's Piers Morgan to Laura Ingraham, from Van Jones to Herman Cain, from Code Pink to Senator Ted Cruz. Paul and many others were concerned that the DOJ would try to use these same arguments to kill "suspicious" U.S. citizens with drones on U.S. soil.

The paper also cited a "public authority justification" for public officials who commit acts that would normally be considered murder or theft. As long as a public official could *excuse* killing an American citizen with a drone, it was neither criminal nor unlawful: "Congress did not intend . . . to criminalize justifiable or excusable killings." Really? Who was Obama kidding?

Cunning people can justify or excuse anything. This white paper effectively dismissed the Constitution entirely and introduced a very slippery slope whereby public officials could use lethal force against any American citizen who irritates them. By this line of reasoning, the president could authorize a drone to zap one of his old girlfriends who bent his heart out of shape. It was embarrassing for our country to have a Department of Justice writing treatises to grant our president such expansive powers. Here we have the Constitution with beautiful amendments like the fourth, fifth, and foureenth that articulate our rights to due process and private property, and Obama wanted to replace those with a white paper that amounted to a trashy murder novella.

This white paper incorrectly cited international law (UN Charter, article 51) instead of the Constitution—to argue that the president or any high-ranking official has the power to authorize force against an American citizen in another country and effectively declare a perpetual global war against terror without congressional oversight. Basically, the DOJ conflated international law with our Constitution.

Americans saw right through this nonsense. We know the Constitution trumps international law. Our government must respect our constitutional rights whether we are at home or abroad. Besides citing UN charters, this white paper cited many *opinions* from various politicians, lawyers, and scholars. Clearly the DOJ could not find sufficient Supreme Court precedent nor constitutional justification for its argument.

Paul's filibuster achieved an answer to the question of whether the president would use lethal force against American citizens on American soil. (Eric Holder sent him a one-word answer: "No.") That was reassuring and Paul brought massive awareness to the drone issue, but we *never* got an answer to the original question: What about American citizens, like Abdulrahman, on *foreign* soil? Obama refused to assure us he would respect our rights of citizenship, including due process, if we are living, vacationing, or working abroad.

Federal judge Rosemary M. Collyer of the United States District Court for the District of Columbia asked the Obama administration: "Are you saying that a U.S. citizen targeted by the United States in a foreign country has no constitutional rights?"[47] The answer Judge Collyer received from the administration's lawyer was obnoxious with a capital O: "We don't want these counterterrorism officials distracted by the threat of litigation."[48] Translation: Obama was not sorry about Abdulrahman and he wanted a court blessing for his administration to kill more Americans abroad without worrying about getting sued by victims' family members.

That's when the good judge should have ordered Obama's arrest. Wearing handcuffs and sitting in prison overnight would have knocked his god-size ego down a notch. Warren Buffett would have paid his bail.

Bull's-eye!

Drone policy was the way Obama's administration threatened to use American citizens for target practice. Cyberpolicy was the way Obama effectively turned our personal identities and our power grid into giant bull's-eyes for global hackers.

First off, Obama specifically targeted millions of young people to sign up for overpriced health insurance on the website HealthCare. gov without informing them that the site was a hacker's dream. "The website got overwhelmed by volume," he said in early October of 2013, brushing aside the site's technical vulnerabilities.

In reality, a month after HealthCare.gov rolled out, the site was essentially a one-stop shop for identity loss. "Hackers are definitely after it," security expert David Kennedy testified before a House panel in November of 2013, "and if I had to guess, based on what I can see . . . I would say the website is either hacked already or will be soon."[49] Here Obama had directed all Americans, particularly Millennials, to enter their personal information into a website that was some *40 percent underdeveloped* (per Centers for Medicare and Medicaid Services deputy chief information officer Henry Chao)—all so he could look like a hero for five minutes.

Fed up with Barack, the typing wizard at *Time* magazine who had written the 2012 cover story "Person of the Year: Barack Obama" called Obama's bluff. *Time*'s journalist quipped that Obama had obfuscated by selling the site's security vulnerabilities as symptomatic of "the popularity of the [web]site" when "the reality, however was far more dire."[50]

When he ran for president in 2008, Obama told tech-savvy young people that "the American Society of Civil Engineers gave our national infrastructure a 'D.'"[51] He vowed to "protect vulnerable targets from terrorism at home" and "modernize our power grid."[52]

Tick. Tock. It's August of 2012 and the power grid is a Stone Age hunk of junk.

Barry has wasted four years forcing taxpayers to spend billions on worthless solar projects instead of addressing the power grid. The American Society of Civil Engineers estimates $107 billion is needed to maintain a U.S. power grid that the *Washington Post* warns is "aging and stretched to capacity."[53] The U.S. power grid became the ticking time bomb that Obama's administration was aware of and failed to address. We are a cyberattack away from businesspeople trapped in elevators; drivers jammed mid-transit without working freeway or traffic lights; and students unable to attend school and not happy about it because their iPhones won't charge, the Internet doesn't work, and untreated sewage is spewing across beaches.

In early 2011, Leon Panetta spoke on Capitol Hill, warning that there had already been "hundreds of thousands" of attempts to take down the U.S. power grid and "We've got to develop . . . a defense against that."[54] Panetta then busied himself with more important matters, such as wagging his finger at the troops. In February of 2013, cybersecurity firm Madiant released an explosive, seventy-six-page report indicating that the Chinese government was sanctioning and responsible for a bulk of the cyberattacks against the U.S. government and American companies. When a Pentagon report also found the Chinese military to be responsible for breaching U.S. security networks, President Obama met with Chinese president Xi Jinping and asked his country to stop hacking American infrastructure. Big surprise: Xi responded by denying China's involvement and asserting China was the *victim*, not the perpetrator, of cyberattacks.[55] Obama looked like a real card.

In the early morning hours of April 16, 2013, a sniper succeeded in knocking out seventeen transformers at a Silicon Valley power substation in less than twenty minutes with 150 rifle rounds. Repairs consumed nearly an entire month in this unprecedented attack. Former Federal Energy Regulatory Commission chairman Jon Wellinghoff labeled the strike a "very well planned, coordinated, and executed attack on a major piece of our electric grid infrastructure."[56]

In October of 2013, the *New York Times* reported that two engineers who "say they hardly qualify as security researchers" had pinpointed critical security vulnerabilities within the country's electrical grid that an amateur hacker could exploit to "inflict a widespread power outage" but "hardly anyone has noticed."[57] The engineers sent the Department of Homeland Security a twenty-page report alerting them to vulnerabilities within the power grid and it took the DHS four months to post a single public advisory, which itself did nothing to solve the problem. Our saving grace was DHS secretary Janet Napolitano. For four years, she had worked night and day to keep us safe, at the incredible pace of a snail.

Obama should have taken proactive measures to revamp our grid— proactive measures such as drastically cutting spending, waste, taxes, and regulations so the private sector would have the flexibility to innovate and improve the grid. No one needed Obama to create another silly government agency. The government's technology expertise extended to full-body scans of grandmothers, toddlers, and good-looking gals. Anything practical? Forget it!

Unfortunately, Obama kept spending money on NSA snooper troopers and TSA creepers who did a fabulous job of scanning our e-mail accounts and patting down our bodies but failed to keep us safe from Chinese hackers or underwear bombers.

The Pentagon sponsored a program to try to train young people to become defensive hackers but this program was bound to fail or only be moderately successful because one of the qualifications to get into the program was that you *couldn't* have hacked anything before (because that is illegal). This automatically eliminated the brightest young techies who were not criminals but nerds, smart enough to hack for the fun of it. There are many intelligent young people out there who do not have the opportunity to channel their skills productively, so they go underground or take to the streets. Some of the biggest advancements in technology have come from smart little pranksters who had the opportunity to channel their abilities constructively.

For example, Apple cofounders Steve Jobs and Steve Wozniak started out as pranksters and hackers who channeled their intelligence and built Apple. Wozniak spent a night in a juvenile detention center for one prank and Jobs was suspended from school more than once.[58] When they were young, they played a hacking prank that allowed them to manipulate AT&T's infrastructure. No harm was done and it was all in good fun, but after that hack they realized they could build Apple.[59]

Al Gore pretended to have invented the Internet. Bill Joy actually invented the supporting code for the Internet. Around the time that Jobs and Woz were up to "trouble," a teenage Joy was in the University of Michigan's Computer Center. Computers were gigantic and insanely expensive to "play on." Joy hacked the system and accrued hours of free programming time, and the knowledge he gained via his prank eventually benefited society.[60]

Our government should have tried to productively harness the talent of young hackers instead of letting it go to waste. We should not reward hacktivists for damaging pranks. Hacking is wrong. However, surely most Americans are glad that Steve Jobs, Bill Joy, and Steve Wozniak did not waste their youth and talent in prison because they were smart and bold enough to experiment with hacking. Plus, don't you question the integrity of DOJ officials who propose using drones against American citizens while acting like they are heroes for hunting down teenage programmers?

Three notable actions Obama took to protect our power grid:

1. Ask China to please cease its cyberattacks.
2. Create a training program for young people to become reverse hackers that excluded the best and brightest from participating.
3. Buy a second dog to defend the White House and give it a fierce name, Sunny.

Bloody, Juicy Gossip

Besides leaving metaphorical ashtrays all over, Barry did something else that smoking presidents like Kennedy never dreamed of doing. Barry literally would not shut up, even on classified matters of national security. He probably quit smoking to be "presidential enough" to appear in public with Michelle, who didn't want him dropping cigarette butts on her designer dresses. He resented this and so, to release his hostility, he turned into a gossipy little snitch.

Obama even went so far as to compromise the safety of generations to come by leaking proprietary information in order to make himself look good.

Naming the SEALs: The 2011 Ch-47 Chinook Shootdown

The SEAL Team 6 members on the mission to kill Osama bin Laden, as well as their family members, have targets on their backs for the rest of their lives. Al-Qaeda knows who to hunt for vengeance.

SEAL Team 6 took out bin Laden on May 1, 2011. Two days later, the White House (via Joe Biden) named the SEALs as responsible for killing bin Laden. This was not an off-the-cuff, jolly jerk remark. It was a prepared speech. That night Panetta jumped for a slice of the attention, telling PBS it was "the SEALs."[61] What a bunch of schoolgirls.

The SEAL Team 6 member who actually shot bin Laden in the forehead and killed him told *Esquire* that this announcement led the media to invade the neighborhood where Team 6 members live and publicize their addresses and favorite local restaurants and bars to the world. Consequently, the SEAL considered legally changing his wife's and children's names to protect their safety, and his wife said she feared a "retaliatory terror attack" on SEAL Team 6 families.[62]

Who knows why Obama's administration named SEAL Team 6, other than that Obama was up for reelection and needed an exciting story to distract Americans from the economy. The more dramatic and dangerous the feat sounded, the better. SEAL Team 6 is an elite unit of an already elite military force. It's nearly impossible to become a SEAL. Only the superhumans among superhumans advance to SEAL Team 6. The fact that SEAL Team 6 was used for this mission made it sound much riskier, impressive, and, frankly, more cool.

Al-Qaeda only took three months to retaliate against SEAL Team 6. On August 6, 2011, twenty-two SEALs were asked to respond to a firefight with the Taliban in a valley of Afghanistan on a chopper that was not built for night raids. As their chopper entered the firefight, the SEALS were banned from using preassault fire because it "damages our [the administration's] efforts to win the hearts and minds of our enemy."[63] Because of Obama's blabbermouth and politically correct rules of engagement, the Taliban gunned down the chopper and thirty Americans died—including twenty-two members of the Millennial Generation. Additionally, twenty-two of the thirty Americans were assigned to the SEALs and included members of SEAL Team 6. Active-duty SEALs represent less than 1 percent (00.17 percent) of the total active-duty military. Losing twenty-two SEALs was a big, big loss.

Twenty-Two SEAL Team Heroes: *

Darrik C. Benson, 28	Nicholas H. Null, 30
Brian R. Bill, 31	Jesse D. Pittman, 27
Christopher G. Campbell, 36	Thomas A. Ratzlaff, 34
Jared W. Day, 28	Robert J. Reeves, 32
John Douangdara, 26	Heath M. Robinson, 34
John W. Faas, 31	Nicholas P. Spehar, 24
Kevin A. Houston, 35	Michael J. Strange, 25
Jonas B. Kelsall, 32	Jon T. Tumilson, 35
Louis Langlais, 44	Aaron C. Vaughn, 30
Matthew D. Mason, 37	Kraig M. Vickers, 36
Stephen M. Mills, 35	Jason R. Workman, 32

Eight U.S. Military Heroes: *

Alexander J. Bennett, 24	Patrick D. Hamburger, 30
John W. Brown, 33	Andrew W. Harvell, 26
David R. Carter, 47	Bryan J. Nichols, 31
Spencer C. Duncan, 21	Daniel L. Zerbe, 28

These SEALs did not need to die. They went into a firefight and obeyed rules of engagement knowing there was little chance they would come out alive. They are bigger heroes for giving up their lives willingly. But how many more Millennial warriors need to die before Obama and his coadjutors are held accountable?

When our special ops teams need to go after more terrorists, we won't have as strong a bench to choose from. Our special ops will be like a soccer team where there are no substitutes and the eleven players on the field have injuries. Any talented young person who was thinking about joining the SEALs will be rethinking this decision. Thanks to Barry's motormouth, we are safer than ever.

---

* Source: *Military Times* Honor the Fallen project, http://projects.militarytimes.com/valor.

Light Your Cigarette

Casual smoking won't kill you. But a nonsmoking president who gets casual about terror and spends his time obsessing over his image *will* leave you vulnerable to lethal violence. That's what Obama did. He left all Americans, particularly the Millennial generation, permanently exposed to terror until we start electing a new breed of politicians.

Obama's one big score against terror was when he told Navy SEALs to risk their lives and take out Osama bin Laden in Pakistan. He made this "tough" call from the comfort of the Situation Room—and he spent the next several months reminding everyone in America that he killed bin Laden and made America a safer place. Obama may have sent to his grave a semiretired terrorist ringleader who was hiding out in a compound full of vacuum-sealed raw opium and self-medicating on herbal Viagra.[64] But, overall, America became a far more dangerous place for Millennials during his presidency. Millennials trusted Obama and he betrayed their trust by letting easily preventable terror occur on his watch and then covering it up or downplaying it.

Someday we will wake up to an America where our president is not a poser. He (or she) will be authentic: a Marlboro Man, a secret keeper, a leader who spends less time perfecting his talking points and more time getting down and dirty and keeping America safe. The sun will rise and we will have a First Lady who will not be posing for pictures for her gardening book while wearing false eyelashes and yachting clothing and holding a rake in a way that no real gardener would ever handle a rake; a First Lady who doesn't gush that military families "take my breath away" and ask, "How is it possible that so many of us know so little about the challenges these families face?" while her husband callously ignores the pain these families experience due to his poor judgment.[65] We will have an executive branch with the judgment to secure our nation against terror attacks instead of a royal court that feigns good judgment. Someday soon.

Go ahead. Light your cigarette. In future elections, enjoy butting out Barry's legacy.

OUR GUN TATTOOS

9

G un-free zones" did not always exist. For many young Americans growing up as recently as the early 1960s (Baby Boomers), guns were culturally accepted as part of everyday life. Many eleven-year-old boys went to school with knives in their pockets. A pocketknife was part of being a boy. It was often a gift from their parents. It was a privilege to carry a knife and you didn't abuse the privilege or you would miss out on the bigger privilege of carrying a hunting rifle. Thirteen-year-old boys in Houston, Texas, used .22 rifles to plink snakes, bullfrogs, and turtles. Seventeen-year-old boys in Syracuse, New York, kept shotguns in their cars at school and hunted game birds like grouse after class. Seventh graders growing up in suburban Los Angeles didn't have as many opportunities to use guns but they weren't afraid of guns; those who wanted to shoot would go to a range or their parents would bring them to a ranch in the desert and let them loose with .22 rifles to shoot at rabbits and quail. Farm kids drove around with unloaded guns openly mounted on their trucks and another gun behind the seat. High school shop teachers let students make "projects" like metal handguns and gun cases and boys would bring their rifles in to class for "show-and-tell."

Across America, boys participated in high school army ROTC, where they shot .22 rifles at ranges connected to their school campus. College students—from Massachusetts to Minnesota—kept cased shotguns in their dorm rooms and used them for hunting on the weekends.

The cultural default was not to assume that people were criminals. The default was to assume that people were innocent until proven guilty. As a result, people had more freedom and more fun, and there was less mass public violence.

* * *

IN the 1920s and early 1930s, mass shootings occurred. But the typical shooter was a hopeless farmer, struggling to provide for his family, who concluded that it would be better for his children to enter eternal paradise prematurely than endure a slow death of starvation.[1] These shooters were different from modern mass shooters in three respects. First, they did not shoot randomly, at strangers in public. Second, their depression stemmed from a sense of helplessness in a dire economy, not schizophrenia or a desire for revenge against social bullies or terrorism.[2] Third, they sought to relieve innocent people of the pain of starvation, not inflict pain.

When JFK was shot in 1963, the nation mourned. Many Baby Boomers, who were schoolchildren at the time, still remember where they were when they heard the news.

One recalls: "I remember it clearly. I was five years old. We were watching the parade on TV and I saw JFK fall over. At first I didn't realize he was shot, but my grandma screamed. She grabbed her Rosary, made the sign of the cross and began praying. I started to cry. My mom was in the kitchen washing the dishes and she came in and started crying." She paused for a moment, then added: "We never knew that he was the playboy that he was. We only knew that he was our first Catholic president and that was a pretty big deal."

Americans wanted to do something to prevent a repeat of such a shocking tragedy.

But three years later, in the summer of 1966, the nation shook again with two mass killings. In July, a hardened criminal and alcoholic named Richard Speck with twenty arrests to his name broke into a Chicago townhouse for nursing students with a knife and a gun. He used the gun to force eight young women into submission. One by one, he garroted the women and used his knife to stop their hearts.[3] In August, a twenty-five-year-old student named Charles Whitman climbed atop a 307-foot tower on the University of Texas at Austin campus and spent eighty minutes randomly spraying bullets, killing sixteen and wounding thirty-one. Whitman had a brain tumor. Modern gun experts attribute the post-1966 acceleration in mass shootings, in part, to the "erosion of community in America."[4]

After these tragedies, more Americans became open to gun control. Even so, they proceeded with caution because, before JFK's assignation, there had been only one major public mass shooting on record in U.S. history according to the *Washington Post*—despite guns being widely available with few restrictions.[5] The 1960s were not that long ago, but our young people have no firsthand memory of this era, where *everyone* used more common sense. The Democrats of the sixties were nothing like Senator Dianne Feinstein, who told *60 Minutes*: "If I could have gotten 51 votes in the Senate of the United States for an outright ban [on semi-automatic firearms], picking up every one of them—Mr. and Mrs. America turn 'em all in—I would have done it!"[6]

Three years after Kennedy's assassination, in 1966, an influential Democrat, Senate majority whip Russell B. Long of Louisiana told the Associated Press: "I have yet to see a gun control bill which would have prevented the assassination of President John F. Kennedy, the killing of the nurses in Chicago or the sniping murders in Texas. These bills might make it more difficult for the murderers to get guns but the man who intends to kill can always get a gun. No matter what we do."[7]

* * *

FAST-FORWARD to 1990. Barack Obama is a young man and George H. W. Bush is president. Bush signed a bad bill that included the Gun Free Zones Act of 1990, which made it a federal crime to carry a firearm within one thousand feet of a school—public, private, or parochial. In 1995, the U.S. Supreme Court declared this law unconstitutional, as a violation of the commerce clause, and it went away. Two days after the Supreme Court's decision, now-president Clinton insisted on bringing the law back. Clinton wanted gun-free zones despite admitting that *twice* the number of high school students carried guns during the three years of the law's existence, from 1990 to 1993.[8] This was not about keeping kids safe. This was about Clinton appearing to keep kids safe so he could get reelected.

Clinton asked his attorney general, Janet Reno, to analyze the Supreme Court's decision and give him a way "to recommend a legislative solution to the problem identified by that decision." Reno sat down at her desk and got straight to work.

What Billy wants, Billy gets. Reno gave Clinton the Gun-Free School Zones Amendments Act of 1995. At Clinton's request, the Democrat-controlled Congress passed this new gun-free zone regulation. It was a beautifully written law, all about saving the children, while assisting its goal of helping Clinton win a second term. Picture a gorgeous ballerina making syntactical pirouettes through the Constitution and a *grand jeté* over common sense.

Schools are not the only places that became gun-free zones in the nineties. So did military bases. Bush Forty-One and Clinton share blame for this.[9]

Twenty years later, Obama became president. By this point, Obama knew the history and the stats about gun-free zones and gun control. He should have known that these measures backfire by leaving young people vulnerable to violence—both in the United States and around the world. For refusing to acknowledge those truths, Obama deserves far more blame than the politicians who passed the first gun control measures. It will take a long time to clean the metaphorical blood that stains Obama's hands.

Obama's Gun Tattoo Parlor

A great metaphor for Obama is that of a tattoo artist. Most tattoo shops let you decide what you want on your body. If you don't walk in with a sketch of your own, the artist can supply you with an array of design options. Tattoo artist President Obama only offered three permanent designs:

$$\mathfrak{Potential\ Criminal}$$

$$\text{POTENTIAL MASS SHOOTER}$$

$$\mathit{Potential\ Schizophrenic\ Gunman}$$

No one would want these tattoos, yet these are the labels Obama used to brand our young people. A tattoo artist uses ink and needles. Obama used lies about guns and unjust gun control laws to brand all Americans, *particularly* young Americans who are students attending school in gun-free zones and many more who are young professionals employed in gun-free "workplaces" such as schools and military bases.

We need to look at the gun control debate in a different way. We need to look at the damage gun control has done to our children and our grandchildren. Not just in terms of keeping them safe, but in branding them as criminals as opposed to the benefit of being presumed innocent before proven guilty. Obama's tattoos have left our youth with a culture of distrust and fear unlike that experienced by previous generations. Comparison of an October 2013 AP-GfK poll and the 1972 General Social Survey reveals that interpersonal trust has fallen markedly among Americans. In 1972, nearly half of Americans said they felt "most people can be trusted," but by 2013, only 32 percent felt they could trust most people and 64 percent of Americans felt "you can't be too careful."[10] By 2013, 62 percent of Americans told pollsters they could not trust the people with whom they shared photos, stories, or videos on social media sites like Facebook and Instagram, leading to the concerning implication that our young people—who have dominated such sites—feel like they cannot even trust their "friends." Here is one of the most overlooked and concerning long-term consequences of Obama's lies about guns and his gun control policies: Young people are being taught to suspect each other of heinous crimes before they get to know each other as friends. Trust is broken before it can form.

The president can't just label all Americans criminals any more than he can label all car drivers as drunk drivers. Because we all have this tattoo, our young teachers can't enter a school with a gun, our young military professionals can't carry a firearm on an army base, and all our young are taught to fear and hate each other, as well as an excellent tool they could use to protect themselves.

* * *

TATTOOS are mainstream among Millennials. It's becoming as common to see a young woman with a tattoo as a young woman with her ears pierced. Many Millennials love tattoos because they *freely choose* them. On the flip side, Millennials are just like their parents and grandparents were at their age in that they despise labels; they don't want to be prejudged or discriminated against. What is the term for labeling and prejudging innocent people as mass murderers? We don't have a term for it in the English language. The *effects* of this form of discrimination are similar to the effects of racism. Let's create our own term. It's a tattoo that all of our young people have but did *not* choose; it's Obama's gun tattoo.

Kids Need to Grow Up Around Guns, Not Fear Guns

For Halloween, Obama always dresses up like a gun. He thinks guns are really scary and he gets mad when hunters laugh at his silly costume.

In previous generations, kids were not afraid of guns. Kids used and handled guns; they knew you had to be careful, but they weren't afraid of guns either. These children knew: "It's a gun. It's not going to shoot someone on its own." Teachers and receptionists were not worried about mass shootings, although guns were easier to obtain. The culture was different. People were more community oriented and children were more respectful—saying "Ma'am" and "Sir" instead of "Hey you!"—and fewer were angry at the world. If you were a spineless criminal, you weren't going to risk attacking a school if there was a good chance a swarm of seventeen- and eighteen-year-old boys would grab their huntin' rifles from their trucks, chase you down, and pump you full of buckshot.

Decades ago, JFK would have been laughed off the stage if he had called a rifle an "assault weapon." Our young people never heard about this time; they did not know that their parents, Baby Boomers, could buy a box of shells for a small-caliber rimfire .22 rifle at the corner gas station at the age of thirteen. They didn't know that kids brought guns to school and went hunting afterward. Our young people were only taught to be afraid of guns. Which doesn't make sense because their parents are (somehow!) still alive.

Obama supported gun-free zones, which teach children to be afraid of a self-defense tool every time they walk through their school doors. He made it sound as if the gun, the inanimate tool, was the criminal. By scaring them, he also deprived them of learning to use the tool for self-defense, as children knew how to do in the fifties and sixties.

A Little Girl Growing Up in a Gun Family

Here is how children who grow up around guns *think*. This is the truth that Obama failed to tell our young people. We'll examine this from the perspective of a little girl who grew up around guns, because that's the perspective of yours truly:

I grew up in a gun family. Hunting was part of my family's culture. Every Thanksgiving, my uncle would bring out a huge tray of wild appetizers—bison, elk, or venison—whatever his latest trophy happened to be. Before we ate store-bought turkey, we had to eat *real* meat. If it was bird, sometimes I would find a BB in the meat. No big deal, it was like finding a stray pit in an olive!

I don't remember our house ever smelling like gunpowder. I only remember feeling safe and happy around gun owners. I thought my father looked equally good in a suit and a tie as in blaze orange and camouflage. I thought it was cool that he would sometimes paint his face in camo before a hunt and that he wore a "fragrance" called "fox urine masking scent." I watched him hang his deer in the garage before he processed it and I helped my mother pack and seal the meat. She did most of the work, but I absorbed important lessons by participating in the process as a child. I saw a dead deer hanging with an open cavity and then a lot of blood and raw animal flesh, so it could have been a gory experience. However, my parents used it as a lesson in health, economics, and conservation. This venison was "organic" meat, free from hormones, so it was very healthy for me to eat. It was also very economical. Moreover, my parents both emphasized how we were respecting the animal by using every bit of meat and not wasting anything. My father enjoyed hunting but he was a purposeful hunter too. He did not want me to think that he shot animals for the heck of it. Later, I watched my father carefully clean and stow his firearms and ammunition. I always understood that his guns and compound bow were *not* toys.

Growing up with mostly male cousins, my sister and I often played outdoor games like "cops and robbers" and "war." Of course we pretended to shoot each other with plastic toy guns. We were playing! No one got hurt, aside from an occasional scraped knee or grass stain. We knew the difference between toy guns and real guns. It never crossed our minds to be afraid of guns or to abuse guns and treat them like toys, because our parents made gun safety crystal clear. Eventually, we took gun safety classes. But the first and best "gun safety" we learned came not from our parents *saying* anything, but from observing how our parents and relatives (the adult gun owners in our lives) *handled* guns. Children learn best by example and we had terrific examples. Because of this, we all grew up to be responsible young adults.

We were not farm kids. We grew up in dense suburbs and could have seriously hurt ourselves or others. But it never crossed our minds to run around with loaded guns; that would be as silly as chopping carrots with a spoon! We saw guns as tools, useful for protection against criminals or hunting in woods and fields.

"Dad, please tell us a bedtime story!" my sister and I would request at night. All his stories were about hunting, his favorite childhood memory. We fell asleep, imagining our father and uncle as little boys, carrying their shotguns and walking through golden cornfields alongside our grandfather on a beautiful autumn morning.

Guns and ammo sounded as innocent to us as counting sheep. This is because our father didn't educate us on gun safety by singing us to sleep with a Snoop Dogg rap song about pistol-whipping pimps, bitches, and AK-47s.

If my brothers so much as shoved my sisters, in the playful way that all brothers do, I remember my father saying: "You don't *ever* hit a girl." He taught them the difference between needless force and meaningful lethal force for self-defense by being a stickler about details. Most of his lessons were actions, not words. His example was so strong and consistent that rap songs, video games, or movies glamorizing violence could never influence my brothers.

My father let us watch violent movies where there are clear-cut good guys, like *Braveheart* and *Gladiator,* but we did not play graphic video games like Call of Duty or Grand Theft Auto. Violent video games were not "banned," but my parents did not buy them for us and we did not buy them for ourselves. We were raised to love nature too much to spend all day on a couch holding a remote control. There is so much violence available instantly on the Internet. But by exposing children to gun safety from a very young age, fathers (and mothers, too) can teach their sons and daughters that force has one purpose: protection.

At night, I felt comforted and safe knowing that my father had guns in the home and at his bedside. A dog, a security system, a high fence, a Taser, a bottle of pepper spray, or—God forbid, as some progressives have suggested—my own urine or vomit could never have provided the same sense of security as knowing that my father had guns. Besides locking our doors, the *only* security we had were my father's guns and that's all I needed to feel safe as a child. I knew it could take the cops up to twenty minutes to respond, but this never bothered me, because I completely trusted my father's ability, even under pressure, to defend us on his own.

* * *

THIS is how a young child thinks who grows up around guns and it is very concerning to think that President Obama indoctrinated our youths to think that guns are evil. Guns are not evil and a "culture of guns" does not turn young people into criminals. It does the opposite; it trains them to use guns properly and be prepared to defend themselves, their friends, and even strangers. Children who grow up around guns learn that a gun is a tool, not a toy. Obama, on the other hand, grew up to sing about pistol-whipping pimps and AK-47s as if they were toys. And this guy thought he could lecture our young people on guns? What a hoot.

What did Obama know about guns? He may have graduated from two Ivy League schools, but he failed Guns 101. At a fundraiser, Obama said that Newtown shooter Adam Lanza used a "fully automatic weapon" at Newtown. Just to refresh Obama's kingly cranium, a fully automatic firearm is one where you can pull the trigger, hold it back, and it will automatically continue to fire rounds until you release the trigger. With a semi-automatic, you need to pull the trigger back each time you fire a round. When Obama can articulate the difference between a semi-auto and full-auto firearm, *then* he can talk about guns and gun-free zones. Until then, give us a break. No one needs a backseat driver, especially a six-year-old who has not yet learned to drive.

Children who grew up in gun families can attest to the fact that a "culture of guns" does not turn young people into criminals. A culture of depression, anger, and abuse can. When children are loved, they usually learn to show love. When children are not loved or they suffer from mental issues, they grow up to act violently or erratically; these unfortunate children use whatever tools are at their disposal, even their own hands, as Erika Menendez did when she pushed a man in front of a New York City subway train because "I thought it would be cool."[11]

No one is afraid of their oven, although hundreds of people die every year from cooking equipment, and this is because we have all been raised around ovens. Our parents let us bake cookies when we were little bambinos but we were also told: "Don't touch the burners" and "Always turn off the burner!" Guns are a tool that children should be exposed to and trained to use, early on, just like ovens.

Progressives will say, "This is why we need more gun control!!!" Well, we definitely need to do something, just not more of the same things we have tried for fifty years that have failed. The answer is bigger than a square of cardboard or an NSA Snooper Trooper performing minute-by-minute, real-time observation of all gun owners. We will get to a solution in this chapter.

Tattooed by Obama: Eagle Scout Arrested in Gun-Free Zone

An Eagle Scout was trying to be a responsible gun owner when he was arrested and kicked out of school because Obama's lies had indoctrinated our culture and labeled him as a potential mass shooter.

David "Cole" Withrow was a sixteen-year-old Eagle Scout and honors student attending a North Carolina high school in April of 2013. He was a few weeks away from graduating. One weekend, Cole went skeet shooting. The following Monday, he drove to school. When he parked his truck in the school parking lot and reached for his book bag, he realized that his unloaded shotgun was still in the truck. He hurried into the school building, where he used a school phone to call his mother, make her aware of the situation, and try to resolve it. His hope was to obtain permission to leave school and bring the firearm back home. As Cole spoke with his mother, a busybody school official listened in: *An unloaded gun in an unoccupied, locked vehicle! That spells DANGER! I don't have anything to do today. No such thing as job security these days. I'll make myself look useful by ratting on this boy!*

Police were called. Cole was arrested, expelled from school, and charged with a felony. The felony was reduced to a misdemeanor when he agreed to the prosecutor's position that he knew the gun was in his car when he drove to school.[12]

An all-around good kid receives a tainted record and is forced to plead guilty to a crime he did not commit. Meanwhile, the Adam Lanzas of the world get to trot through the front door of schools and shoot to kill. Who are gun-free zones serving?

And where was President Obama? Just three months earlier, he had released a photo to prove he enjoyed the hobby of skeet shooting "all the time." Also, on the campaign trail, Obama had told young people he would protect their Second Amendment right to "participate in a variety of shooting sports, such as sporting clays, skeet, target, and trap shooting."[13]

How Obama Used Guns to Buy Votes

His entire life, Obama exploited guns—to make himself look cool, and for political advancement. As president, he would take actions to control guns, actions that, at heart, he *knew* were unethical, illogical, and unconstitutional. When he was a high school student, he *chose* to defend the pro-gun-rights argument for class and won the debate because he did such an excellent job of making his case.[14]

When Obama was an adult (by age, not maturity), he was proud to announce that he sang his baby daughter a rap song that portrayed AK-47s as toys and pistols as the tools of pimps. A few years later, when he was running for president and needed to win the votes of Millennials, he promised that he would protect their Second Amendment rights. Obama summarized his vision for America as president in a preelection book where he outlined his "plan" for America, including a plan to "Protect the Second Amendment."[15]

Barack Obama believes the Second Amendment creates an indi-
vidual right, and he greatly respects rights of Americans to bear
arms. As President, he will protect the rights of hunters and other
law-abiding Americans to purchase, own, transport, and use guns.

He gave speeches on the campaign trail, promising that "I believe in the Second Amendment, and if you are a law-abiding gun owner, you have nothing to fear from an Obama administration!"

When he was safely reelected president, and concerned about his legacy, he told lies about guns so he could look like a hero of children by pushing bans on semi-automatic firearms. What did he care if average Americans living in Middle America couldn't defend themselves from intruders? He would have armed Secret Service protection for perpetuity!

Young people voted for Obama thinking he would protect their right to self-defense and the right to hunt. He let them down. And now they and their children will live with consequences they did not bargain for, labels and branding that could haunt them for the rest of their life—like a tattoo they never authorized.

The Shooters

Five of the twelve deadliest mass shootings on record in American history occurred when Obama was president.[16] Who were the men who pulled the trigger? Let's take a look.

- Binghamton, New York, Immigration Services Center shooting, 2009. (Thirteen dead, four wounded, shooter kills self.)
  - *Shooter:* Forty-one-year-old Jiverly Antares Wong, mentally unstable and delusional.
- Fort Hood Shooting, 2009. (Thirteen dead, thirty-two wounded.)
  - *Shooter:* Major Nidal Hasan, who "displayed erratic behavior," isolation, and unreliability during his military career. The

FBI was aware of his communications with al-Qaeda member Anwar al-Awlaki.[17]

- Tucson, Arizona, grocery store shooting, 2011. (Six dead, thirteen wounded.)*
  - *Shooter:* Twenty-two-year-old Jared Loughner, diagnosed with schizophrenia; displayed delusionary, isolated, and erratic behavior before shooting.[18]
- Aurora, Colorado, movie theater shooting, 2012. (Twelve dead, seventy injured.)
  - *Shooter:* Twenty-four-year-old James Holmes, counseled by a psychiatrist who notified the police one month prior to the shooting of his homicidal statements and threats, and the danger he posed to the community.[19] Upon arrest, Holmes played "puppets" with the paper bags shielding the gunshot residue on his hands while a detective interrogated him.[20]
- Sandy Hook Elementary School shooting, 2012. (Twenty-six dead; shooter also kills his mother and himself.)
  - *Shooter:* Twenty-year-old Adam Lanza, diagnosed in childhood with conditions that made him more vulnerable to anger and anxiety: sensory integration disorder (SID) and Asperger's. His babysitter said he threw unnatural tantrums and Lanza's mother instructed the sitter to "keep an eye on him at all times and never turn my back or even go to the bathroom or anything like that, which I found odd."[21] In the last years of his life, Lanza holed himself up in his room, playing violent video games such as School Shooting. He blocked the sunlight from his windows with garbage bags and relied on e-mail to converse with his own mother.[22]
- D.C. Navy Yard shooting, 2013. (Twelve dead, eight wounded. Police kill shooter.)

---

*Tucson is included in this list because it was widely covered by the media and thus most people are familiar with the story, although it is not one of the largest mass shootings in U.S. history.

— *Shooter:* Thirty-four-year-old Aaron Alexis was dismissed from the navy reserves because of repeated misconduct. He was hired as a military contractor despite an arrest for vandalizing a car with a gun, an arrest for improper discharge of a firearm, and a history of delusions and prior poor performance in the navy reserves. His contractor clearance let him bypass armed guards at entry. Under Obama, the number of security clearances rose 15 percent after 2010, and by 2013 there were 4.9 million total clearances in issuance.[23] According to *Time,* when Bush was in office in 2006, it took an average of 165 days to receive a security clearance; four years later, under Obama, it took just 53 days.

These six shootings were not the only mass shootings that occurred during the Obama administration, just those that ranked among the largest in U.S. history and are also best known. In each of these shootings, the gunman had mental health issues. In every shooting except for Tucson, he also went to a gun-free zone to commit his crime. In Tucson, Loughner went to the grocery store parking lot in broad daylight, maintaining the pattern of demonstrating a disregard for the law and also acting out of the norm for the usual criminals we face as a society, who tend to have a rational fear of repercussions, such as jail time.

These shooters are not your average American or your average gun owner. They also broke every law there was to break. They stole guns (Lanza stole his mother's gun and Alexis stole his second gun from a security guard). They used contraband weapons (Alexis skirted the law by using a shotgun with a sawed-off barrel). They entered gun-free zones with guns (all, except Loughner, who opened fire in broad daylight). All of them operated firearms while mentally ill. All of them committed murder. How many laws did a mass shooter need to break for Obama to wake up?

The Fort Hood shooting and D.C. Navy Yard shooting were preventable crimes. There were warning signs that the Obama administration knew about and failed to act upon for politically correct reasons.

The FBI knew Hasan was in communication with al-Qaeda and the military knew of his poor performance, and the Pentagon failed to act.

Former New York City mayor Rudy Giuliani pointed out that Barack Obama has "institutionalized political correctness to the detriment of the safety of the American people." Giuliani also said, "Bureaucracy [FBI and other law enforcement agencies] is very sensitive to what goes on at the top. And the signal being sent to this bureaucracy, whether it's the military in the case of Hasan or law enforcement in the case of the Boston bombing, is, boy, you better be very, very careful about how you classify people. So careful that you are so far on the side of caution that you neglect doing basic things . . . like they did with Major Hasan, promoting him all the way up through the military."[24]

Likewise, the military was aware of Alexis's track record of misbehavior and mental instability. The Defense Department admitted to missing "red flags" and a navy admiral forced Alexis's commander to grant him honorable discharge instead of general discharge, which contributed to his being hired back as a military contractor and granted security clearance.[25]

We'll give Obama this much: Fort Hood *was* a workplace. But, Obama lost us by calling Hasan's shooting "workplace violence" instead of "terrorism." He lost us when he delayed Hasan's trial for over three years. He lost us when he took our money and paid a terrorist a salary.[26] (Usually that would be called paying an assassin.) Obama put terrorism on par with a disgruntled employee who opens a hundred cans of tuna, sneaks into his boss's office, and sprinkles tuna fish everywhere.

Even Obama's own party had to criticize his methods. Representative Chaka Fattah of Pennsylvania excoriated the Obama administration for using "political correctness" to classify Fort Hood as "workplace violence" instead of "terrorism," tiptoeing around Hasan's "extremist" beliefs, and denying combat-level benefits and Purple Heart awards to the injured victims.[27]

Back to the shooters. They were all mentally disturbed and Hasan was in contact with al-Qaeda. Our young people who are students or teachers or work on military bases are lumped into the same category as these shooters. Because of gun-free zones and gun control, Millennials are all tattooed as potential criminals, like Hasan. This is silly, and dangerous, public policy.

Sorry Barack, Your Lies About Guns Ain't Bulletproof

C ome on! Let's go to the shooting range! Leave your ammo at home. You won't need brass this time. Words are our bullets. We're shooting up Obama's lies about guns. For splattering targets, we have five bull's-eyes, *each* marked with one of Obama's gun lies. Ready, aim, fire!

Obama Lie #1: Gun Owners Are "Bitter Clingers"

Gun owners are from diverse backgrounds, and it's condescending to try to put them all in one category. Yet that's what Obama did. He said that all Midwest gun owners are "bitter" about the economy and political system, after being misled by the Clinton and Bush administrations about job creation—so they cling to guns or religion.[28]

Obama was sending the message that guns and faith are abnormal; that Americans who own guns or believe in God are angry kooks who would probably shoot your eye out before they turned the other cheek.

POINT ONE: Obama far outdid Clinton and Bush on lying to Americans about jobs. More than his predecessors, Obama did a super-cali-fragi-listic-expi-ali-docious job of tanking the economy. Obama not only insulted gun owners by calling them bitter, but the foundation he constructed for their supposed bitterness was about as flimsy as his paper gun-free zone signs.

POINT TWO: Most Americans have faith in God and most Americans pray, so there's nothing abnormal or exclusive to gun owners about faith. Many Americans are members of churches where they express their love for God in a community, something the Obamas made a big show of doing while he ran for president and then effectively stopped doing once he became president.

Obama Lie #2: Semi-Automatic Rifles Are "Assault Weapons"

There is no such thing as an "assault weapon" or "assault rifle." These are made-up terms beloved by Obama and his gun control cheerleaders like former New York City mayor Michael (Mickey) Bloomberg. Six days after the Newtown tragedy, Bloomberg went on ABC's *Nightline* to discuss gun control and made himself sound very silly.

Nightline anchor Cynthia McFadden asked Bloomberg whether his definition of an "assault weapon" would ban pistols. He responded: "No, but pistols are different [from "assault weapons"]. You have to pull the trigger each time. An assault weapon, you basically hold it, it goes: *BADUTDUTDUTDUT!*" McFadden corrected him: "No, those are *fully* automatic weapons." Unembarrassed, Bloomberg went on to share his sage advice: "Don't try to go for a gun. You've got someone pointing a gun at you, you think you're gonna be able to outshoot them?! That's one of the stupidest things I've ever heard!" When McFadden pointed out the hippocracy of his anti-gun views: "There are men with guns out there to make sure that you're safe," Bloomberg didn't bat an eye: "Yeah, absolutely."

Oh Mickey! What a pity you don't understand guns. Don't shoot your eye out Mickey!

Obama, Bloomberg, and their girlfriend Senator Dianne Feinstein unfairly targeted AR-15s and other semi-automatic firearms, calling them "assault weapons." FBI data shows that a hammer or a fist is more likely to be used as an "assault" weapon than any kind of rifle.[29] Should we cut off our hands? And then, when we don't have hands, should we hold a stick in our mouth instead of a hammer when we need to drive a nail through the wall and hang a painting? C'mon!

It is arbitrary to call an AR-15 or a semi-automatic rifle more dangerous than a handgun. An AR-15 has a longer barrel than a handgun, which means it can shoot farther, more accurately, long range. But an AR-15 is also big, meaning that you can't conceal it easily. A female al-Qaeda member could be wearing a sundress and have a pistol holstered on her thigh and no one would know. A terrorist could not conceal an AR-15 by holstering it to her thigh.

Whatever object or substance a crazy person is using to attack you is the most dangerous one. Scalding water is more dangerous than bullets if that's what is being sprayed on you. The danger depends on the *situation*, not cosmetics.

We've all been in a public place before and witnessed a situation where a stranger falls and collapses due to a heart attack or faintness and, inevitably, a generous off-duty doctor or nurse in the crowd rushes forward to aid the stranger in need. Gun owners who are carrying concealed in a public place behave the same way. A gun owner's natural instinct is to *protect*, not to assault. That is why the term "assault weapon" was so harmful for our young people to hear, especially from a man with as much weight as the president of the United States.

Many hunters keep guns for personal protection and prefer to use compound bows to hunt certain animals, like deer. Whether a hunter uses a gun or a bow, he or she grants the animal a more merciful death than Mother Nature—who offers slow and painful deaths by starvation, disease, or the claws of predators. This is why it was hilarious to hear Michael Bloomberg liken deer hunters to lazy pigs who may as well use dynamite to blow up their deer. What a moronic and immoral thing to suggest!

Hunting is all about the preparation, camaraderie, enjoyment of the great outdoors, and the pursuit of the beast, not an assault on it. Hunters eat what they kill too. Little Mikey B. can buy himself a free-range organic hamburger and think he's a great guy, but the man who goes one extra step and uses his own hands to kill the animal that provides the organic, free-range meat is somehow a menace to society? Get real! For the sake of our kids. Please.

Guns are never for assaulting people (or animals). Guns are tools for defense and conscientious recreation. The people you use a gun to shoot are the kind Bloomberg says not to: armed criminals who are in your face, threatening you. He who fires first lives.

Obama Lie #3: Gun-Free Zones Keep Kids Safe

Obama never admitted that he needed to reconsider the price of gun-free zone regulations.

There is no evidence that gun-free zones or cardboard signs deter mass shooters, either in the United States or around the world. No matter what language you use to print "Gun-Free Zone" on a sign—be it English, French, German, Japanese, or Korean—the signs never stop criminals from killing children.[30]

Criminologist, lawyer, and retired professor Don B. Kates Jr. wrote after the Newtown tragedy: "There is no known instance of a terrorist or lunatic surrendering to the unarmed victims he was killing. In contrast, had one armed parent been present [at Sandy Hook Elementary] 20 small children could be alive today."[31] A gun is the lone equalizer in the face of an irrational gunman.

Obama made a speech where he slandered gun owners, saying they "willfully lied" about his gun control proposals. Several days *before* that speech, the *New York Times* reported how police were now advising Americans to take an active response, such as "fighting back" during a mass attack, including "shooting" the "perpetrator."[32] But you can't fight back very easily if you are in a gun-free zone, can you?

Obama Lie #4: Backgound Checks Keep Kids Safe

Background checks have never been proven to help. Major Hasan passed a background check. Jared Loughner passed a background check. Aaron Alexis passed a background check. Neither existing background check law nor the Manchin-Toomey bill Obama pushed for (which would have expanded mandatory background checks for gun purchases, including firearms bought online or at gun shows) would have prevented these men from committing mass murder.

Obama's administration said this would save lives. There is no hard data showing that expanded background checks will protect children from insane people. Dr. John Lott has shown that "There is no real scientific evidence among criminologists and economists that background checks actually reduce crime."[33]

Lott wrote about Obama's lies in the *National Review* in January of 2013: "Obama made many other false statements during his talk. He asserted that 'over the last 14 years [background checks] kept 1.5 million of the wrong people from getting their hands on a gun.' But these were only 'initial denials,' not people prevented from buying guns."[34]

We need to reform the existing background check system before we add more layers of bureaucracy to it, otherwise we will be holding innocent people back from obtaining a gun while failing to address why people like James Holmes seek guns.

Obama Lie #5: "Easy" Availability of Guns Explains Higher Gun-Related Crime Compared to Other Countries

No other advanced nation endures this kind of violence—none. Here in America, the murder rate is three times what it is in other developed nations. The murder rate with guns is ten times what it is in other developed nations. . . . What's different in America is it's easy to get your hands on a gun—and a lot of us know this. But the politics are difficult, as we saw again this spring.[35] —President Obama, September 2013, memorial for victims of D.C. Navy Yard shooting

Obama left out one teensy weensy detail: This was a lie.

Crime is high in other countries; the criminals just don't necessarily use guns. Five days after Obama spoke, NPR released an article showing that Russia has far fewer guns in circulation than the United States (under 13 million vs. 300 million) and about 58 percent more murders.[36] In Russia, there are bans on full-auto and semi-auto firearms and very strict background checks to obtain handguns or shotguns; there are 9 guns to every 100 Russians versus 100 guns to every 100 Americans.[37] Yet, the result of all this gun control is that Russia still suffers mass shootings and has 58 percent more murders than the U.S. according to the latest data available.

Russia is not the only phenomenon disproving Obama's claim. Two criminologists and professors emeritus, Don B. Kates Jr. and Gary Mauser, published a study in the *Harvard Journal of Law and Public Policy* in 2007 that has yet to be refuted, showing:

There is no social benefit in decreasing the availability of guns . . .

*One study asserts that Americans are more likely to be shot to death than people in the world's other 35 wealthier nations. While this is literally true, it is irrelevant—except, perhaps to people terrified not of death per se but just death by gunshot. A fact that should be of greater concern—but which the study fails to mention—is that per capita murder **overall** is only half as frequent in the United States as in several other nations where **gun** murder is rarer, but murder by strangling, stabbing, or beating is much more frequent [emphasis in original].*[38]

"Most Americans are unaware that gun crime is markedly lower than it was two decades ago," reported the Pew Research Center in May of 2013.[39] Here Obama was scaring Americans about guns while, in fact, gun violence was way down. Compared to 1993, gun homicides *dropped 49 percent* by 2010 and assaults, sex crimes, and robberies committed with a firearm had collectively *dropped 75 percent* by 2011. Plus, most people who died by firearm were not victimized, they were depressed, and used the firearm to commit suicide instead of other means.

Another finding from Pew: under 1 percent of all gun homicides are mass shootings.

Despite the fact that gun crime was declining, only 12 percent of Americans thought it was declining; 82 percent of Americans thought crime had increased or plateaued.[40] Gee, wonder why! Maybe because, listening to Obama, you could think a "bitter" hunter with a fully automatic AR-15 was hiding behind every corner ready to go *badudududut!*

* * *

THAT was fun! We did a great job of putting bullets through Obama's lies about guns. Bull's-eye every time! That was nice target practice. But it's not enough. Now, we need to leave the "shooting range" and put our skills to work in the real world. We need to use our words—our bullets—to offer a better solution. Obama's oratorical solution to violence is more gun control laws. We can do better than that.

As gun owners, we need to offer a real solution to solve *all* needless death. The children who died at Newtown are angels. Their lives matter as do the lives of the troops who are dying, one a day, from suicide.

Below is a two-pronged solution that politicians should embrace because it will protect our freedoms, increase peace, and save lives. And even if the only thing politicians care about is winning votes, well, it does that too. Because this solution will *actually*, not theoretically, save lives.

Fewer Gun Laws

Terrorists and insane people are not afraid of the penalties associated with breaking laws: jail and death. Mass shooters get satisfaction from preying on the vulnerable; they are not looking to fight, they are looking to kill. You can't "scare" these people away from killing with the threat of imprisonment or death. You can only impede them (let teachers carry) and proactively prevent them from reaching violent depression (love each other).

Israel experienced great success in deterring school violence by allowing school officials to be armed.[41] Every public shooting in the United States since 1950 in which more than three people died took place where guns were banned; the one exception is the Tucson shooting.[42] That's amazing.

The philosopher Thomas Aquinas argues that great carefulness must be exerted in creating new laws: "Wherefore . . . in establishing new laws, there should be evidence of the benefit to be derived, before departing from a law which has long been considered just."[43] Since the beginning of time, humans have had the natural right to self-defense. In other words, the Second Amendment simply reinstates a law that has long been considered just and we have yet to see evidence of the benefits to be derived from gun control laws. This is not surprising; gun control is unnatural and sound human law is based on natural law.

The right to self-defense is a *civil right*. Progressives—the same ones who did not want Obama to use drones against innocent children in the Middle East or Americans at home—should join us in standing against laws that restrict this natural, civil right.

Love, Love, Love: Fewer Gun Laws, More Love

Guns are the reactive, defensive answer to evil in the world. We also need love.

Sometimes it appears as though evil is "spreading," such as when we hear stories about the Newtown tragedy. How could this happen to our children? However, what is happening is people are choosing not to love or are struggling to love, because they are mentally ill, arrogant, or afraid. Evil is less powerful than love. Evil is nothing. Love is real. Love spreads and consumes like a wildfire. We need to start setting sparks. A wildfire begins with a spark.

We have tried background checks. We tried banning the manu-facturing of firearms and magazines (thanks, Bill Clinton!). We tried gun-free zones, as have many other countries around the world. Countries like Russia have experimented with stricter background checks and more gun control than we have. The result? Mass violence.

David Nathan, a doctoral candidate in counseling psychology at the University of Saint Thomas, pointed out after Newtown:

> *No one has the power to keep guns away from everyone who would use them on innocent people. . . . Every single young man who com-mitted mass murder over the past few years had a mental illness. We will never know what would have happened if someone had reached out to them [with counseling or friendship] before they acted.*[44]

We can all play a role in ending mass violence, murder, and suicide. Our role is loving more, not passing laws.

Loving the Mentally Unstable

M ost mentally ill people are *not* violent. One way we can love the mentally ill and prevent them from becoming violent is to encourage them to be open with their feelings. They need to trust a counselor so that they will take their medications and keep coming back for therapy. This means *not* putting all mentally disturbed people on a national registry as some politicians and lobbyists have suggested. Most states do their own reporting, and we need to be careful not to dissuade depressed people from seeking the help they need, if we hope to keep our kids safe.

Our treatment of the mentally ill begins in childhood, when parents and society at large have decisions to make about treatment. Some questions for parents to think about: Are we being too politically correct as a society, trying to "mainstream" children with severe physical or mental challenges? Is it right for little Jessica who has a need to take up one teacher for one year? Is it fair to our teachers to ask them to teach thirty-five students at one level plus another student at a different level during certain periods of the day? It is extraordinarily tough to have a special needs child and such parents ought to be commended for their love and sacrifice. For children who may have violent tendencies, that individual attention might be the strategy that keeps them from becoming a violent adult. At the same time, it is also frustrating for other parents who feel like their child and their child's teacher are being stretched thin.

Many of us cannot imagine raising a challenging or mentally unstable child, although I do have the parallel experience of caring for and loving a person whose illness—Alzheimer's—caused them to speak and act violently. Yes, Alzheimer's comes later in life, but there are children out there who call their mothers "bitches" and threaten to "kill" them—exactly like an Alzheimer's patient can behave toward a caretaker.[45] These children do not understand how they are treating their mothers any more than dementia patients who used to be sweet, loving, and proper know that they are swearing and hitting. My search for solutions comes from seeking better ways to care for our mentally ill—young, old, and in between. We cannot pretend that special needs children are not special needs. Some mentally unstable persons, especially those prone to physical and verbal violence, like an Alzheimer's patient, *cannot* be "mainstreamed."

There used to be state-run hospitals for the mentally ill. However, one of the last bills that John F. Kennedy signed, the Community Mental Health Act of 1963, eliminated most state hospitals. This was known as "deinstitutionalization." The mentally ill were to be transitioned into community mental health centers. Two thousand centers, each housing 100,000 individuals, were supposed to be built by 1980 but only 768 were built by 1989.[46] Many of the mentally ill ended up crowding the streets of big cities like New York instead.

There needs to be a balance between "mainstreaming" and institutionalizing the mentally ill, whether they are children or adults. When JFK leaned too far toward idealism, we ended up in a situation where we had mentally ill people, not in improved facilities but *homeless* and unable to take care of themselves. Unfortunately, the Community Mental Health Act of 1963 strayed too far from common sense and the endeavor unintentionally hurt the mentally ill instead of improving their lives. With the majority of state hospitals closed, some of today's special needs parents are told that their best option is to throw their child into *prison.*[47] We need a better way, and it needs to involve *parents*. Mark Mattioli, father of six-year-old Sandy Hook Elementary School victim James Mattioli testified: "Parenting is where we need to focus our attention. We do not need complex laws."[48]

Mainstreaming is often not fair to the mentally ill person either—to ask them to be what they cannot be. Mainstreaming misses the beauty of their illness. For example, an Alzheimer's person never holds a grudge. How beautiful is that? They also won't tell secrets; you can talk something out with another human being and rest assured that it is forgotten fifteen minutes later. Likewise, there are undiagnosed children who are *geniuses*, but prone to violence. A genius does not need conventional school; he or she needs to be challenged so a special gift of music or mathematics can flow, and without endangering others. By trying to mainstream the education of mentally abnormal people, we could miss the beauty in the "abnormal," while stretching our teachers too thin and shortchanging our students without issues. To solve this problem of mass violence, we need to start by loving our mentally ill in a way that avoids the dangerous trap of political correctness.

Obama, meanwhile, won a high school debate by articulating the benefits of gun rights but was too afraid to admit that gun-free zones don't work—and the result was Newtown. He institutionalized political correctness in his intelligence bureaucracy, and the result was Fort Hood.

Barry must have dipped his pacifier into a solution of political correctness every night before Michelle tucked him in with his security blanket.

* * *

OBAMA could not make up his mind about guns. One morning he was recreating by skeet shooting; the next, he was sticking his head in the sand while an Eagle Scout was arrested for enjoying the same hobby. Obama also struggled to piece together the facts about gun control in a logical manner and make real, lasting strides in reducing mass violence. Even further, he unfortunately lacked the leadership skills to ensure our young people understood how to safely use and could freely access the tools (guns) they needed to defend themselves and prevent violence. Obama never acknowledged that gun-free zones backfire, despite the statistical evidence proving they fail. He observed five of the biggest mass shootings in U.S. history, and while all occurred in gun-free zones, he lied and said we needed more of the same.

Obama never displayed a consistent moral opposition to guns. He wanted to go skeet shooting, but he didn't want anyone else to go skeet shooting. He held up scary-*looking* guns like AR-15s and called them assault weapons because that was easy to pitch to the public, especially if you don't tell the public that AR-15s are rarely used in gun homicides.[49]

Obama may not have *set out* to get young people shot, but he also didn't seem to care if they did. If he had cared, he would have dropped the gun control, which left children vulnerable to violence. But, as with

Clinton, gun control was his big opportunity to *look* like he cared. He chose to try to *look* like he cared by sending our young people to prepare for a gunfight with a cardboard "gun-free zone" sign.

Criminals opt for and use the most modern and advanced weapon technology they can get their hands on (guns). When Obama did not defend a young person's right to use a gun, he was attacking the most effective far-range tool of self-defense, and this was very immoral. Firearms can wound and deter from dozens of feet away. Electronic control devices like Tasers can put young people in a compromising position because the assailant must be within ten to fifteen feet. Fists, knives, clubs, and bats require the attacker to be practically standing next to the victim (unless she happens to be a champion knife thrower). By this time, it will be too late.

Children already see and hear guns used violently in video games, movies, and music; why didn't Obama want to counter that by allowing them to see guns used properly and safely? Because he was not about safety, he was about Barry. Unlike Obama, everyday Americans like you and me can fight back against violence in our culture, and against damaging labels that haunt our children and wear away the basic trust that holds our personal and professional relationships together.

Three things we can do to end needless violence and remove our gun tattoos:

1. Love each other.
2. Teach children gun safety.
3. Overturn failed gun control laws like gun-free zone regulations and stop passing more laws that violate our civil right to self-defense.

This route will be harder than writing laws. Love is tough and also takes time, which is why we know it will work. Short-term solutions like laws make things worse. We need a long-term solution and it is love and justice. Since we cannot prevent all evil in the world, we still need guns to defend our natural right to life.

Removing Obama's "gun tattoos" from our youths will be a painstaking process, just like removing ink tattoos. Most Millennials have not had the benefit of growing up around guns. Millennials have grown up in a culture of fear and distrust that helps politicians win votes, and also gets young people killed. Over time, by spreading a message that is rooted in facts—and *love*—we can recapture the freedom and community of the early 1960s.

Obama only represented *himself,* instead of representing American values. He acted like he cared about keeping American children safe and then pushed gun control legislation that left our children vulnerable to carnage. He acted like he cared about keeping Americans safe from terrorism and then he treated al-Qaeda-coached murderers like Nadal Hasan better than American warriors. If Obama wanted to go down as The American President Who Hated America, he did everything right.

ROARIN' MUSCLE CARS 10

've penned a few lyrics to give us an anthem for reclaiming our dreams and freedom:

Jump in my GTO! Let's find a stretch of open road.
We'll race the Chevy Super Sports.
Big engines. High horsepower. Rock 'n' Roll. Turn it up!

Let's go for a ride in the 442! We'll show 'em how much torque we got.
Drive-ins. Cream sodas. Waitresses on roller skates. Cruising the strip!

Rev the Chevelle! We'll outroar the surf.
Gunning the twists. Hugging the cliffs. Pacific Coast Highway!

Loving God. Working hard. Having fun.
Feeling the rush of freedom!

Barack Obama said he would take our young people forward. Forget forward. Forget following a man without a moral compass. Let's go back to a culture of *freedom!* We can't turn back the clock. We can't erase the damage that Obama did to our young people. Turning back the clock on our technological advances, our medical breakthroughs, the civil rights struggle, and the multitude of other positive changes our country has made isn't the answer. Millennials today have bene-fited from the opportunities made possible by those advances. We *can* go back in the sense that we can learn from what worked in the past and ask ourselves, why were we so eager to "change"? What was great about life in the early 1960s, culturally, that we wish we hadn't changed for the sake of changing? Freedom. We've gradually given up our own freedom to politician after politician looking to win votes; and each suc-cessive politician has taken away more of our independence, more easily. Enough. We're throwing on the brakes. In this chapter, we'll discuss how we can revitalize our lives and move toward our dreams by unlock-ing an American culture of entrepreneurship; pride in our nation; fact-based and faith-driven lifestyles; reputable political representatives; and openness to honest dialogue.

These are our youths. This is our land. This is our money. And we're taking our freedom back. Here's how:

Feelin' Hot Rod Confidence

Not every young person had a gun in the 1960s. Many young peo-ple, especially those who lived in big cities without easy access to hunting land, were more likely to have another symbol of freedom. Muscle cars. Classy, sporty cars with a lot of pep—thanks to big engines and high horsepower. Hot rods like the GTO, 442, Chevy Super Sport, Chevelle SS, Trans Am, and Dodge Charger attracted young people into car showrooms because of their racing power and the independent lifestyle they represented.

Cars have been an expression of freedom for forever. You can go wherever you want to go, crank your music as high as you want, and see the other side of every hill. You can *fly*. Cars reflect our mindset and our culture. Muscle cars represented the confidence Americans had in their God-given right to be free. The confidence of a muscle car is a feeling that penetrates your whole body. You get behind that piece of metal—not plastic—and you step on the gas. You hear the rumble. *Bddddduuurrrrr!* You feel proud. You feel freedom, that get-up-and-go! You feel like life is good.

Cars were very big in the sixties. All the cool bands wrote songs about cars: "G.T.O." (Ronny & the Daytonas); "409," "Little Deuce Coupe," "Fun, Fun, Fun," and "Shut Down" (Beach Boys); "Drag City" and "The Little Old Lady from Pasadena" (Jan and Dean). In the sixties, teens couldn't *wait* until they could get their driver's licenses. It's interesting to contrast this with today, when historic numbers of teenagers are choosing *not* to get their drivers' licenses because they prefer to let their parents drive them around.[1] Parents could cut the umbilical cord and tell teens to get their butts into driver's ed, but driving sounds boring to young people because many modern cars, especially electric cars, are not cool. The only time the Chevy Volt was hot was when it set itself on fire. Thanks to faux environmentalists like Jolly Green Barack, electric cars represent a vise grip, not freedom. Green cars will be cool when the government gets out of the way and private entrepreneurs improve their price, look, and functionality. Until then, no one wants to drive or write songs about cars resembling the red and yellow "Little Tikes Cozy Coupe."

We keep giving men and women in D.C. our freedom. Men and women with less business experience, less common sense, and less interest in the truth than us. We know, after learning the truth about Barack Obama, that most government bureaucrats do not care about our children or us. They can't do basic math (think senior IRS official Lois Lerner: "I'm not good at math!"). They are in power because they got lucky: important people wrote letters of recommendation for them and other important people caved to their whining for unearned promotions, helping them sail through life by the seat of their pants (think Obama). These people are not leaders and they are ruining our children's future.

The Little Old Lady from Pasadena was the "terror of Colorado Boulevard" because she was a speed demon and shut down all the guys who would race her on the strip. We should be the terror of Pennsylvania Avenue and shut down the politicians who hug our children, lie to our children, take our children's votes, and then leave our children in the dust.

Competition Clutch

When Americans looked at Barack Obama, they saw a man with his nose in the air, test-driving a Chevy Volt—a car that would erupt in flames after government crash tests. When Americans looked at their president, they saw a former community organizer in a yellow hard hat meandering through a government-subsidized solar panel factory that he knew would go bust.

When Americans listened to Obama, they heard a former smoker who now achieved his high by talking down to them: "We could save all the oil that they're talking about getting off drilling if everybody was just inflating their tires, ah, and, and getting regular tune ups, you could actually save just as much!" They observed a man who did everything he could to stand in the way of America utilizing her natural resources like shale, coal, natural gas, and oil that could make us independent of Middle Eastern oil and allow us to create jobs and dominate the world. And when Americans heard President Obama rambling about how he "fumbled" and needed to "win back" his "credibility" after breaking his promises for Obamacare, they lost their confidence in the dominance of America.

Americans living in the JFK era had 100 percent confidence that other countries took America seriously. They knew our allies would do business with us and communist efforts would crumple if they encountered American resistance. The president of Brazil wasn't canceling trips to meet with the president of the United States because of NSA Snooper Troopers. *That* happened under Obama. Neither our allies nor our enemies take us seriously anymore thanks to Obama, our first adolescent president.

Next time we elect a president (or any politician), we all need to come together—including the conventional media and Hollywood, whose livelihoods depend on freedom. Let's join the same team, Team Freedom, and elect a president with the metal to come through in the clutch instead of a man who is willing to drag his country into World War III to salvage his ego and his "red line" ultimatum. In the future, let's look for men and women to lead us who possess certain qualities that Obama lacked:

(Actual) experience: Youth can allure, as Obama's did, but maturity is priceless. We don't need any more children in Washington. We also should be wary of incumbents with so-called "experience," in politics, which means they have spent twenty years refining their white lies, family history, and hugs. We need representatives who can relate to us because they have *recently* done what *we* do everyday: work hard; save money; build companies; listen to and care for our families, friends, and clients. Being able to "relate" to us is not enough: we should look for ingenuity in finance, science, medicine, or foreign policy. For terrific talkers can be poor *doers*.

Game plan: Obama never had a plan; he had promises. Next time, let's demand a plan.

Courage: The dastardliest trait Obama possessed was cowardice. He cowered under political correctness, enabling American death and misery. Think Fort Hood; Benghazi; the 2011 Chinook shootdown that killed thirty Americans and twenty-two SEALs; the D.C. Navy Yard shooting; record numbers of U.S. service members lost to suicide and suffering from PTSD; Lieutenant Clint Lorance sentenced to twenty years in prison; and the festering of absent fatherhood and joblessness.

Love for America: This means respect for our law, the U.S. Constitution. Politicians who want to be European aristocrats or pseudo-preachers do not understand that the founders wanted individuals and states to have more freedom in spheres where Obama tried to exert control: health care; marriage; free speech; energy; and, the dollar, which he and Ben Bernanke manipulated in ways that helped the rich get richer and the poor poorer.

Workin' and Savin' for a Brand-New 409

Young people worked on their muscle cars all the time in the fifties and sixties. Cars weren't computerized, making it simpler to work on them. They had no power windows or seats, no air conditioning and certainly no air-conditioned seats. This manual system was not as dependable as our modern computerized systems, but many people still work on their own engines today. By tinkering on their cars and changing their own oil, they learned self-sufficiency and saw the fruits of their labor. As young adults, our parents were proud to work hard and save money. Their efficient spirit was reflected in the era's hit songs, including the Beach Boys' "409," which *glamorized* youths who worked and saved their "pennies" and "dimes" to buy a "brand new 409."

Fun was often about finding an open piece of asphalt and showing off how much torque you had in your engine, and then getting a good night's sleep so you could go to work, save up for a hot rod, and then put yourself through college, launch a career, and buy a home. Most young people growing up in the sixties knew that if they worked hard, *anything was possible.* Our young people feel the opposite; they feel like no matter how hard they work, success is often luck of the draw: Obama and his wife held up entertainers as role models of successful "businesspeople" who became rich by getting lucky; men who rose to fame by rapping about drug abuse, domestic battery, and violence; a woman who made millions by shaking her booty and pitching soda pop. These are not very realistic or healthy careers. Barack and Michelle should have encouraged young people to think realistically and recognize that success comes through hard work, not luck.

'57 Chevy

Obama's promises about hope and jobs were empty and his policies set Millennials further behind than before. Is there still a chance for our young people to achieve their dreams and find fulfilling careers?

Absolutely. Even in this terrible economy, with the odds against them, young people *can* reach their goals and fulfill their dreams.

In the late fifties and into the sixties, many teenage boys who wanted a new muscle car but could not afford one decided to get innovative. They bought a used car—the '57 Chevy—which had a fantastic body style and everyone loved the looks of it: its lines, chrome, and flaring rear fender. Guys souped up the engine, raked it, added different mufflers to enhance the sound, or added a cool paint job in the hot color combinations, like aqua and white. Young people did all of this on their own in their garages and ended up with the same results as those who could afford new wheels—all because of their ingenuity. Today, there are more '57 Chevys on the road than there were in 1957; the car is an American icon.

Our young people can do something similar: we can achieve financial independence and fulfilling careers by thinking outside the box. It won't be easy, it won't be conventional, but we can do it and here are some places to begin:

BE OPEN TO ALL THREE FORMS OF ENTREPRENEURSHIP: In late 2013, *Entrepreneur* magazine featured a Rasmussen College report showing that 71 percent of Millennials say they would like to leave their "regular" jobs and become their own bosses and that 60 percent of Millennials intended to jump ship within two years.[2] The biggest reason Millennials gave for these desires? *Freedom.*

As a nation we need to channel this pioneering desire in a way that is uniquely best for each young person. For some Millennials, their desire to work for themselves stems from being underutilized and unchallenged. For other young professionals, experts say their discontent at work stems from a lack of self-awareness or understanding of their options. I believe there are three ways to be an entrepreneur in America:

1. *Traditional:* Starting a business on your own. This is the hardest route and requires a distinct personality type and an amazing business plan. Natural (traditional) entrepreneurs tend to be responsible, driven, nimble, persistent, and, most of all, free

spirits. They will give up sleep and social activities to hit their goal. They have a nearly spiritual belief that they are offering the world a product or service, energizing them in the face of obstacles. An entrepreneur's work is so important for society, and requires such enormous passion, because he or she creates jobs that *last*—not temporary green gigs. Steve Jobs described the work ethic and vision of a faux entrepreneur shortly before he died: "people call themselves 'entrepreneurs' when what they're really trying to do is launch a start-up and then sell or go public, so they can cash in and move on. They're unwilling to do the work it takes to build a real company, which is the hardest work in business . . . . a company that will stand for something a generation or two from now."[3]

2. *Hybrid:* Existing companies—from Fortune 500 companies to tiny start-ups—need hybrid entrepreneurs. These are young professionals who click with their company's vision. Then, they go above and beyond their job description to use their passion and creativity to spearhead new products, solutions, or services that enhance client satisfaction and profitability. Existing companies should capitalize on Millennials' desire to innovate and encourage them to trailblaze within the company. Young people will find fulfillment, companies will retain top talent, and clients will be more satisfied. It's a win-win-win.

Research shows that entrepreneurs who launch companies in their forties, not their twenties, have the greatest chance of achieving success.[4] For some young people, hybrid entrepreneurship is an essential stepping-stone into traditional entrepreneurship down the road; their corporate job is a "workshop" where they will develop the maturity and experience to make it on their own.

A report conducted by Harris Interactive in 2011 found that young people between the ages of twenty-one and thirty-one said they desired "a sense of meaning" in their careers more than any other factor.[5] Millennials are attracted to entrepreneurship because they view it as a way to create a meaningful path for themselves; but meaningful work can be found in existing organizations too. For example, a Marine sniper like Sergeant Rob Richards, who innovated on the battlefield, is a hybrid entrepreneur in a meaningful career. Same with a young doctor who heals her patients, or a salesman who figures out how to profit by saving his clients money with his product or services. Basically, a hybrid entrepreneur is anyone who does his or her job passionately and successfully.

3. *Social:* Stay-at-home parents, young people who care for their aging relatives, and young people who start nonprofits are all social entrepreneurs. A parent who homeschools is effectively running his or her own school, and this is a full-time, high-value job. Likewise, a young person who starts an educational nonprofit (assuming the corrupt IRS approves it!) is innovating by promoting intellectual diversity while stimulating learning and open dialogue. It is also possible, with a strong support system in place, to be a social *and* hybrid or traditional entrepreneur simultaneously.

By staying open to all three routes to entrepreneurship, our young people will ensure that they choose the right path for their individual talents, interests, and personality.

So, after openness, what's next?

FIND WHAT YOU LOVE TO DO: The most essential step to finding lifelong entrepreneurial success is to determine what you *love* to do. Because, when you love (80 percent of) what you do, you will work most efficiently: you will be working in your "zone." Staying open to all possibilities will ensure that you don't close a door too early. For example, as a girl I once told my mother that I "hated" writing and would "never" become a writer. She offered me good advice: "Never say never." Thankfully, I took her advice and scribbled for fun and then for a city newspaper and discovered (to my surprise) that I loved journalistic writing.

I have received helpful advice from wise and generous mentors over the years and have also acquired a few valuable life lessons in my ongoing journey toward a fulfilling entrepreneurial career. When I was a college student, a mentor who is a successful, self-made entrepreneur gave me this advice: "Always be doing something else." So, I kept up my writing on the side, starting a conservative student newspaper on my college campus, while exploring different careers and completing a variety of internships. Another mentor told me: "Explore as many careers as you can during college. People are more willing to advise you when you're young, and, if you make a mistake, it won't matter." These were great kernels of wisdom that I appreciate to this day.

As a college student, there is enormous pressure to hone in on your lifelong career within two short years. So many of us are interested in more than one career, making it challenging to choose one to spend the rest of our life in. Declaring a professional track almost feels like being forced to pick a marriage partner! What I found is that, if you have multiple interests, the way to discover what you love to do is by jumping in and trying everything you are interested in.

As a sophomore, I explored finance and medicine through an internship as a financial auditor for a large medical device company and through an externship involving clinical shadowing. As a junior and senior, I explored law, by interviewing lawyers, as well as commercial real estate with both brokerage and property management internships. All this time, I was still writing editorial columns for my college newspaper so I would be keeping my options open by "doing something else" that I knew I enjoyed. Throughout your journey of scouting out career options, keep in mind that if you consistently feel underutilized, it's a sign that you are not in the right field; you cannot *love* what you are doing, you can only *like* it, and need to persevere in exploring.

The best advice I can offer to young people trying to discover what they love to do is: Jump in! *Just go for it.* You'll never find what you love to do, and consequently what you are best at, until you try. Early and often. Explore internships while you're a college student. Of course, thanks to Obama's economy, it's hard to find paid internships or to justify taking a nonpaid internship if you are acquiring college debt. Even if you are on academic scholarship, you want to maximize your time—by doubling up. Blend your higher education and your professional exploration together; ask your professors if they will let you do "experiential learning" (I did this twice) where you *actively* explore and do a paid or unpaid internship or externship in a field such as law, business, or medicine while meeting with a professor one on one, reading business-related texts and writing papers that connect your real-world work experience to theory.

If you are a young professional who was recently laid off or if you are a recent graduate who has been job hunting for many months, here are four buoys to keep up your hopes. First, half the battle is staying energized and never giving up faith in yourself or your future. Good things really do happen to decent, hardworking people because all employers want can-do attitudes. Create your own luck by keeping up your search with a smile, and word will spread. Second, drink lots of tea. Not by yourself; invite others out for coffee or tea. It's far more affordable than breakfast, lunch, or happy hour. Try to buy your mentor's drink; it's good form. A four-dollar coffee with one executive could lead to another contact, which could lead to a job. Third, write thoughtful e-mails when requesting meetings and send handwritten thank-you notes after every meeting. One executive who has generously mentored me for years said this the first time we met: "Do you know why I agreed to meet with you?" She didn't wait for me to answer. "I get so many e-mails from young professionals asking me to meet them so they can 'pick my brain,' and some request dinner, assuming dinner's on me too," she said. "That entitlement drives me crazy. Your e-mails were thoughtful and I could tell you would respect my time." When looking for contacts who will lead you to a job, genuine words can open doors. If you're already doing all of these things, here's one more nugget: Look for neglected markets. We'll eventually need many conscientious caretakers for Baby Boomers who enjoy their active, independent lifestyles and won't want to retire to sterile nursing homes or assisted living facilities. We'll need more aides, nurses, and doctors who specialize in geriatrics, and more innovative entrepreneurs to care for our maturing population. Millennials have big hearts and a desire for meaningful work; there's opportunity here, as well as in other neglected markets.

For young professionals who are already in the workplace and still looking to find what they love to do, there are many options. The best route is volunteering to take on challenging projects. Spearhead your own projects to create solutions and expose yourself to *every angle* of the career you *think* you want to pursue. If there are multiple departments within your company, e-mail executives within those departments and offer to take them to breakfast or lunch and learn more about their niche. Join committees or take on leadership roles within your professional industry where you will make connections and also expose yourself to new ideas. I chaired national and state "young professional" commercial real estate committees for our trade association. I also participated in a public policy committee, where I listened to seasoned developers walk us through the ridiculous regulations they had to jump through or the years they had to spend negotiating with city bureaucrats over a development project. Chair the committee: I immediately raised my hand at every chance to lead. This added tasks to my day job, but I found that the chair gains the most, regardless of any extra work. By taking on extra leadership roles, you will be acting as a hybrid entrepreneur and helping your company while learning lifelong skills that you will need to start your own venture one day.

Position Yourself, Immediately, as a Go-Getter

If you dream of being an entrepreneur, you'll benefit from interfacing with seasoned experts who are far older than you, who were in your shoes at one point, and can offer you direction. But, just like you won't improve as basketball player if the coach won't give you any playing time, you won't be able to improve as a professional if the VPs and the CEOs won't take a risk on you and let you cut your teeth on work that's a bit more challenging than you can handle. It is a risk for a VP to hand a junior colleague a big, high-profile assignment. To earn the privilege to work on challenging assignments and learn entrepreneurial skills, immediately position yourself as a go-getter.

One summer during college, I was doing typical commercial property management intern work (cold calls, filing, data entry, and special projects). I kept things interesting by keeping my eyes peeled for trends in the data that I was working with, and discovered a trend that I felt certain the executives would want to know about. On my own time, I created a PowerPoint presentation analyzing the implications of the data and asked my supervisor, a vice president, if she would be interested in hearing it. She was.

My boss then recruited her boss and another VP to listen to me present a second time. Ultimately, they did not implement my full proposal. But by going the extra mile behind the scenes, I gained their trust as an intern. They offered me a full-time job upon graduation, and for the rest of my time at this firm, I was tapped by upper management to work on special projects, including confidential research on new acquisitions for the CEO. These extra projects helped me learn and grow, as I was working side by side with some of the most experienced directors within the company. Basically, by working as a hybrid entrepreneur, you will acquire the skills you will need to do what 71 percent of Millennials say they want to do, which is to start their own business someday. I would not have gained these valuable learning experiences if I had not pushed myself to pioneer within an existing company as an intern.

Do What Scares You—It Might Become What You Love

As you move toward success, particularly entrepreneurial success, take time to do what you (think you) fear. For instance, if you avoid public speaking, do that. Several times a month, as a college intern and then as a full-time employee, I made myself participate in a public speaking program for the brokers at our firm. Most interns did not participate but this was the best decision I ever made. Each speech became more fun as I focused more on engaging my audience and less on my racing heart. If your company has a public speaking program, by all means participate. Even if you're in a role that does not require regular presenting, such as engineering or accounting, the skills and confidence you gain will spill over into your life and career. If your company lacks such a program, form your own or consider joining Toastmasters.

Many people only achieve about 70 to 85 percent of their career potential and it's *not* because they are in the wrong field; it's because they are in the right field, but they never forced themselves to break a sweat. Break a sweat, and take yourself to 100 percent.

Gotta Be Cool, Now Power Shift

Baby Boomers and Gen Xers who supervise or lead Millennials in the workplace will advance their own careers and improve corporate bottom lines by helping young people achieve their desire to become entrepreneurs. If you are a Boomer or Gen Xer and notice that a young person who normally has enormous energy is behaving aloof or disinterested, it could be that they've begun to feel like they have no way to give everything they have to offer. Rather than losing this young professional to traditional entrepreneurship (before they are ready) or to another company with a better offer, try to challenge them at *your* company.

Sometimes Millennials feel like their ideas are unwanted, so they shut down, negatively impacting everyone because great ideas are discarded before they materialize. Invite your junior colleagues to participate in executive meetings and on big projects and encourage them to pipe up if they have an idea, even if they think it might be "off the wall." That said, be sure you set a high bar too. Young professionals enjoy a challenge and will feel more fulfilled if they need to "earn" the right to be involved, because this will push them to show up at meetings well prepared, having read up on the latest industry news in trade journals or having analyzed key data on their own ahead of time.

Seasoned professionals, parents, and teachers can help fill the "role model gap" that the Obamas helped create—by more aggressive mentoring. Young people want so badly to achieve success, but hardly anyone is telling them that it comes through hard work. Parents and supervisors: tear out a success story about a young entrepreneur from the newspaper or a magazine and give it to your child or employee. Encourage them to read about inspirational entrepreneurs like Steve Jobs who achieved success through innovation and hard work, not by twerking.

Encourage your young employees, students, or children to engage in public policy as well. My supervisors *encouraged* me to participate on that public policy committee and cheered my decision to chair the young professionals committees. By participating, I traveled across the country and witnessed the political challenges of doing business in different major geographic markets firsthand; I also collaborated with other businesspeople in D.C. to educate our politicians on the benefits of lower taxes and common sense regulations. For a young woman, this was an invaluable learning experience; the blinders came off and I realized that job-generating business projects are often held up by taxes, regulations, or ignorant politicians who believe they're "saving the earth" from the (non–scientifically proven) dangers of human-caused warming. For example, developers would be awarded for incorporating a high level of "sustainable resources" into building materials—where a young tree felled *locally* could be considered more sustainable timber than an old tree felled and trucked from an overgrown, ready-to-erupt-in-flames forest. I learned that sententious bureaucrats looking to make themselves *look and feel* like they are shattering "glass ceilings" will push developers to grant an arbitrary number of contracts to female-owned or minority-owned businesses—regardless of the availability of minority-owned firms that offer more competitive rates and greater expertise than other firms. Expose your employees to public policy issues and draw the connection for them so they see how superfluous bureaucracy and taxes make it hard for you to do business or increase their salaries. My supervisors were professional, without letting political correctness stop them from educating me. For example, one executive "educated" me by stopping me in the hall to debate newsworthy topics impromptu: "So Kieffer, what do you think about . . . ," which forced me to always be on my toes; he also regularly e-mailed me with lessons from our founding fathers.

By educating your junior associates, and explaining the connection between government regulation and their jobs, salaries, and promotions, you will motivate them to be engaged citizens or possibly even run for political office someday. You will groom future civic leaders with solid business experience under their belts and boatloads of common sense, which is far more valuable to our country than boatloads of community organizing.

Daddy, Take the T-Bird Away

Obama never understood the value of money, but in his arrogance, he thought himself an economic whiz. So, he caused his recession to drag on forever by spending more and creating new taxes like Obamacare. It pays to teach children the value of money. You never know . . . they might become president one day!

Today, it is common to hear parents and grandparents complain about "entitlement" in young people. This is a valid complaint. Young people have it easy in some ways and need to learn what it means to work and earn their keep. We *can* teach our children that they are capable of more than they think. To get them started, they need the adults in their lives to hold them accountable because they won't realize their capabilities if their best friend is a tablet or if their parents do all the housework while they text. It is didactic for children and young adults to pitch in around the house, and parents should not feel like they are the personal assistants to their progeny.

If parents and grandparents pass along their work ethic, young people won't fall into the trap of thinking they deserve something for nothing. Your parents made you save your pennies and dimes for your 409. You know the sense of pride and fulfillment that comes from setting a goal and working and saving to achieve that goal. Let your child or

grandchildren have the same chance to feel the pride of *earning* a modern version of a brand-new 409. Let them feel that giddy-up!

Drag City

Young Americans would go out to a stretch of empty road and race
each other in their muscle cars in the sixties. This was not necessarily "legal," but kids did it all the time and everyone knew it. Street
racing or "drag racing" was a huge part of the allure of muscle cars. It
was the thrill of "Who's gonna get there first?"

There were rules in the 1960s, but everyone understood that laws
don't stop criminals. Instead of bazillions of laws, previous generations
had strong families and parents taught their children three basic rules:

1. The Golden Rule
2. The Ten Commandments
3. Eat Your Brussels Sprouts

Today, our young people have so many laws that it is overwhelming; it is crippling. The NSA Snooper Troopers, the TSA Creepers, and
Obama's Gun Tattoos have caused our young people to clam up. They
are afraid to speak their minds, even among their friends; they self-
censor. We do not have free speech in America if young people refrain
from sharing certain remarks via text because they fear the NSA.

If we want more rules, we'll write them ourselves. For now, we need
to pare down to the basics. Let's elect politicians who will honor our
existing laws (natural and constitutional), such as our right to own and
carry guns for self-defense, before concocting ineffective and unjust laws
like Obamacare and gun-free zone legislation. As our Founding Father
Patrick Henry once said, "Everyone who is able may have a gun."[6]

We need fewer taxes and regulations so that young people can dig
themselves out of this mess by becoming entrepreneurs. The fact that
the United States has the highest corporate income tax rate in the G20
is threatening entrepreneurship and job growth.[7] Let's have a new goal—

the lowest corporate income tax rate in the G20—and watch how many young people start businesses!

Helping our veterans succeed as entrepreneurs is one more reason to lower taxes and regulations that burden small businesses. Entrepreneurship is also a proven way for veterans to battle postcombat stress, find a job in this difficult economy, and utilize their unique leadership skills. Almost one in ten small businesses is owned by veterans, and vets are 45 percent more likely to start businesses than individuals without a military background.[8]

By voting in local elections, by choosing strong candidates, and by utilizing our voices to educate our friends, colleagues, and legislators, we will make America the most, not the least, competitive place to do business. *Let's burn up that quarter mile!*

Freedom of Faith

Today, parents and young people alike have become skeptical of public worship. Pew Research released a major study in October of 2013 indicating that a historic number of American Jews are losing their religion and not passing it along to their children: One in four Jews say they do not believe in God and two thirds of Jews do not belong to a synagogue. Young American Jews (Millennials) are the most likely to say that, while they are proud of their Jewish heritage, they have "no religion."[9] The Jewish faith is hardly alone in this regard. Since 1990, the number of Americans who self-identify as having no religion has doubled; 16 percent of all Americans say they have no religion.[10] Researchers say this does not mean these Americans have abandoned faith in God. Rather, this increasing trend of "no religion" indicates that some Americans are losing confidence in the value of public spiritual fellowship.

We all crave happiness and serenity in our fast-paced world. How do we go about relaxing our hearts and minds?

A weekly visit to church is a wonderful way to give ourselves a little spa time. If we open ourselves to the benefits of attending church, we may find that we grow more blissful while our children become more respectful. What could we lose? Let's explore the benefits of spiritual fellowship:

BOOSTS HAPPINESS: Gallup found a link between church attendance and higher feelings of happiness and lower feelings of negativity compared to those who don't attend church regularly.[11] By watering down the way we express our faith publicly, we may have lost some happiness.

HELPS CHILDREN THINK METAPHYSICALLY: Worship-based activities are sometimes dismissed as "irrational." However, a child who attends church may be exposed to a wider world of ideas than that encountered in school or day care, a world with the reason-based thinking of philosophers like Augustine of Hippo:

Augustine was a playboy. His mother, Monica, would weep and pray; Augustine rolled his eyes. He was very smart; he loved philosophy and logic and spent years experimenting with various ideologies. Augustine was highly influenced by Plato, and Plato's renowned student, Aristotle. Eventually, he shocked his mother and chose Christianity as his primary philosophy. In his book, the *Confessions*, he perfected Plato's famous leaky vessel analogy: "You [God] arouse us so that praising you may bring us joy, because you have made us and drawn us to yourself, and our heart is unquiet until it rests in you."[12]

In faith-based activities, children often benefit by encountering metaphysics and the same high-level, reason-based thinking as classical philosophers like Aristotle and Plato.

HELPS CHILDREN DEVELOP VISION: As much as we want our children to be physically active, we will benefit from balancing athletics with spiritual calisthenics. Let's help our youths take the long-term view and see their participation in sports as one activity, among many, that makes them successful.

HELPS CHILDREN LEARN RESPECT: Church and synagogue activities can help children learn how to behave in public by training them to behave in an orderly manner for an entire hour, every week, from a young age. These activities will help youngsters build their "tolerance" for etiquette and acquire skills that will transfer over to their behavior in other public places, like airplanes and restaurants.

OFFERS EMOTIVE BENEFITS: Have you heard the story of the 9/11 cross? Two days after 9/11, on September 13, 2001, an excavator named Frank Silecchia found two weighty intersecting steel beams shaped like a cross and standing upright, defying gravity, amid the rubble of the World Trade Center. Every Sunday for nearly a year, from bitterly cold winter nights to warm spring mornings, a Catholic priest, the Reverend Brian Jordan, led services at the cross. Christians, Jews, Buddhists, and Muslims all found comfort in the cross. "People who believed or didn't believe. It was a matter of human solidarity," explained Reverend Jordan. The Jewish director of New York's Office of Emergency Management said: "Intellectually, you knew it's just two pieces of steel, but you saw the impact it had on so many people, and you also knew it was more than steel."[13]

We are visual, tactile creatures; sensing and feeling icons can remind us of our personal ideals. Stained-glass windows. Flickering candles. A little girl closing her eyes in prayer. These visuals, like the 9/11 cross, can edify us, unify us, and move us to live with purpose.

PROVIDES MOTIVATION: Public fellowship is motivational—just like going to work in a physical building where you are surrounded by colleagues or going to high school in a building where you are surrounded by peers and have the instruction of teachers. As you see others work toward improving themselves, it motivates you to improve yourself.

PROVIDES SUPPORT: When we face a challenge—whether it's a calculus problem in school or a presentation for work—it is helpful to have a wise, experienced person like a teacher or supervisor who can offer helpful insight. Likewise, if we are struggling to overcome an unpleasant habit or situation in our personal lives, it is beneficial to have a confidant like a pastor—a kind counselor with experience advising other people going through similar struggles.

BEATS THE ALTERNATIVE: What good has it done us to water down our faith? We feel dispirited by the enormous challenges we face, thanks to corrupt politicians like Obama. Millennials, and their parents who help foot their bills, are inordinately stressed by their lack of opportunities for financial independence. Many of our young people are further burdened by a culture without present fathers. We *all* need something to lift us out of the here and now. We need our creator, our God.

Winning the Race

Republicans have been unlucky in the past two presidential elections. One major reason for this is that the GOP continues to lose the youth vote. Let's explore how we can win the race.

Which American president do you think Millennials view most favorably? *Hint:* It's not Obama. The Pew Research Center found that by November of 2011, Millennials were most likely to rank Clinton as the "president who has done the best job" in their lifetime.[14] You would think Millennials would prefer the president *they* voted for and invested their energy to get out the vote for (Obama) over a president like Clinton whom they were too young to vote for—or even remember with 100 percent clarity.

You'll recall that Millennials began having buyer's remorse as soon as Obama was reelected. They voted for him with less enthusiasm the second time around, and perhaps many of them *would* have voted for the Republican candidate if they had been stronger (more on this in a moment). You'll also remember from our first chapter that the *economy* is the *number one* issue for Millennials. So, the logical reason why 61 percent of Millennials ranked Clinton as their first or second choice for best president compared to just 37 percent who chose Obama is because they are mindful of Clinton's economy. Certainly, Reagan deserves some credit for Clinton's strong economy and Clinton's own policies actually ravaged our economy in ways that (lucky for him) did not come to light until after he left office, as we discussed in chapter 5. If Democrats run Hillary Clinton in 2016, she'll have a massive head start in winning the youth vote—being married to their all-time favorite president. We should not fall into the trap of presuming that Millennials' anger or frustration *with Obama* will make it easier for us to win the youth vote. That said, I think there are several concrete steps the GOP can take to win back the trust of young people.

We have more resources now and so we can do a better job of educating our young people about the next presidential nominee than we were able to with Barack Obama. This book is a start, as it begins to expose the truth about Hillary and her party, using language and stories that Millennials can relate to—showing how her decisions and her party's policies *hurt them*. As Rush Limbaugh said on his talk show in late 2013: "If you do not fully understand your opponent, you'll never know what it takes to defeat them . . . . I'm [going to keep educating Americans and I'm] not going to assume that everyone knows what it takes to defeat her [Hillary]."

The reason Millennials like Bill Clinton has more do to with what they *have heard* about his accomplishments while in office than the entirety of his legacy (perception can be as important as reality). Millennials remember that Clinton left a budget surplus; they remember that their parents had jobs and they vaguely remember that Clinton spent less recklessly than Obama. Fiscally conservative Millennials also remember that Clinton was sometimes willing to reach across the aisle (think welfare reform), explaining a trend that the *Economist* pointed out in late 2013: "young Republicans have a soft spot for [Clinton]."[15] This tells us that the GOP can appeal to young voters by playing to one of its strengths and nominating a presidential candidate who can demonstrate consistent fiscal accountability. But that's only the beginning.

Contrary to popular opinion, conservatives will not appeal to young voters by watering down their core values. We have solid, beneficial beliefs; we simply need to do a better job of explaining to Millennials why we hold these values, and how they will benefit by sharing them. We can win the youth vote by showing young people that we are the Party of Options because we believe in the Constitution and states' rights. In the Constitution, we have answers to issues like legalizing gay marriage that respect human dignity and equality—while also respecting free speech and freedom of religion, as we saw in chapter 6. Obama's party is the Party of No: No guns (except to protect Michael Bloomberg). No private health care (except maybe for Harry Reid and his staffers). No jobs (except for billionaire "green" opportunists like Elon Musk and Eric Schmidt). No freedom of religion (except for terrorists like Nidal Hasan). No free speech (except for Eric Holder and Jay-Z). No soda pop (except for Beyoncé). No privacy (except for Obama and Tiger on the golf course).

What young person will want to be a Democrat once they see how few options the Democratic Party offers? Let's meet Millennials where they are; let's educate them; and let's invite them over to our side, while staying true to our core values.

We will also attract Millennials by running candidates who project consistency, which is a form of transparency—a trait that is very important to Millennials.

To appeal to young voters, the GOP would be wise to avoid candidates who seem like flip-floppers, as Romney unfortunately did due to championing RomneyCare and changing his position on abortion. Such candidates do not exude transparency and will struggle to win Millennial voters.

We also could benefit from being more welcoming toward our allies instead of attacking so-called "grassroots," "independent," or "tea party" conservatives. By dismissing some of its natural friends, the GOP is becoming its own bully and preventing itself from expanding into a tent that is big enough for *more* people—*young* people—to enter without feeling claustrophobic. In the 2008 and 2012 elections, many GOP moneymen as well as conservative talking heads wasted money and time attacking their own: candidates like Herman Cain and Ron Paul, very early on in the race. This gave Obama an edge because many young people liked Cain and Paul and they were turned off by watching high-profile members of the GOP attack these two men instead of going after the obvious target: Barack Obama.

We need to stop pouncing on our own friends and grassroots candidates before they have a chance to shine because young people gravitate toward the grassroots. Instead of seeing our more creative candidates as "extreme," we should welcome them into the party for they have the ability to attract and energize the young.

Pedal to the Floor, Let 'Em Hear You Roar!

You can never overestimate the power of your own voice. It's easy to fall into the trap of thinking: "What can my one little voice do?" Don't think like that. It's self-defeating and you've lost before trying. It's all about how you use your voice, not how many voices you have.

You have good ideas and you are ~~just as smart~~ *way smarter* than the average politician. A good rule of thumb is that a politician who makes a career out of being a politician does so because he or she likes sales but isn't a strong enough salesperson to sell real goods or services, so they sell promises instead. Most politicians are not that bright. You need to speak up or they will implement their ideas, which will not be as intelligent as your ideas.

There's no point to living in America if you don't exercise your right to free speech. Politicians need to hear you. One way to talk is by voting. Another way is by withholding your money from subpar political campaigns. (As long as politicians lie, we've got to keep taking the T-bird away!) The best way is by calling your representatives or by starting an informative website that holds your representatives accountable.

Professors also need to hear from us. They hug trees and recycle every minuscule item, from toilet paper rolls to tea bags, and then they litter by throwing their trash, like political correctness, into the minds of our young people. Donors: Speak with students on the campuses where you donate and get the scoop before you write another check. Colleges roll out the red carpet when you come to visit, so you need to do your own sleuthing. College and graduate students: You have very powerful voices within your institutions because your schools are concerned about their public image and tuition coffers. Your tuition money talks: speak up if you believe you are receiving an inferior education. Empower yourselves and promote intellectual diversity by starting a club, newspaper, or website that gives you and your friends an outlet to debate important topics outside of class.

The best way to preserve your freedom of speech is to openly exercise free speech. Talk it up!

G.T.O.

JFK's private narcissism was self-cannibalizing. Clinton's narcissism made him look like a goof-off instead of a leader. Obama's narcissism was *immoral*, destroying the careers, hopes, and dreams of 95 million young Americans—an entire generation—all so that he could become powerful. His defenders will inevitably claim that he did not *set out* to permanently damage the Millennial generation in his quest to seize and maintain political control. But so what? Is Obama a *better* guy if he just didn't care whether he hurt young people? He knew the consequences of his words and actions. He knew innocent young warriors would die. He knew young people would go jobless, lose access to quality health care, and become unable to afford home ownership. He acted anyway. Obama was not *out* to get young people killed, but if they died in a drone strike in the Middle East or in a mass shooting at home due to his incompetency, it did not appear to bother him.

In his arrogance, Obama got in over his head on the economy and destroyed it. He got in over his head on reforming health care and passed a plan that would annihilate high-quality health care. He got in way over his head on foreign policy and our brave young warriors paid the price with their blood. He encouraged Millennials to drown in student loan debt while they received worthless degrees and graduated without job prospects. He damaged fatherhood. He made decisions that compelled young people to "shack up" with their parents instead of moving on with their lives. He covered up and lied about Benghazi. He lied about energy and wasted our money on job-killing projects instead of stepping back and letting private entrepreneurs innovate in freedom. He encouraged young people to turn into Facebook-trolling zombies.

He drank beer in his presidential man cave with Bo. Occasionally, he snuck a cigarette.

We will remember Barack Obama. Just like we will always remember Bernie Madoff.

This story is your story; this story is my story. This is our story of how Obama seduced an entire generation through two consecutive elections only to leave them worse off than all previous generations. It will remain relevant for as long as charming opportunists walk planet Earth. This is every American's self-help story on how to sight a charmer and secondly on how to shut down that stud or siren when he or she gets grabby. Grabby for our freedom.

Millennials will pick up the pieces of their shattered dreams and build new careers and dreams. It will not be easy. Most young people will need to adjust and work harder and longer than ever. But we know we can do it. We have hot-rod confidence. We will dig ourselves out of this mess through our hard work and passion, and an entrepreneurial spirit.

* * *

HERE's a version of "G.T.O." that I wrote especially for Barack Obama. Let's sing it!

> *Barry, you've been talking yourself up for the past six years.*
> *Saying all these things you're gonna do for my peers.*
> *Well, they never came to pass and we gotta contend on the road.*
> *You in your Chevy Volt. Versus me in my G.T.O.*
> *Little Barry, gonna shut you down.*
> *When I turn it on, wind it up, blow it out, G.T.O.!*

Notes

Dear Barack Obama

1. Peter Schweizer, "GAI Report: Presidential Calendar: A Time-Based Analysis," Government Accountability Institute, April 28, 2013, http://www.g-a-i.org /gai-report-presidential-calendar-a-time-based-analysis/.

1: Operation Pickup Line

1. Zeke J. Miller, "The Politics of the Millennial Generation," *Time*, accessed May 14, 2013, http://swampland.time.com/2013/05/09/millennial-politics/.
2. David Hancock, "Clinton Cheated 'Because I Could,'" CBS News, June 16, 2004, http://www.cbsnews.com/8301-18563_162-623570.html.
3. Mimi Alford, *Once Upon a Secret: My Affair with President John F. Kennedy and Its Aftermath* (New York: Random House, 2012), 40–45, 47–50, 101–2.
4. Ann Coulter, *High Crimes and Misdemeanors: The Case Against Bill Clinton* (Washington, D.C.: Regnery, 1998), 33, 51–55, 71–72, 83–89; Ken Starr, "Where Are They Now: The Clinton Impeachment," *Time*, January 9, 2009, http://www.time.com/time/specials/packages/article/0,28804,1870544 _1870543_1870469,00.html.
5. Bill Clinton, *My Life* (New York: Knopf, 2004), 811.
6. Andrew Morton, *Monica's Story* (New York: St. Martin's Press, 1999), 113–14.
7. Walter Isaacson, *Steve Jobs* (New York: Simon & Schuster, 2011), 39, 192–93, 272, 278, 516–17, 544–46.
8. Morton, *Monica's Story*, 59, 63.
9. Tom Agan, "Embracing the Millennials' Mind-Set at Work," *New York Times*, November 9, 2013, http://www.nytimes.com/2013/11/10/jobs/embracing-the -millennials-mind-set-at-work.html.
10. Miller, "The Politics of the Millennial Generation."
11. Emily Alpert, "What's in Millennials' Wallets? Fewer Credit Cards," *Los Angeles Times*, May 18, 2013, http://articles.latimes.com/2013/may/18/local/la-me -credit-cards-millennials-20130519.
12. Amy Chozick, "Longing to Stay Wanted, MTV Turns Its Attention to Younger Viewers," *New York Times*, June 17, 2013, http://www.nytimes.com/2013/06 /18/business/media/longing-to-stay-wanted-mtv-turns-its-attention-to-younger -viewers.html.
13. David Horowitz, *Barack Obama's Rules for Revolution: The Alinsky Model* (Sherman Oaks, CA: David Horowitz Freedom Center, 2009), 3–15.

14. David Maraniss, *Barack Obama: The Story* (New York: Simon & Schuster, 2012), 552.

15. Serge Kovaleski, "Obama's Organizing Years, Guiding Others and Finding Himself," *New York Times*, July 7, 2008, http://www.nytimes.com/2008/07/07/us/politics/07community.html.

16. Maraniss, *Barack Obama*, 511–12, 552.

17. Ibid., 552.

18. Kovaleski, "Obama's Organizing Years."

19. Helen Kennedy, "A Starry-Eyed Stalker: Monica a Mixture of Vixen, Innocent," Philly.com, September 14, 1998, http://articles.philly.com/1998-09-14/news/25757593_1_lewinsky-presidential-seal-bill-clinton.

20. Jodi Kantor, "Teaching Law, Testing Ideas, Obama Stood Slightly Apart," *New York Times*, July 30, 2008, http://www.nytimes.com/2008/07/30/us/politics/30law.html.

21. Barack Obama, *Change We Can Believe In: Barack Obama's Plan to Renew America's Promise* (New York: Three Rivers Press, 2008), 200–201, 228, 241, 269, 204–5, 230, 256, 248.

22. Sharon Terlep, "Test Explodes Electric-Car Battery, Injuring General Motors Lab Worker," *Wall Street Journal*, April 11, 2012, http://online.wsj.com/article/SB10001424052702304444604577337704120872184.

23. Marc Lallanilla, "How Do Wind Turbines Kill Birds?," Yahoo! News, May 14, 2013, http://news.yahoo.com/wind-turbines-kill-birds-190145748.html; Ben Wolfgang, "Wind-Power Subsidy Spared Cuts," *Washingtion Times*, January 3, 2013, http://www.washingtontimes.com/news/2013/jan/3/wind-power-subsidy-spared-cuts/.

24. Obama, *Change We Can Believe In*, 209.

25. Kantor, "Obama Enthralled Students."

26. "Most Voters Say News Media Wants Obama to Win," Pew Research Center , October 22, 2008, http://www.people-press.org/2008/10/22/most-voters-say-news-media-wants-obama-to-win/.

27. L. Brent Bozell III, "Liberal Media Helped Obama Win Presidency by Ignoring or Downplaying Crucial Issues," *Watchdog*, December 2008.

28. Ibid.; Daniel J. Wakin, "Quieter Lives for 60's Militants, but Intensity of Beliefs Hasn't Faded," *New York Times,* August 24, 2003, http://www.nytimes.com/2003/08/24/nyregion/quieter-lives-for-60-s-militants-but-intensity-of-beliefs-hasn-t-faded.html.

29. Media Research Center, "Liberal Media's Barack Obama Bias Is Quotable in New MRC Report," *Watchdog*, December 2008.

30. Joe Klein, "The Fresh Face," *Time*, October 15, 2006, http://content.time.com/time/subscriber/article/0,33009,1546362-1,00.html.

31. Media Research Center, "Liberal Media's Barack Obama Bias Is Quotable."

32. Rush Limbaugh, "Sexy Rock Star Obama Whines About His Ears," *Rush Limbaugh Show*, December 13, 2006, http://www.rushlimbaugh.com/daily /2006/12/13/sexy_rock_star_obama_whines_about_his_ears4.

33. Matthew Balan, "Newsweek's Thomas: 'Slightly Creepy Cult of Personality' Around Obama," NewsBusters, November 6, 2008, http://newsbusters.org/ blogs/matthew-balan/2008/11/06/newsweek-s-thomas-slightly-creepy-cult -personality-around-obama.

34. Kathleen McClellan, "Now Am I Allowed to Criticize Obama on Drones & Assassination & Military Commissions & Secret Memos Expanding Secret Surveillance Powers??," microblog, *@Kath_McClellan*, November 6, 2012, https://twitter.com/Kath_McClellan/status/266036927558475776.

35. "New York Times Editorial Board Says Administration Has 'Lost All Credibility,' " Fox News, June 6, 2013, http://www.foxnews.com/politics/2013/06/06 /new-york-times-editorial-board-says-administration-has-lost-all-credibility/.

36. Barack Obama, *Dreams from My Father: A Story of Race and Inheritance* (New York: Three Rivers Press, 2004), 122–23.

37. Obama, *Change We Can Believe In*, 237–38.

38. Noah Rothman, "Dana Perino: Unlike Obama, Bush Thought Late Night Shows Not 'A Place Where the President Should Be,' " Mediaite, April 23, 2012, http://www.mediaite.com/tv/dana-perino-unlike-obama-bush-thought-late -night-shows-not-a-place-where-the-president-should-be/.

39. Bill Carter, "As Obama Accepts Offers, Late-Night Television Longs for Romney," *New York Times*, October 28, 2012, http://www.nytimes.com /2012/10/29/business/as-obama-accepts-offers-late-night-television-longs-for -romney.html.

40. Devin Dwyer, "Obama Talks Donald Trump, Tigers With Jay Leno on 'Tonight Show,' " ABC News (blogs), October 25, 2012, http://abcnews.go.com /blogs/politics/2012/10/obama-talks-donald-trump-tigers-with-jay-leno-on -tonight-show/.

41. James Montgomery, "Barack Obama Fields Your Questions, Reps the Roots on 'Ask Obama,' " October 26, 2012, http://www.mtv.com/news/articles/1696356 /ask-obama-live-interview-recap.jhtml.

42. Michael Scherer, "2012 Person of the Year: Barack Obama, the President," *Time*, December 19, 2012.

43. Michael Scherer, "A Rich Man's Game," *Time*, August 13, 2012.

44. Scherer, "2012 Person of the Year."

45. Michael Scherer, "Friended: How the Obama Campaign Connected with Young Voters," *Time*, accessed March 22, 2014, http://swampland.time .com/2012/11/20/friended-how-the-obama-campaign-connected-with-young -voters/.

46. Ibid.

47. Feifei Sun, "Teen Moms Are Taking over Reality TV. Is That a Good Thing?" *Time*, July 10, 2011, http://www.time.com/time/magazine/article /0,9171,2081928,00.html.

48. Claire Atkinson, "O-Bummer! MTV Tunes out Prez Campaign," *New York Post*, September 27, 2011, http://www.nypost.com/p/news/business/bummer _mtv_tunes_out_prez_campaign_qWhWvs5wajz7IXAGl0xGzM.

49. Jodi Kantor, "On a Day That's Anything But Normal, Obama Girls Appear Just That," *New York Times*, January 21, 2013, http://www.nytimes.com /2013/01/22/us/politics/on-a-day-thats-anything-but-normal-obama-girls -appear-just-that.html.

50. Dalton Conley, "Wired for Distraction: Kids and Social Media," *Time*, March 19, 2011, http://www.time.com/time/magazine/article /0,9171,2048363,00.html.

51. Austin Considine, "Twitter Followers For Sale," *New York Times*, August 22, 2012, http://www.nytimes.com/2012/08/23/fashion/twitter-followers-for-sale .html.

52. Geoffrey Mohan, "Facebook Is a Bummer, Study Says," *Los Angeles Times*, August 14, 2013, http://articles.latimes.com/2013/aug/14/science/la-sci-sn -facebook-bummer-20130814.

53. "Katy Perry Talks Body Image, Fame and Politics in Rolling Stone Cover Story," *Rolling Stone* website, July 7, 2011, http://www.rollingstone.com/music /news/katy-perry-talks-body-image-fame-and-politics-in-rolling-stone-cover -story-20110622.

54. Tim Appelo, "Poll: Katy Perry Influences Young Voters More than Older Voters," *Hollywood Reporter*, November 3, 2012, http://www.hollywood reporter.com/news/poll-katy-perry-more-credible-386176.

55. Monica Langley, "Eva Longoria's Next Role: Hispanic Activist in Washington," *Wall Street Journal*, January 18, 2013, http://online.wsj.com/article/SB1000142 4127887323783704578247792990982484.html.

56. Scherer, "2012 Person of the Year."

57. Isaacson, *Steve Jobs*, 546.

58. Obama, *Change We Can Believe In*, 197.

59. Jodi Kantor, "A Candidate, His Minister and the Search for Faith," *New York Times*, April 30, 2007, http://www.nytimes.com/2007/04/30/us/politics/30 obama.html.

60. Obama, *Change We Can Believe In*, 210.

61. Michael Scherer, "Moneyball," *Time*, March 18, 2013.

62. Ibid.

63. Peter Lattman, "Duke Energy Power Play Provokes an Uproar," DealBook, July 6, 2012, http://dealbook.nytimes.com/2012/07/06/uproar-over-c-e-o-s -ouster-at-merged-energy-giant/.

64. Scherer, "Moneyball."

65. Morton, *Monica's Story*, 123.

2: Fired Before They Even Interviewed

1. Ann Coulter, *High Crimes and Misdemeanors: The Case Against Bill Clinton* (Washington, D.C.: Regnery, 1998), 27–28.

2. Bill Clinton, *My Life* (New York: Knopf, 2004), 802.

3. Ibid., 803, 811.

4. "Millennials in Adulthood: Detached from Institutions, Networked with Friends," (Washington, D.C.: Pew Social and Demographic Trends, March 7, 2014) www.pewsocialtrends.org/files/2014/03/2014-03-07_generations-report -version-for-web.pdf

5. Peter Ferrara, "Economically, Could Obama Be America's Worst President?," *Forbes*, June 2, 2013, http://www.forbes.com/sites/peterferrara/2013/06/02 /economically-could-obama-be-americas-worst-president/.

6. Niraj Chokshi, "The State Jobs Recovery Is Nowhere Near Where It Should Be," *Washington Post*, September 23, 2013, http://www.washingtonpost.com /blogs/govbeat/wp/2013/09/23/the-state-jobs-recovery-is-nowhere-near-where -it-should-be/.

7. Ferrara, "America's Worst President?"

8. Ibid.

9. Barack Obama, *Change We Can Believe In: Barack Obama's Plan to Renew America's Promise* (New York: Three Rivers Press, 2008), 248.

10. Barack Obama, "Remarks of President Barack Obama—Address to Joint Session of Congress," WhiteHouse.gov, February 24, 2009, http://www .whitehouse.gov/the_press_office/Remarks-of-President-Barack-Obama -Address-to-Joint-Session-of-Congress.

11. "15.8% of Young People Still Out of Work in January," (Arlington, VA: Genera- tion Opportunity, February 7, 2014), Generationopportunity.org/press/15-8-of -young-people-still-out-of-work-in-January/.

12. Mike Patton, "The Real Story of Job Creation," *Forbes*, November 2, 2012, http://www.forbes.com/sites/mikepatton/2012/11/02/the-real-story-of-job -creation/.

13. Catherine Ruetschlin and Tamara Draut, *Stuck: Young America's Persistent Jobs Crisis*, Demos, 2013, http://www.demos.org/publication/stuck-young-americas -persistent-jobs-crisis, p. 13.

14. Paul Wiseman, "New Jobs Disproportionately Low-Pay or Part-Time," Yahoo! News, August 4, 2013, http://news.yahoo.com/jobs-disproportionately-low -pay-part-time-162103614.html.

15. David Leonhardt, "The Idled Young Americans," *New York Times*, May 3,

2013, http://www.nytimes.com/2013/05/05/sunday-review/the-idled-young -americans.html.

16. Diana Furchtgott-Roth, "The Unemployment Crisis for Younger Workers," Manhattan Institute for Policy Research, *Issues 2012*, no. 14, May 2012, http://www.manhattan-institute.org/html/ir_14.htm.

17. Brian Domitrovic, "Obama Is Repeating JFK's Mistakes," *Forbes*, September 12, 2011, http://www.forbes.com/sites/briandomitrovic/2011/09/12/obama -is-repeating-jfks-mistakes/.

18. Geoffrey Perret, *Jack: A Life Like No Other* (New York: Random House, 2001), 358.

19. Bruce Bartlett, "When Tax Cuts Were a Tough Sell," *Economix* (blog), January 22, 2013, http://economix.blogs.nytimes.com/2013/01/22/when-tax-cuts -were-a-tough-sell/.

20. Domitrovic, "Repeating JFK's Mistakes."

21. Leonhardt, "Idled Young Americans."

22. Obama, *Change We Can Believe In*, 235.

23. Ibid., 244.

24. Pauline Jelinek, "Report: Richest 7% Got Richer during Recovery," Associated Press, April 23, 2013, http://bigstory.ap.org/article/report-richest-7-got-richer -during-recovery.

25. Constantine von Hoffman, "Wealth of Most Americans Down 55% Since Recession," CBS News, May 31, 2013, http://www.cbsnews.com/8301-505123 _162-57587033/wealth-of-most-americans-down-55-since-recession/.

26. Ben S. Bernanke, "What the Fed Did and Why: Supporting the Recovery and Sustaining Price Stability," *Washington Post*, November 4, 2010, http://www .washingtonpost.com/wp-dyn/content/article/2010/11/03/AR2010110307372 .html?hpid=topnews.

27. "Buyer of Saks Assembling Upscale Giant," *Houston Chronicle*, July 30, 2013, http://www.houstonchronicle.com/business/article/Buyer-of-Saks-assembling -upscale-giant-4694508.php.

28. Annie Lowrey, "The Rich Get Richer Through the Recovery," *Economix* (blog), September 10, 2013, http://economix.blogs.nytimes.com/2013/09/10/the-rich -get-richer-through-the-recovery/.

29. von Hoffman, "Wealth of Most Americans."

30. Andrea Sachs, "Intern Nation," *Time*, September 12, 2011, http://www.time .com/time/magazine/article/0,9171,2091366,00.html.

31. Jim Tankersley, "Vanishing Workforce Weighs on Growth," *Washington Post*, April 6, 2013, http://articles.washingtonpost.com/2013-04-06/business /38324296_1_workforce-job-market-heidi-shierholz.

32. U.S. Census Bureau, "Income, Poverty and Health Insurance Coverage in the United States: 2012," news release, September 17, 2013, http://www.census .gov/newsroom/releases/archives/income_wealth/cb13-165.html.

33. U.S. Bureau of Labor Statistics, *Labor Force Characteristics by Race and Ethnicity, 2008*, November 2009, http://www.bls.gov/cps/cpsrace2008.pdf; *Labor Force Characteristics by Race and Ethnicity, 2012*, October 2013, http://www .bls.gov/cps/cpsrace2008.pdf.

34. Brad Plumer, "These Ten Charts Show the Black-White Economic Gap Hasn't Budged in 50 Years," *Washington Post*, August 28, 2013, http://www.washing tonpost.com/blogs/wonkblog/wp/2013/08/28/these-seven-charts-show-the -black-white-economic-gap-hasnt-budged-in-50-years/.

35. U.S. Bureau of Labor Statistics, *Labor Force Characteristics* (2008 and 2012).

36. Daniel Henninger, "Henninger: Meet Generation Jobbed," Wonder Land, *Wall Street Journal*, May 8, 2013, http://online.wsj.com/article/SB100014241278873 23826804578469572442880176.

37. U.S. Census Bureau, "Income, Poverty and Health Insurance in the United States: 2009 (Highlights)," http://www.census.gov/hhes/www/poverty/data /incpovhlth/2009/highlights.html; U.S. Census Bureau Public Information Office, "Income, Poverty and Health Insurance Coverage in the United States," http://www.census.gov/newsroom/releases/archives/income_wealth/cb13-165 .html].

38. Obama, *Change We Can Believe In*, 226.

39. Ibid., 225–26.

40. Michelle Obama, *American Grown: The Story of the White House Kitchen Garden and Gardens Across America.* (New York: Crown, 2012), 5, 12, 14–15.

41. John Carpenter, "Cops Probe Chicago Shooting Death's Connection to Evanston Cases," Homicide Watch Chicago, *Chicago Sun-Times*, May 14, 2013, http://homicides.suntimes.com/2013/05/14/cops-probe-chicago-shooting -deaths-connection-to-evanston-cases/.

42. "Is the Era of Identity Politics Over?," *Hannity*, Fox News, June 21, 2013, http://www.foxnews.com/on-air/hannity/2013/06/24/era-identity-politics -over.

43. Obama, *Change We Can Believe In*, 253.

44. Veronique de Rugy, "Assessing the Department of Energy Loan Guarantee Program," Mercatus Center, George Mason University, June 19, 2012, http:// mercatus.org/publication/assessing-department-energy-loan-guarantee-program.

45. Craig D. Idso et al., "Scientific Critique of IPCC's 2013 'Summary for Policy-makers'" (Nongovernmental International Panel on Climate Change, October 2013), http://heartland.org/sites/default/files/critique_of_ipcc_spm.pdf.

46. Bryan Walsh, "Tower of Power," *Time*, June 24, 2013, http://www.time.com /time/magazine/article/0,9171,2145499,00.html.

47. David Brown, "Nuclear Power Is Safest Way to Make Electricity, according to Study," *Washington Post*, April 2, 2011, http://articles.washingtonpost.com /national/nuclear-power-is-safest-way-to-make-electricity-according-to-2007 -study/2011/03/22AFQUbyQC_story.html Bryan Walsh, "Radioactive

Green: *Pandora's Promise* Rethinks Nuclear Power," *Time*, June 21, 2013, http://science.time.com/2013/06/21/radioactive-green-pandoras-promise -rethinks-nuclear-power/.

48. Barack Obama, "Transcript of President Obama's Remarks on Energy at University of Miami," FOX News Insider, February 23, 2012, http://foxnews insider.com/2012/02/23/full-text-transcript-of-president-obamas-remarks-on -energy-at-university-of-miami.

49. "Plans for New Nuclear Reactors Worldwide," World Nuclear Association, March 1, 2013, http://www.world-nuclear.org/info/Current-and-Future -Generation/Plans-For-New-Reactors-Worldwide/.

50. U.S. Department of Energy Loan Programs Office, list of discontinued projects, DOE website, accessed December 3, 2013, http://lpo.energy.gov/our-projects /discontinued-projects/.

51. Michael Grunwald, "A Bump on the Road to Green," *Time*, May 16, 2013, http://business.time.com/2013/05/16/a-bump-on-the-road-to-green/; Matthew Rocco, "Source: A123 Thrown Under the Bus for Fisker Meltdown," Fox Business, June 6, 2013, http://www.foxbusiness.com/industries/2013/06/06/ source-a123-thrown-under-bus-for-fisker-meltdown/.

52. Tom Hals and Ben Klayman, "Chinese Firm Wins A123 despite U.S. Tech Transfer Fears," Reuters, January 29, 2013, http://www.reuters.com/article /2013/01/29/us-a123-wanxiang-approval-idUSBRE90S0JN20130129.

53. Ryan Randazzo, "First Solar Loans Criticized," *USA Today*, March 21, 2012, http://www.usatoday.com/USCP/PNI/Business/2012-03-21-PNI0321biz-first -solarPNIBrd_ST_U.htm.

54. Matthew L. Wald, "House Panel to Cite New Flaw in Energy Loans," *New York Times*, March 19, 2012, http://www.nytimes.com/2012/03/19/us/politics /house-panel-to-cite-new-flaw-in-energy-loans.html.

55. Ibid.

56. Stephen Clark, "Solar Project That Received $1.2 Billion Federal Loan Sponsored by Financially Troubled Firm," Fox News, October 12, 2011, http://www .foxnews.com/politics/2011/10/12/solar-firm-that-received-12-billion-federal -loan-plagued-by-financial-problems-702546811/.

57. Reuters, "Abound Solar Files to Liquidate in Bankruptcy," Reuters, July 2, 2012, http://www.reuters.com/article/2012/07/02/us-aboundsolar-bankruptcy -idUSBRE86118020120702.

58. "Abound Solar Cleanup Could Cost Nearly $4M," *Washington Free Beacon*, October 4, 2013, http://freebeacon.com/abound-solar-cleanup-could-cost -nearly-4m/.

59. Steven Church, "Evergreen Solar Seeks Bankruptcy With Plans to Sell Itself," Bloomberg News, August 15, 2011, http://www.bloomberg.com/news/2011 -08-15/evergreen-solar-seeks-bankruptcy-protection-with-debt-of-486-5 -million.html; "Solyndra Not Sole Firm to Hit Rock Bottom Despite Stimulus

Funding," Fox News, September 15, 2011, http://www.foxnews.com/politics
/2011/09/15/despite-stimulus-funding-solyndra-and-4-other-companies-have
-hit-rock-bottom/.

60. "Beacon Power Finds Buyer, US Could Recover Some Funds," Reuters, February 6, 2012, http://www.reuters.com/article/2012/02/06/beacon -idUSL2E8D6HOE20120206.

61. "Solyndra Not Sole Firm."

62. David Louie, "Solyndra Settles with Fired Workers for $3.5 Million," KGO-TV, San Francisco, August 13, 2012, http://abclocal.go.com/kgo/story?section= news/business&id=8772384.

63. Eric Lipton and Matthew L. Wald, "E-Mails Reveal Early White House Worries Over Solyndra," *New York Times*, October 3, 2011, http://www .nytimes.com/2011/10/04/us/politics/e-mails-reveal-white-house-concerns-over -solyndra.html.

64. Matthew Daly, "Obama Donor Discussed Second Solyndra Loan with White House," *Denver Post*, November 10, 2011, http://www.denverpost.com/business /ci_19302224.

65. Michael Scherer, "The Solyndra Syndrome," *Time*, October 10, 2011, http:// www.time.com/time/magazine/article/0,9171,2095546,00.html.

66. Scott Wilson, "White House Orders Review of Energy Department Loans amid Solyndra Fallout," *Washington Post*, October 28, 2011, http://articles.washing tonpost.com/politics/white-house-orders-independent-review-of-energy -loans/2011/10/28/gIQASsrPQM_story.html.

67. Matthew L. Wald, "Solyndra Executives to Invoke Fifth Amendment Rights," *New York Times*, September 20, 2011, http://www.nytimes.com/2011/09/21 /science/earth/21solar.html.

68. U.S. Department of Energy, list of discontinued projects.

69. Scott Woolley, "Tesla Is Worse Than Solyndra," *Slate*, June 29, 2013, http:// www.slate.com/articles/business/moneybox/2013/05/tesla_is_worse_than _solyndra_how_the_u_s_government_bungled_its_investment.single.html.

70. Carol D. Leonnig and Joe Stephens, "Federal Funds Flow to Clean-Energy Firms with Obama Administration Ties," *Washington Post*, February 14, 2012, http://www.washingtonpost.com/politics/venture-capitalists-play-key-role-in -obamas-energy-department/2011/12/30/gIQA05raER_story.html.

71. Ibid.; U.S. House of Representatives Committee on Oversight and Government Reform, "The Department of Energy's Disastrous Management of Loan Guarantee Programs Staff Report," U.S. House of Representatives–112th Congress, March 20, 2012, http://oversight.house.gov/wp-content/uploads /2012/03/final-doe-loan-guarantees-report.pdf.

72. Ibid.

73. Mascoma Corporation, amended SEC registration statement (Form S-1, Amendment no. 3), list of non-employee directors, March 13, 2012, http://

www.sec.gov/Archives/edgar/data/1345691/000119312512112205/
d230618ds1a.htm; Gregory T. Huang, "Cleantech VC Hemant Taneja Moves
to Bay Area, Talks Investment Strategy at General Catalyst," *Xconomy*, February 17, 2011, http://www.xconomy.com/boston/2011/02/17/cleantech-vc
-hemant-taneja-moves-to-bay-area-talks-investment-strategy-at-general-catalyst;
Bloomberg Businessweek, "Executive Profile: Hemant Taneja," *Businessweek*,
February 28, 2014, http://investing.businessweek.com/research/stocks/private
/person.asp?personId=8577651&privcapId=170951109&previousCapId=27159
&previousTitle=CURIS%20INC.

74. Mascoma Corporation, SEC registration statement (Form S-1), "Risk Factors,"
September 16, 2011, http://www.sec.gov/Archives/edgar/data/1345691
/000119312511250417/d230618ds1.htm.

75. Mascoma, amended SEC registration statement, 14.

76. David Shaffer, "Minnesota Loses Cellulosic Ethanol Venture," *StarTribune*,
February 18, 2012, http://www.startribune.com/business/139541448.html.

77. Andy McGlashen, "As Key Partner Departs, Future Dims for Michigan
Cellulosic Biofuel Plant | Midwest Energy News," *Midwest Energy News*,
August 6, 2013, http://www.midwestenergynews.com/2013/08/06/as-key
-partner-departs-future-dims-for-michigan-cellulosic-biofuel-plant/; Jarrett
Skorup and Matthew Needham, "'Green' Company Awarded Up to $120
Million Promised 70 Jobs—Creates Just Three Jobs in Three Years," CAP
CON, Mackinac Center for Public Policy, June 25, 2012, http://www
.MichiganCapitolConfidential.com/17123.

78. "Mascoma Withdraws Biofuel IPO, Citing 'Market Conditions,'" *BusinessWeek*,
March 22, 2013, http://www.businessweek.com/news/2013-03-22/mascoma
-withdraws-biofuel-ipo-citing-market-conditions-.html; Katie Fehrenbacher,
"Mascoma Finally Realizes Going Public Is Not a Good Idea," GigaOM,
March 27, 2013, http://gigaom.com/2013/03/27/mascoma-finally-realizes
-going-public-is-not-a-good-idea/.

79. Warren Johnston, "Mascoma Corp. Loses a $50 Million Partner: Valero Pulls
Out of Michigan Project," *Valley News*, August 11, 2013, http://www.vnews
.com/news/business/8003877-95/mascoma-corp-loses-a-50-million-partner
-valero-pulls-out-of-michigan-project.

80. McGlashen, "Key Partner Departs."

81. Raven Clabough, "EPA Worked With Enviro Groups to Kill Keystone XL
Pipeline," *The New American*, January 23, 2014, http://www.thenewamerican
.com/tech/environment/item/17463-epa-worked-with-enviro-groups-to-kill
-keysone-xl-pipeline.

82. Sean Cockerham and Erika Bolstad, "WASHINGTON: State Department
Opens Door to Keystone XL Pipeline Approval | Environment | McClatchy
DC," McClatchy DC, March 1, 2013, http://www.mcclatchydc
.com/2013/03/01/184628/state-department-opens-door-to.html; Lucia Graves,

"State Department Moves Forward on Construction of Keystone XL Oil Pipeline," *Huffington Post*, August 26, 2011, http://www.huffingtonpost.com /2011/08/26/state-department-keystone-xl-oil-pipeline_n_938138.html; Elana Schor, "EPA Seeks Expanded Review of Proposed Oil Sands Pipeline," *New York Times*, June 7, 2011, http://www.nytimes.com/gwire/2011/06/07/07 greenwire-epa-seeks-expanded-review-of-proposed-oil-sand-60126.html.

83. Fareed Zakaria, "Build That Pipeline!," *Time*, March 7, 2013, http://swamp land.time.com/2013/03/07/build-that-pipeline/.

84. "Buffett, Gates and Munger Talk Energy, Business School," FOX Business, May 7, 2012, http://video.foxbusiness.com/v/1626194240001/buffett-gates -and-munger-talk-energy-business-school/#sp=show-clips.

85. Ibid.

86. Travis Hoium, "What Value Does Warren Buffett See in Solar?" *The Motley Fool*, April 17, 2013, http://www.fool.com/investing/general/2013/04/17/what -value-does-warren-buffett-see-in-solar.aspx.

87. Obama, *Change We Can Believe In*, 253.

88. Isaacson, *Steve Jobs*, 544.

89. "Corporate Tax Rates Table," KPMG.com, 2006–2014, http://www.kpmg .com/global/en/services/tax/tax-tools-and-resources/pages/corporate-tax-rates -table.aspx.

90. Kevin McCoy, "Apple CEO Defends Tax Tactics at Senate Hearing," *USA Today*, May 26, 2013, http://www.usatoday.com/story/money/business/2013 /05/21/apple-tax-hearing/2344351/.

91. Keyser Marston Associates, *Economic and Fiscal Impacts Generated by Apple in Cupertino: Current Facilities and Apple Campus 2*, May 2013, http://www.apple .com/pr/pdf/apple_economic_impact_on_cupertino.pdf, p. 6.

92. Bob McIntyre, "Big No-Tax Corps Just Keep on Dodging," Citizens for Tax Justice, April 9, 2012, http://www.ctj.org/pdf/notax2012.pdf.

93. Obama, *Change We Can Believe In*, 202.

94. Phil Gramm and Steve McMillin, "The Debt Problem Hasn't Vanished," *Wall Street Journal*, May 21, 2013, http://online.wsj.com/article/SB10001424127887 324787004578494864042754582. "The Daily History of the Debt Results, Historical Returns from 01/20/2009-03/22/2014," www.savingsbonds.gov

95. Salim Furth, "High Debt Is a Real Drag," Heritage Foundation, February 22, 2013, http://www.heritage.org/research/reports/2013/02/how-a-high-national -debt-impacts-the-economy.

96. Carmen M. Reinhart, Vincent R. Reinhart, and Kenneth S. Rogoff, "Public Debt Overhangs: Advanced-Economy Episodes Since 1800," *Journal of Economic Perspectives* 26, no. 3 (August 2012): 69–86, doi:10.1257/jep.26.3.69.

97. John F. Cogan and John B. Taylor, "Stimulus Has Been a Washington Job Killer," *Wall Street Journal*, October 3, 2011, http://online.wsj.com/article /SB10001424052970204138204576600630985154132.

98. Roger Crombie, "What US Govt. Economic Involvement Means in Real Terms," *Royal Gazette*, September 26, 2009, http://www.royalgazette.com /article/20090926/BUSINESS/309269988.

99. John Detrixhe, "U.S. Loses AAA Credit Rating as S&P Slams Debt Levels, Political Process," Bloomberg News, August 6, 2011, http://www.bloomberg .com/news/2011-08-06/u-s-credit-rating-cut-by-s-p-for-first-time-on-deficit -reduction-accord.html; Anne Gibson, "Report: How Young Are Shut Out of Owning Home," *New Zealand Herald*, June 11, 2013, http://www.nzherald .co.nz/business/news/article.cfm?c_id=3&objectid=10889675.

100. Richard Fry et al., "The Rising Age Gap in Economic Well-Being," Pew Research Pew Social & Demographic Trends, November 7, 2011, http://www .pewsocialtrends.org/2011/11/07/the-rising-age-gap-in-economic-well-being/.

101. Brad Tuttle, "Talk About 'Old Money': Old Folks Got Richer, Young People Much Poorer Over the Years," *Time*, November 9, 2011, http://business.time .com/2011/11/09/talk-about-old-money-old-folks-got-richer-young-people -much-poorer-over-the-years/; C. Eugene Steuerle et al., "Lost Generations? Wealth Building among Young Americans," Urban Institute, March 15, 2013, 1–3, http://www.urban.org/publications/412766.html; Annie Lowrey, "Do Millennials Stand a Chance in the Real World?," *New York Times*, March 26, 2013, http://www.nytimes.com/2013/03/31/magazine/do-millennials-stand -a-chance-in-the-real-world.html.

3: Young and Hellthy

1. Mimi Alford, *Once Upon a Secret: My Affair with President John F. Kennedy and Its Aftermath* (New York: Random House, 2012), 78–79, 99–100, 105, 146.

2. Frank Newport, "Americans' Views of Healthcare Quality, Cost, and Coverage," Gallup Politics, November 25, 2013, http://www.gallup.com/poll/165998 /americans-views-healthcare-quality-cost-coverage.aspx.

3. Sheryl Gay Stolberg, "Insurance Mandate May Be Health Bill's Undoing," *New York Times*, November 15, 2011, http://www.nytimes.com/2011/11/16/health /policy/insurance-mandate-may-be-health-bills-undoing.html.

4. Jeffrey M. Jones, "In U.S., 45% Favor, 48% Oppose Obama Healthcare Plan," Gallup Politics, accessed May 16, 2013, http://www.gallup.com/poll/126521/ Favor-Oppose -Obama-Healthcare-Plan.aspx.

5. "Kaiser Health Tracking Poll: April 2013," Kaiser Family Foundation, accessed May 14, 2013, http://kff.org/health-reform/poll-finding/kaiser-health-tracking -poll-april-2013/.

6. Zeke Miller, "The Politics Of The Millennial Generation," *Time*, accessed May 9, 2013, http://swampland.time.com/2013/05/09/millennial-politics/.

7. "Senate Health Bill Would Up Costs for Millions in Middle Class, Analysis Finds," Fox News, March 11, 2010, http://www.foxnews.com/politics/2010/03/11/senate-health-care-raises-taxes-middle-class-analysis-finds.

8. Kevin Sack, "Health Plan from Obama Spurs Debate," *New York Times*, July 23, 2008, http://www.nytimes.com/2008/07/23/us/23health.html; Obama, *Change We Can Believe In*, 204.

9. Kevin Sack, "Young Adults Make Gains in Health Insurance Coverage," *New York Times*, September 21, 2011, http://www.nytimes.com/2011/09/22/us/young-adults-make-gains-in-health-insurance-coverage.html.

10. ObamaCare Impact: Physician Written Responses. June 2013 AAPS Survey for KK - 284 Physician Responses, interview by Katie Kieffer, June 22, 2013 Katie Kieffer, Obamacare Impact Survey, survey of physician and surgeon members of the American Association of Physicians and Surgeons: Tucson, AZ, June 22–25, 2013. The called out physician quotes in this chapter are from this survey.

11. Obama, *Change We Can Believe In*, 44.

12. Darlene Superville, "Obama Pitches New Health Care Law in California," Yahoo! News, June 8, 2013, http://news.yahoo.com/obama-pitches-health-care-law-california-175412055.html.

13. Drew Gonshorowski, "How Will You Fare in the Obamacare Exchanges?," Heritage Foundation, October 16, 2013, http://www.heritage.org/multimedia/infographic/2013/10/how-will-you-fare-in-the-obamacare-exchanges.

14. Alyene Senger, "Obamacare: Projected Premium Increases by State," *The Foundry* (Heritage Foundation blog), March 18, 2013, http://blog.heritage.org/2013/03/18/obamacare-projected-premium-increases-by-state/.

15. Brad Jacobson, "Obama Received $20 Million from Healthcare Industry in 2008 Campaign," The Raw Story, January 12, 2010, http://www.rawstory.com/rs/2010/01/12/obama-received-20-million-healthcare-industry-money-2008/.

16. Natasha Singer, "Harry and Louise Return, with a New Message," *New York Times*, July 16, 2009, http://www.nytimes.com/2009/07/17/business/media/17adco.html.

17. Peter Baker, "Obama Was Pushed by Drug Industry, E-Mails Suggest," *New York Times*, June 8, 2012, http://query.nytimes.com/gst/fullpage.html.

18. Singer, "Harry and Louise Return."

19. Obama, *Change We Can Believe In*, 210.

20. David D. Kirkpatrick, "White House Affirms Deal on Drug Cost," *New York Times*, August 5, 2009, http://www.nytimes.com/2009/08/06/health/policy/06insure.html.

21. Obama, *Change We Can Believe In*, 46.

22. Alan Fram, "Big Pharma Wins Big with Health Care Reform Bill," *Huffington Post*, March 29, 2010, http://www.huffingtonpost.com/2010/03/29/big-pharma-wins-big-with_n_516977.html.

23. Timothy P. Carney, "Dems Tap Drug Maker Millions for PhRMA-Friendly Bill," *Washington Examiner*, March 7, 2012, http://washingtonexaminer.com /article/15976.

24. Mike Allen, "Massive Campaign for Obama Hits Air," Politico, August 13, 2009, http://www.politico.com/news/stories/0809/26076.html.

25. Paul Blumenthal, "The Legacy of Billy Tauzin: The White House-PhRMA Deal," *Huffington Post*, February 12, 2010, http://www.huffingtonpost.com /paul-blumenthal/the-legacy-of-billy-tauzi_b_460358.html.

26. Fram, "Big Pharma Wins Big."

27. Bruce Japsen, "ObamaCare Will Bring Drug Industry $35 Billion In Profits," *Forbes*, May 25, 2013, http://www.forbes.com/sites/brucejapsen/2013/05/25 /obamacare-will-bring-drug-industry-35-billion-in-profits/.

28. Kate Pickert, "Is Your Plan In Play?," *Time*, December 2, 2013.

29. "Small Business and Obamacare," *Wall Street Journal*, November 12, 2013, http://online.wsj.com/news/articles/SB10001424052702303460004579192102 917020082.

30. Barack Obama, *The Audacity of Hope* (New York: Crown Publishers, 2006), 290.

31. "Assessing the Healthcare Rollout," Ozymandias, November 12, 2013, http:// www.ozy.com/c-notes/assessing-the-healthcare-rollout-with-bill-clinton/3639 .article.

32. James Madera to Monica Jackson, April 1, 2013, comments on proposed student loan affordability regulations, http://www.ama-assn.org/resources/doc /washington/medical-student-loans-comment-letter-01april2013.pdf.

33. Patience Haggin, "Doctor Shortage?," *Time*, August 13, 2012, http://www .time.com/time/magazine/article/0,9171,2121086,00.html.

34. Scott Gottlieb, "The Doctor Won't See You Now. He's Clocked Out," *Wall Street Journal*, March 14, 2013, http://online.wsj.com/newsarticles/SB10001424 127887323628804578346614033833092.html.

35. Ibid.

36. Ibid.

37. Zeke J. Miller, "And Now, the Selling of Obamacare," *Time*, June 20, 2013, http://swampland.time.com/2013/06/20/and-now-the-selling-of-obamacare/.

38. Shawn Tully, "What Tummy Tucks Can Teach Us about Health Care Reform," CNN Money, May 23, 2013, http://features.blogs.fortune.cnn.com/2013/05 /23/what-tummy-tucks-can-teach-us-about-health-care-reform/.

39. Christopher Snowbeck, "Twin Cities Doctors Bypass Insurers; Patients Charged Directly for Care," TwinCities.com, accessed May 16, 2013, http://www .twincities.com/politics/ci_22462995/doctors-at-edina-practice-say-direct-pay -cures.

40. Lou Magdon, "The Great Healthcare Debate: A Medical Student's Perspective,"

Association of American Physicians and Surgeons website, June 20, 2013, http://www.aapsonline.org/index.php/site/article/the_great_healthcare _debate_a_medical_students_perspective/.

41. Ibid.

4: Flipping Students the Bird

1. David Maraniss, *Barack Obama: The Story* (New York: Simon & Schuster, 2012), 300.
2. "News Photographer Arnie Sachs; Took Pictures of 11 Presidents," obituary, *Washington Post*, November 7, 2006, http://www.washingtonpost.com/wp-dyn /content/article/2006/11/06/AR2006110601080.html.
3. Maraniss, *Barack Obama*, 355–56.
4. Bill Clinton, *My Life* (New York: Knopf, 2004), 199.
5. Maraniss, *Barack Obama*, 347–48, 355–57; Jodi Kantor, "Teaching Law, Testing Ideas, Obama Stood Slightly Apart," *New York Times*, July 30, 2008, http://www.nytimes.com/2008/07/30/us/politics/30law.html.
6. Alexandra Starr, "Case Study," *New York Times*, September 19, 2008, http:// www.nytimes.com/2008/09/21/magazine/21obama-t.html.
7. Ibid.
8. Ibid.
9. Kantor, "Teaching Law."
10. Ibid.
11. Mimi Alford, *Once Upon a Secret: My Affair with President John F. Kennedy and Its Aftermath* (New York: Random House, 2012), 79, 99, 115, 135.
12. Andrew Morton, *Monica's Story* (New York: St. Martin's Press, 1999), 84.
13. Richard Vedder, Christopher Denhart, and Jonathan Robe, *Why Are Recent College Graduates Underemployed? University Enrollments and Labor-Market Realities*, Center for College Affordability and Productivity, January 1, 2013, http://centerforcollegeaffordability.org/uploads/Underemployed%20 Report%202.pdf.
14. Barack Obama, speech on the "American Dream," Bettendorf, Iowa, November 7, 2007, http://edition.cnn.com/2007/POLITICS/12/21/obama.trans .americandream/.
15. Barack Obama, *Change We Can Believe In,* (New York: Three Rivers Press, 2008), 251.
16. Ibid., 237.
17. Barack Obama, "A Letter to My Daughters," *Parade*, January 18, 2009, http:// www.parade.com/37592/parade/barack-obama-a-letter-to-my-daughters/.
18. Jane E. Brody, "Commuting's Hidden Cost," *New York Times*, October 28, 2013, http://well.blogs.nytimes.com/2013/10/28/commutings-hidden-cost/.

19. Jon Marcus, "Community College Grads out-Earn Bachelor's Degree Holders," *CNN Money*, February 26, 2013, http://money.cnn.com/2013/02/26/pf /college/community-college-earnings/index.html.

20. Ibid.

21. Malcolm Gladwell, *Outliers: The Story of Success* (New York: Little, Brown/Back Bay Books, 2011), 36–37, 67.

22. Barack Obama, commencement speech at Morehouse College, transcript, *Washington Wire*, May 20, 2013, http://blogs.wsj.com/washwire/2013/05/20 /transcript-obamas-commencement-speech-at-morehouse-college/.

23. Ethan Bronner, "Law Schools' Applications Fall as Costs Rise and Jobs Are Cut," *New York Times*, January 30, 2013, http://www.nytimes.com/2013/01/31 /education/law-schools-applications-fall-as-costs-rise-and-jobs-are-cut.html.

24. Ibid.

25. Debra Cassens Weiss, "Average Debt of Private Law School Grads Is $125K; It's Highest at These Five Schools," *ABA Journal*, March 28, 2012, http://www .abajournal.com/news/article/average_debt_load_of_private_law_grads_is _125k_these_five_schools_lead_to_m/.

26. Catherine Rampell, "Only Half of First-Time College Students Graduate in 6 Years," *Economix* (blog) February 26, 2013, http://economix.blogs.nytimes.com /2013/02/26/only-half-of-first-time-college-students-graduate-in-6-years/.

27. Brad Plumer, "Student Debt Beginning to Drag down Economy," *Columbus Dispatch*, April 28, 2013, http://www.dispatch.com/content/stories/business /2013/04/28/student-debt-beginning-to-drag-down-economy.html. Ashley Pratte, "Updated: 2013 Youth Misery Index (YMI) Released on Fox and Friends," *The New Guard* blog, January 8, 2014, www.yaf.org/YouthMisery Index2013Report.aspx.

28. Shahien Nasiripour, "Obama Student Loan Policy Reaping $51 Billion Profit," *Huffington Post*, May 14, 2013, http://www.huffingtonpost.com/2013/05/14 /obama-student-loans-policy-profit_n_3276428.html.

29. John Hechinger, "Taxpayers Fund $454,000 Pay for Collector Chasing Student Loans," Bloomberg News, May 15, 2012, http://www.bloomberg.com/news /2012-05-15/taxpayers-fund-454-000-pay-for-collector-chasing-student-loans .html.

30. John Hechinger, "Obama Cuts Student-Debt Collector Commissions to Aid Borrowers," Bloomberg News, March 19, 2013, http://www.bloomberg.com /news/2013-03-19/obama-cuts-student-debt-collector-commissions-to-aid -borrowers.html.

31. Shahien Nasiripour, "Student Loan Rates Boost Government Profit As Debt Damps Economy," *Huffington Post*, April 9, 2013, http://www.huffingtonpost .com/2013/04/09/student-loan-rates-debt-economy_n_3048216.html.

32. Sarah Wheaton, "With Students as Backdrop, Obama Warns of Doubling of

Loan Rates," *New York Times*, May 31, 2013, http://www.nytimes.com/2013 /06/01/education/with-students-as-backdrop-obama-warns-of-doubling-of -loan-rates.html.

33. Scott Jaschik, "Moving Further to the Left," *Inside Higher Ed*, October 24, 2012, http://www.insidehighered.com/news/2012/10/24/survey-finds -professors-already-liberal-have-moved-further-left.

34. Ariel Kaminer, "The Last Refuge From Scandal? Professorships," *New York Times,* May 4, 2013, http://www.nytimes.com/2013/05/05/education/ in-disgrace-yet-in-demand-as-college-teachers.html.

35. Patrick Svitek, "Class Sex Toy Demonstration Causes Controversy," *Daily Northwestern*, February 28, 2011, http://dailynorthwestern.com/2011/02/28 /campus/campusarchived/class-sex-toy-demonstration-causes-controversy/.

36. Tyler Kingkade, "Deandre Poole Keeps FAU Job After 'Stomp on Jesus' Controversy," *Huffington Post*, June 24, 2013, http://www.huffingtonpost. com/2013/06/24/deandre-poole-fau-stomp-on-jesus_n_3490263.html

37. Daniel J. Wakin, "Quieter Lives for 60's Militants, but Intensity of Beliefs Hasn't Faded," *New York Times*, August 24, 2003, http://www.nytimes .com/2003/08/24/nyregion/quieter-lives-for-60-s-militants-but-intensity-of -beliefs-hasn-t-faded.html.

38. Michael Moynihan, "How 1960s Radicals Ended Up Teaching Your Kids," *Daily Beast*, April 10, 2013, http://www.thedailybeast.com/articles/2013/04/10 /how-1960s-radicals-ended-up-teaching-your-kids.html.

39. GfK Roper Public Affairs & Media, *What Will They Learn: GfK Roper Public Affairs & Corporate Communications Survey on Behalf of ACTA*, survey, August 5, 2011, http://whatwilltheylearn.com/public/pdfs/RoperFindings.pdf.

40. American Council of Trustees and Alumni (ACTA), *What Will They Learn?* 2012–2013 Ratings, http://www.whatwilltheylearn.com/.

41. "Transcript: Obama's Commencement Speech at Ohio State," May 6, 2013, transcript, http://blogs.wsj.com/washwire/2013/05/06/transcript-obamas -commencement-speech-at-ohio-state/tab/print/.

42. Maggie Galehouse, "Before You Text, Ask This: Is Other Person as Hip to Tech as You?" *Houston Chronicle*, March 1, 2011, http://www.chron.com/life/article /Before-you-text-ask-this-Is-other-person-as-hip-1691981.php.

43. Diana Middleton, "Students Struggle for Words," *Wall Street Journal*, March 3, 2011, http://online.wsj.com/article/SB100014240527487034099045761746517 80110970.html.

44. Alina Tugend, "What It Takes to Make New College Graduates Employable," *New York Times*, June 28, 2013, http://www.nytimes.com/2013/06/29/your -money/a-quest-to-make-college-graduates-employable.html.

45. Alex Newman, "Common Core: A Scheme to Rewrite Education," *New American*, August 8, 2013.

46. Ibid.

47. Michael Cogan, *Exploring Academic Outcomes of Homeschooled Students* University of St. Thomas, 2009, http://www.airum.org/docs/presentations /2009-Cogan.pdf.

5: The New "Shacking Up"

1. Jonathan Alter, "The Power and the Glitz," *Newsweek*, May 25, 1998.

2. Constantine von Hoffman, "Wealth of Most Americans Down 55% Since Recession," CBS News, May 31, 2013, http://www.cbsnews.com/news /wealth-of-most-americans-down-55-since-recession/.

3. Christopher S. Rugaber, "US Home Prices Rise 12.2 Percent, Best in 6 Years," *The Big Story*, July 30, 2013, http://bigstory.ap.org/article/us-home-prices-rise -122-percent-best-6-years.

4. Richard Fry, "A Rising Share of Young Adults Live in Their Parents' Home: A Record 21.6 Million in 2012," Pew Research Social & Demographic Trends, August 1, 2013, http://www.pewsocialtrends.org/2013/08/01/a-rising-share-of -young-adults-live-in-their-parents-home/.

5. Ibid.

6. Hope Yen, "Is U.S. Becoming a Granny State?," TwinCities.com, August 26, 2011, http://www.twincities.com/national/ci_18759892.

7. Floyd Norris, "Easing U.S., Slowly, Out of Home Financing," *New York Times*, February 28, 2013, http://www.nytimes.com/2013/03/01/business/report-lays -out-plan-to-reduce-government-role-in-home-financing.html.

8. David Streitfeld and Gretchen Morgenson, "Building Flawed American Dreams," *New York Times*, October 18, 2008, http://www.nytimes.com/2008 /10/19/business/19cisneros.html.

9. Tamara Jones, "Henry & Linda: A Painful Story of Public Service and Private Anguish," *Washington Post Magazine*, February 22, 1998, 1–5, http://www .washingtonpost.com/wp-srv/politics/special/cisneros/stories/cis022298.htm.

10. Ibid., 6–7.

11. Ibid., 7.

12. Ibid., 5–6.

13. Tamara Jones, "Henry & Linda: A Painful Story of Public Service and Private Anguish," *Washington Post Magazine*, February 22, 1998, 11 and 14-15, http://www.washingtonpost.com/wp-srv/politics/special/cisneros/stories /cis022298.htm.

14. Matthew Vadum, *Subversion Inc.: How Obama's ACORN Red Shirts Are Still Terrorizing and Ripping Off American Taxpayers* (Washington, D.C.: World NetDaily, 2011), 140–141.

15. Bill Clinton, *My Life* (New York: Knopf, 2004), 454.

16. "The Cisneros Plea," *New York Times*, September 8, 1999, http://www.nytimes .com/1999/09/08/opinion/the-cisneros-plea.html.

17. Streitfeld and Morgenson, "Building Flawed American Dreams."

18. Ibid.

19. William J. Clinton, "Remarks on the National Homeownership Strategy," June 5, 1995. Online by Gerhard Peters and John T. Woolley, *The American Presidency Project*, http://www.presidency.ucsb.edu/ws/?pid=51448.

20. Steven A. Holmes, "Fannie Mae Eases Credit To Aid Mortgage Lending," *New York Times*, September 30, 1999, http://www.nytimes.com/1999/09/30 /business/fannie-mae-eases-credit-to-aid-mortgage-lending.html.

21. "Reagan's Legacy: Our 25-Year Boom," Investors Business Daily, online at Real Clear Markets, April 10, 2009, http://www.realclearmarkets.com/articles /2009/04/reagans_legacy_our_25year_boom.html.

22. Helen Thomas, *Thanks for the Memories, Mr. President: Wit and Wisdom from the Front Row at the White House* (New York: A Lisa Drew Book/Scribner, 2002), 137–38.

23. Streitfeld and Morgenson, "Building Flawed American Dreams."

24. Ibid.

25. Ibid.

26. Ibid.

27. Vadum, *Subversion Inc.*, 51.

28. Ibid., 51, 172.

29. Ibid., 172.

30. Ibid., 184–87.

31. Ibid., 177.

32. Stephanie Strom, "On Obama, Acorn and Voter Registration," *New York Times*, October 10, 2008, http://www.nytimes.com/2008/10/11/us/politics/11acorn .html.

33. Stanley Kurtz, *Radical-in-Chief: Barack Obama and the Untold Story of American Socialism* (New York: Simon & Schuster, 2012), 221.

34. Vadum, *Subversion Inc.*, 59.

35. Jim Rutenberg, "Acorn's Woes Strain Its Ties to Democrats," *New York Times*, October 15, 2009, http://www.nytimes.com/2009/10/16/us/politics/16acorn .html.

36. Christopher Borrelli, "Remembering 'Blues Brothers' 30 Years Later," *Chicago Tribune*, June 16, 2010, http://articles.chicagotribune.com/2010-06-16 /entertainment/ct-live-0616-blues-brothers-20100616_1_jane-byrne-blues -brothers-mayor-richard-j-daley.

37. John Gibson and FoxNews.com, "Barack Obama's Fannie Mae/Freddie Mac Connection," Fox News, September 16, 2008, http://www.foxnews.com /story/2008/09/16/barack-obama-fannie-maefreddie-mac-connection.

38. David Goldman, "3 AIG Execs Get Bonus OK from Pay Czar," CNN Money, October 23, 2009, http://money.cnn.com/2009/10/22/news/companies/aig _bonuses_feinberg/.

39. Jim Puzzanghera and Nathaniel Popper, "TARP Pay Czar Criticizes Big Bank Bonuses but Won't Seek Refund of Bailout Money," *Los Angeles Times*, July 24, 2010, http://articles.latimes.com/2010/jul/24/business/la-fi-executive-comp -20100724.

40. Edmund L. Andrews, "U.S. Sets Big Incentives to Head Off Foreclosures," *New York Times*, March 4, 2009, http://www.nytimes.com/2009/03/05/business /05housing.html.

41. Ilyce Glink and Samuel Tamkin, "Knowing the Difference between HARP and HAMP," *Chicago Tribune*, April 13, 2012, http://articles.chicagotribune.com /2012-04-13/marketplace/sns-201204061600--tms--realestmctnig-a20120413 apr13_1_home-affordable-refinance-program-harp-homeowners-hope-hotline.

42. David Streitfeld, "U.S. Mortgage Relief Effort Is Falling Short of Its Goal," *New York Times*, August 20, 2010, http://www.nytimes.com/2010/08/21 /business/economy/21housing.html.

43. Shahien Nasiripour and Arthur Delaney, "Extend and Pretend: The Obama Administration's Failed Foreclosure Program," *Huffington Post*, August 4, 2010, http://www.huffingtonpost.com/2010/08/04/extend-and-pretend-the-ob_n _668609.html?page=1.

44. Daniel Wagner and Derek Kravitz, "S&P Downgrades Fannie and Freddie, US-Backed Debt," Yahoo! Finance, August 8, 2011, http://finance.yahoo.com /news/SP-downgrades-Fannie-and-apf-1344749763.html.

45. Derek Kravitz, "Home-Buying Season the Worst in at Least 50 Years," Yahoo! Finance, September 26, 2011, http://finance.yahoo.com/news/Homebuying -season-the-worst-apf-308078857.html.

46. Annie Lowrey, "Treasury Department Faulted in Effort to Relieve Homeown- ers," *New York Times*, April 12, 2012, http://www.nytimes.com/2012/04/12 /business/economy/treasury-department-faulted-in-effort-to-relieve-home owners.html.

47. C. Eugene Steuerle et al., "Lost Generations? Wealth Building among Young Americans," Urban Institute, March 15, 2013, 1–3, http://www.urban.org /publications/412766.html.

48. Nathaniel Popper, "Behind the Rise in House Prices, Wall Street Buyers," DealBook, June 3, 2013, http://dealbook.nytimes.com/2013/06/03/behind -the-rise-in-house-prices-wall-street-buyers/.

49. Ibid.

50. Neal Cavuto and Sam Zell, "Sam Zell: I'm Cynical About Housing Recovery," Fox Business, August 6, 2013, http://video.foxbusiness.com/v/2589815600001 /sam-zell-im-cynical-about-housing-recovery/.

51. Lawrence Yun, "The Latest Homeownership Rate," *Economists' Outlook*, July 30, 2013, http://economistsoutlook.blogs.realtor.org/2013/07/30/the -latest-homeownership-rate/.

52. Lisa Prevost, "Home Loans for Millennials," *New York Times*, June 13, 2013, http://www.nytimes.com/2013/06/16/realestate/home-loans-for-millennials .html.

53. Shaila Dewan, "New Defaults Trouble a Mortgage Program," *New York Times*, July 24, 2013, http://www.nytimes.com/2013/07/25/business/new-defaults -trouble-a-mortgage-program.html.

54. Norris, "Easing U.S., Slowly, Out of Home Financing."

55. Steve Jordon, "Mortgage Lending at Risk If Rules Not Delayed, Banker Says," *Omaha World-Herald*, September 25, 2013, http://www.omaha.com/apps/pbcs .dll/article?AID=/20130925/MONEY/130929269/1697.

56. Ibid.

57. Nick Timiraos, "Higher Rates Aren't Enough to Stall Housing," *Wall Street Journal*, July 21, 2013, http://online.wsj.com/article/SB1000142412788732426 3404578615771412506206.html.

58. Constance Rosenblum, "First Rentals: Native New York Style," *New York Times*, May 17, 2013, http://www.nytimes.com/2013/05/19/realestate/first -rentals-native-new-york-style.html.

59. Claire Bushey, "Young Professionals Live with Roommates Longer; Effects of Recession, Later Marriages," *Crain's Chicago Business*, March 14, 2011, http:// www.chicagobusiness.com/article/20110312/ISSUE03/303129986/young -professionals-live-with-roommates-longer-effects-of-recession-later-marriages.

60. Ibid.

61. Meta Brown and Sydnee Caldwell, "Young Student Loan Borrowers Retreat from Housing and Auto Markets," *Liberty Street Economics* (blog), Federal Reserve Bank of New York, April 17, 2013, http://libertystreeteconomics.new yorkfed.org/2013/04/young-student-loan-borrowers-retreat-from-housing-and -auto-markets.html; Nin-Hai Tseng, "More Bad News for Student Loan Borrowers," CNN Money, April 22, 2013, http://finance.fortune.cnn.com /2013/04/22/student-loan-debt-borrowing/.

62. Fry, "Rising Share of Young Adults."

63. E. Scott Reckard, "Are Millennials a Window of Opportunity or a Closed Door for Home Builders?," *Los Angeles Times*, June 7, 2013, http://articles.latimes .com/2013/jun/07/business/la-fi-house-debt-20130607.

64. "Median Age of Reader in Cosmopolitan vs. New York Times (Daily) vs. Wall Street Journal," Readership Survey, MRI+ database, Spring 2013, accessed June 6, 2013, http://www.mriplus.com/site/index.aspx?AspxAutoDetectCookie Support=1.

65. Fry, "Rising Share of Young Adults."

66. Bethany Heitman, "5 Ways to Survive Moving Back in with Your Parents," *Cosmopolitan*, accessed September 18, 2013, http://www.cosmopolitan.com /advice/tips/living-with-your-parents.

67. "Depression and Anger Can Plague Recent University Graduates," Science Daily, May 13, 2008, http://www.sciencedaily.com/releases/2008/05 /080513112355.htm.

68. Victor Schwartz, "Recent College Grads: From Frustration to Clinical Depression," *Huffington Post*, July 17, 2012, http://www.huffingtonpost.com/dr -victor-schwartz/college-grads-clinical-depression_b_1679759.html.

69. Sharon Jayson, "Who's Feeling Stressed? Young Adults, New Survey Shows," *USA Today*, February 6, 2013, http://www.usatoday.com/story/news/nation /2013/02/06/stress-psychology-millennials-depression/1878295/.

70. *Stress in America: Missing the Health Care Connection*, American Psychological Association, accessed May 22, 2013, http://www.apa.org/news/press/releases /stress/2012/full-report.pdf.

71. *Young, Unemployed and Optimistic: Coming of Age, Slowly, in a Tough Economy* (Washington, D.C.: Pew Research Social & Demographic Trends, February 9, 2012), http://www.pewsocialtrends.org/files/2012/02/young-underemployed- and-optimistic.

72. Emily Alpert, "Millennial Generation is Persistently Optimistic," *Los Angeles Times*, July 7, 2013, http://articles.latimes.com/2013/jul/07/local /la-me-millennial-optimism-20130708.

73. Steuerle et al., "Lost Generations?"

74. Jones, "Henry & Linda," 2.

6: Why Fathers Matter

1. D'Vera Cohn et al., "Barely Half of U.S. Adults Are Married—A Record Low," Pew Research Social & Demographic Trends, December 14, 2011, http://www .pewsocialtrends.org/2011/12/14/barely-half-of-u-s-adults-are-married-a-record -low/.

2. David Tuller, "A Different Kind of Fatherhood," *Well*, June 16, 2013, http:// well.blogs.nytimes.com/2013/06/16/a-different-kind-of-fatherhood/.

3. Walter Isaacson, *Steve Jobs* (New York: Simon & Schuster), 91.

4. Belinda Luscombe, "Another Cause of Early Puberty in Girls: Absent Dads," *Time*, September 17, 2010, http://healthland.time.com/2010/09/17/another -cause-of-early-puberty-in-girls-absent-dads/; Darby Saxbe, "Why Are American Girls Reaching Puberty Faster?" Oprah.com, January 1, 2009, http://www .oprah.com/health/Why-Are-American-Girls-Reaching-Puberty-Faster.

5. "Like Father, like Son: Men More Likely to Cheat on Wives If Their Fathers Were Unfaithful, Survey Shows," *Mail Online*, June 27, 2011, http://www

.dailymail.co.uk/sciencetech/article-2008368/Cheating-runs-family--future
-father-law-unfaithful-likely-husband-too.html.

6. Sara McLanahan et al., "Strenthening Fragile Families," policy brief, The
Future of Children, Fall 2010, http://futureofchildren.org/futureofchildren
/publications/docs/20_02_PolicyBrief.pdf.

7. *Fragile Families and Child Wellbeing Study Fact Sheet, 2007–2010,* http://www
.fragilefamilies.princeton.edu/documents/FragileFamiliesandChildWellbeing
StudyFactSheet.pdf.

8. "CNN's Don Lemon Says More than 72 Percent of African-American Births
Are out of Wedlock," PolitiFact, July 27, 2013, http://www.politifact.com
/truth-o-meter/statements/2013/jul/29/don-lemon/cnns-don-lemon-says-more
-72-percent-african-americ/.

9. Barack Obama, *Change We Can Believe In* (New York: Three Rivers Press,
2008), 235–36.

10. Andréa Ford and Lon Tweeten, "Changing Faces," *Time,* December 19, 2012.

11. McLanahan et al., "Strenthening Fragile Families."

12. Kathryn Kost and Stanley Henshaw, *U.S. Teenage Pregnancies, Births and
Abortions, 2008: State Trends by Age, Race and Ethnicity,* Guttmacher Institute,
March 2013, http://www.guttmacher.org/pubs/USTPtrendsState08.pdf.

13. U.S. Bureau of Labor Statistics, *Labor Force Characteristics by Race and
Ethnicity, 2012,* October 2013, http://www. bls.gov/cps/cpsrace2012.pdf.

14. Frank Newport, "Hillary Clinton, Barack Obama Most Admired in 2012,"
Gallup Politics, December 31, 2012, http://www.gallup.com/poll/159587
/hillary-clinton-barack-obama-admired-2012.aspx.

15. Michael D. Shear, "Obama Starts Initiative for Young Black Men, Noting His
Own Experience," *New York Times,* February 27, 2014, http://www.nytimes
.com/2014/02/28/us/politics/obama-will-announce-initiative-to-empower
-young-black-men.html.

16. Christopher Andersen, *Barack and Michelle: Portrait of an American Marriage*
(New York: William Morrow, 2009), 210.

17. Jann S. Wenner, "A Conversation with Barack Obama," July 10–24, 2008,
Jann Wenner website, http://www.jannswenner.com/Archives/Barack_Obama
.aspx.

18. Beverley Lyons and Laura Sutherland, "The Razz: It's a Super Day for Snoop,"
Daily Record, February 5, 2008, Features section.

19. Kia Makarechi, "Snoop Dogg on Obama & Romney: Rapper Explains His
Vote in List Posted on Instagram," *Huffington Post,* October 5, 2012, http://
www.huffingtonpost.com/2012/10/05/snoop-dogg-obama-romney-instagram
_n_1942724.html.

20. Etan Vlessing, "Snoop Dogg on Why He Supports Barack Obama," *Hollywood
Reporter,* September 8, 2012, http://www.hollywoodreporter.com/news/
toronto-2012-snoop-dogg-barack-obama-368891.

21. Ian S. Port, "The State of Snoop Dogg: An Awkward Gangstafari," *SF Weekly*, April 17, 2013, http://www.sfweekly.com/2013-04-17/music/snoop-doggy -dogg-rastafari-reggae-snoop-lion/.

22. Sasha Frere-Jones, "Surfin': Laptop Sins Yield Pallid Confessions," *The New Yorker*, June 2, 2008.

23. Jocelyn Vena and Shaheem Reid, "Usher Recalls Stealing Barack Obama's Candy Bar," MTV Newsroom, January 19, 2009, http://newsroom.mtv .com/2009/01/19/usher-recalls-stealing-barack-obamas-candy-bar/; Jayson Rodriguez and Shaheem Reid, "When Usher Met Barack Obama . . . ," MTV Newsroom, January 19, 2009, http://newsroom.mtv.com/2009/01/19/when -usher-met-barack-obama/.

24. Vena and Reid, "Usher Recalls Stealing," "When Usher Met Barack Obama."

25. Danielle Lawler, "FaBulous Does . . . A Hip-Hop Dance Lesson with Usher," *News of the World*, July 3, 2011, national edition, Features.

26. Louise Boyle and Lydia Warren, "Inside the White House After-Party: How the President Took Part in a Gangnam Style Dance Off and Michelle Grooved to 'Single Ladies' at Celebrity-Packed Bash," Mail Online, January 21, 2012, http://www.dailymail.co.uk/news/article-2266156/Inauguration-2013-party -Obama-Ushers-Gangnam-Style-dance-Michelle-grooves-Beyonce.html.

27. Wenner, "Conversation with Barack Obama."

28. Jayson Rodriguez and Sway Calloway, "Ludacris Says He and Tiger Woods Should Talk," MTV.com, February 25, 2010, http://www.mtv.com/news /articles/1632690/ludacris-tiger-woods-should-talk.jhtml.

29. George Rush et al., "Signing More Than Checks for a Star-Struck Obama," *Daily News*, March 7, 2007 (sports final edition, "Gossip" section).

30. Gordon Smart, "Prez Rep Raps Jay-Z for Brag," *Sun*, April 13, 2013 (national edition, editoral section).

31. Brennan Murray, "Barack Obama and Jay-Z: The History of an Unlikely Friendship," *Telegraph*, April 13, 2013.

32. Rose Lilah, "Jay Z Talks Blue Ivy's Influence on His Music & Kanye West," *HotNewHipHop*, July 19, 2013, http://www.hotnewhiphop.com/jay-z-talks -blue-ivy-s-influence-on-his-music-and-kanye-west-news.6475.html.

33. Jayson Rodriguez, "Jay-Z, Behind The Rhymes: Hidden Britney Spears Reference Is Just One Trick of Hov's Trade," MTV.com, November 27, 2007, http://www.mtv.com/news/articles/1575127/jay-zs-voice-less-than-10-admits .jhtml.

34. Julia Rubin, "How Heroin Is Invading America's Schools," *Teen Vogue*, September 1, 2013, http://www.teenvogue.com/my-life/2013-09/teen-heroin.

35. Kia Makarechi, "Obama Says 'Beyonce Could Not Be A Better Role Model for My Girls' As Event With Jay-Z Nets $4 Million," *Huffington Post*, September 19, 2012, http://www.huffingtonpost.com/2012/09/19/obama-beyonce-role -model-jay-z-4-million_n_1896368.html.

36. Michelle Obama, *American Grown: The Story of the White House Kitchen Garden and Gardens Across America* (New York: Crown, 2012), 180.

37. Andersen, *Barack and Michelle*, 80.

38. Beth Kassab, "The Difference between Christopher Lane and David Guerrero," *Orlando Sentinel*, September 4, 2013, http://articles.orlandosentinel.com/2013 -09-04/news/os-osceola-shootings-beth-kassab-20130904_1_walt-disney-world -trayvon-martin-random-shootings.

39. Lizette Alvarez, "Martin Was Shot as He Leaned over Zimmerman, Court Is Told," *New York Times*, July 9, 2013, http://www.nytimes.com/2013/07/10/us /teenager-was-over-zimmerman-as-he-was-shot-expert-says.html.

40. Lizette Alvarez, "Juror Says Zimmerman 'Got Away With Murder,'" *New York Times*, July 25, 2013, http://www.nytimes.com/2013/07/26/us/juror-says -zimmerman-got-away-with-murder.html.

41. "Brooklyn Residents Hold Rally Calling for End to 'Knockout Game' Assaults," CBS New York, November 29, 2013, http://newyork.cbslocal .com/2013/11/29/brooklyn-residents-to-hold-rally-calling-for-end-to-knockout -game-assaults/.

42. Percent who favor same-sex marriage by age group, 2001–2013 (graph), "Changing Attitudes on Gay Marriage," Pew Research Religion & Public Life Project, June 2013, http://features.pewforum.org/same-sex-marriage-attitudes /slide2.php; percent who oppose or favor same-sex marriage (overall) 2001– 2013 (graph), "Changing Attitudes on Gay Marriage," Pew Research Religion & Public Life Project, June 2013, http://features.pewforum.org/same-sex -marriage-attitudes/.

43. Percent who favor same-sex marriage by age group, Pew Research; percent who oppose or favor same-sex marriage (overall), Pew Research.

44. Jeffrey Kluger, "Too Old to Be a Dad?," *Time*, April 22, 2013, http://www .time.com/time/magazine/article/0,9171,2140795,00.html.

45. Dylan Griffiths, "Americans Giving Up Passports Jump Sixfold as Tougher Rules Loom," Bloomberg Personal Finance, August 9, 2013, http://www .bloomberg.com/news/2013-08-09/americans-giving-up-passports-jump -sixfold-as-tougher-rules-loom.html.

46. Fry, "A Rising Share of Young Adults Live in Their Parents' Home: A Record 21.6 Million in 2012," Pew Research Social & Demographic Trends, August 1, 2013, http://www.pewsocialtrends.org/2013/08/01/a-rising-share-of-young -adults-live-in-their-parents-home/; Constantine von Hoffman, "Wealth of Most Americans Down 55% Since Recession," CBS News, May 31, 2013, http://www.cbsnews.com/8301-505123_162-57587033/wealth-of-most -americans-down-55-since-recession/; Paul Wiseman, "New Jobs Dis-proportionately Low-Pay or Part-Time," Yahoo! News, August 4, 2013, http://news.yahoo.com/jobs-disproportionately-low-pay-part-time-162103614 .html.

47. Lauren Sandler, "Having It All Without Having Children," *Time*, August 12, 2013, http://www.time.com/time/magazine/article/0,9171,2148636,00.html.

48. Cohn et al., "Barely Half of U.S. Adults Are Married."

49. Kim Parker, "The Boomerang Generation," Pew Social & Demographic Trends, March 15, 2012, http://www.pewsocialtrends.org/2012/03/15/the-boomerang -generation/.

50. Paul Taylor, et al, "Millennials in Adulthood: Detached from Institutions, Networked with Friends," Pew Social & Demographic Trends, March 7, 2014, http://www.pewsocialtrends.org/files/2014/03/2014-03-07_generations-report-version-for-web.pdf.

51. Eliana Dockterman, "Cities' Growth Outpaces Suburbs' for First Time Since 1920s" *Time*, July 2, 2012, http://newsfeed.time.com/2012/07/02/cities-growth-outpaces-the-suburbs-for-the-first-time-since-the-1920s/.

52. Michelle Castillo, "Almost Half of First Babies in U.S. Born to Unwed Mothers," CBS News, March 15, 2013, http://www.cbsnews.com/8301-204_162 -57574599/almost-half-of-first-babies-in-us-born-to-unwed-mothers/.

53. "First Premarital Cohabitation in the United States: 2006–2010 National Survery of Family Growth," *National Health Statistics Reports*, no. 64, April 4, 2013, http://www.cdc.gov/nchs/data/nhsr/nhsr064.pdf.

54. Kluger, "Too Old to Be a Dad?"

7: Steamrolling the Foxholes

1. Mike Dorning, "Obama Reaches across Decades to JFK," *Chicago Tribune*, October 4, 2007, http://articles.chicagotribune.com/2007-10-04/news /0710040214_1_kennedy-speechwriter-kennedy-comparison-jack-kennedy.

2. Geoffrey Perret, *Jack: A Life Like No Other* (New York: Random House, 2001), 111–12.

3. Ibid., 113.

4. "Lieutenant John F. Kennedy, USN," Naval History and Heritage Command website, June 18, 2002, http://www.history.navy.mil/faqs/faq60-2.htm.

5. Ibid.

6. David L. Holmes, *Faiths of the Postwar Presidents: From Truman to Obama* (Athens: University of Georgia Press, 2012), 224–25.

7. Ibid.

8. Lara Logan, "Hank Crumpton: Life as a Spy," CBS News, May 13, 2012, http:// www.cbsnews.com/8301-18560_162-57433105/hank-crumpton-life-as-a-spy/.

9. Richard Miniter, *Losing Bin Laden: How Bill Clinton's Failures Unleashed Global Terror* (Washington, DC: Regnery, 2003), xviii–xix.

10. Barack Obama, *The Audacity of Hope*, (New York: Crown, 2006), 129.

11. Ibid., 210.

12. Christopher Andersen, *Barack and Michelle: Portrait of an American Marriage* (New York: William Morrow, 2009), 204–5.

13. Ibid.

14. Barack Obama, *Change We Can Believe In* (New York: Three Rivers Press, 2008), 196–97.

15. Andersen, *Barack and Michelle*, 256.

16. Obama, *Change We Can Believe In*, 230.

17. "Obama and Wright Controversy Dominate News Cycle," Pew Research Center for the People and the Press, March 27, 2008, http://www.people-press.org /2008/03/27/obama-and-wright-controversy-dominate-news-cycle/.

18. Perret, *Jack: A Life Like No Other*, 111–12.

19. Michael Hastings, "Bowe Bergdahl: America's Last Prisoner of War," *Rolling Stone*, June 7, 2012, http://www.rollingstone.com/politics/news/americas-last -prisoner-of-war-20120607.

20. Matthew Rosenberg, "Karzai Says He Was Assured C.I.A. Would Continue Delivering Bags of Cash," *New York Times*, May 4, 2013, http://www.nytimes .com/2013/05/05/world/asia/karzai-said-he-was-assured-of-cash-deliveries-by -cia.html.

21. Ibid.

22. Ernesto Londoño, "Scrapping Equipment Key to Afghan Drawdown," *Washington Post*, June 19, 2013, http://www.washingtonpost.com/world/asia_pacific /scrapping-equipment-key-to-afghan-drawdown/2013/06/19/9d435258-d83f -11e2-b418-9dfa095e125d_story.html.

23. Hastings, "Bowe Bergdahl."

24. Ibid.

25. Ibid.

26. Ibid.

27. "Bowe Bergdahl's Family Gets Call from Obama, Assured U.S. Trying to Free Soldier Captured in Afghanistan," *Oregonian*, August 9, 2012, http://www .oregonlive.com/pacific-northwest-news/index.ssf/2012/08/bowe_bergdahls _family_gets_cal.html.

28. Nate Rawlings, "The Return of Bowe Bergdahl? Taliban Suggest Prisoner Swap of Last Remaining U.S. POW," *Time*, June 21, 2013, http://world.time.com /2013/06/21/the-return-of-bowe-bergdahl-taliban-suggest-prisoner-swap-of -last-remaining-u-s-pow/.

29. Aryn Baker and Nate Rawlings, "Bring Our Son Home," *Time*, May 28, 2012, http://content.time.com/time/magazine/article/0,9171,2115061,00.html.

30. John Miller, "Taliban Offer Adds Urgency to Idaho POW Rally," Yahoo! News, June 22, 2013, http://news.yahoo.com/taliban-offer-adds-urgency-idaho-pow -rally-081600377.html.

31. Dan Lamothe, "General: More than 100 Kills for Some Marine Snipers," *Battle*

Rattle, September 1, 2011, http://blogs.militarytimes.com/battle-rattle/2011/09/01/general-more-than-100-kills-for-some-marine-snipers/.

32. David Maraniss, *Barack Obama: The Story* (New York: Simon & Schuster, 2012), 494–95.

33. David Martosko, James Nye, and Daniel Bates, " 'It Made Him Look like a Butler': Retired General Blasts President Obama for Ordering U.S. Marine to Break Military Rules by Holding an Umbrella," *Mail Online*, May 16, 2013, http://www.dailymail.co.uk/news/article-2325893/President-Obama-makes-U-S-Marine-break-rules-does-look-happy-it.html.

34. Alissa J. Rubin, "8 Soldiers Die in Attacks in Afghanistan," *New York Times*, May 4, 2013, http://www.nytimes.com/2013/05/05/world/asia/blast-kills-7-soldiers-in-afghanistan.html.

35. James Dao and Andrew W. Lehren, "Baffling Rise in Suicides Plagues the U.S. Military," *New York Times*, May 15, 2013, http://www.nytimes.com/2013/05/16/us/baffling-rise-in-suicides-plagues-us-military.html.

36. Nancy Gibbs and Mark Thompson, "The War on Suicide?" *Time*, July 23, 2012, http://www.time.com/time/magazine/article/0,9171,2119337,00.html.

37. Colonel John G. Baker, "Saving Lives by Caring," *Marine Corps Gazette*, August 2013, http://www.mca-marines.org/gazette/article/saving-lives-caring.

38. Paul John Scott, "The Military's Billion-Dollar Pill Problem," *Men's Journal*, December 1, 2012, http://www.mensjournal.com/magazine/the-militarys-billion-dollar-pill-problem-20130116.

39. Patricia Kime, "Pentagon to Limit Antipsychotic Drugs for PTSD," *Army Times*, May 3, 2012, http://www.armytimes.com/article/20120503/NEWS/205030316/Pentagon-limit-antipsychotic-drugs-PTSD.

40. Obama, *Change We Can Believe In*, 211, 200.

41. Henry C. Jackson, "Obama Focuses on Seniors, Veterans in Positive Ads," *Big Story*, May 23, 2012, http://bigstory.ap.org/content/obama-focuses-seniors-veterans-positive-ads.

42. "2013 Member Survey," Iraq and Afghanistan Veterans of America, accessed September 4, 2013, http://iava.org/files/2013survey/IAVAMemberSurvey2013.pdf.

43. Karen Jowers, "Female Vets Benefit from Entrepreneur Program," *Marine Corps Times*, September 24, 2013, http://www.marinecorpstimes.com/article/20130924/JOBS03/309240014/Female-vets-benefit-from-entrepreneur-program.

44. Mark Thompson, "Guess the VA Does Have a Paperwork Problem," *Time*, August 10, 2012, http://nation.time.com/2012/08/10/guess-the-va-does-have-a-paperwork-problem/.

8: Where There's a Nonsmoker

1. David Maraniss, *Barack Obama: The Story* (Simon & Schuster, 2012), 293–94, 540.

2. "Obama Sells Himself as the New JFK," *Washington Post*, October 3, 2007, http://voices.washingtonpost.com/44/2007/10/post-109.html.

3. Geoffrey Perret, *Jack: A Life Like No Other* (New York: Random House, 2001), 372.

4. Ibid., 373–74, 379.

5. Barack Obama, *Change We Can Believe In: Barack Obama's Plan to Renew America's Promise* (New York: Three Rivers Press, 2008), 240.

6. "Unclassified Version of the Accountability Review Board Report," *New York Times*, December 18, 2012, 18–19, http://www.nytimes.com/interactive/2012/12/18/us/19benghazi-report.html?ref=politics; "Review of the Terrorist Attacks on U.S. Facilities in Benghazi, Libya, September 11-12, 2012 Together With Additional Views" by the Senate Select Committee on Intelligence, U.S. Senate, 113th Congress. Place: D.C. Date of Report Release: 1/15/14. Accessed 1.26.14 URL: http://www.intelligence.senate.gov/benghazi2014/benghazi.pdf.

7. "Background Briefing on Libya," press release, October 9, 2012, U.S. Department of State, http://www.state.gov/r/pa/prs/ps/2012/10/198791.htm; "Accountability Review Board Report," 21.

8. Chris Stephen, "US Consulate Attack in Benghazi: A Challenge to Official Version of Events," *Guardian*, September 9, 2013, http://www.theguardian.com/world/2013/sep/09/us-consulate-benghazi-attack-challenge.

9. CCP Xhagen, "A Tribute to Sean 'Vile Rat' Smith," *EVE Community*, September 13, 2012, http://community.eveonline.com/news/dev-blogs/73406.

10. "Accountability Review Board Report," 21, 36.

11. "Accountability Review Board Report."

12. The Mittani, "RIP: Vile Rat," *TheMittani.com*, September 12, 2012, http://themittani.com/news/rip-vile-rat.

13. Ibid.

14. Ibid.

15. "Accountability Review Board Report," 22.

16. Ibid., 23.

17. "Background Briefing on Libya."

18. Nancy A. Youssef, "Libyans, Diplomats: CIA's Benghazi Annex a Secret," *Seattle Times*, November 12, 2012, http://seattletimes.com/html/nationworld/2019670396_benghazi13.html.

19. Ibid.

20. "Background Briefing on Libya."

21. Youssef, "Libyans, Diplomats."

22. "Transcript: Whistle-blower's account of Sept. 11 Libya terror attack," Fox News, May 8, 2013, http://www.foxnews.com/politics/2013/05/08/transcript-whistle-blower-account-sept-11-libya-terror-attack/.

23. "Libyan President to NBC: Anti-Islam Film Had 'Nothing to Do with' US Consulate Attack," NBC News, September 25, 2012, http://worldnews.nbc

news.com/_news/2012/09/26/14105135-libyan-president-to-nbc-anti-islam
-film-had-nothing-to-do-with-us-consulate-attack.

24. Hisham Matar, "What Was Really Behind the Benghazi Attack?," *The New Yorker* (blogs), September 13, 2013, http://www.newyorker.com/online/blogs /comment/2012/09/what-was-really-behind-the-benghazi-attack.html.

25. James Rosen, "The Benghazi Transcripts: Top Defense Officials Briefed Obama on 'attack,' Not Video or Protest," Text.Article, FoxNews.com, January 14, 2014, http://www.foxnews.com/politics/2014/01/14/benghazi-transcripts-top -defense-officials-briefed-obama-on-attack-not-video-or/.

26. Jake Tapper, "U.S. Security Official in Libya Tells Congressional Investigators About 'Inappropriately Low' Security at Benghazi Post," *Political Punch* (blog), ABC News, October 10, 2012, http://abcnews.go.com/blogs/politics/2012 /10/u-s-security-official-in-libya-tells-congressional-investigators-about -inappropriately-low-security-at-benghazi-post/.

27. "Sharyl Attkisson Tweets House Report; Reveals Hillary Clinton Lied under Oath about Benghazi; Update: WH Altered Talking Points," *Twitchy*, April 23, 2013, http://twitchy.com/2013/04/23/sharyl-attkisson-tweets-house-report -reveals-hillary-clinton-lied-under-oath-about-benghazi/.

28. Jonathan Karl, "Exclusive: Benghazi Talking Points Underwent 12 Revisions, Scrubbed of Terror Reference," *The Note* (blog), ABC News, May 10, 2013, http://abcnews.go.com/blogs/politics/2013/05/exclusive-benghazi-talking -points-underwent-12-revisions-scrubbed-of-terror-references/.

29. Senate Select Committee on Intelligence, U.S. Senate, 113th Congress, *Review of the Terrorist Attacks on U.S. Facilities in Benghazi, Libya, September 11-12, 2012 Together With Additional Views* (Washington, D.C., January 15, 2014), http://www.intelligence.senate.gov/benghazi2014/benghazi.pdf.

30. Ibid.

31. "Accountability Review Board Report," 29.

32. Susan Cornwell and Mark Hosenball, "U.S. Officer Got No Reply to Requests for More Security in Benghazi," Reuters, October 9, 2012, http://www.reuters .com/article/2012/10/09/us-libya-usa-idUSBRE89815N20121009.

33. "Transcript: Whistle-blower's account of Sept. 11 Libya terror attack," FoxNews .com, May 8, 2013, http://www.foxnews.com/politics/2013/05/08/transcript -whistle-blower-account-sept-11-libya-terror-attack/.

34. Caroline May, "Benghazi Whistle-Blower a Democrat, Voted for Hillary and Obama Twice," *Daily Caller*, May 11, 2013, http://dailycaller.com/2013/05/11 /benghazi-whistle-blower-a-democrat-voted-for-hillary-and-obama-twice/.

35. Hugo Gye, " 'Did Your Son Always Have Balls the Size of Cue Balls?' Biden's Bizarre Question Angers Father of Navy SEAL Who Died in Benghazi Attack," *Mail Online*, October 26, 2012, http://www.dailymail.co.uk/news/article -2223554/Did-son-balls-size-cue-balls-Bidens-bizarre-question-father-Navy -SEAL-died-Benghazi-attack.html.

36. Sean Hannity, "Benghazi Victim's Father: 'The Difference Is Credibility,'" Fox News, May 7, 2013, http://www.foxnews.com/on-air/hannity/2013/05/08/benghazi-victims-father-difference-credibility.

37. "Impeachment Support Soars as Voters Say Feds 'Out of Control,'" *New American*, June 17, 2013, 6.

38. Drew Griffin, Kathleen Johnston, and Jake Tapper, "Exclusive: Dozens of CIA Operatives on the Ground during Benghazi Attack," *The Lead* (blog), CNN, August 1, 2013, http://thelead.blogs.cnn.com/2013/08/01/exclusive-dozens-of-cia-operatives-on-the-ground-during-benghazi-attack/.

39. Eric Schmitt, "C.I.A. Said to Aid in Steering Arms to Syrian Opposition," *New York Times*, June 21, 2012, http://www.nytimes.com/2012/06/21/world/middleeast/cia-said-to-aid-in-steering-arms-to-syrian-rebels.html; Michael R. Gordon and Mark Landler, "Backstage Glimpses of Clinton as Dogged Diplomat, Win or Lose," *New York Times*, February 2, 2013, http://www.nytimes.com/2013/02/03/us/politics/in-behind-scene-blows-and-triumphs-sense-of-clinton-future.html; C. J. Chivers and Eric Schmitt, "Arms Airlift to Syrian Rebels Expands, With Aid From C.I.A.," *New York Times*, March 24, 2013, http://www.nytimes.com/2013/03/25/world/middleeast/arms-airlift-to-syrian-rebels-expands-with-cia-aid.html; Griffin, Johnston, and Tapper, "Dozens of CIA Operatives."

40. Joel B. Pollak, "Hillary Misled Congress—But Not Under Oath," *Breitbart*, May 9, 2013, http://www.breitbart.com/Big-Peace/2013/05/09/Hillary-Misled-Congress-But-Not-Under-Oath.

41. Steve Kroft et al., "Obama and Clinton: The 60 Minutes Interview," CBS News, January 27, 2013, http://www.cbsnews.com/8301-18560_162-57565734/obama-and-clinton-the-60-minutes-interview/.

42. Nasser al-Awlaki, "The Drone That Killed My Grandson," *New York Times*, July 17, 2013, http://www.nytimes.com/2013/07/18/opinion/the-drone-that-killed-my-grandson.html; Tom Junod, "Obama's Administration Killed a 16-Year-Old American and Didn't Say Anything About It: This Is Justice?," *Esquire*, July 9, 2012, http://www.esquire.com/blogs/politics/abdulrahman-al-awlaki-death-10470891.

43. Michael Isikoff, "Justice Department Memo Reveals Legal Case for Drone Strikes on Americans," NBC News, February 4, 2013, http://investigations.nbcnews.com/_news/2013/02/04/16843014-justice-department-memo-reveals-legal-case-for-drone-strikes-on-americans.

44. Christopher Andersen, *Barack and Michelle: Portrait of an American Marriage* (New York, NY: William Morrow, 2009), 212–13.

45. Mark Mazzetti, "A Secret Deal on Drones, Sealed in Blood," *New York Times*, April 6, 2013, http://www.nytimes.com/2013/04/07/world/asia/origins-of-cias-not-so-secret-drone-war-in-pakistan.html.

46. Craig Whitlock, "FBI Has Received Aviation Clearance for at Least Four

Domestic Drone Operations," *Washington Post*, June 20, 2013, http://articles.washingtonpost.com/2013-06-20/world/40089990_1_u-s-airspace-drone-puma-ae.

47. Scott Shane, "Judge Challenges White House Claims on Authority in Drone Killings," *New York Times*, July 19, 2013, http://www.nytimes.com/2013/07/20/us/politics/judge-challenges-white-house-claims-on-authority-in-drone-killings.html.

48. Ibid.

49. Michael Tennant, "Up to 40 Percent of Healthcare.gov Still in Development, Says CMS Official," *New American*, November 22, 2013, http://www.thenewamerican.com/usnews/health-care/item/16997-up-to-40-percent-of-healthcare-gov-still-in-development-says-cms-official.

50. Michael Scherer, "More Than a Glitch," *Time*, November 4, 2013.

51. Obama, *Change We Can Believe In*, 255.

52. Ibid.

53. Ashley Halsey III, "Aging Power Grid on Overload as U.S. Demands More Electricity," *Washington Post*, August 1, 2012, http://articles.washingtonpost.com/2012-08-01/local/35493997_1_power-grid-power-plants-new-nuclear-plants.

54. Richard A. Serrano, "U.S. Intelligence Officials Concerned about Cyber Attack," *Los Angeles Times*, February 11, 2011, http://articles.latimes.com/2011/feb/11/nation/la-na-intel-hearing-20110211.

55. "Obama Seeks China Cooperation on Hacking That Xi Denies," Bloomberg Politics, June 8, 2013, http://www.bloomberg.com/news/2013-06-08/obama-seeks-china-cooperation-on-hacking-that-xi-denies.html.

56. Michael Martinez, "Sniper attack on Silicon Valley power grid spurs security crusade by ex-regulator," CNN, February 7, 2014, http://www.cnn.com/2014/02/07/us/california-sniper-attach-power-substation/.

57. Nicole Perlroth, "Electrical Grid Is Called Vulnerable to Power Shutdown," *Bits* (blog), October 18, 2013, http://bits.blogs.nytimes.com/2013/10/18/electrical-grid-called-vulnerable-to-power-shutdown/.

58. Walter Isaacson, *Steve Jobs* (New York: Simon & Schuster, 2011), 23–26.

59. Ibid., 27–30.

60. Malcolm Gladwell, *Outliers: The Story of Success* (New York: Little, Brown, 2008), 36–37, 42–47, 67.

61. Mark Thompson, "The Outing of the SEALs Has SecDef Ticked Off," *Time*, May 13, 2011, http://nation.time.com/2011/05/13/the-outing-of-the-seals-has-secdef-ticked-off/.

62. Phil Bronstein, "The Man Who Killed Osama Bin Laden . . . Is Screwed," *Esquire*, February 11, 2013, http://www.esquire.com/features/man-who-shot-osama-bin-laden-0313.

63. "SEAL Hero's Mom: 'Hearts and Mind of Our Enemy' More Valuable to Gov't

'Than My Son's Blood,'" Breitbart News Network, May 10, 2013, http://www
.breitbart.com/Breitbart-TV/2013/05/10/SEAL-Heros-Mom-Hearts-and-
Mind-of-Our-Enemy-Is-More-Valuable-to-This-Government-Than-My-Sons
-Blood.

64. Bronstein, "The Man Who Killed Osama"; Helen Kennedy, "Osama Bin Laden
Wasn't on Kidney Dialysis, Took Herbal Viagra While Living in Compound,"
New York Daily News, May 8, 2011, http://www.nydailynews.com/news/world
/osama-bin-laden-wasn-kidney-dialysis-herbal-viagra-living-compound-article
-1.141224.

65. Elizabeth Dias, "I Am Thankful For . . . ," *Time*, December 9, 2013.

9: Our Gun Tattoos

1. Matt Crenson, "Mass Shootings More Common since 1960s," Boston.com,
April 21, 2007, http://www.boston.com/news/education/higher/articles/2007
/04/21/mass_shootings_more_common_since_1960s/?page=1.

2. Ibid.

3. "A Mass Murderer Leaves Eight Women Dead," History.com, July 14, 1966,
http://www.history.com/this-day-in-history/a-mass-murderer-leaves-eight
-women-dead.

4. Crenson, "Mass Shootings More Common."

5. "Deadliest U.S. Shootings," *Washington Post*, September 16, 2013, http://www
.washingtonpost.com/wp-srv/special/nation/deadliest-us-shootings/.

6. Rome Hartman, "What Assault Weapons Ban? CBS '60 Minutes' Video," CBS
News, August 1, 1999, http://www.cbsnews.com/video/watch/?id=7380236n&
tag=api

7. "Gun Bill Is Blocked by Lack of Quorum," *New York Times*, August 18, 1966,
http://select.nytimes.com/gst/abstract.html?res=F40E17F83D58117B93CAA81
783D85F428685F9.

8. "Attack Real Gun Problem," *USA Today*, editorial, June 3, 1995.

9. John Lott, "Time to Put an End to Army Bases as Gun-Free Zones," Fox News,
November 10, 2009, http://www.foxnews.com/opinion/2009/11/10/john-lott
-ft-hood-end-gun-free-zone.

10. Connie Cass, "In God We Trust, Maybe, but Not Each Other," Yahoo! News,
December 2, 2013, http://news.yahoo.com/god-trust-maybe-not-other
-135752394.html.

11. Colleen Long, "Subway Shoving Suspect: I Was Having a Bad Day," Associated
Press, January 19, 2013, http://abclocal.go.com/wabc/story?section=news
/local/new_york&id=8936549.

12. "Chancellor Falwell Renews Support to NC Teen in Gun Possession Case,"
Liberty News Service, May 17, 2013, http://www.liberty.edu/news/?PID=
18495&MID=90812.

13. Obama, *Change We Can Believe In*, 176.

14. Maraniss, *Barack Obama*, 298–99.

15. Obama, *Change We Can Believe In*, 176–77.

16. "Deadliest U.S. Shootings."

17. Anne Flaherty, "Pentagon Finds Mistakes by Officers over Hasan," Boston.com, January 15, 2010, http://www.boston.com/news/nation/washington/articles /2010/01/15/us_official_officers_may_get_hit_for_base_rampage/; "Fort Hood: Diversity Rules," *New York Post*, October 29, 2012, http://www nypost.com/2012/10/29/fort-hood-diversity-rules.

18. "Jared Loughner Grew Erratic and Delusional in Months before Shooting, Documents Say," *San Jose Mercury News*, March 27, 2013, http://www .mercurynews.com/ci_22883229/jared-loughner-grew-erratic-and-delusional -months-before.

19. "James Holmes' Psychiatrist Warned of Threat before Attack," Associated Press, April 4, 2013, http://www.foxnews.com/us/2013/04/04/james-holmes -psychiatrist-warned-threat-before-attack/.

20. Dan Elliott, "Detective: Holmes Played Puppets with Paper Bags," *Big Story*, January 8, 2013, http://bigstory.ap.org/article/colo-shooting-families-listen -police-testimony.

21. Amy Powell, "Connecticut School Shooting: Adam Lanza's Babysitter Noticed Odd Behavior," ABC News, December 16, 2012, http://abclocal.go.com/kabc /story?section=news/national_world&id=8923027.

22. Jeffrey Kluger, "Sandy Hook's Chilling Final Chapter," *Time*, December 9, 2013.

23. Mark Thompson, "Unchecked Agression: The Navy Yard Attack and Our Broken Security-Vetting System," *Time*, September 30, 2013.

24. Rudy Giuliani and Sean Hannity, "Giuliani Warns of 'Institutionalized Political Correctness,'" transcript, Fox News, April 24, 2013, http://www .foxnews.com/on-air/hannity/2013/04/25/giuliani-warns-institutionalized -political-correctness.

25. Trip Gabriel and Thom Shanker, "Officials Never Learned of Police Doubts on Gunman's Stability," *New York Times*, September 18, 2013, http://www .nytimes.com/2013/09/19/us/hagel-orders-reviews-of-security-procedures -and-clearances.html.

26. Scott Friedman, "Accused Fort Hood Shooter Paid $278,000 While Await-ing Trial," NBC 5 Investigates, May 20, 2013, http://www.nbcdfw.com/ investigations/Accused-Fort-Hood-Shooter-Paid-278000-While-Awaiting-Trial -208230691.html.

27. Ned Berkowitz, "Dem Blames 'Political Correctness' for Fort Hood 'Workplace Violence' Controversy," ABC News (blog), May 7, 2013, http://abcnews.go .com/blogs/headlines/2013/05/dem-blames-political-correctness-for-fort-hood -massacre-controversy/.

28. Saira Anees, "Obama Explains Why Some Small Town Pennsylvanians Are 'Bitter,'" ABC News (blog), April 11, 2008, http://abcnews.go.com/blogs /politics/2008/04/obama-explains-2/.

29. "Murder Victims by Weapon, 2007–2011," Crime in the United States 2011, Federal Bureau of Investigation, http://www.fbi.gov/about-us/cjis/ucr/crime -in-the-u.s/2011/crime-in-the-u.s.-2011/tables/expanded-homicide-data-table-8.

30. Don B. Kates Jr., "Gun Free Zones: A Prevalent Delusion," Independent Institute, May 14, 2013, http://www.independent.org/newsroom/article.asp?id=3616.

31. Ibid.

32. Erica Goode, "In Mass Attacks, Public Now Advised to Take Action," *New York Times*, April 6, 2013, http://www.nytimes.com/2013/04/07/us/in-a-shift-police -advise-taking-an-active-role-to-counter-mass-attacks.html.

33. John Lott, "Fact vs. Fiction on Background Checks and the Gun Control Debate," Fox News, April 9, 2013, http://www.foxnews.com/opinion/2013 /04/09/fact-vs-fiction-on-background-checks-and-gun-control-debate/.

34. John Lott, "The '40 Percent' Myth," *National Review Online*, January 24, 2013, http://www.nationalreview.com/articles/338735/40-percent-myth-john-lott.

35. Barack Obama, "President Obama's Remarks at Navy Yard Memorial Service" (full text), CBS DC, September 22, 2013, http://washington.cbslocal. com/2013/09/22/full-text-president-obamas-remarks-at-navy-yard-memorial -service/.

36. Corey Flintoff and James Glynn, "The U.S. Has More Guns, But Russia Has More Murders," *Parallels* (blog), NPR, September 21, 2013, http://www.npr .org/blogs/parallels/2013/09/19/224043848/the-u-s-has-more-guns-but-russia -has-more-murders.

37. Ibid.

38. Don B. Kates and Gary Mauser, "Would Banning Firearms Reduce Murder and Suicide? A Review of International and Some Domestic Evidence," *Harvard Journal of Law & Public Policy*, Vol. 30, No. 2, Spring 2007, http://www.gary mauser.net/pdf/KatesMauserHJPP.pdf.

39. D'Vera Cohn et al., "Gun Homicide Rate Down 49% Since 1993 Peak; Public Unaware," Pew Research Social & Demographic Trends, May 7, 2013, http:// www.pewsocialtrends.org/2013/05/07/gun-homicide-rate-down-49-since-1993 -peak-public-unaware/.

40. D'Vera Cohn et al., "Barely Half of U.S. Adults Are Married—A Record Low," Pew Research Social & Demographic Trends, December 14, 2011, http://www .pewsocialtrends.org/2011/12/14/barely-half-of-u-s-adults-are-married-a-record -low/.

41. Kates, "Gun Free Zones."

42. John Lott, "Did Colorado Shooter Single Out Cinemark Theater Because It Banned Guns?" Fox News, September 10, 2012, http://www.foxnews.com /opinion/2012/09/10/did-colorado-shooter-single-out-cinemark-theater/.

43. St. Thomas Aquinas, *Treatise on Law* (Washington, DC: Regnery, 1956).

44. David Nathan, "Research Points the Way: Reach out," TwinCities.com, December 26, 2012, http://www.twincities.com/ci_22256585/david-nathan-research -points-way-reach-out.

45. Liza Long, "I Am Adam Lanza's Mother: My Son Threatens to Kill Me; I've Tried Everything; Everything Is Not Enough," *Pittsburgh Post-Gazette*, December 23, 2012, http://www.post-gazette.com/stories/opinion/perspectives /i-am-adam-lanzas-mother-my-son-threatens-to-kill-me-ive-tried-everything -everything-is-not-enough-667485/.

46. Daniel Patrick Moynihan, "Promise to the Mentally Ill Has Not Been Kept," *New York Times*, May 22, 1989, http://www.nytimes.com/1989/05/22/opinion /l-promise-to-the-mentally-ill-has-not-been-kept-211189.html.

47. Long, "I Am Adam Lanza's Mother."

48. Daniel Greenfield, "Father of Sandy Hook 6-Year-Old: 'Gun Laws Are Not the Problem, Personal Responsibility Is,'" *FrontPage Mag*, January 29, 2013, http:// frontpagemag.com/2013/dgreenfield/father-of-sandy-hook-6-year-old-gun-laws -are-not-the-problem-personal-responsibility-is/.

49. "Murder Victims by Weapon, 2007–2011."

10: Roarin' Muscle Cars

1. Joel Stein, "I Brake for Teenage Drivers," *Time*, September 23, 2013.

2. Andrea Huspeni, "Millennials Are Snubbing the Corporate World for Entrepreneurship," *Entrepreneur*, September 23, 2013, http://www.entrepreneur.com /article/228464.

3. Walter Isaacson, *Steve Jobs* (New York: Simon & Schuster, 2011), 569.

4. Michelle Wright, "Entrepreneurs: Nature or Nurture?" *Telegraph*, November 20, 2013, http://www.telegraph.co.uk/finance/businessclub/10462559 /Entrepreneurs-nature-or-nurture.html.

5. Emily Esfahani Smith and Jennifer L. Aaker, "Millennial Searchers," *New York Times*, November 30, 2013, http://www.nytimes.com/2013/12/01/opinion /sunday/millennial-searchers.html.

6. Virginia Convention on the Ratification of the Constitution, June 1788, Quotes by Patrick Henry, Patrick Henry Center for Individual Liberty, http://www .patrickhenrycenter.com/quotes.aspx.

7. Catherine Clifford, "U.S. Remains Dominant Force in Global Entrepreneurship . . . For Now," *Entrepreneur*, August 28, 2013, http://www.entrepreneur .com/article/228128.

8. Tasha Cunningham, "Veterans Find Opportunity in Entrepreneurship," *Miami Herald*, September 2, 2013, http://www.miamiherald.com/2013/09/01/v -fullstory/3600624/veterans-find-opportunity-in.html.

9. Laurie Goodstein, "Poll Shows Major Shift in Identity of U.S. Jews," *New York*

Times, October 1, 2013, sec. U.S., http://www.nytimes.com/2013/10/01/us /poll-shows-major-shift-in-identity-of-us-jews.html.

10. Amy Sullivan, "The Rise of the Nones," *Time*, March 12, 2012, http://content .time.com/time/magazine/article/0,9171,2108027,00.html.

11. Chaeyoon Lim, "In U.S., Churchgoers Boast Better Mood, Especially on Sundays," GALLUP Well-Being, March 22, 2012, http://www.gallup.com /poll/153374/churchgoers-boast-better-mood-especially-sundays.aspx.

12. Saint Augustine, *Confessions*, ed. John E. Rotelle, trans. Maria Boulding, vol. 1 (Hyde Park, NY: New City Press, 2004).

13. Sally Jenkins, "9/11 Memorials: The Story of the Cross at Ground Zero," *Washington Post*, September 8, 2011, http://articles.washingtonpost.com/2011 -09-08/politics/35418445_1_frank-silecchia-crane-operators-ground-zero.

14. "Millennials Rank Clinton Highly Among Modern Presidents," Pew Research Center, February 18, 2013, http://www.pewresearch.org/daily-number /millennials-rank-clinton-highly-among-modern-presidents/.

15. "The Clinton Effect," *Economist*, November 2, 2013, http://www.economist .com/news/united-states/21588913-young-recall-clinton-boom-not-scandals -clinton-effect.

ACKNOWLEDGMENTS

Dreams come true with hard work, faith, and solid teammates. I achieved my dream of writing a book that I hope advances liberty—with the help of a wonderful team.

Thank you to my best friends: two loving parents, two brilliant and beautiful sisters, and two ever-teasing yet very talented brothers.

Thank you and high fives to my bright and supportive editor, Stephanie Knapp. Heartfelt thanks to my kind and masterful publisher, Tina Constable. Thanks to Dominick Anfuso (vice president and executive editor)—a man who was born to champion great books. Thanks to art director Michael Nagin for your perseverance and creativity in developing the perfect cover. Thanks to the talented and enthusiastic Aussie-American on my team, Campbell Wharton (associate publisher). Thank you to my vivacious and nimble publicity and marketing team of Tammy Blake (publicity director), Megan Perritt (senior publicist), Julie Cepler (marketing director), and Gianna Sandri (marketing associate). Thanks to my teammates at Crown who have worked so hard behind the scenes: Maria Spano (managing editor), Norman Watkins (senior production manager), designer Barbara Sturman (the woman behind this book's clean and powerful design), and Rosalie Wieder (my meticulous copyeditor). It's been delightful and exciting to work with all of you!

I appreciate the encouragement, advice, or feedback that I received from: Audra Otto, Lawrence Pobuda, Joseph Flynn, Les Knoke, Jason Lewis, Sue Jeffers, Mitch Berg, John Hawkins, Brad Carlson, my cousin Ryan, Rob Loftus, Larry Flodin, Shawn Johnson, Jerry and Linda Holty, Jill Johnson, and Jan Preble.

Thank you to Octagon's amazing Tom Repicci and extraordinary John Ferriter for discovering me in the heart of the Midwest and motivating me by your zest for the best.

Abundant thanks to my agent Dan Strone, CEO of Trident Media

Group. In you, I have had the immense joy of working side-by-side with an entrepreneur and professional whose phenomenal talent, high character, and impeccable standards have inspired me to work at my full potential. Dan, like Poseidon, you hold the glinting trident.

An encore of thanks to my brother "The Colonel" and especially to my father, who teethed me on talk radio. *Deus gubernat navem.*

KATIE KIEFFER is a political commentator, popular public speaker, and a weekly columnist at Townhall.com. She has a background in journalism and business. Kieffer is a member of the Ladies of Liberty Alliance Speakers Bureau, and she has been featured on NRA News, CNBC, MSNBC, and the Fox Business Network.

Kieffer's father raised her on talk radio—and her mother homeschooled her through the eighth grade. Her high school selected her to be the school's ambassador at the American Legion Auxiliary Girls State. She began her professional writing career as a high school senior, when she was selected to write editorial columns for the *St. Paul Pioneer Press*. As a college student, Kieffer founded and edited an independent journal of thought and opinion, the *St. Thomas Standard*. Katie graduated summa cum laude with a dual major from the University of St. Thomas.

Kieffer spent several years working in the commercial real estate industry, during which time she won numerous public speaking awards and held multiple state and national leadership roles, including chairing NAIOP's national Young Professionals Forum of rising stars.

Kieffer is very passionate about promoting free speech and entrepreneurship. Due to her investigative research and interviews with troops, veterans, and military families facing the challenge of PTSD—as well as her three-and-a-half-year experience of caring for a relative who suffers from Alzheimer's—Katie has developed a strong concern for those who struggle with mental illness and their caretakers. In her free time, Kieffer enjoys traveling, meeting new people, running, and working out—especially in the great outdoors.